T0320145

Theoretical Foundations of Corporate Finance

Theoretical Foundations of Corporate Finance

João Amaro de Matos

Princeton University Press
Princeton and Oxford

Library of Congress Cataloging-in-Publication Data

Amaro de Matos, João, 1961-
   Theoretical foundations of corporate finance/João Amaro de Matos.
      p.   cm.
   Includes bibliographical references and index.
   ISBN 0-691-08794-6 (alk. paper)
      1. Corporations—Finance. I. Title.

   HG4014 .A4 2001
   338.6′041—dc21
                                        2001032104

British Library Cataloging-in-Publication Data is available

This book has been composed in New Baskerville

Printed on acid-free paper. ∞

www.pup.princeton.edu

Printed in the United States of America

10   9   8   7   6   5   4   3   2   1

Contents

List of Figures   **xi**

Preface   **xiii**
   0.1   Intended Audience   xiv
   0.2   Organization of the Text   xv
   0.3   Acknowledgments   xvi

Part I   **Foundations**   **1**

1 Valuation   **3**
   1.1   Valuation under Certainty   5
      1.1.1   The Robinson Crusoe Economy   5
      1.1.2   Time Preferences   7
      1.1.3   Production Opportunities   8
      1.1.4   The Role of Capital Markets   9
      1.1.5   Consumption and Investment with
             Capital Markets   11
      1.1.6   The Value of an Investment Project   14
      1.1.7   Multiperiod Economy with Capital Markets   15
      1.1.8   Exercises   17
   1.2   Valuation under Uncertainty   18
      1.2.1   One-Period Model   18
      1.2.2   Value and the Absence of Arbitrage   22
      1.2.3   Arbitrage Opportunities and Investment   23
      1.2.4   Value and the Martingale Measure   24
      1.2.5   Beta Values   26
      1.2.6   Exercises   28
   1.3   Multiperiods and Flexibility under Uncertainty   29
      1.3.1   The Multiperiod Setting   30
      1.3.2   Real Options   33

| | 1.3.3 | Some General Properties of Options........... | 34 |
| | 1.3.4 | Exercises................................. | 37 |

2 Optimal Capital Structure   **39**
2.1		The MM Propositions.............................	40
	2.1.1	The Irrelevancy Statement...................	40
	2.1.2	Cost of Capital.............................	42
	2.1.3	The MM Propositions with Taxes.............	44
	2.1.4	Empirical Evidence.........................	46
	2.1.5	Exercises.................................	47
2.2		Personal and Corporate Taxation...................	48
	2.2.1	Demand for Bonds.........................	49
	2.2.2	Supply of Bonds...........................	50
	2.2.3	The Equilibrium...........................	51
	2.2.4	Comparing with MM.......................	53
	2.2.5	Changes in Taxations: An Alternative Equilibrium...............................	54
	2.2.6	Empirical Evidence.........................	57
	2.2.7	Exercises.................................	58

Part II   **Agency and Information**   **59**

3 Implications for Capital Structure   **61**
3.1		The Role of Agency Costs........................	62
	3.1.1	Agency Costs of Outside Equity..............	64
	3.1.2	Principal–Agent Problems...................	66
	3.1.3	Agency Costs of Debt......................	71
	3.1.4	Empirical Evidence.........................	75
	3.1.5	Exercises.................................	77
3.2		Informational Asymmetries.......................	78
	3.2.1	Managers' Signaling because of Fee Schedules...	79
	3.2.2	When Managers Are Also Investors............	82
	3.2.3	Signals Conditioned by Investment Opportunities...............................	85
	3.2.4	Stock Repurchase as a Signal................	89
	3.2.5	Empirical Evidence.........................	93
	3.2.6	Exercises.................................	95

4 Payout Policy   **97**
4.1		Dividend Policy................................	98
	4.1.1	Another Irrelevancy Proposition..............	98
	4.1.2	Alternative Valuations.......................	100
	4.1.3	Growth Rates.............................	102

		4.1.4	Relaxing Certainty	103
		4.1.5	Dividends and Taxes	104
		4.1.6	Empirical Evidence	105
		4.1.7	Exercises	109
	4.2	Dividends and Information		110
		4.2.1	The Informational Content of Dividends	110
		4.2.2	A Signaling Model	111
		4.2.3	A Consistent Signaling Model	114
		4.2.4	Empirical Evidence	116
		4.2.5	Exercises	119
	4.3	Stock Repurchases		119
		4.3.1	Trends in Payout Policies	120
		4.3.2	Reasons for Stock Repurchases	121
		4.3.3	Empirical Evidence	122
5	**Financial Contracting**			**125**
	5.1	Contracting and Allocation of Control		126
		5.1.1	The Model	127
		5.1.2	Entrepreneur Control	129
		5.1.3	Investor Control	131
		5.1.4	Contingent Control	133
		5.1.5	Financing Contracts	133
		5.1.6	Exercises	134
	5.2	Debt Contract Design		134
		5.2.1	Extending the Model	134
		5.2.2	The Case of Many Creditholders	137
		5.2.3	The Choice of the Duration	139
		5.2.4	The Effect of Seniority	146
		5.2.5	Exercises	148
Part III		**Capital Restructuring**		**149**
6	**Going Public**			**151**
	6.1	The Going Public Decision		152
		6.1.1	The Model	152
		6.1.2	The Equilibrium	154
		6.1.3	Empirical Evidence	160
		6.1.4	Exercises	160
	6.2	Underpricing and Information Asymmetries		160
		6.2.1	Asymmetry between Issuers and Underwriters	162
		6.2.2	Asymmetry between Investors	163
		6.2.3	Reputation of Bankers and Uncertainty	165
		6.2.4	How Underwriters Become Informed	167

6.2.5   Legal Liabilities   171
6.2.6   Empirical Evidence   172
6.2.7   Exercises   175

7 Going Private   177
7.1   Stock Repurchases   177
7.2   Leveraged Buyouts   179
7.2.1   The Mechanism of Leveraged Buyouts   179
7.2.2   A Model for MBOs   181
7.2.3   Empirical Evidence   186
7.2.4   Exercises   189

8 Mergers and Acquisitions   191
8.1   Tender Offers and the Free-Rider Problem   192
8.1.1   Largely Diffused Ownership   193
8.1.2   The Role of a Large Shareholder   196
8.1.3   Uncertain Outcome of a Takeover   199
8.1.4   The Optimal Size of α before a Takeover   201
8.1.5   Exercises   205
8.2   Merger Bids   205
8.2.1   Competition between Bidders   206
8.2.2   Choosing the Means of Payment   207
8.2.3   Cash as a Preemptive Instrument with
Many Bidders   212
8.2.4   The Choice of Takeover Methods   214
8.2.5   Empirical Evidence   218
8.2.6   Exercises   223

Part IV   Appendices   225

A Optimization Principles   227
A.1   Unconstrained Optimization   227
A.2   Constrained Optimization   228
A.2.1   Equality Constraints   228
A.2.2   Inequality Constraints   231

B Notions of Game Theory   233
B.1   Introduction   233
B.2   Informational Equilibrium   234
B.3   The Revelation Principle   238

C Suggested Solutions **241**
C.1 Valuation 241
      C.1.1 Valuation under Certainty 241
      C.1.2 Valuation under Uncertainty 244
      C.1.3 Valuation of Flexibility 250
C.2 Optimal Capital Structure 251
      C.2.1 The MM Propositions 251
      C.2.2 Personal and Corporate Taxation 255
C.3 Implications for Capital Structure 255
      C.3.1 The Role of Agency Costs 255
      C.3.2 Informational Asymmetries 260
C.4 Payout Policy 261
      C.4.1 Dividend Policy 261
      C.4.2 Dividend and Information 263
C.5 Financial Contracting 266
      C.5.1 Contracting and Allocation of Control 266
      C.5.2 Debt Contract Design 267
C.6 Going Public 268
      C.6.1 The Going Public Decision 268
      C.6.2 Underpricing and Information Asymmetries 268
C.7 Going Private 270
      C.7.1 Leveraged Buyouts 270
C.8 Mergers and Acquisitions 271
      C.8.1 Tender Offers and Free-Rider Problem 271
      C.8.2 Merger Bids 276

Notes **279**

Bibliography **285**

Index **297**

List of Figures

1.1   The Region of Admissible Consumptions in a
      Robinson Crusoe Economy...................... 5
1.2   The Region of Admissible Consumptions in a
      Robinson Crusoe Economy with an Investment Schedule   8
1.3   The Region of Admissible Consumptions in the
      Presence of Capital Markets..................... 10
1.4   The Region of Admissible Consumptions in a
      Robinson Crusoe Economy with an Investment
      Schedule and Capital Markets.................... 14
1.5   The Binomial Tree of States for the First Two Periods... 31
1.6   The Binomial Tree for the Underlying Project Value.... 32
2.1   The Equilibrium in Miller's Model................. 51
2.2   The Change of Equilibrium in Miller's Model with
      Underutilization of Tax Shields and Deadweight Costs . . 56
3.1   The Regions of Investment and No-Investment
      Decisions According to Myers and Majluf's Model...... 87

Preface

This book tries to fill a gap in the existing range of textbooks in the field of corporate finance. It is meant to serve as a theory-oriented core text in corporate finance for teaching at a postgraduate or advanced graduate level. A typical use would be as the main textbook in a one-semester course in corporate finance in a Ph.D. program in finance. The text covers the standard syllabus of such a course, with a range of topics such as investment valuation, debt-equity structure, dividend policy, financial contracts, the pricing of IPOs, and corporate restructuring. These are the main topics in corporate finance, each of great practical relevance and each requiring a nontrivial use of key analytical tools and ideas from finance theory. Masters courses in any of these topics may benefit from using this book, which provides a unique integrated framework for this field together with an accessible set of exercises and their solutions.

The material used in corporate finance courses is typically a set of original research papers in the area, chosen according to the taste of the instructor. Some of the papers, however, are unavoidable and constitute the core of the field. In particular, a remarkable collection of papers in this category was edited by Bhattacharya and Constantinides (1989a,1989b). More recently, two volumes were edited by Brennan (1996) in the same spirit. These works have proven to be very useful to students as well to researchers in modern financial theory. This book does not intend to substitute for the original research in the area. On the contrary, the idea is to stimulate the search for the original sources by relating all these works in a uniform language and presenting exercises that refer directly to the discussed papers.

The writing style and presentation are semiformal, mixing discursive motivation and derivation with consistent mathematical notation and simple formal manipulations in a unifying framework. Compared with typical MBA-style corporate finance books, this one is relatively short and concise. Its underlying philosophy is neither to describe the state of the art by providing the most recent results, nor to be exhaustive in the coverage of such a vast subject as corporate finance, but rather to center on the core contributions to the field, emphasizing the way in which the modeling of the relevant issues in corporate finance developed over time.

0.1 Intended Audience

This text addresses a numerate graduate or advanced undergraduate student in finance. The distinctive feature of this book is that it is designed to fit a program directed to the foundations of corporate finance rather than a program aimed at financial practitioners. The emphasis is on theoretical models and related empirical evidence, rather than on practical rules and details of institutional arrangements. Also, the text does not presume extensive prior knowledge of mathematics, economics, or finance. However, it does presume a general familiarity with rigorous mathematical reasoning in general and calculus in particular.

The analytical tools used in the text relate to fundamental theoretical concerns such as asymmetric information, signaling problems, and principal–agent problems of general relevance that feature in many other areas of theoretical finance apart from corporate finance.

The text routinely and systematically applies optimization techniques from calculus to choice problems in corporate finance. Applications of these techniques are direct and brisk so students definitely will have to have some familiarity with Lagrangian optimization, first-order conditions, and marginalist thinking in general to be able to follow the main thread of the argument. An appendix on optimization presenting the required concepts is provided. The text also routinely uses basic integration rules. Students are presumed to be familiar with these techniques or else to receive extra tuition in the mathematical prerequisites from outside the book.

Much of the theory of corporate finance depends on the use of game theory, and the text makes frequent reference to ideas and results from this field of economics. General references for the applications of game theory to corporate finance can be found in Thakor (1991) and in Allen and Morris (2001). An appendix sets up the principles of game theory, although the key ideas are concretely introduced in each specific application. Students who have encountered game theory before will recognize the ideas and are likely to benefit from their familiarity with the territory. However, students with no prior knowledge of the field are given a concrete economic motivation whenever a game-theoretical idea is used.

0.2 Organization of the Text

The text is divided in three main parts. In Part I, the foundations of the theory characterizing the optimal capital structure are established. Chapter 1 presents the principles of valuation under certainty and under uncertainty, introducing at the end the notion of real options and continuous-time valuation. Chapter 2 discusses the seminal work of Modigliani and Miller, showing how the introduction of tax deductibility of interest leads to the trade-off theory of capital structure. The tax advantage of debt relative to the expected level of bankruptcy costs would seem to be such that firms should use more debt than what is actually observed in the market. It has been argued that, in particular, Modigliani and Miller's assumptions of perfect markets and perfect information are too strong to explain the real mechanism of value creation underlying corporate financial decisions.

The literature evolved by considering the impact of asymmetric information and agency problems, which is the content of Part II. Chapter 3 analyzes how these factors affect the optimal capital structure, examining different types of conflicts of interest and discussing the role of signaling in financial decisions. A survey of this subject in Harris and Raviv (1991) includes an extensive bibliography. Chapter 4 starts from the observation of Modigliani and Miller that dividends might convey information to exploit a certain number of theoretical models that tried to explain this issue. Payout policy is discussed within the context of information asymmetry, with a particular focus on share repurchases. A very complete and recent overview of this particular field can be found in Lease et al. (2000). Finally, some implications of such asymmetries in writing financial contracts is discussed in Chapter 5. Subjects such as allocation of power and control are closely related to the contractual nature of the relationship among people within the organizations. In particular, the incomplete character of contracts is shown to play a relevant role in understanding the nature of debt and equity. A more in-depth analysis of these questions can be found in Hart (1995).

Part III of this text concerns financial restructuring, trying to answer questions such as what leads a firm to change its capital structure, concentrating or diluting equity ownership. Chapter 6 discusses the going public phenomenon, why it happens, and possible explanations for IPOs' underpricing. Getting answers to these questions is an important step in understanding the role of stock markets, as stressed by Pagano Marco and Röell (1996) in their representative collection of recent research papers in this field. Chapter 7 goes through the related subject of going private, where stock repurchases are revisited, the LBO process is characterized, and a model for MBOs is presented. Finally, Chapter 8 goes through the underlying theoretical models of mergers and acquisitions. Updated and extensive references to the issues discussed in these last two chapters can be found in Weston, Siu, and Johnson (2001).

This book's structure reflects a particular choice of the subjects. Some topics that have become central in the literature of corporate finance, such as corporate control, are present, but in a transverse way. More or less specific references to this issue are made in chapter 3's discussion of the impact of agency problems on capital structure and on financial contracts as well as in all chapters in Part III, which refers to restructuring.

The text proceeds by carefully going through a sequence of related models, each building and expanding on the earlier ones. Notation is simple and consistent throughout the entire book. Key economic assumptions are displayed and highlighted as Assumption 2.1, Assumption 2.2, and so on and are stated verbally with a minimum amount of mathematical symbolism. Mathematical derivations are given in a semiformal style that mixes economic intuition with mathematical manipulation; some results are especially displayed as propositions, but many important results are stated discursively within the regular flow of the main text.

0.3 Acknowledgments

Finally, it is obvious that a book such as this could never have been written without the help of many people. Many thanks to Sudipto Bhattacharya, Olivier Cadot, Paolo Fulghieri, Pekka Hietala, Pierre Hillion, Kevin Kaiser, Diogo Lucena, and Paulo Soares de Pinho. I owe special thanks to the Ph.D. students involved in the project, particularly to Ana Lacerda, but also to Ulrik Pelle, Rita Cardim, and Jesper Langmak, with whom most of the exercises were developed. Pedro Pita Barros, Ricardo Brito, and Marcelo Fernandes kindly took time to read substantial parts of the manuscript, providing insightful comments. John Huffstot made a careful revision of the text.

Very special thanks are due to some people without whom the simple idea of this work would not even exist. First, recognition goes to Theo Vermaelen, who taught me this subject at INSEAD and forced me to go through all the fundamental papers in Corporate Finance. Also, Paula Antão provided outstanding assistance during the whole writing process over a two-year period, becoming an essential link between me and the students. Finally, José Miguel Gaspar provided the material for the appendix about game theory, and João Sobral do Rosário did similar work for the appendix about principles of optimization.

Finally, I would like to thank the institutions where this work has been developed—first, INSEAD (in particular, its Finance Department).

There I found a place, time, resources, and motivation to study corporate finance during my Ph.D. work. Also I appreciate the use of its facilities in Singapore, where part of the final revisions was done during the Summer of 2000. I especially would like to mention the support of the INSEAD staff, especially that of Susan Damesin (in Singapore) and of Sharon Horry (in Fontainebleau). Also, the enthusiasm of the School of Economics of the Universidade Nova de Lisboa, where I taught this course in the past years, was very helpful. I thank in particular its dean, José Neves Adelino, and both José Ferreira Machado and Mário Páscoa, who directed the Ph.D. program at different times during that period. Last but not least, I thank Célia Alves, who provided the necessary secretarial support.

PART I
Foundations

1
Valuation

THIS CHAPTER DISCUSSES the main principles and implications that should underline a rational choice of an investment policy. It will be argued here that the objective of any investor is to maximize his/her wealth, expressed as the capacity to consume. From this principle two things follow. The first is that an investment project is acceptable if the investor has additional consumption choices with the project that he/she would lack without it. The second is that optimality of an investment policy implies that such policy makes as broad as possible the set of accessible consumption paths over time. As for a criterion of acceptability of a project, one measures how much the set of consumption paths is enlarged for that given investment project. This measure is the net value of the project. When choosing investments, one should only take projects with positive net value. When comparing equally risky investments, one should always prefer the investment with the largest net value. Consider now the case of a decision of a firm's management about whether or not to invest in a project. When the cash flows of the investment project are properly defined, the net value of the project is exactly the same as the increase in the firm's value. Given perfect capital markets, the owners of the firm will unanimously support the acceptance of all projects with positive net value.

This chapter is divided into three parts. The first part is very much constructed on the basis of well-known texts such as Hirshleifer (1970) and is focused on the case of certain future cash flows and endowments. Starting with a one-period economy with no trade, it presents the natural constraints to choose the optimal path of consumption. The possibility of investing part of the initial endowment is then introduced. It is argued that the only acceptable investments are those that enlarge the set of possible consumption paths. Immediately after that conclusion, the existence of investment possibilities is ignored just for the next subsection, in order to introduce and isolate the effect of financial markets. This allows us

3

to illustrate the role of these markets in broadening the set of consumption paths by the fact that they make it possible to transact consumptions at different moments, according to the time preferences of the agents. More possibilities of investments enlarge the ability to increase the value of firms. An investment schedule in the presence of financial markets is then considered and it is shown that an optimal choice of investment leads to a value that is at least as good as it was in the absence of financial markets. Moreover, it is shown that the decision about how much to invest and which projects one should invest in is completely independent of the time preference consumption of the investors. An extension to multiperiods is then made.

The second part of this chapter analyzes the implications of uncertainty for these results. A very simple and brief approach is taken here. The notion that no additional consumption paths can be obtained without a positive cost is introduced. This principle, known as the absence of arbitrage opportunities, has implications for the market value of any stream of uncertain cash flows. Namely, any such stream is shown to be valued as the expected discounted cash flows under an artificially constructed probability measure. The final step in the second section is to define certain classes of equivalence among uncertain streams of cash flows by introducing the concept of beta-evaluation. The way in which the subject is presented here has roots in the original approach developed by Arrow (1964). Almost every text in financial economics, such as Huang and Litzenberger (1988), Pliska (1997), and Dothan (1990), covers this topic in great detail. This part follows the synthetic structure of the first chapter of Duffie (1996).

Finally, the third section is devoted to a very important aspect that determines the value of any project under uncertainty. The issue here is the fact that whoever decides whether or not to invest in a project usually has some flexibility. This flexibility unambiguously increases the value of the future uncertain stream of cash flows as valued before, and therefore increases the worth of the projects to be valued. The fact is that as time goes by, uncertainty is gradually resolved. In many real circumstances, the investor may postpone the decision to invest in a project that, if started now, would give him/her a negative net value. If the realization of uncertainty becomes more favorable in the future, the option of investing later in the very same project may reveal it to be attractive. In a similar way, if investment has been made at time 0 in a positive–net-value project and the realization of uncertainty becomes unfavorable (so that the value becomes negative), the investor may, for example, cancel the project, in this way eliminating some of the future bad results (a negative value) at that point in time. In other words, the possibility of canceling the project should imply an overall higher value for the project, in the sense that it eliminates some bad outcomes. The usual references for this subject are the books by Dixit and Pindyck (1994) and by Trigeorgis (1996).

1.1 Valuation under Certainty

In this section the criteria for investment decisions under certainty are discussed. The analysis made herein follows the traditional setup of the problem that may be found in Hirshleifer (1958) among others.

1.1.1 The Robinson Crusoe Economy

Suppose that there is an individual who, just like Robinson Crusoe, has been left alone on an island. He lives in a one-period economy, defined by two points in time: now and the future (say, one year from now). The fact that he is alone means, in essence, that there is no one to trade with. He is given endowments in a nonperishable good. Let X denote the initial endowment and Y denote the promised future endowment. Given this situation, Robinson faces a problem—namely, to choose how much to consume today, x, as compared to how much to consume in the second period, y. Clearly, one must have

$$y \leq Y + X - x \tag{1.1}$$

together with $0 \leq x \leq X$ and $0 \leq y \leq Y + X$. This region of admissible consumptions is illustrated in Figure 1.1.

Let us assume that his time preferences for consumption are fully characterized by a utility function $U(x, y)$ defined in R_+^2 and that the

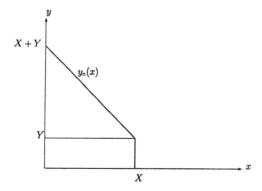

Figure 1.1. *The Region of Admissible Consumptions in a Robinson Crusoe Economy*

solution for this problem is given by maximizing $U(x, y)$ subject to the preceding conditions. In order to make this mechanism solution operational, the following assumption is made:

Assumption 1.1.1. *The utility function $U(x, y)$ is continuous and twice differentiable in its two arguments.*

Within this context the derivatives with respect to the first and second arguments are denoted, respectively, by U_1 and U_2. The second derivatives are denoted accordingly, and we incorporate the usual assumption that

Assumption 1.1.2. *Utility functions increase in both arguments at decreasing rates.*

In other words, both U_1 and U_2 are positive, and both U_{11} and U_{22} are negative. Therefore, in maximizing the utility, no waste of resources will be allowed at the end of the period, meaning that the constraint (1.1) is binding. Instead of the general inequality, strict equality relating y to x must hold at the optimal solution, defining for every current level of consumption x the optimal consumption in the future as

$$y_o(x) = Y + X - x. \tag{1.2}$$

It is then important to characterize the optimal consumption at time 0, x_o^*, given by the optimization of the utility in x. Thus, subject to $0 \le x \le X$, as illustrated in Figure 1.1, one finds the optimal consumption at time $t = 0$ satisfying

$$x_o^* = \arg \max U[x, y_o(x)].$$

Some important and desirable properties for x_o^* must be ensured. The first one is uniqueness of the solution. Negative convexity of U with respect to x ensures that the optimal solution is unique.

Assumption 1.1.3. *The utility function $U(x, Y + X - x)$ is strictly concave as a function of x.*

Also, notice that the uniqueness of this solution implies that for all $x \ne x_o^*$,

$$U(x_o^*, Y + X - x_o^*) > U(x, Y + X - x).$$

With this in mind, one may show that

$$x_o^* = \arg \max U[x, y_o(x)] = \begin{cases} 0 & U_1(0, Y + X) \le U_2(0, Y + X) \\ X & U_1(X, Y) \ge U_2(X, Y) \\ x^* & \text{otherwise,} \end{cases}$$

where x^* is the solution of $U_1(x^*, Y + X - x^*) = U_2(x^*, Y + X - x^*)$. Notice that the first two solutions are corner solutions. The first solution corresponds to a strong preference for postponing consumption; at that point, any decrease in future consumption has more impact in the utility than the correspondent increase in current consumption. The second solution denotes a strong preference for current consumption. In this case total utility decreases as current consumption is diminished from level X. Finally, the last solution comes out from the usual first-order condition

$$U_1(x^*, Y + X - x^*) - U_2(x^*, Y + X - x^*) = 0. \tag{1.3}$$

1.1.2 Time Preferences

Consider now the following problem: For a given level of utility $u = U(x, y)$ obtained by consuming x today and y in the future, one may ask how much current consumption Robinson is willing to sacrifice for future consumption, keeping the same level of utility. In other words, since u is fixed, this is simply solved by making

$$du = 0 = dU(x, y) = U_1(x, y)dx + U_2(x, y)dy$$

or

$$\frac{dy}{dx} = -\frac{U_1(x, y)}{U_2(x, y)} < 0.$$

This ratio dy/dx is called the *marginal rate of substitution* between consumption today and consumption in the future. It measures how much future consumption must be sacrificed to obtain one more unit of consumption today, keeping utility constant.

The negative sign of this ratio is quite intuitive. If current consumption decreases, for utility to be kept at the same level, future consumption has to increase. Variations in current and future consumption must thus have opposite signs. Moreover, if there is a time preference for earlier consumption, one would require that future consumption increase by a higher amount than the decrease in current consumption. Somehow this would compensate for waiting, and one would have $dy/dx \leq -1$. Therefore, at the optimal choice of consumption levels in both periods, define the positive number ρ such that

$$\frac{dy}{dx} = -(1 + \rho) \tag{1.4}$$

where this factor ρ measures the time preference for earlier consumption. This implies that at the optimal point $(x_o^*, Y + X - x_o^*)$ satisfying equation (1.3), d^2y/dx^2 is positive, which is left to prove as an exercise.

1.1.3 Production Opportunities

Up to now, Robinson Crusoe has not considered any production alternative for his initial endowment. But how would his decision change if he had the possibility of making productive investments that have positive returns at the end of the period? Consider therefore the possibility of making investments at time $t = 0$. The following assumption about the available investment schedule is made:

Assumption 1.1.4. *At an investment level I, assume that an additional marginal investment has a marginal nonincreasing rate of return $\varphi(I)$, which is always positive.*

If at time 0 there is an endowment X, for an initial consumption x there is the possibility of a total investment $X - x$ made at that point in time. This leads to a total amount y_p for consumption at time 1 given by

$$y_p(x) = Y + \int_0^{X-x} [1 + \varphi(I)] dI$$
$$= Y + (X - x) + \int_0^{X-x} \varphi(I) dI$$
$$> Y + X - x = y_o(x).$$

Notice that for any level of consumption x at time 0, the level of consumption y at time 1 is always strictly greater than the value $Y + X - x$ when no investment schedule is available, as shown in Figure 1.2. From this construction it follows that the decision about how much to consume in the first and second periods will be made on this line $y_p(x)$, which can be easily shown to decrease in x at a decreasing rate as Figure 1.2 suggests. This is left as an exercise.

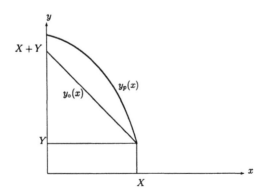

Figure 1.2. *The Region of Admissible Consumptions in a Robinson Crusoe Economy with an Investment Schedule*

1.1.4 The Role of Capital Markets

Ignore for now the existence of an investment schedule such as the one just described. But now consider that the island has been invaded and that Robinson still lives in a one-period economy, but with the difference that there are now many agents.

The existence of different people trading means that there is a market for trading time preferences. Some people may want to consume at time $t = 0$ more than their endowment allows them to do. Some other agents, however, may initially have more than they are willing to consume at that point in time. The former agents will be willing to exchange some of their future endowment for part of the latter's current endowment.

In equilibrium the interaction of demand and supply for endowments at different times should determine a price for transferring consumption from time $t = 0$ to $t = 1$. This price represents a premium for postponing consumption. Clearly, Robinson may leave an amount ϕ of his current consumption to get it back in the future with a premium of ϕr, proportional to ϕ.

Recall that it has been assumed that the utility function is increasing in current and future consumption (i.e., Robinson prefers more wealth to less). Therefore, with this premium ϕr, Robinson will be better off lending his current consumption than keeping it for his own use in the future if and only if

$$U(X - \phi, Y + \phi(1 + r)) \geq U(X, Y).$$

The positiveness of the proportionality constant r, termed the *interest rate*, provides the right incentive for such exchanges to happen given the decrease in the first argument of the utility function.

The maximum amount that Robinson could lend would be X, in which case his current consumption would be null. In the future he would have Y plus the initial endowment X back with the premium rX, a total amount $Y + X(1 + r)$. The amount $X(1 + r)$ is denominated the *future value* of X.

Alternatively, he may wish to consume in the present more than his current endowment X by an additional amount ϕ, say, that someone in the market is willing to lend him. This may happen provided that he pays it back from his future endowment Y plus a premium of ϕr. Under these circumstances, the maximum possible ϕ in this case would be $Y/(1 + r)$. This amount is called the *present value* of Y.

The issue here is to determine how this possibility affects Robinson's consumption decisions. Given the endowment pair (X, Y), the current consumption is not bounded anymore by X. This bound can be augmented to $0 \leq x \leq X + Y/(1 + r)$. It is then said that the pair of

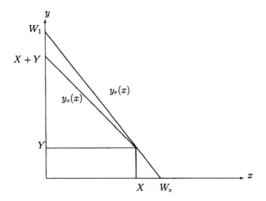

Figure 1.3. *The Region of Admissible Consumptions in the Presence of Capital Markets*

endowments (X, Y) generates a *current wealth* of $W_o = X + Y/(1 + r)$, which reflects the maximum possible current consumption. In the same fashion, future consumption is bounded by $0 \le y \le Y + X(1 + r)$ as illustrated in Figure 1.3, and one defines the *future wealth* of endowments (X, Y) as $W_1 = X(1 + r) + Y$, which reflects the maximum possible future consumption.

This situation may be compared with that of the previous section, where there was an investment schedule with a positive (decreasing) marginal rate of return $\varphi(I)$ for the level of investment I. Here, it follows that the marginal rate of return is a positive constant r. This leads to a total amount y_r for consumption at time 1 given by

$$y_r(x) = Y + \int_0^{X-x} [1 + r] dI$$

$$= Y + (X - x)(1 + r)$$

$$> Y + X - x = y_o(x).$$

Figure 1.3 illustrates this inequality. Notice that W_o can be easily identified with the intercept of the straight line $y_r(x)$ with the x axis, whereas W_1 is the intercept with the y axis. Note also that the existence of markets allows the choice of any point on the straight line $(x, y_r(x))$. Any chosen point on this line has the following important property: The current consumption plus the present value of the future consumption add up to the current wealth generated by the endowment pair (X, Y). In other words,

$$x + \frac{y_r(x)}{1 + r} = X + \frac{Y}{1 + r}.$$

Thus, all points on the straight line $(x, y_r(x))$ are associated with the same level of wealth, W_o. This straight line is called *market line*. Then, as before, it is simple to show that $x_r^* = \arg \max U[x, y_r(x)]$ is given by

$$x_r^* = \begin{cases} 0 & U_1[0, Y + X(1+r)] \le (1+r)U_2[0, Y + X(1+r)] \\ X + \frac{Y}{1+r} & U_1[X + Y/(1+r), 0] \ge (1+r)U_2[X + Y/(1+r), 0] \\ x^* & \text{otherwise,} \end{cases}$$

the interpretation being identical as for x_o^*, and x^* now being the solution of $U_1(x^*, Y + X - x^*) = (1+r)U_2(x^*, Y + X - x^*)$. In other words, now the marginal ratio of substitution must be $-(1+r)$ at the optimal point of consumption, thus leading to $r = \rho$, the parameter ρ being defined in equation (1.4).

The effect of capital markets may be read from the expression of $y_r(x)$. For any level of current consumption x, the fact that $y_r(x) \ge y_o(x)$ implies that consumption in the future can be greater with than without the capital markets. Since the presence of capital markets implies that future and current consumption can be exchanged, this means that current consumption can also increase from its original maximum X up to the level of current wealth. Thus, the optimal choice has a greater level of utility with financial markets than without them.

1.1.5 Consumption and Investment with Capital Markets

Now consider the same one-period economy with many agents, again including an investment schedule. Assume that there are different time preferences. Also, demand and supply are assumed to exist for both current and future consumption. This leads to an equilibrium value for the discount factor r reflecting the premium that one gets for postponing consumption. Being determined in equilibrium, this premium is exactly how much one must pay to consume earlier. In the presence of an investment schedule, it is also reasonable to make the following assumption:

Assumption 1.1.5. *The infimum of the marginal decreasing rate of return $\varphi(I)$, which is always positive, is smaller than the interest rate r.*

In other words, after a certain amount of investment, it is more interesting to invest in the financial market than in the investment schedule.

Up to now, only two types of investment have been considered: an investment schedule as analyzed in section 1.1.3 and the capital markets as just described. Now a more general situation is considered since there are *two* different places to invest: the production schedule and the financial markets.

Given the endowment pair (X, Y), the existence of financial markets allows us to borrow money for investment. Let ϵ be the amount to be invested in the investment schedule. Thus, consuming x at the initial time $t = 0$, the amount available for the investment is $X - x$. If the required investment ϵ is greater than $X - x$, the amount $\epsilon - (X - x)$ must be borrowed from the bank. This implies that at time $t = 1$ the investor must pay back $[\epsilon - (X - x)](1 + r)$ to the bank. If, on the other hand, the required investment ϵ is smaller than $X - x$, the amount $(X - x) - \epsilon$ must be lent to the bank. Hence, in any case, the future consumption will be given by

$$y(x) = Y + \int_0^\epsilon [1 + \varphi(I)]dI - [\epsilon - (X - x)](1 + r) \qquad (1.5)$$

$$= X + Y - x + \int_0^\epsilon \varphi(I)dI - [\epsilon - (X - x)]r. \qquad (1.6)$$

Then the problem is to maximize the utility $U(x, y)$ subject to the possibilities allowed by the production schedule or, equivalently, maximizing $U(x, y(x))$ with $y(x)$ given by equation (1.5), subject to $\epsilon \geq 0$. Maximization must be performed with respect to x and ϵ. It is simple to check that the first-order condition with respect to ϵ does not depend on x and y, leading to an optimal value ϵ^* of ϵ given by

$$\epsilon^* = \begin{cases} 0 & r \geq \varphi(0) \\ \varphi^{-1}(r) & \varphi(0) \geq r. \end{cases}$$

This result may be interpreted as follows: The optimal level of investment ϵ^* does not depend on the preferences of the agents over the levels of consumption in both periods. A rational agent maximizing his/her utility will invest in all available investment projects up to the level where the marginal rate of return equals the market interest rate, r. From that point on, the agent prefers to lend money in the market at that interest rate.

The fact that the market rate r is the threshold that determines up to what point an investment project is interesting establishes a very important role for the capital markets. Markets actually become the term of comparison for analyzing investments in the sense that if one's nonconsumed current wealth has not been invested, it may be invested in the market at the rate r. For that reason, the market rate is often referred to as the *cost of opportunity of capital* or simply *cost of capital.*

The fact that the preceding optimal solution for the investment level depends only on the market rate r and is completely independent of consumption levels leads to the following proposition:

Proposition 1.1.1 (Fisher separation). *The optimal production decision is determined by an objective market criterion independently of individuals' subjective preferences that define their consumption decisions.*

This result has strong implications in that the structure of any investment policy can be seen as a sequential decision in two phases. In the first phase, one chooses the level of investment. In the second, a decision is made about the intertemporal consumption path, or how much to consume at each point in time. Therefore, the level of investments is decided independently of the consumption preferences, but the level of possible consumption depends on the investment decision.

The consumption problem should actually be solved as follows: First, define the function

$$f(x, y) = x + y - X - Y - \int_0^\epsilon \varphi(I)dI + r[\epsilon - (X - x)]. \qquad (1.7)$$

Then the problem is to maximize the utility $U(x, y)$ subject to the possibilities allowed by the production schedule, described from equation (1.5) as $f(x, y) = 0$. One may find the optimal solution either by constructing the Lagrangean

$$\mathcal{L}(x, y) = U(x, y) - \lambda f(x, y)$$

and then working out the first-order conditions $U_1 = \lambda f_1$ and $U_2 = \lambda f_2$ or, equivalently, by maximizing $U[x, y(x)]$ with $y(x)$ given by equation (1.5). This last formulation reduces to a one-dimensional optimization in x. The first-order condition is $U_1 + U_2 y' = 0$, implying once again that the marginal rate of substitution at the point of optimal consumption should be $-(1+r)$. This leads once more to $r = \rho$, the parameter ρ being defined in equation (1.4).

Once the optimal level x of initial consumption is determined, the future consumption is maximized for an investment level ϵ^*. The optimal value ϵ^* of investment leads to a total amount $y_f(x)$ for consumption at time 1 given by

$$y_f(x) = \begin{cases} Y + (X - x)(1 + r) & r \geq \varphi(0) \\ Y + (X - x)(1 + r) + \int_0^{\varphi^{-1}(r)} [\varphi(I) - r]dI & r \leq \varphi(0). \end{cases}$$

It is a very important and intuitive result that for a given level of current consumption x,

$$y_f(x) \geq y_p(x) \geq y_o(x), \qquad (1.8)$$

which can be checked by simple inspection. This means that the introduction of financial markets allows a larger range of current and future consumption alternatives for the economic agents, as illustrated in Figure 1.4. Thus, the existence of financial markets leads to a choice of optimal solutions of investment and consumption choices with higher levels of utilities for the agents as compared with the case where no such markets exist.

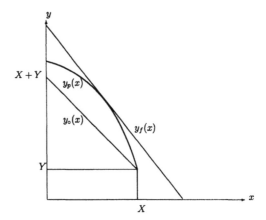

Figure 1.4. *The Region of Admissible Consumptions in a Robinson Crusoe Economy with an Investment Schedule and Capital Markets*

1.1.6 The Value of an Investment Project

In an earlier subsection the consumption problem was analyzed in the absence of an investment schedule, leading to an optimal consumption at $t = 1$ expressed by $y_r(x)$. One may wonder where would $y_r(x)$ be placed in the set inequalities (1.8).

Formally the problem may be solved very simply by noticing that the consumption decision is based on the optimization of the utility $U(x, y_f(x))$, in the case of determining $y_f(x)$, and on maximizing $U(x, y_r(x))$ in the case of $y_r(x)$. Comparing $y_r(x)$ with $y_f(x)$, one notices that the difference between them is expressed as

$$y_f(x) - y_r(x) = \int_0^{\varphi^{-1}(r)} [\varphi(I) - r] dI$$

if there are projects more interesting than the financial markets, or as zero otherwise. The important thing is that this difference is independent of the optimal choice of x and y. Thus, the introduction of an investment works as if the future endowment Y were shifted by

$$\Delta = \begin{cases} 0 & r \geq \varphi(0) \\ \int_0^{\varphi^{-1}(r)} [\varphi(I) - r] dI & r \leq \varphi(0) \end{cases}$$

This means that the introduction of the investment schedule is equivalent to increasing the future wealth by Δ. In other words, the current wealth is increased by $\Delta/(1 + r)$.

Given an investment schedule, its *net present value* (NPV) is defined as the increase in the current wealth generated by the investment. In this case, for the given investment schedule φ,

$$\text{NPV}(\varphi) = \frac{\Delta}{1+r}.$$

Notice that if the investment schedule does not allow return rates greater than r, its NPV is null. In other words, the corresponding investments are rationally ignored. It follows that

Proposition 1.1.2. *It is rational to invest in a project if its net present value is positive.*

This is simply another way of saying that the optimal level of investment is ϵ^*. By construction, this is also equivalent to saying that one should invest in a project if its marginal rate of return is at least equal to r.

A corollary of this proposition is that the optimal level of investment is the one that maximizes the present wealth of the agents or, in other words, is the level of investments that maximizes their capacity to generate higher levels of consumption from the pair (X, Y) for both periods.

Corollary 1.1.1. *The optimal investment decision is the one that maximizes the current wealth of the agents.*

1.1.7 Multiperiod Economy with Capital Markets

There is no mystery in how to generalize these ideas to a multiperiod economy. Suppose now that there is a two-period economy with capital markets together with production arising from a given investment schedule. Introducing z as the consumption at time $t = 2$ and Z as the endowment at that point in time, the formalism follows the earlier sections. Let ϵ_0 and ϵ_1 be the amounts invested at times $t = 0$ and $t = 1$, respectively. The consumption problem should actually be solved as follows: Analogously to equation (1.7), one may define the pair of functions

$$f(x, y) = x + y - X - Y - \int_0^{\epsilon_0} \varphi(I)dI + r[\epsilon_0 - (X - x)]$$

and

$$g(y, z) = y + z - Y - Z - \int_0^{\epsilon_1} \varphi(I)dI + r[\epsilon_1 - (Y - y)].$$

Then the problem is to maximize the utility $U(x, y, z)$ subject to the possibilities allowed by the production schedule, described as $f(x, y) = 0$ and $g(y, z) = 0$. The optimal solution is found by constructing the Lagrangean

$$\mathcal{L}(x, y, z) = U(x, y, z) - \lambda f(x, y) - \gamma g(y, z)$$

and then working out the first-order conditions with respect to x

$$U_x = \lambda f_x = \lambda(1+r),$$

with respect to y

$$U_y = \lambda f_y + \gamma g_y = \lambda + \gamma(1+r)$$

and, finally, with respect to z

$$U_z = \gamma g_z = \gamma.$$

These first-order conditions lead to

$$U_y = \frac{U_x}{1+r} + U_z(1+r)$$

with the optimal investment at each period being

$$\epsilon_0^* = \epsilon_1^* = \begin{cases} 0 & r \geq \varphi(0) \\ \varphi^{-1}(r) & \varphi(0) \geq r. \end{cases}$$

This result confirms the Fisher separation principle once more. Now, since the investment policy is just the same as in the case of a one-period economy, it follows that the investment schedule increases the wealth of the investor in each period by

$$\Delta = \begin{cases} 0 & r \geq \varphi(0) \\ \int_0^{\varphi^{-1}(r)} [\varphi(I) - r]\, dI & \varphi(0) \geq r. \end{cases}$$

Therefore, at time $t = 0$ the investor may ask the bank for an additional amount of $\Delta/(1+r)$ to be paid at $t = 1$ with the results from the initial investment plus $\Delta/(1+r)^2$ to be paid at $t = 2$ with the results from the investment at time $t = 1$. Therefore, the present net value of the project is again written as the increase in wealth at time 0 generated by the investment,

$$\text{NPV}_T = \frac{\Delta}{(1+r)} + \frac{\Delta}{(1+r)^2}.$$

The valuation principle developed in this section works for an arbitrary number of periods. In particular, ignoring the presence of production schedules, let $X_o, X_1, \ldots, X_n$ denote the endowments or simply a sequence of cash flows at times $0, 1, \ldots, n$, respectively. If r is the interest rate per period, the lines of constant wealth (the market lines as previously defined) become hyperplanes with the equation for the present value

$$PV = X_o + \frac{X_1}{1+r} + \frac{X_2}{(1+r)^2} + \cdots + \frac{X_n}{(1+r)^n}$$

$$= \sum_{i=0}^{n} \frac{X_i}{(1+r)^i}.$$

This expression may be easily generalized for the case where there are different market interest rates in different time periods. Let r_t denote the constant interest rate between times t and $t+1$. In this case, the equation for the market lines is again a hyperplane expressed as

$$PV = X_\circ + \frac{X_1}{1+r_\circ} + \frac{X_2}{(1+r_\circ)(1+r_1)} + \cdots + \frac{X_n}{\Pi_{j=0}^{n-1}(1+r_j)}$$

$$= X_\circ + \sum_{i=1}^{n} \frac{X_i}{\Pi_{j=0}^{i-1}(1+r_j)}.$$

1.1.8 Exercises

1. Consider a Robinson Crusoe economy in one period without an investment schedule. Show that $x_\circ^*$ is given by the expression in the text.
2. Consider a Robinson Crusoe economy in one period without an investment schedule. Prove and interpret the fact that d^2y/dx^2 is positive at the optimal point $(x_\circ^*, Y + X - x_\circ^*)$ satisfying the equivalent of equation (1.3) in the presence of time preference.
3. Consider a Robinson Crusoe economy in one period with an investment schedule. Show that $y_p(x)$ is decreasing in x with a negative second derivative.
4. Show that the optimal value of the investment in financial markets is given by the expression for ϵ^* in the text.
5. Prove Corollary 1.1.1.
6. Show how to get the expression for $y_f(x)$.
7. Show the inequalities in relation (1.8).
8. Prove Proposition 1.1.2.
9. Consider an economy with two agents, A and B, who live in a one-period economy defined by two points in time. The preferences of agents A and B are represented respectively by $U^A(x, y) = x^2y$ and $U^B(x, y) = xy^2$, where x is the level of consumption now and y is the level of consumption in the future. They are given equal endowments. Each one receives 100 now and 48.46 in the future. Both agents have the possibility of making productive investments with return given by $\varphi(I) = -I + 10$.
    (a) What is the optimal level of investment by each agent?
    (b) Is that dependent on the preferences of each agent?
    (c) How much does each one wish to consume now as a function of the interest rate?
    (d) Verify that in equilibrium $r = 0.2$.

1.2 Valuation under Uncertainty

The principles already developed may well be extended to situations in which the future outcome is not certain. Suppose that Robinson Crusoe now has a bundle of investment projects available to him, but he is not sure of the outcome of any of them. This section addresses how this uncertainty affects his optimal decision of consumption and investment.

In other words, considering that there are several available projects, and that each of them requires an initial investment I_i and has an intrinsic present value of V_i, this section will describe conditions under which the decision about whether or not to invest depends only on whether or not V_i is greater than I_i. In order to do that one must know how to properly characterize the value V_i of each project, given the uncertainty underlying their payoffs. This is the main purpose of this section.

It will be assumed that financial markets are available in the context of an exchange economy. In that setting conditions will be established so that the analysis under uncertainty may be focused strictly on the valuation process of the projects and not on the consumption path.

1.2.1 One-Period Model

The expression *future uncertainty in a one-period economy* means that someone investing at time $t = 0$ is not sure of the market conditions at $t = 1$. Both the endowment and the investment's payoff at that point in time depend on the particular conditions of nature at $t = 1$. Uncertainty is thus described by a set of states belonging to a finite sample space $\Omega = \{w_1, w_2, \ldots, w_K\}$, where each state w_j occurs with probability $p(w_j)$, denoted for simplicity as p_j. Also, if $x \in R^K$ is a random variable in Ω, let

$$E(x) \equiv \sum_{j=1}^{K} x_j p_j$$

denote the expectation of x under the probability measure p.

The notion of utility must be refined under uncertainty. In Section 1.1, utility was introduced as a real function $U(x, y)$, increasing and differentiable in the present consumption x and in the future consumption y. Here, however, future consumption is a random variable. Let $y \in R^K$ denote a *consumption plan* (i.e., the vector of possible consumptions at time $t = 1$), with the j-th component $y_j \equiv y(w_j)$ denoting consumption in state j. In this setting utility must be a real function $U^*(x, y)$ defined on R^{K+1}, allowing us to define preferences over different plans of consumption. Comparing two different consumption plans, y and z, the utility function U^* of an individual must be constructed in a way such that

$$U^*(x, y) > U^*(x, z)$$

if this individual prefers plan y to plan z. In more formal terms, the individual's preferences are said to have a utility representation if there is a function U^* with the preceding property. A commonly accepted utility representation is the *von Neumann-Morgenstern utility function*,

$$U^*(x, y) = EU(x, y) = \sum_{j=1}^{K} U(x, y_j)p_j,$$

also known as the *expected utility function*. Notice that under a *certain consumption plan*, where consumption is a sure thing or, in other words, y_j is a constant k independent of j, $U^*(x, y) = U(x, k)$ and the utility function under certainty is recovered.

The *certainty equivalent* of an uncertain consumption plan y can be defined as the certain consumption plan γ with the same expected utility as y. In other words, $U^*(x, y) = U(x, \gamma)$.

An agent is said to be *risk-averse* if, for any consumption plan y, the certainty equivalent γ is smaller than $E(y)$ or

$$EU(x, y) < U[x, E(y)].$$

It follows that the utility function U must be concave. If, on the other hand, an agent has a utility such that the certainty equivalent of a risky consumption plan is greater than the expected future consumption, the agent is said to be *risk-seeking* and U must be convex. Finally, risk-neutrality characterizes an agent that is indifferent between a certain consumption plan and a risky plan, provided that the expected consumption coincides with the certain consumption. In this case, the utility function U must be linear.

Now, consider the consumption problem in a one-period setting under uncertainty. Regarding the endowments, define $Y_j \equiv Y(w_j)$ as the endowment received at $t = 1$ in state $j = 1, 2, \ldots, K$. Also, instead of having one single project to consider for investment, assume that the investor faces a bundle of N different one-period projects. Each of these projects has an initial value V_i, $i = 1, \ldots, N$, and at time $t = 1$ pays $\Gamma_i(w_j)$ in state $j = 1, 2, \ldots, K$. For simplicity of notation, let $\Gamma_i(w_j)$ be denoted by Γ_{ij}. These values define a value vector $V \in R^N$ and a payoff $N \times K$ matrix Γ, given by

$$\Gamma = (\Gamma_1, \Gamma_2, \ldots, \Gamma_K) = \begin{bmatrix} \Gamma_{11} & \Gamma_{12} & \cdots & \Gamma_{1K} \\ \Gamma_{21} & \Gamma_{22} & \cdots & \Gamma_{2K} \\ \vdots & \vdots & \ddots & \vdots \\ \Gamma_{N1} & \Gamma_{N2} & \cdots & \Gamma_{NK} \end{bmatrix}$$

where Γ_j denotes the N-dimensional column vector of payoffs in state j.

An investment decision amounts to choosing a portfolio of projects, namely a vector $\theta \in R^N$ with one component for each project. It follows that a portfolio has market value $V^\top\theta = \sum_i V_i\theta_i$ and payoff vector $\Gamma^\top\theta \in R^K$. In other words, for a given choice of θ, consumption at $t = 0$ is

$$x(\theta) = X - V^\top\theta \tag{1.9}$$

and consumption at $t = 1$ will be

$$y(\theta) = Y + \Gamma^\top\theta, \tag{1.10}$$

where y is a K-dimensional vector, with the j-th component y_j denoting consumption in state j.

From the consumption point of view, this setting of uncertain outcomes poses new problems. If we suppose that an agent has a specific consumption target y for $t = 1$, the choice of θ should be made in such way as to satisfy

$$\Gamma^\top\theta = y - Y$$

or, more explicitly,

$$\begin{bmatrix} \Gamma_{11} & \Gamma_{21} & \cdots & \Gamma_{N1} \\ \Gamma_{12} & \Gamma_{22} & \cdots & \Gamma_{N2} \\ \vdots & \vdots & \ddots & \vdots \\ \Gamma_{1K} & \Gamma_{2K} & \cdots & \Gamma_{NK} \end{bmatrix} \begin{bmatrix} \theta_1 \\ \theta_2 \\ \vdots \\ \theta_N \end{bmatrix} = \begin{bmatrix} y_1 - Y_1 \\ y_2 - Y_2 \\ \vdots \\ y_K - Y_K \end{bmatrix}. \tag{1.11}$$

It has been assumed that N projects are available, but when analyzing the consumption problem it is reasonable to consider only projects with linearly independent payoffs. In other words, suppose that there is a project k such that its payoff in any state of nature can be written as a combination of the payoffs of the other available projects. Then, holding an investment in project k is not relevant since such a position can be substituted for by holding a portfolio of the other projects, as defined by the linear combination of payoffs.

Formally, consider a portfolio choice θ. If there exists a real vector $\alpha \in R^N$ such that $\alpha_k = 0$ and $\Gamma_{kj} = \sum_{i \neq k} \alpha_i\Gamma_{ij}$, the $t = 1$ consumption is the same as if the chosen portfolio were θ^* with $\theta_k^* = 0$ and $\theta_i^* = \theta_i + \alpha_i\theta_k$. In that sense we say that project k is *redundant*. Hence, let N be the number of projects with linearly independent payoffs—that is, such that there is no real vector $\alpha \in R^N$ such that $\sum_i \alpha_i\Gamma_{ij} = 0$.

The existence of a solution to the system of K equations on N independent variables θ as described in equation (1.11) depends only on the number of linearly independent lines of the matrix $\Gamma^\top$ (or the number of linearly independent columns of Γ). It is a standard result from linear algebra that a unique solution θ to the preceding system of equations exists for any vector $(y - Y)$ if and only if $K = N$. When a unique solution is possible, the market is said to be *complete* at time $t = 0$. Otherwise, is said to be *incomplete* at that point in time.

In other words, completeness of the market is equivalent to having the number of projects with linearly independent payoffs N equal to the number of states K.

Using this notation and assuming as before that the investors maximize strictly increasing, concave, differentiable utility functions, the optimal portfolio choice can be characterized as follows: Let $U(x, y)$ be one such utility function. Then an optimal portfolio must maximize the expected utility, satisfying

$$\max_{\theta} E[U(x, y)] \equiv \max_{\theta} E\{U[x(\theta), y(\theta)]\}$$

subject to the constraints (1.9) and (1.10). First-order conditions imply that at the optimal portfolio choice

$$dE(U) = 0 \Rightarrow -U_x V^\mathsf{T} + E(U_y \Gamma^\mathsf{T}) = 0.$$

The interpretation of this condition is simple. The amount of utility decrease because consumption was diminished at $t = 0$ must be compensated by the increased expected utility due to the larger future consumption.

In other words, an optimal portfolio choice links the N-dimensional value vector of the projects V to the $N \times K$ matrix of future payoffs by the relationship

$$V = \sum_{j=1}^{K} p_j \Gamma_j \frac{\partial U/\partial y_j}{\partial U/\partial x} = \sum_{j=1}^{K} \Gamma_j \psi_j,$$

where

$$p_j \frac{\partial U/\partial y_j}{\partial U/\partial x} \equiv \psi_j > 0 \tag{1.12}$$

given the assumption that utilities are strictly increasing. The interpretation for the components of the K-dimensional vector ψ is as follows: We defined Γ_{ij} as the payoff of project i in state j. Suppose that such payoff increases to $\Gamma_{ij} + 1$. This implies that the value of the project would change from V_i to $V_i + \psi_j$. Therefore, ψ_j measures the change in value of any project for a unitary increase of the payoff in state j. For that reason the K-dimensional vector ψ is termed the vector of *state-prices* and ψ_j is called the price of state j.

1.2.2 Value and the Absence of Arbitrage

Under the assumption that all agents have increasing utility functions in their wealth, simple economic considerations can be developed.

An *arbitrage opportunity* is a portfolio θ such that initial consumption is not reduced below X and, still, future consumption may be greater than Y. Hence, if all agents have increasing utility functions in their wealth and choose portfolios so as to optimize their utilities, an existing arbitrage opportunity would be the optimal portfolio choice for all such agents. In this way, an unbounded demand for that portfolio would be generated, allowing unbounded future consumption with no sacrifice of present consumption.

However, by construction an arbitrage opportunity is a portfolio θ such that $V^{\top}\theta \leq 0$ and, therefore, at least one of the components of θ is negative. This means that any holder of such a portfolio would be selling at $t = 0$ a project without holding the claim to its payoff at $t = 1$. If all the agents were optimally holding the arbitrage opportunity, they would all be selling that project, and there would be no one to whom they could sell it. It follows that in an exchange economy with several agents optimizing their utilities under the preceding assumptions, arbitrage opportunities cannot exist for they generate an inconsistent collective behavior.

The absence of arbitrage opportunities implies that any portfolio θ such that the K-dimensional vector of payoffs $\Gamma^{\top}\theta$ is positive in all states of nature must also satisfy $V^{\top}\theta \geq 0$. There is a mathematical result known as Farka's lemma[1] that states that this is true if and only if there exists a vector $\lambda \in R_+^K$ of strictly positive components such that

$$V = \Gamma\lambda.$$

Thus, one easily identifies each component λ_j with the state-prices ψ_j, in the case where utilities are differentiable. Notice that the reasoning to get to state-prices here is independent of any differentiability assumption involving the utility functions, as it is the interpretation of the components of ψ as state-prices. This result is summarized in the following:

Proposition 1.2.1. *The absence of arbitrage opportunities is equivalent to the existence of a strictly positive vector of state-prices $\psi \in R_+^K$ such that $V = \Gamma\psi$.*

Under the absence of arbitrage opportunities, it is clear that a redundant project such that $\Gamma_{kj} = \sum_{i \neq k} \alpha_i \Gamma_{ij}$ has value

$$V_k = \sum_{j=1}^{K} \sum_{i \neq k} \alpha_i \Gamma_{ij} \psi_j = \sum_{i \neq k} \alpha_i V_i.$$

It follows that restraining the number of projects to those with linearly independent payoffs does not affect the consumption possibilities of the investors at times $t = 0$ and $t = 1$. Otherwise stated, the only reason for considering redundant projects, given that they provide a payoff similar to a portfolio of the other projects, would be if they were cheaper than the equivalent portfolio, allowing a larger initial consumption. Under absence of arbitrage opportunities, this is not possible.

Whether or not the vector ψ of state-prices is uniquely defined depends once more on the number of independent lines of the matrix Γ, defined as the number of projects with linearly independent payoffs, N. Again, if the market is complete at $t = 0$, the K components of ψ solve a system of $K = N$ independent linear equations. In other words, the vector of state-prices is clearly uniquely defined as

$$\psi = \Gamma^{-1} V.$$

1.2.3 Arbitrage Opportunities and Investment

Markets being complete or not may have implications regarding the separation between the investment and consumption decision. In fact, under the absence of arbitrage opportunities, the required investment $I^\top \theta$ in a portfolio θ must equal its value $V^\top \theta$. Otherwise an arbitrage opportunity exists, allowing an increase of current consumption by

$$(V - I)^\top \theta,$$

for fixed future consumption or, equivalently, increasing future consumption by

$$(V - I)^\top \theta (1 + r),$$

for fixed current consumption. In the language of the first section of this chapter, $(V - I)^\top \theta$ would be the net present value of such an arbitrage opportunity.

Hence, market *completeness* together with the absence of arbitrage opportunities implies that all investments have zero net present value. In other words, if markets are complete, then any portfolio θ is a redundant security, and there is no special θ^* that improves the set of intertemporal consumption possibilities.

However, under *incomplete* markets V is not uniquely defined, since there is a family of possible vectors of state-prices. Consider that markets are incomplete and that both

$$\psi^1 \equiv \{\psi_j^1\} \quad \text{and} \quad \psi^2 \equiv \{\psi_j^2\}$$

are possible vectors of state-prices. Then, two possibly different vectors of values would exist—namely, $V^1 = \Gamma^\top \psi^1$ and $V^2 = \Gamma \psi^2$.

In this case, if $(V^1)^\top \theta \neq (V^2)^\top \theta$ for a given portfolio θ, then there is a positive net present value at least with respect to one of the state-price vectors. Suppose, without loss of generality, that $(V^1 - I)^\top \theta = 0$. In that case, under ψ^2

$$(V^2 - I)^\top \theta \neq 0.$$

If $(V^2 - I)^\top \theta > 0$, the investment in the portfolio θ has a positive net present value of $(V^2 - I)^\top \theta$. If $(V^2 - I)^\top \theta < 0$, a positive net present value strategy would be to sell at time $t = 0$ the portfolio θ by $I^\top \theta$, paying the respective payoff $\Gamma^\top \theta$ at time $t = 1$.

The issue here is that, given the nonuniqueness of the state-prices under market incompleteness, the value of a portfolio may be not uniquely defined, allowing for positive net present value investments.

1.2.4 Value and the Martingale Measure

Assume the existence of an investment such that its payoff is a constant and therefore does not depend on state of nature to be realized in the future. Such an investment is said to be *risk-free*. As in section 1.1, assume that for each unit invested at time 0, a number $(1 + r)$ of consumption units are received at time 1. It then follows from Proposition 1.2.1 that

$$1 = (1 + r) \sum_{j=1}^{K} \psi_j$$

and the value vector may be rewritten as

$$V = \frac{1}{1+r} \Gamma \pi, \tag{1.13}$$

where π is an K-dimensional vector with components

$$\pi_i = \psi_i \bigg/ \sum_{j=1}^{K} \psi_j.$$

By construction it follows that $\pi_i \in [0, 1]$ and $\sum_{i=1}^{K} \pi_i = 1$. Therefore, π may be interpreted as a probability vector in the space of the states of nature. In that case, the value of each project reads from the preceding expression as its expected discounted payoff, the expectation being defined under the probability measure π and the discounting using the risk-free interest rate.

When the expectation of future values coincides with the present value, the value process is said to follow a *martingale*. From equation (1.13) the payoffs discounted at the risk-free rate follow a martingale under the π-measure. For that reason, the π-measure is termed a *martingale measure*.

Also by construction, uniqueness of the probability measure π depends on the market being complete. If markets are not complete, different probability measures may arise leading to different value vectors V.

Given equation (1.13), the value of an arbitrary portfolio θ is given by

$$V^{\mathsf{T}}\theta = \frac{1}{1+r}\sum_{j=1}^{K}\pi_j(\Gamma^{\mathsf{T}}\theta)_j. \tag{1.14}$$

The vector of probabilities π does not necessarily correspond to the vector of real probabilities of occurrence of the different states of nature. Notice that the vector π is a theoretical construct that appears from the absence of arbitrage possibilities.

A natural point to raise is whether it would be possible to write the present value of an uncertain future cash flow as its discounted expected payoff, but now using the real probabilities of occurrence of the different states. The answer is yes, this is possible to do. However, if one changes the probabilities into the real ones and if the value is assumed to be the same as that which does not allow for arbitrage opportunities, the discount factor will have to be different from the preceding risk-free rate. This section shows how to make such an adjustment.

Given the original set of states of nature $\Omega = \{w_1, w_2, \ldots, w_K\}$, where each state w_i occurs with probability p_i, one may write

$$V_i = \Gamma_i\psi = \sum_{j=1}^{K}\Gamma_{ij}\psi_j = \sum_{j=1}^{K}\Gamma_{ij}\delta_j p_j,$$

where the factor $\delta_j = \frac{\psi_j}{p_j}$ is called the *state-price deflator*. Under complete markets, both ψ and p being unique, the resulting state-price deflator vector δ is also unique. It follows from the definition of the state-price vector in (1.12) that the state-price deflator is simply the ratio of marginal utilities

$$\delta_j = \frac{\partial U/\partial y_j}{\partial U/\partial x},$$

measuring the ratio of increased future utility in state j per decreased current utility.

A portfolio on the available investment projects may then be valued as the weighted sum of the corresponding expected deflated payoffs

$$V^{\mathsf{T}}\theta = \sum_{i=1}^{N}\sum_{j=1}^{K}\delta_j p_j\Gamma_{ij}\theta_i = \sum_{j=1}^{K}\delta_j p_j(\Gamma^{\mathsf{T}}\theta)_j = E(\delta^{\mathsf{T}}\Gamma^{\mathsf{T}}\theta).$$

Notice that this expression compares with equation (1.14) in the sense that it gives the same value. The difference, however, is that here *real* probabilities are used instead of the martingale measure π.

1.2.5 Beta Values

The present value of the portfolio has to be calculated as an expectation because it is not known ex-ante which state of nature will be realized. Thus, a weighted average over all possible outcomes is required. Ex-post, however, one knows exactly which state has been realized (say, state j) and may compare the resulting payoff $(\Gamma^\top\theta)_j$ of holding that portfolio with the value initially paid, $V^\top\theta$. The measure of such comparison is known as the total return on the portfolio, defined as

$$R^\theta_j = \frac{(\Gamma^\top\theta)_j}{V^\top\theta},\tag{1.15}$$

which is clearly a random variable. Notice that if it is possible to choose a portfolio θ such that its payoff is independent of the future state of nature or, in other words, such that $(\Gamma^\top\theta)_j$ is independent of j, then it follows that

$$V^\top\theta = \sum_{j=1}^{K}\delta_j p_j(\Gamma^\top\theta)_j = (\Gamma^\top\theta)_1\sum_{j=1}^{K}\delta_j p_j = \frac{(\Gamma^\top\theta)_1}{1+r}$$

where use has been made of the equality

$$E(\delta) = \sum_{j=1}^{K}\delta_j p_j = \sum_{j=1}^{K}\psi_j = \frac{1}{1+r},$$

which means that the expected deflator is the risk-free discount rate. The return on the preceding portfolio will be denoted by R and is given by $R = 1 + r$. Such a portfolio is risk-free by construction and, as one would expect, for each unit invested at time 0 it gives back $(1+r)$ units at $t = 1$. This is what the total return measure tells.

In the case of a risky portfolio, the return is a random variable, whose expected value may be obtained from the expression

$$\mathrm{cov}(R^\theta, \delta) = E(R^\theta\delta) - E(R^\theta)E(\delta)$$

or, equivalently,

$$E(R^\theta) - \frac{E(R^\theta\delta)}{E(\delta)} = -\frac{\mathrm{cov}(R^\theta, \delta)}{E(\delta)}.$$

Since

$$E(R^\theta\delta) = \sum_{j=1}^{K}\frac{(\Gamma^\top\theta)_j}{V^\top\theta}\delta_j p_j = \frac{\sum_{j=1}^{K}(\Gamma^\top\theta)_j\delta_j p_j}{V^\top\theta} = 1,$$

it follows that

$$E(R^\theta) - R = -\frac{\mathrm{cov}(R^\theta, \delta)}{E(\delta)}.\tag{1.16}$$

This equality gives the expression for how much more return is expected from a portfolio of risky investments when compared to a risk-free investment. It may simplify into a more familiar relationship by taking a particular portfolio θ^* such that $\delta = \Gamma^\top \theta^*$. In that case,

$$\text{var}(\Gamma^\top \theta^*) = \text{cov}(\Gamma^\top \theta^*, \Gamma^\top \theta^*).$$

Now denote by $R^* = (\Gamma^\top \theta^*)/V^\top \theta^*$ the return on this particular portfolio. Multiplying both sides of the preceding equality by δ, dividing by $(V^\top \theta^*)^2$, and recalling that $\delta = \Gamma^\top \theta^*$, one gets

$$\delta = \frac{\text{cov}(R^*, \delta)}{E(\delta)} \frac{R^*}{\text{var}(R^*)} E(\delta)$$

or still

$$\delta = -[E(R^*) - R]\frac{R^*}{\text{var}(R^*)} E(\delta).$$

Using the linearity of the covariance operator, it then follows that

$$-\frac{\text{cov}(R^\theta, \delta)}{E(\delta)} = \frac{\text{cov}(R^\theta, R^*)}{\text{var}(R^*)}[E(R^*) - R],$$

which, together with equation (1.16), leads to the state-price model

$$E(R^\theta) - R = \beta_\theta[E(R^*) - R], \tag{1.17}$$

with

$$\beta_\theta = \frac{\text{cov}(R^\theta, R^*)}{\text{var}(R^*)}. \tag{1.18}$$

This so-called beta model states that the excess expected return on any arbitrary portfolio is proportional to the excess expected return on the portfolio θ^*. Portfolios with the same proportionality coefficient β are said to be in the same *class of risk* and β is said to be a measure of the systematic risk of portfolios with respect to the given portfolio θ^*. Notice in particular that the existence of a portfolio satisfying $\delta = \Gamma^\top \theta^*$ relies on the assumption that markets are complete.

Going back to the original problem of evaluating a project, recall from equation (1.15) that

$$V^\top \theta E(R^\theta) = E(\Gamma^\top \theta)$$

and, hence, the value of any portfolio of projects is simply written as

$$V^\top \theta = \frac{1}{E(R^\theta)} E(\Gamma^\top \theta),$$

the expected discounted payoff of the portfolio.

There are two main differences between the interpretation of this equation and the interpretation of equation (1.14). Although they provide the same vector, this last equation uses the *real* probabilities for the occurrence of the different states of nature. Also, the expected cash flow generated by the portfolio of projects is discounted not at the risk-free rate but at the expected return that is adjusted for the class of risk of the considered portfolio.

1.2.6 Exercises

1. Prove that if there is a strictly positive vector of state-prices $\psi \in R^K$ such that $V = \Gamma\psi$, then there are no arbitrage opportunities.
2. Derive the expression

$$-\frac{\text{cov}(R^\theta, \delta)}{E(\delta)} = \frac{\text{cov}(R^\theta, R^*)}{\text{var}(R^*)}[E(R^*) - R].$$

3. When developing the beta-valuation model, it is stated that the existence of a portfolio satisfying $\delta = \Gamma^\top \theta^*$ relies on the assumption that markets are complete. Explain why.
4. Consider two agents, A and B, who live in a one-period economy defined by two points in time. They are given endowments at both points in time. Both agents have the possibility of making productive investments. However, there is uncertainty with respect to the return of this investment in the future. With probability p it is $F_1(\epsilon)$ and with probability $1 - p$ it is $F_2(\epsilon)$. As a consequence, an agent who makes a productive investment cannot be certain about the future consumption. With probability p agent i can consume y_i^1 and with probability $1 - p$ can consume y_i^2. Their preferences are described by a utility function $V_i = EU_i(x, y)$ where $U_i(x, y)$ has the properties described in section 1.1. Find sufficient conditions for the level of investment to be independent of the preferences and of the endowments of the agents.
5. Consider a one-period economy with two possible states of nature at time $t = 1$. The risk-free rate in this economy is 1%. There is a project (call it project 1) in this economy with value today of 6.7 and payoffs $\Gamma_{11} = 10$ and $\Gamma_{12} = 5$.
    (a) Compute the vector of state-prices when there are no arbitrage opportunities.
    (b) Consider another project (project 2) with payoffs $\Gamma_{21} = -2$ and $\Gamma_{22} = 4$. The investment necessary to do project 1 is 5; to do project 2, we must invest 2. Will an agent invest in both projects?
6. Consider a two-period model with two assets: a risk-free asset that pays R in each state of nature and a risky asset that pays D in the first state

of nature and U in the second state. Suppose that the price of each asset is equal to 1.

   (a) Under what condition is this a complete market problem?
   (b) Show that under this condition, a market is free of arbitrage if and only if $D < R < U$.

7. Consider the following one-period model with two agents (A and B). At time $t = 0$ each agent chooses how to allocate his/her initial endowment (5) between the risk-free asset and a project. At time $t = 1$ there are three possible states of nature with equal assigned probabilities. The endowment of agent A is 1 in all states of nature, while agent B has an endowment of 1 in the second state of nature and of 2 in the others. Each agent maximizes a utility function of the form $U(x, y) = u(x) + \sum_{i=1} p_i u(y_i)$ where $u(w) = w^{0.5}$. The riskless asset has a rate of return of 1%. The project has an initial cost of 85 and payoffs $(60, 120, 95)$ in each of the three states of nature.

   (a) Compute the optimal portfolio for each agent.
   (b) Is the vector of state-prices of this economy unique? Justify.
   (c) Suppose that there is a new project available in this economy with payoffs $(50, 70, 30)$. If the arbitrage-free price of this project is 38.02, what are the state-prices in this economy? Are they different between agents?

1.3 Multiperiods and Flexibility under Uncertainty

The valuation principle described previously is at the basis of any work in finance. It accounts for two things: the time value of money and uncertainty. In order to illustrate the principle, a procedure was proposed to evaluate projects under complete markets. One must simply discount the future cash flow associated with the project at a suitable rate and subtract the cost of investment. If this difference is positive, the project is valuable; otherwise, it is not.

This section discusses how to extend this principle to several periods. Particular attention is devoted to the fact that, as uncertainty is resolved, the possibility of managerial flexibility in decision making may have an impact on the initial value of projects.

Whenever dealing with uncertainty, the possibility of not taking into account all the factors that generate value to a project exists. An initial decision with respect to a project does not necessarily avoid the possibility of later additional decisions. This is an essential feature that distinguishes the valuation problem in a setting of several time periods.

Taken from that point of view, the classical analysis of the value of a project based on the net present value as introduced in the earlier sections sounds incomplete. Alternative approaches are then required so as to accommodate this issue. This is done here within the framework of net present value.

1.3.1 The Multiperiod Setting

Consider a project that is supposed to work for a long period of time, with initial value $V(0)$. A partition of this period is considered characterizing a sequence of points in time $t = 0, 1, \ldots$. In order to characterize the value of the project, an underlying uncertainty structure over time is required.

For simplicity, the value of the project will be described as following what is known as a *binomial tree*. Assume that at each point in time t, future uncertainty is characterized by the sample space $\Omega = \{w_+, w_-\}$, reflecting the existence of only *two* states of nature at time $t + 1$. The probabilities are taken as $P(w_+) = p$ and $P(w_-) = 1 - p$. For sake of interpretation, in one of the states the value of the project is assumed to increase, and in the other state to decrease. Moreover, the value of the project at any point in time is assumed to be determined only by the number of times that its value increased.

A tree is formally defined as a pair (Ξ, Λ), where Ξ is a set of nodes and Λ is a set of arcs linking such nodes. Under this setting, a *node* is defined as the pair (j, t), with $0 \le j \le t$. More specifically, a node (j, t) represents a possible state of nature at time t. The *arcs* are defined under this binomial setting by the pairs of nodes of the form $[(j, t); (j, t + 1)]$ or $[(j, t); (j + 1, t + 1)]$.

The initial node is $(0, 0)$. Seen from $t = 0$, at $t = 1$ there are two possible states denoted as $(1, 1)$ and $(0, 1)$, depending on whether the value of the project increased or decreased with respect to its initial value. At time $t = 2$ there are in principle four possible states, two for each of the possible states at $t = 1$. In fact, from state $(1, 1)$, the value of the project may increase, leading to state $(2, 2)$, but may also decrease, leading to $(1, 2)$. Similarly, from state $(0, 1)$, one can achieve either state $(1, 2)$ or $(0, 2)$. Notice that two of these four states collapse into the same one, leaving only three distinct states at $t = 2$. One such tree is said to be *recombining*.

More formally, this property can be rephrased as follows: Given a binomial tree (Ξ, Λ) with a node $(j, t) \in \Xi$ with $0 < j < t$, this tree is said to be recombining if both $[(j, t-1); (j, t)] \in \Lambda$ and $[(j-1, t-1); (j, t)] \in \Lambda$. Figure 1.5 depicts this property.

Finally, markets are taken as complete at any point in time in the sense that there is always a one-period risk-free asset besides the project.

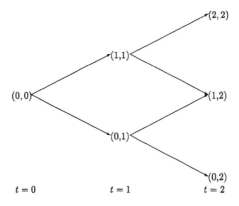

Figure 1.5. *The Binomial Tree of States for the First Two Periods*

Let j be the number of times up to date t that the value of the project increased. At each node, the value of the project is denoted by $V_j(t)$, and the payoff matrix for the next period by

$$\Gamma_j(t) = \begin{bmatrix} V_j(t) & V_{j+1}(t) \\ R & R \end{bmatrix}$$

with $R = 1 + r$ reflecting the discount rate of the risk-free project. Under the absence of arbitrage opportunities, there exists $\psi(j, t) \in R^2$ such that

$$\begin{bmatrix} V_j(t) \\ 1 \end{bmatrix} = \Gamma_j(t+1)\psi(j, t), \tag{1.19}$$

fully characterizing the value of the project at any node. Figure 1.6 shows the tree for the time evolution of the project's value.

The *binomial model* is a further simplification of this structure. It establishes the existence of rates U and D such that

$$V_{j+1}(t+1) = UV_j(t)$$

and

$$V_j(t+1) = DV_j(t).$$

Under the assumption that $U \geq D$, absence of arbitrage opportunities implies that $U > R > D$. The particular feature of this model is that the state-price vector $\psi(j, t)$ is independent of j and t. In fact, equation (1.19) becomes simply

$$\begin{bmatrix} 1 \\ 1 \end{bmatrix} = \begin{bmatrix} U & D \\ R & R \end{bmatrix}\psi.$$

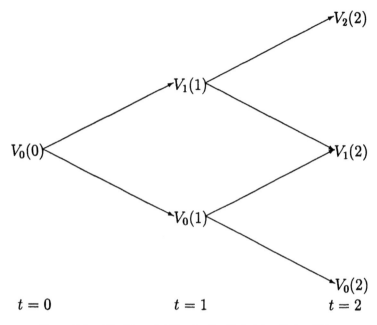

Figure 1.6.   *The Binomial Tree for the Underlying Project Value*

Solving for ψ, it is easily seen that the martingale measure is characterized by

$$\pi = \frac{R - D}{U - D},$$

and the value of a project can simply be written as a function of its future payoffs after n periods as

$$V = \frac{1}{R^n} \sum_{j=0}^{n} \binom{n}{j} \pi^j (1 - \pi)^{n-j} V_j(n). \qquad (1.20)$$

Of course, this value could be written with the real probabilities p and $1-p$, provided that the discount rate would be suitably adjusted for its class of risk. If the project requires an initial investment of I, its net present value (NPV) at time $t = 0$ would be given by

$$\text{NPV} = V - I.$$

The project would be accepted if and only if NPV > 0.

1.3.2 Real Options

When dealing with the net present value of a project, the cash flow is discounted at the rate corresponding to the risk of the project. Every element of this cash flow is discounted as if the project started at a certain point in time and went over several time periods, ending at its maturity.

The fact is that as time goes by, uncertainty is gradually resolved. In many real circumstances, if the realization of uncertainty becomes unfavorable, management may, for example, cancel the project, eliminating in that way some of the bad results that led to the very high discounted rates. In other words, the possibility of canceling the project should imply an overall lower rate of discount and thus a higher value for the project.

This point is easily illustrated in the context of the binomial tree in Figure 1.6. Consider a project starting at time $t = 0$. Its present value is simply

$$V = V_1(1)\psi(1, 0) + V_0(1)\psi(0, 0). \tag{1.21}$$

Now, assume that the investor has the option to cancel the project at $t = 1$ and let $\widehat{V}$ be the present value of the same project, but now incorporating this option. In that case, the investor goes on with the project at $t = 1$ if and only if its value is positive at that point in time. If

$$[x]^+ = \max\{0, x\}$$

denotes the positive part of x, then the value of the project at time $t = 0$ now is

$$\widehat{V} = [V_1(1)]^+\psi(1, 0) + [V_0(1)]^+\psi(0, 0) \geq V.$$

The positive difference $\widehat{V} - V$ is the value of the option to cancel the project. It is also known as the *option premium.*

A similar story can be told if one considers the option to defer the decision of investment. There may be projects that have a current negative net present value, but look like very good projects in the future depending on what happens (in other words, provided that uncertainty will be resolved in a favorable way). Therefore, if one has the option to postpone the decision of investment, the real value of the project is certainly higher than having the all-or-nothing alternative of investing now. The difference in value is precisely the option premium.

This can also be illustrated in the setting of a binomial tree. Consider the case of the preceding project requiring an investment I. The net present value of the project is then

$$\text{NPV} = V - I$$

with V given as in (1.21). Suppose that the investor has the alternative to wait one year until $t = 1$ to decide whether or not to invest in the same project. The option to invest at $t = 1$ thus has a net present value

$$\text{NPV}^* = [V_1(1) - I]^+ \psi(1, 0) + [V_0(1) - I]^+ \psi(0, 0).$$

With the option to postpone, the investment is made at $t = 0$ only if $\text{NPV} \geq \text{NPV}^*$. If, on the other hand, $\text{NPV}^* \geq \text{NPV}$ with $\text{NPV}^* > 0$, then the investment is made only at $t = 1$, if at all. In any case the net present value of the project with the option to delay investment may be written as

$$\text{NPV} + [\text{NPV}^* - \text{NPV}]^+ \geq \text{NPV}.$$

Many other examples of such real options can be given.[2] Other typical examples are the option to expand an investment at some future point in time, the option to temporarily shut down the project, and the option to switch operating modes at multiple decision points.

One thing is true for all these examples, however. An option obviously always has a positive value since it is a right, not an obligation. In other words, to hold an option leads necessarily to a (nonstrictly) positive payoff. Hence, the value of a project plus one or more of such options is always worth more than the original project.

1.3.3 Some General Properties of Options

A European option is generally defined as the right to buy or to sell an asset with initial value $V(0)$ at a given point in the future T termed its *maturity* for a price I, known as its *exercise price*. A *call* option is the contract to buy; a *put* option is the contract to sell. If at maturity there are K different states, its payoff is given by

$$[V_j(T) - I]^+$$

for $j = 1, 2, \ldots, K$. Let C and P denote respectively the values of a call and a put option at time $t = 0$. Under the absence of arbitrage opportunities C is given by

$$C = \sum_{j=1}^{K} \psi_j [V_j(T) - I]^+. \tag{1.22}$$

Similarly

$$P = \sum_{j=1}^{K} \psi_j [I - V_j(T)]^+.$$

Using the fact that $[x]^+ - [-x]^+ = x$, a relation between P and C is readily obtained as

$$C - P = \sum_{j=1}^{K} \psi_j [V_j(T) - I] = V(0) - \frac{I}{R},$$

known as the *put–call parity relation*. Therefore, given the value of a call, the value of the corresponding put with the same maturity and exercise price is automatically determined. For that reason, our analysis here is centered on the call options.

Regarding the value of a call in (1.22), C is clearly a decreasing function of the exercise price I. Also, by construction there are natural lower bounds given by $C \geq 0$ and

$$C = \sum_{j=1}^{K} \psi_j [V_j(T) - I]^+ \geq \sum_{j=1}^{K} \psi_j [V_j(T) - I] = V(0) - \frac{I}{R}.$$

Hence,

$$C \geq \left[V(0) - \frac{I}{R} \right]^+.$$

A natural upper bound is also obtained as

$$C = \sum_{j=1}^{K} \psi_j [V_j(T) - I]^+ \leq \sum_{j=1}^{K} \psi_j V_j(T) = V(0).$$

It follows from these two bounds that $I = 0 \Rightarrow C = V(0)$ and $V(0) = 0 \Rightarrow C = 0$. In other words, if there is no investment required in the future, the option to invest in a project is the present value of its future payoffs. On the other hand, if a project is worthless, the option to invest in that project should be worthless, as well.

Some other properties can be derived within the context of specific models. Here, a heuristic approach is used in the context of a one-period binomial model.

The first result to be derived is that the value of a call option is larger for larger values of the underlying project. To see this, let U and $D < U$ denote the increasing and decreasing rates as before, and let V be the initial value of the project underlying the option. Then

$$C = \frac{1}{R} [\pi C_1(1) + (1 - \pi) C_0(1)], \tag{1.23}$$

where $C_1(1) = [UV - I]^+$ and $C_0(1) = [DV - I]^+$. There are three situations to verify. First, if $DV \geq I$, clearly

$$\frac{dC}{dV} = \frac{1}{R} [\pi U + (1 - \pi) D] = 1.$$

Second, if $UV \geq I > DV$,

$$\frac{dC}{dV} = \frac{\pi U}{R} = \frac{RU - UD}{RU - RD} \Rightarrow 1 \geq \frac{dC}{dV} \geq 0.$$

Finally, if $I \geq UV$,

$$\frac{dC}{dV} = 0.$$

In any case, the statement

$$1 \geq \frac{dC}{dV} \geq 0 \tag{1.24}$$

is always true.

Another result that is particularly relevant for later applications is that the value of a call option increases with the variance of the returns of future payoffs. Consider the return

$$R_j = \frac{V_j(1)}{V(0)}.$$

This return is U with probability p and is D with probability $(1 - p)$. The expected return is thus

$$\varepsilon = pU + (1 - p)D,$$

and the variance of the return is

$$\sigma^2 = (U - D)^2 p(1 - p).$$

For fixed expected return ε, it is possible to characterize the sensitivity of a call value to changes in the volatility. This amounts to calculating

$$\frac{dC}{d\sigma} = \frac{\partial C}{\partial U} \frac{dU}{d\sigma} + \frac{\partial C}{\partial D} \frac{dD}{d\sigma}$$

$$= \frac{1}{R} \left\{ \frac{\partial \pi}{\partial U} [C_1(1) - C_0(1)] + \pi \left[\frac{\partial C_1(1)}{\partial U} - \frac{\partial C_0(1)}{\partial U} \right] \right\} \frac{dU}{d\sigma}$$

$$+ \frac{1}{R} \left\{ \frac{\partial \pi}{\partial D} [C_1(1) - C_0(1)] + \pi \left[\frac{\partial C_1(1)}{\partial D} - \frac{\partial C_0(1)}{\partial D} \right] \right.$$

$$+ \left. \frac{\partial C_0(1)}{\partial D} \right\} \frac{dD}{d\sigma}. \tag{1.25}$$

The ingredients for this expression must be calculated by steps. First, it is simple to verify that

$$\frac{\partial \pi}{\partial U} = -\frac{\pi}{U - D} \quad \text{and} \quad \frac{\partial \pi}{\partial D} = -\frac{1 - \pi}{U - D}.$$

Also, from $d\varepsilon = 0$ we get

$$p\,dU + (1-p)\,dD = 0.$$

On the other hand, the expression for σ^2 gives

$$d\sigma = \sqrt{p(1-p)}(dU - dD).$$

These last two expressions together allow us to write

$$\frac{dU}{d\sigma} = \sqrt{\frac{1-p}{p}} \quad \text{and} \quad \frac{dD}{d\sigma} = -\sqrt{\frac{p}{1-p}}.$$

Noticing that

$$C_1(1) - C_0(1) = \begin{cases} 0 & \text{if } I \geq UV \\ UV - I & \text{if } UV > I \geq DV \\ (U-D)V & \text{if } DV > I \end{cases}$$

together with

$$\frac{\partial C_1(1)}{\partial U} - \frac{\partial C_0(1)}{\partial U} = \begin{cases} 0 & \text{if } I \geq UV \\ S & \text{if } UV > I \end{cases}$$

and

$$\frac{\partial C_1(1)}{\partial D} - \frac{\partial C_0(1)}{\partial D} = \begin{cases} 0 & \text{if } I \geq DV \\ -V & \text{if } DV > I, \end{cases}$$

it is possible to conclude by substitution in (1.25) that

$$\frac{dC}{d\sigma} = \sqrt{\frac{1-p}{p}} \frac{\pi}{U-D}(I - VD) + \sqrt{\frac{p}{1-p}} \frac{1-\pi}{U-D}(UV - I) > 0$$

$$\text{if } UV > I \geq DV$$

and is zero otherwise. It then follows that as future returns are more variable, all the other parameters being fixed, the value of a call option increases.

1.3.4 Exercises

1. In the binomial model, show that if $V \neq \frac{1}{R}[\frac{R-D}{U-D}V_1(1) + \frac{U-R}{U-D}V_0(1)]$, there is an arbitrage opportunity.
2. Suppose that there is no risk-free asset in the preceding discrete-time setting. Would it be possible to choose a portfolio such that the value of this portfolio at date $t = 1$ would fit the payoff of the option described in the text? How many assets are necessary and what characteristics should they have in order to fit the payoff of the option?
3. Show that when the volatility changes, for fixed expected return ε, π can either increase or decrease.

4. Consider exercise 1.2.5 of the previous section.

    (a) Suppose you have the option to defer the decision of investment in project 1—that is, you can either invest today or invest in the project at time $t = 1$. The cost is the same—that is, it costs 5. What is the best strategy: to invest today or to wait one period?

    (b) Assume now that project 2 can be canceled at time $t = 1$. Will you invest in that project?

2

Optimal Capital Structure

THE PREVIOUS CHAPTER described the investment decision as an optimization problem. Based on the cash flow associated with a specific investment project and on the intertemporal cost of money, expressed as the interest rate, agents decide whether or not to invest in order to maximize their wealth. As explained at length, the cost of money plays a central role in the valuation of a project in the sense that it reflects the cost of opportunity of the money invested. The point of the next two chapters is that different types of money sources may be available to finance a project, with possibly different costs of opportunities. Therefore, the financing choice of a project may be seen as a source of additional value and a strategic variable in the optimization of investment decisions.

The *capital structure* of a project in general, or of a firm, more specifically, reflects the structure of the financial sources used in the project. Funds to keep the project going may be generated internally by the project itself or externally. In order to raise external capital, firms have essentially two alternatives: either issue stock or issue debt. Most of the effort of the financial decision making process is centered on the determination of the optimal capital structure of a corporation, that is to say, on the decision of the optimal ratio of debt to equity.

Modigliani and Miller (1958) gave a central contribution to this question with their famous propositions (hereinafter the MM propositions). The first of their results states that under some strict assumptions, such as the absence of taxes, the structure of capital is irrelevant for determining the value of firms in equilibrium. This is so since, given the assumptions of MM's model, they demonstrate that arbitrage profits could arise for individuals able to do "home-made" leverage from unlevered undervalued firms or, alternatively, to undo leverage of undervalued levered firms. Since in equilibrium arbitrage profits are not allowed, levered and unlevered firms should have equal value, and therefore the debt-equity ratio is irrelevant. The introduction of corporate taxes in this context, discussed by Modigliani and Miller (1958, 1963), allows firms to deduct the interest on debt in computing taxable profits. This generates tax advantages for debt that would induce firms to be completely financed through debt. The fact that this is not observed in practice led several authors, starting with Modigliani and Miller themselves, to argue for the relevance of bankruptcy costs. This factor, together with other possible costs associated with debt, could therefore explain the debt-equity ratios observed in the market. The work of Modigliani and Miller will be described in some detail in Section 2.1. However, some years later, Miller argued with convincing market figures that bankruptcy costs are in general of too small a magnitude to affect the equilibrium to be sustained. He suggested a different equilibrium, based on demand and supply of bonds induced by differentiated taxes for individuals and corporations. In Section 2.2 this equilibrium is described and compared with that of MM.

2.1 The MM Propositions

Modigliani and Miller (1958, 1963) have worked out a set of rather strict conditions under which the structure of capital does not affect the actual value of the firms. Of course, it is never claimed that the real world follows these assumptions. What is hoped is that by modeling the universe of the firms in such a way, and by relaxing the assumptions one by one, it is possible to identify and discuss the weight or relevance of each of the different factors in the search for an optimal capital structure.

2.1.1 The Irrelevancy Statement

Assume that a firm starts at time $t = 0$ and has payoffs $\Gamma_j(t)$ in state j at any point in time t, with $j = 1, 2, \ldots k(t)$ denoting the possible states of nature at time t.

In the setting to be considered here, it is assumed that markets do not allow for arbitrage opportunities and also that markets are perfect, in the sense that there are no frictions of any type, taxes included. Also, there are two ways to finance the firm: either through equity only or through equity together with debt. When debt is issued, the firm is said to be *levered*; otherwise it is *unlevered*.

Equityholders and debtholders have different claims on the final payoff of the firm. Debtholders, also known as *bondholders* or *creditors*, buy a debt contract issued by the firm giving them the claim to a face value F at time T. If at that point in time the state of nature is such that $\Gamma_j(T)$ is less than F, the firm is said to go *bankrupt*, in which case the creditholder will receive $\Gamma_j(T)$, if positive. Let $V_j(T)$ denote the positive part of $\Gamma_j(T)$, or $V_j(T) \equiv [\Gamma_j(T)]^+$. *Bankruptcy* is then defined by the set of states of nature where the firm is unable to pay its debt. The payoff to a debt instrument in the j-th state of nature is thus

$$B_j(T) = \min\{F, V_j(T)\}.$$

If K is the number of possible states of nature at time T, then, under the absence of arbitrage opportunities, there exists a strictly positive vector $\psi \in R^K$ such that the present value of the debt is

$$B = \sum_{j=1}^{K} \psi_j B_j(T).$$

Notice that, if there is no state leading to bankruptcy, $B_j(T) = F$ and the preceding expression implies that

$$B = F \sum_{j=1}^{K} \psi_j \Rightarrow B = \frac{F}{R}. \tag{2.1}$$

In other words, in the absence of bankruptcy, debt is contracted at the risk-free rate. On the other hand, given the positiveness of the vector ψ, the existence of bankruptcy in some states of nature leads to

$$B < \frac{F}{R}.$$

This means that F should be discounted at a higher rate than the risk-free rate in order to provide the no-arbitrage value of the debt.

The equityholders, on the other hand, are the true owners of the firm, having the right to receive what is left from the payoff of the firm once the creditholders are paid, provided that the remaining value is positive. They may issue *shares* in order to transact this residual claim, in which case the equityholders are also known as *shareholders*. The positiveness of this residual claim constitutes a protection to shareholders and is termed *limited liability*. In other words, the payoff to equityholders in state j is

$$\begin{aligned} S_j(T) &= [\Gamma_j(T) - \min\{F, V_j(T)\}]^+ \\ &= V_j(T) - \min\{F, V_j(T)\} \\ &= \max[0, V_j(T) - F], \end{aligned} \tag{2.2}$$

implying that

$$V_j(T) = S_j(T) + B_j(T).$$

The present value of the equity is thus

$$S = \sum_{j=1}^{K} \psi_j S_j(T).$$

In this setting, it is clear that the value of the unlevered firm V_u is equal to the value V_l of a levered firm since

$$V_l = S + B = \sum_{j=1}^{K} \psi_j [B_j(T) + S_j(T)] = \sum_{j=1}^{K} \psi_j V_j(T) = V_u$$

This result is known as the first proposition of Modigliani and Miller and may be stated as

Proposition 2.1.1 (MM1). *The market value of any firm is independent of its capital structure*

$$V_l = V_u. \tag{2.3}$$

This statement implies that if equity is not sufficient to finance a firm, debt can be contracted without affecting the value of the project. Also, the consumption of equityholders is not bounded by the fact that they are investing in the project. In fact, equity may be used for consumption and replaced in the capital structure by debt without any side effect on the total value of the firm.

2.1.2 Cost of Capital

Consider now the situation of an unlevered firm. Its cost of capital is simply the expected return on equity. By construction

$$R_s^u = \frac{EV_j(T)}{V}$$

where $V \equiv V_l = V_u$. From Chapter 1 it is known that under complete markets there is a portfolio θ^* such that its expected return is $E(R^*)$, allowing us to write

$$R_s^u = R + \beta_s^u [E(R^*) - R],$$

where β_s^u is the systematic risk of equity in the unlevered firm, as defined in (1.18).

In a levered firm one must consider the *cost of debt*, that is, the expected return to debt

$$R_b = \frac{EB_j(T)}{B}.$$

Under the absence of bankruptcy possibilities, $EB_j(T) = F$ and expression (2.1) implies that $R_b = R$. The presence of bankruptcy, however, leads to $R_b > R$, implying the existence of a systematic risk β_d that is different from zero, as defined by equation (1.18).

Also, there is the *cost of equity*, given by the expected return to equity

$$R_s = \frac{ES_j(T)}{S}.$$

Rewriting this last term,

$$R_s = \frac{E[V_j(T) - B_j(T)]}{S} = \frac{R_s^u V}{S} - \frac{R_b B}{S} = R_s^u + (R_s^u - R_b)\frac{B}{S}.$$

This result is known as the second proposition of Modigliani and Miller:

Proposition 2.1.2 (MM2). *The expected return on equity is equal to the expected return R_s^u for a pure equity stream, plus a premium related to the financial risk equal to the debt-to-equity ratio times the spread between R_s^u and R_b. That is to say,*

$$R_s = R_s^u + (R_s^u - R_b)\frac{B}{S}. \tag{2.4}$$

In other words, the cost of equity changes linearly with the debt-equity ratio B/S. From this expression, the systematic risk of equity in the unlevered firm can be obtained from the linearity of the covariance operator as

$$\beta_s = \beta_s^u\left(1 + \frac{B}{S}\right) - \beta_d\frac{B}{S}.$$

Finally, the *average cost of capital* is defined as

$$\bar{R} = \frac{E[S_j(T) + B_j(T)]}{S + B} = \frac{S}{S + B}R_s + \frac{B}{S + B}R_b$$

and is expressed as the weighted average of the cost of equity and the cost of debt. The weights turn out to be the relative values of equity and debt with respect to the total value. Clearly, this average cost of capital has a correspondent systematic risk given by

$$\bar{\beta} = \frac{S}{S + B}\beta_s + \frac{B}{S + B}\beta_d.$$

2.1.3 The MM Propositions with Taxes

The presence of frictions and, in particular, the presence of taxes may drastically change the preceding conclusions. In this section it is assumed that firms pay taxes at a rate $\tau \in [0, 1]$.

Consider the case of a levered firm. In that case, let T be the point in time where both taxes and the creditholders are paid. In case of bankruptcy, no taxes are paid; otherwise, the firm pays $\tau[V_j(T) - F]$. In other words, in any case the taxes are calculated in state j as

$$\theta_j^\tau(T) = \tau[V_j(T) - F]^+.$$

Under the absence of arbitrage opportunities, the present value of taxes is then

$$\theta^\tau = \tau \sum_{j=1}^{K} \psi_j [V_j(T) - F]^+.$$

The debtholders will receive in state j

$$B_j(T) = \min\left\{ F, \left[V_j(T) - \theta_j^\tau(T) \right]^+ \right\} = \min\{F, V_j(T)\},$$

exactly the same payoff as without taxes. The equityholders are left in state j with

$$S_j^\tau(T) = V_j(T) - B_j(T) - \theta_j^\tau(T). \tag{2.5}$$

It follows that

$$V = S^\tau + B + \theta^\tau \tag{2.6}$$

where

$$S^\tau = \sum_{j=1}^{K} \psi_j S_j^\tau(T).$$

The Main Result
Given the payoffs in the presence of taxes, the value of the unlevered firm is

$$V_u^\tau = (1 - \tau) \sum_{j=1}^{K} \psi_j V_j(T).$$

In the case of the levered firm, the firm generates for equity and debtholders the value

$$V_l^\tau = \sum_{j=1}^{K} \psi_j [S_j^\tau(T) + B_j(T)].$$

Notice from (2.5) that

$$S_j^\tau(T) + B_j(T) = (1 - \tau)V_j(T) + \tau V_j(T) - \theta_j^\tau(T)$$
$$= (1 - \tau)V_j(T) + \tau\{V_j(T) - [V_j(T) - F]^+\}$$
$$= (1 - \tau)V_j(T) + \tau \min\{V_j(T), F\}.$$

In other words,

$$V_l^\tau = (1 - \tau)\sum_{j=1}^{K} \psi_j V_j(T) + \tau \sum_{j=1}^{K} \psi_j B_j(T)$$
$$= V_u^\tau + \tau B.$$

This result is known as the proposition of Modigliani and Miller under taxes and is summarized as

Proposition 2.1.3. *Under the absence of arbitrage opportunities and in the presence of taxes, the value of the firm increases linearly with the level of debt as*

$$V_l^\tau = V_u^\tau + \tau B. \tag{2.7}$$

This decomposition of the value of the firm affects the different costs of capital.

Cost of Capital under Taxation
The fact that the payoff to the debtholders is exactly the same as in the case with no taxes implies that the cost of debt is the same, as is its systematic risk. The cost of equity, however, is affected by the payment of taxes. By construction

$$R_s^\tau = \frac{ES_j^\tau(T)}{S^\tau} = \frac{E[V_j(T) - B_j(T) - \theta_j^\tau(T)]}{S^\tau}$$
$$= \frac{R_s^u V}{S^\tau} - \frac{R_b B}{S^\tau} - \frac{E\theta_j^\tau(T)}{S^\tau}.$$

Use of equality (2.6) simplifies this expression to

$$R_s^\tau = R_s^u + (R_s^u - R_b)\frac{B}{S^\tau} + \frac{R_s^u \theta^\tau - E\theta_j^\tau(T)}{S^\tau},$$

from which expression (2.4) is recovered by making $\tau = 0$. This is a general expression, allowing for the possibility of bankruptcy. A particular case can be worked out considering that there is no bankruptcy in any state. Under this assumption,

$$\theta_j^\tau = \tau[V_j(T) - B_j(T)], \forall j$$

leading to

$$\theta^\tau = \tau[V - B]$$

and

$$E\theta_j^\tau(T) = \tau[R_s^u V - RB],$$

where $R_b = R$, given the absence of default. Substituting in the expression for R_s^τ gives the equivalent to Proposition MM2 with taxes:

$$R_s^\tau = R_s^u + (R_s^u - R)\frac{B}{S^\tau}(1 - \tau).$$

The systematic risk of equity in this case is then

$$\beta_s^\tau = \beta_s^u\left[1 + \frac{B}{S^\tau}(1 - \tau)\right].$$

Finally, the average after-tax cost of capital is defined as

$$\bar{R}^\tau = \frac{E[V_j(T)(1 - \tau)]}{S^\tau + B} = R_s^\tau\frac{S^\tau}{S^\tau + B} + R_b\frac{B}{S^\tau + B}.$$

2.1.4 Empirical Evidence

According to equation (2.7), this theory suggests that there is a big incentive for firms to be financed only through debt. The existence of tax advantages for debt financing is clear from equation (2.7). The value of levered firms is always greater than the value of unlevered equivalent firms. This increase in value is usually termed *debt tax shield.*

The evidence for the existence of a relation between debt-equity ratios and tax shields is mixed. In fact, there are other variables (depreciations, net operating losses, carryforwards, and investment tax credits, for example) that provide similar sorts of tax advantages as the debt tax shield.

Models predict that firms with more taxable income and fewer non-debt advantages from taxes should present higher debt-equity ratios.

In contrast to such predictions, some studies[1] show that the more non-debt tax shields firms have, the more debt they seem to have.

As Barclay and Smith (1999) stress, however, these results cannot lead to conclusions about the irrelevancy of taxes in the capital structure decisions. In fact, the results are difficult to interpret because they are ambiguous. The tax variables may be seen as crude proxies for the firms' effective marginal rate and, therefore, possibly highly correlated with other variables that influence the choice of capital structure.

As an example, consider a firm with a high level of depreciation. Typically, it will be a firm with mainly tangible fixed assets and, thus, with low contracting costs associated with debt financing. This is so, since tangible fixed assets provide good collateral. Evidence reported in the study just cited above is perfectly compatible with this type of interpretation.

Additional recent studies have dealt carefully with this issue. Mackie-Mason (1990) found more solid evidence that firms with a high marginal tax rate are more likely to issue debt than firms in with a low marginal tax rate. In another attempt to avoid the problem of variables that are crude proxies for marginal tax rates, Graham (1996) developed a specific simulation method to provide an extremely sophisticated measure of such rates. Using those firms' marginal tax rates, evidence is found of a positive relation between changes in debt-equity ratios and those rates.

Therefore, evidence tends to support the idea that the existence of taxes does somehow affect the capital structure decisions. However, the impression that one might come away with—namely, that firms have the incentive to raise external capital only in the form of debt—is not correct. In reality, firms are never fully financed with debt. The reason is that there are typical costs associated with debt, such as the flotation costs and the costs of bankruptcy. As the level of debt increases, the higher the probability is that firms will not be able to pay their debt obligations. Aware of that, the debtholders increase the required premium, increasing the cost of capital. These costs increasing with debt may well offset the tax advantage here described, leading to the equilibrium structure observed in the market.

Modigliani and Miller's framework does not take these effects into account. Therefore, the correctness of their results is to be understood in the strict context of their assumptions.

2.1.5 Exercises

1. Let a firm start at time $t = 0$ and have projects with payoffs $\Gamma_j(T) = [10\ 8\ 6]$ for the three different states of nature at time $t = T$. The firm is partially financed with debt with face value $F = 5$ and pays taxes at rate $\tau = 0.4$. Assume that the three different states of nature have

equal assigned probabilities. There are no arbitrage opportunities and the vector of state prices is $\psi = [0.3\ 0.25\ 0.44]$.

    (a) Check propositions MM1 and MM2. Compute the weighted average of the costs of debt and equity.

    (b) Suppose now that $F = 7$, that is, the firm will be bankrupt if state of nature $j = 3$ occurs. How do the values of debt, equity, and the firm change? Compute the weighted average of the costs of debt and equity and compare them with the previous case.

2. Show how to explore arbitrage opportunities when $V_l \neq V_u$, if individuals can borrow capital with the same characteristics as firms.

3. Modigliani and Miller (1958) developed their theory under some different assumptions. They assumed that debt had an infinite life and that each period the firm had to pay interest on debt equal to rD. Moreover, firms could deduct the interest on debt in computing taxable profits. The return to the stockholders is defined as the time average of an infinite stream of payoffs and given by X. How would you obtain proposition MM1 with and without taxes?

4. In the context of the previous exercise, suppose that an individual in the economy faces a borrowing interest rate $\bar{r}$ and a lending interest rate $\underline{r}$ such that $\bar{r} > r > \underline{r}$, where r is the corporate interest rate. What happens to MM1?

5. Suppose that any time an individual wants to sell/purchase assets (bonds and shares), he must pay a fixed amount T of transaction costs. In the context of Modigliani and Miller (1958), what is the effect of these transaction costs on MM1?

2.2 Personal and Corporate Taxation

As discussed in this chapter's introduction, Miller (1977) argued that bankruptcy costs are not relevant enough to justify the debt-equity ratios observed in the market.

    The U.S. corporate tax savings were around 48 cents per dollar at the time of Miller's paper—34 cents now, after the tax reforms in 1986—and the basis for comparison with bankruptcy costs was a familiar number around 20 cents per dollar. The point that Miller raises is that this 20% is applicable to *individuals*, not to firms. Actually, for large, publicly held corporations, that figure does not hold. An empirical study by Warner (1977) using a sample of 11 railroads reports an average bankruptcy cost of around 5.3 cents per dollar invested, presenting a strong inverse size effect: The largest corporation had a cost of 1.7%.

The fact that the debt-equity rate has a stable behavior through time and does not explode to infinity, as the Modigliani and Miller theory suggests, remains to be explained.

The idea of Miller in (1977) to explain this fact is quite simple. Taxes on interest income and dividends are higher than taxes on capital gains (most of which can be deferred). Hence, companies would issue debt to investors who either are tax-exempted or pay little tax, and would issue equity to high–tax-bracket investors. The equilibrium value for the return on the bonds would be defined by the condition that firms would not increase returns above the level at which the saving in taxes to the investors exceeded the firms' corporate tax liability.

On the basis of Miller's argument, there is the underlying assumption that taxes are differentiated. Consider here that besides the tax on corporate profits under which interest payments are deductible, hereby denoted by τ_c, there are also personal income taxes denoted by τ_b and τ_s that are applicable, respectively, to bonds and to shares.

Under this assumption it is possible to describe the equilibrium suggested by Miller. In what follows, rates of return will be used instead of total returns, as before.

2.2.1 Demand for Bonds

To study the demand for bonds, consider the existence of two types of bonds: fully tax-exempt bonds, with equilibrium rate of return r_o, and the other bonds, which are not tax-exempt and have a required rate of return r_b. The after-tax rate of return on these latter bonds is $(1 - \tau_b)r_b$. There is demand for the nonexempt bonds provided that this after-tax rate of return is greater than r_o. This means that

$$r_b \geq \frac{r_o}{1 - \tau_b}.$$

Consider a firm that raises equity at a cost of capital before taxes denoted by ρ. If this equity is within the same class of risk as the tax-exempt bonds, with rate of return r_o as just described, one would require the same rate of return for the equity after paying the taxes due. Thus

$$r_o = (1 - \tau_s)(1 - \tau_c)\rho.$$

If a small amount of *aggregate* debt is issued, it can be sold for relatively low rates of return, that is, the bonds will be owned by *tax-exempt* investors. In this case, $\tau_b = 0$ and the demanded rate of return to the bonds is at its lowest possible level, $r_b^d = r_o$.

Increasing the amount of issued debt will require bondholders in higher tax brackets. Thus, the average τ_b paid by the investors is an increasing function of the aggregate issued debt,

$$\tau_b \equiv \tau_b(B) \text{ such that } \tau_b'(B) \geq 0.$$

As a consequence, the *demanded rate of return* on the bonds becomes

$$r_b^d \equiv r_b^d(B) = \frac{r_\circ}{1 - \tau_b(B)}, \tag{2.8}$$

which is an increasing function of B since

$$\frac{dr_b^d(B)}{dB} = \frac{dr_b^d}{d\tau_b(B)} \tau_b'(B) = \frac{r_\circ}{(1 - \tau_b)^2} \tau_b'(B) \geq 0.$$

2.2.2 Supply of Bonds

From the supply side, corporate taxable firms prefer to issue debt in comparison to equity as long as the bonds are cheaper than equity. In this case firms require a before-tax rate of return r_b that is smaller than the minimum before-tax rate of return $r_\circ$ required by investors on equity.

In other words, corporations prefer to raise capital through bonds if

$$r_b \leq \rho. \tag{2.9}$$

Hence, firms are willing to supply bonds whenever the rates of return r_b satisfy

$$r_b \leq \frac{r_\circ}{(1 - \tau_s)(1 - \tau_c)}.$$

The maximum value of the available rates of return r_b is taken as the *supplied rate of return* r_b^s for bonds,

$$r_b^s = \frac{r_\circ}{(1 - \tau_s)(1 - \tau_c)}. \tag{2.10}$$

The aggregate supply of bonds as a function of the aggregate debt is therefore described by a straight line defining a constant level of rate of return, independent of the aggregate level of debt.

2.2.3 The Equilibrium

The equilibrium that follows from the preceding supply and demand curves for rates of return on bonds is achieved at a debt level B^* and a rate of return on bonds r_b^* satisfying

$$r_b^* \equiv r_b^s = r_b^d(B^*).$$

The solution of this equation is illustrated graphically in Figure 2.1.

Given that r_b^s is constant, equal to ρ, it follows that

$$r_b^* = \rho \quad \text{and} \quad B^* = [r_b^d]^{-1}(\rho),$$

where $[r_b^d]^{-1}$ denotes the *inverse function* of $r_b^d(x)$. In terms of the tax rates, since

$$\rho = \frac{r_o}{(1 - \tau_s)(1 - \tau_c)} \quad \text{and} \quad \rho = r_b^d(B^*) = \frac{r_o}{[1 - \tau_b(B^*)]},$$

the equilibrium relation may be rewritten as

$$(1 - \tau_s)(1 - \tau_c) = 1 - \tau_b(B^*). \tag{2.11}$$

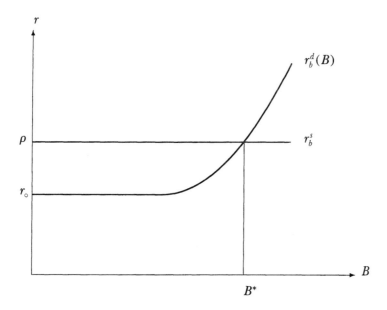

Figure 2.1. *The Equilibrium in Miller's Model*

But perhaps the most striking aspect of Miller's equilibrium is that, although there is an optimal level of aggregate debt in the economy, there will be *no tax advantage for any particular firm to issue either debt or equity*. To see why, notice that to raise a certain amount K of capital, one can issue either debt or equity. In the first case, the stockholders pay back $r_b(1 - \tau_c)K$, whereas in the second, they pay $\rho(1 - \tau_c)K$. But since in equilibrium $r_b^* = \rho$, there is no relative advantage in one form of raising capital with respect to the other.

Alternatively, the relative advantage of leverage for stockholders, G_L, is written as

$$G_L = [\rho(1 - \tau_c) - r_b^*(1 - \tau_c)]K$$

$$= \left[1 - \frac{(1 - \tau_s)(1 - \tau_c)}{1 - \tau_b(B^*)}\right] \frac{r_o K}{(1 - \tau_s)}.$$

The equilibrium relation between the tax rates expressed in (2.11) implies that $G_L = 0$, which is to say, there is no advantage of leverage for the stockholders.

The nature of this equilibrium is strongly driven by the existence of personal taxations. Following Hamada and Scholes (1985), this will be called the *after-tax* equilibrium. However, as stressed by some authors,[2] the U.S. federal tax statutes allow for many different ways of saving and investing at *before-tax* rates of return. The result is that the *effective* personal tax rate applicable may be zero. In this case, one would expect to retrieve the results of Miller and Modigliani that firms will have incentive to be totally financed through debt.

In fact, making personal tax rates equal to zero (i.e., all tax rates except the corporate tax rate τ_c), it follows that the riskless rate under this condition will be greater than r_o in equation (2.9) and will be given by r_o' satisfying

$$r_o' = \rho(1 - \tau_c) > r_o.$$

Also, the supply curve for bonds defined in (2.10) becomes a straight line at the constant level ρ, independent of the aggregate debt level,

$$r_b^s = \rho = \frac{r_o'}{1 - \tau_c}, \qquad (2.12)$$

and the demand curve for bonds in equation (2.8) becomes the parallel straight line at the constant value

$$r_b^d = r_o' = \rho(1 - \tau_c). \qquad (2.13)$$

Thus, in the before-tax model of Modigliani and Miller, equilibrium is reached only at an infinite amount of debt issued, since demand and supply are constants independent of the level of aggregate debt. This leads to a corner solution of 100% debt.

Notice moreover that $r_b^s \geq r_b^d$. This inequality will be strict as long as the constant values of r_b^d and r_b^s are different. If they are equal, both investors and firms will be indifferent to the amount of bonds issued. Comparing equations (2.13) and (2.12), one notices that this may happen in two cases: if $\tau_c = 0$, in which case the result of Proposition MM1 is retrieved, or if $r_o' = 0$.

For a noncorner solution of the before-tax equilibrium (i.e., to avoid the corner solution of 100% of debt financing), an additional assumption introducing some market imperfection would be required, such as leverage-related costs that increase with the *aggregate* debt issued. As noted by Hamada and Scholes (1985), and as will be extensively discussed, the nature of these costs can be multiple (e.g., bankruptcy costs, contracting or monitoring costs, information and signaling costs, differential flotation costs, incomplete markets costs). Which of these costs are relevant is an empirical issue. Whatever the true nature of the costs of debt is, they will lead firms to be willing to reduce the rate of return on bonds as B increases.

In such a case, the supply curve given in expression (2.12) will change into a decreasing function of the aggregate debt level B, $r_b^s(B)$, that will eventually cross the demand level $r_b^d = r_o'$ at some point, defining in that way a *before-tax equilibrium debt*

$$B^* = [r_b^s]^{-1}(r_o')$$

and an *equilibrium rate of return on bonds*

$$r_b^* = r_o'.$$

2.2.4 Comparing with MM

The existence of these two competing theories to explain the equilibrium rate of return on bonds is compatible with the existence of possibly different types of marginal investors defining equilibrium. If these marginal investors can wash out the effect of personal taxation as suggested by Miller and Scholes (1978), the before-tax theory will dominate. Otherwise, in the presence of effective personal taxes, Miller's after-tax equilibrium will be the relevant one.

Notice that the two equilibria are quite different. As stressed before, in the *after-tax* equilibrium, the riskless rate r_o is smaller than the risk-free rate r'_o in the *before-tax* equilibrium. This will be reflected in quite different costs of capital, as described in Hamada and Scholes (1985).

The cost of capital is given by the expected rate of return on a project at which a marginal investor would be indifferent between investing or not. From equation (1.17) in Chapter 1, the risk premium on a given project is proportional to the *systematic risk* β_p of the project. If R^* is the expected return on the portfolio with respect to which β is defined, for the after-tax theory this means that

$$E(R_p^{at}) - r_o = \beta_p[E(R^*) - r_o],$$

whereas for the before-tax theory this result reads

$$E(R_p^{bt}) - r'_o = \beta_p[E(R^*) - r'_o],$$

where $r_o = (1 - \tau_s)r'_o$. Notice that the market portfolio may not be the same when taxes are considered. From these two relationships it is evident that the costs of capital associated with the two equilibria discussed here may be quite different, depending on the values of the various parameters.

2.2.5 Changes in Taxations: An Alternative Equilibrium

Once Modigliani and Miller established their result describing the tax advantages of debt, most of the research in the field of corporate finance involved the relevant costs that could define an optimal debt-equity ratio.

However, the arguments raised in the initial analysis of Miller's bond market equilibrium point to the possibility that there might be no real tax advantages. Hence, the costs previously discussed are apparently balancing a nonexistent advantage.

In order to solve this incompatibility, Miller (1977, p. 271) hinted at the origin of an alternative source of debt advantage. The point is that companies in default will not yield the issuing stockholders the whole interest deduction on debt, their tax shield. If that is the case, the rate of return on bonds supplied by the stockholders will tend to be lower than the rate of return given in (2.10) in order to account for this cost, and the relation between the tax rates will no longer be satisfied. Finally, there seems to exist a natural tax advantage of debt.

This idea has been worked out especially by DeAngelo and Masulis (1980). Their theory is essentially an analysis of the supply side of a generalized after-tax equilibrium. There are two main forces lowering the supplied rate of return on bonds as the aggregate debt increases; the first is the underutilization of tax shields and the second is the leverage-related deadweight costs driven from the before-tax equilibrium.

In the work of DeAngelo and Masulis, uncertainty with respect to the underutilization of tax shields is incorporated, and some substitutes for interest deductions are introduced, such as depreciation, to serve as tax shields. Thus, taxes can be shielded in this context not only by issuing debt but also, for instance, by purchasing depreciable equipment.

To isolate the effect of the underutilization of tax shields, assume that the investment decisions are already made and that the probability distribution of the operating earnings is determined exogenously. In that case, additional borrowing will increase the probability that some tax shields will not be fully used. The incremental value of tax shields decreases, implying a decreasing slope for the supply curve of taxable corporate bonds. Using the same principle as in describing the demand for bonds, the expression for the supply curve (2.10) is changed by considering the *effective* corporate tax τ_c as a *decreasing* function of the aggregate debt level B:

$$\tau_c \equiv \tau_c(B) \text{ such that } \tau_c'(B) \leq 0.$$

As a consequence, the supplied rate of return on the bonds becomes

$$r_b^s \equiv r_b^s(B) = \frac{r_o}{[1 - \tau_c(B)](1 - \tau_s)},$$

which is a *decreasing* function of B since

$$\frac{dr_b^s(B)}{dB} = \frac{dr_b^s}{d\tau_c(B)}\tau_c'(B) = \frac{r_o}{1 - \tau_s}\frac{\tau_c'(B)}{(1 - \tau_c)^2} \leq 0.$$

Therefore, the equilibrium described by Miller is changed. For the same demand curve, now there is a decreasing supply curve lowering the optimal aggregate amount of debt (say, B') and the equilibrium return rate on bonds. In other words, as suggested by Miller, the costs of underutilizing the tax shields are shifted to bondholders in the form of a lower risk-adjusted equilibrium rate of return.

The underutilization of the tax shield generates a deadweight cost, since some of the interest deduction goes to waste. However, this is not the only factor lowering the supply curve. In what follows, a general model incorporating possibly different types of deadweight costs related to leverage is presented. Let $d(B)$ denote these deadweight costs, d being an increasing function of B. Then, the supply curve previously given will become

$$r_b^s(B, d) = \frac{r_o}{[1 - \tau_c(B)](1 - \tau_s)} - d(B),$$

which decreases faster with the total amount of debt B than before because of the additional term $-d(B)$. The new equilibrium return rate

r_b'' will be at the point where demand equals supply for a new equilibrium debt level B'':

$$r_b'' = \frac{r_\circ}{1 - \tau_b(B'')} = \frac{r_\circ}{[1 - \tau_c(B'')](1 - \tau_s)} - d(B'').$$

This new equilibrium is illustrated in Figure 2.2 and compared to the original equilibrium in Miller's model. The new proposed equilibrium defines implicitly the equilibrium deadweight cost d'' as the value satisfying

$$r_b'' = \frac{r_\circ}{[1 - \tau_c(B'')](1 - \tau_s)} - d''(B'').$$

Equivalently, $r_\circ$ is given by

$$r_\circ = (d'' + r_b'')[1 - \tau_c(B'')](1 - \tau_s),$$

which can be rewritten as

$$\frac{r_\circ}{r_b''} = \left(1 + \frac{d''}{r_b''}\right)[1 - \tau_c(B'')](1 - \tau_s). \tag{2.14}$$

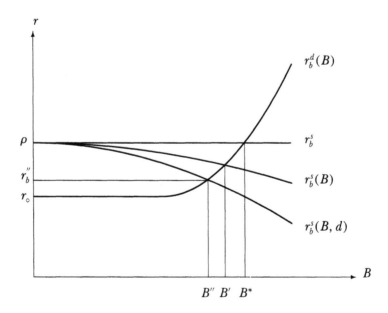

Figure 2.2.   *The Change of Equilibrium in Miller's Model with Underutilization of Tax Shields and Deadweight Costs*

From this equation it is clear that the equilibrium return rate on bonds decreases both with an increase in the deadweight costs d'' and with a decrease in the effective corporate tax rate τ_c due to the underutilization of the tax shields. Therefore, in this generalized Miller's equilibrium there is an increase in the marginal tax advantage of bonds, because both effects imply the decrease in the equilibrium supply of bonds.

2.2.6 Empirical Evidence

The existence of an optimal capital structure under the generalized tax model is an empirical issue, depending on how economically significant the costs are. From equation (2.14), testable implications can be drawn from the theory. It is seen that the ratio between the risk-free rate and the equilibrium rate of return on the bonds, r_o/r_b^*, is positively related to d^* and negatively related to $\tau_c(B)$. But these are both economywide ex-ante variables sensitive to macroeconomic conditions. In a recession, d^* is expected to increase because of higher probability of default. At the same time, $\tau_c(B)$ should decrease because corporations are expected to earn less, and therefore the risk of underutilizing their tax shield is higher. The two effects go in the same direction and lead to the prediction of an increase in the ratio r_o/r_b^*. In sum, in an unfavorable economic situation, corporations are not willing to pay high rates of return on the issued bonds. This prediction is consistently supported by a paper by Buser and Hess (1986). Using monthly yield data on newly issued one-year prime-grade municipal (tax-free) securities as a proxy for r_o and using U.S. Treasury securities from 1959 to 1982 as a measure of r_b^*, they find that the ratio r_o/r_b^* is negatively related to the aggregate level of industrial production. Also, in a more direct measure, they estimate the marketwide *default premium* , which reflects the market expectation of corporate default and hence relates directly to the expectation of the ex-ante deadweight cost d^*. Consistent with equation (2.14), the ratio r_o/r_b^* is found to be positively related to the default premium at the significance level of 0.0001. This time series analysis therefore provides strong evidence that the costs considered are relevant and affect the rate of return on the bonds.

Also, there are cross-sectional testable implications from the theory. Assuming that the deadweight costs may be represented by different functions $d(B)$ for different types of corporations, some firms may reach the optimal cost d^* defined by equilibrium faster than others. Therefore, the firms first achieving the critical value will have less leverage. In other words, firms more likely to encounter financial distress tend to borrow less, and firms less likely to encounter financial distress should borrow more. Consistent evidence of this prediction is found in the work of Castanias (1983), in which a significant negative relation between observed leverage and historical failure rates is reported. Also, Bradley, Jarrell, and Kim (1984) show that long-run average debt ratios are significantly negatively related to earnings volatility. This is compatible with the balancing theory discussed here, since the probability of financial distress for a given degree of financial leverage should increase with the variability of the earnings. Hence, there seems to be some evidence providing support for the generalized Miller's equilibrium.

2.2.7 Exercises

1. Show that in the presence of personal income tax and corporate income tax, the gain from leverage to stockholders is given by the expression

$$G_L = \left[1 - \frac{(1 - \tau_c)(1 - \tau_s)}{1 - \tau_b} \right] B$$

   where B denotes the market value of the debt in the leveraged firm.

2. In the presence of underutilization of a tax shield or leverage-related deadweight costs, the after-tax equilibrium model discussed in Kim (1989) says that the equilibrium is reached at a value of t_c lower than the top tax rate. In this case, what is the best strategy for companies at the top corporate tax rate?

PART II
Agency and Information

3

Implications for Capital Structure

Reading Chapter 2, it might seem that in the presence of a tax system firms should be fully financed with debt, taking advantage of the tax shields. Although there is some evidence to support the importance of taxes in the decision of how much debt a firm should issue, the explanation for the debt-equity ratio on the basis of the tax structure is not entirely satisfactory for several reasons. Among these, the costs leading to the tax equilibria previously discussed are very hard to determine accurately. Besides, since debt has been used for a long time, way before the creation of the described tax system, a theory looking for costs able to offset the advantages of the tax system is necessarily incomplete.

Alternative explanations for the existence of an optimal capital structure have been developed introducing some more realistic aspects of the decision problem defining the optimal capital structure. This chapter presents the two main streams developed in the 1970s and 80s—namely, that capital structure is optimally designed by taking into account the existence of costs of agency (i.e., costs due to conflict of interest among the agents involved in the financial decisions) and costs due to asymmetry of information.[1]

The issue of *agency costs* is addressed in Section 3.1. One of the main components of the costs of raising funds is the difference of interests of the agents involved. Debtholders, new shareholders, old shareholders, and managements all enter into negotiations for different reasons. Bringing them into agreement is costly in the sense that it is very difficult to reach a first-best solution for any of them. Concessions are required to achieve at least a second-best solution. Very roughly speaking, the difference between the value of the firm in what would be an ideal contracting situation and what is viable through negotiation is referred to as *agency costs*. Optimal capital structure requires finding the optimal debt-equity ratio minimizing these costs. Agency models are among the most successful models in generating relevant implications.

In Section 3.2 a different but related stream of thought is described, relating the costs associated with informational asymmetries to the design of capital structure. This approach assumes that managers and/or insiders have private information about the investment opportunities of the firm and related cash flows. The asymmetry of information with respect to other economic agents may have two types of impact. First, managers may use their choice of capital structure as a credible signal to the market of their private information. Second, the information asymmetry may lead to some inefficiencies in the financing decisions of the firms, and alternatives of capital structure may be used to mitigate those effects.

3.1 The Role of Agency Costs

This section discusses the approach to agency costs according to which the structure of debt-equity ratios may have roots in the existence of conflicts of interest among agents within the firms. Two particular types of conflict and associated costs are discussed here. The first type refers to conflicts between managers and shareholders, and the second to conflicts between shareholders and debtholders.

First, let us analyze the nature of the conflict between managers and shareholders. Assume for simplicity that managers have no shares (i.e., no right to residual claim). The owners of the firm are thus the shareholders. Therefore, any effort from the managers to improve the firm's profit will benefit the shareholders but not the managers. On the other hand, the managers will bear all the cost of that effort. Seen from this point of view, the managers do not have any incentive to work in the best interest of the shareholders. The fact that managers have different goals from shareholders may generate a cost—namely, the cost to the shareholders of monitoring the management. The existence of these conflicts of interest may therefore lower the value of the firms due to the extra costs incurred.

The monitoring problem can be solved,[2] assuming that there is an optimal *fee schedule* to be paid to the management for its services. The optimality criterion used is to maximize the expected utility of the shareholders constrained by the fact that the equilibrium fee should provide the management with at least a minimum attractive level of expected utility and take into account that managers are also utility maximizers in the choice of their actions.

Within this context, for a given fee schedule including a punishment in the case of bankruptcy, it can be shown[3] that the performance of the management will be related to the debt-equity ratio. The higher this ratio, the higher the risk of bankruptcy, and therefore the more efficient the management should be in order to avoid the penalty. Hence, the cost of monitoring, reflected in the fee schedule, has a direct relationship to the optimal capital structure. The relationship of this type of problem to the optimal debt-equity ratio may come in many different ways. For instance, it may seem reasonable to assume that shareholders would appreciate a high level of debt. The reason is that a large debt commits the firm to a series of cash payments that would prevent the management from wasting any free cash flow of the firm in any inconvenient way, (i.e., in any way that would not be in the best interest of the shareholders).[4] This mechanism would lower the cost of monitoring.

A different type of conflict, known as *risk shifting*, exists between shareholders and debtholders.[5] For instance, when debt is issued at very high levels, there is a clear conflict between the owners of the firm and the debt issuers. This happens because the choice of any investment project is at the risk of the creditholders. Actually, the best interest of shareholders is to invest in projects that may yield very high payoffs, even if they have a low probability. If it works, the shareholders will pay the debt and keep the residual claim. If it does not work, the debtholders bear the cost. In other words, the value of equity increases with the riskiness of investments. The search for risky investments, however, is not necessarily equivalent to the search for the best, positive-NPV projects. This incentive that equityholders have to choose risky investments may lead to an *overinvestment* problem, which includes the acceptance of negative-NPV projects. This lowers the value of the firm, representing an agency cost of debt.

Another sort of agency cost of debt reflects the fact that equityholders have no incentive to invest new capital, not even in positive-NPV projects when the firm is highly levered. This is known as the *underinvestment problem*. The reason is that when leverage is very high, the residual claim will probably be zero and those who are most likely to benefit from any investments are the creditholders.[6]

Up to now, all the described costs of agency are due to debt. However, when issuing equity, there are also costly effects. The first, and easiest to describe, is that there is an opportunity cost of not issuing debt, thereby losing its associated tax advantage. A different effect is that when issuing equity, the inside shareholders lower their fraction of the total claim on the outcomes of the firm. As discussed in the next section, this situation may lead to a decrease in the residual claim of the firm. Aware of that, the new shareholders will be willing to pay an amount taking into account the expected decrease in the value of the firm.

The total agency costs of raising external funds may therefore be decomposed into two main streams. There are costs associated with debt and costs associated with equity. As the leverage level of the firm increases, the former increases monotonically as the latter decreases. These effects should add to the tax benefits of debt when looking for an optimal capital structure.

3.1.1 Agency Costs of Outside Equity

Consider a firm where the manager owns a fraction of the equity. This manager-owner will make operating decisions maximizing the joint effect of two different sources of utility. The manager's utility will be assumed to be generated not only by the benefits derived from pecuniary returns, but also by some nonpecuniary aspects of the manager's activity. Examples of nonpecuniary aspects are the physical appointments of the office, the kind and amount of contributions to charity, attractiveness of the staff, nature of personal relationship with employees, and an excellent computer.

When the owner-manager sells equity to outsiders, a typical agency problem arises because of the difference of interests between him/her and the outside shareholders.

Consider a firm generating a flow with present market value $\overline{V}$, and let F denote the market value of the stream of the manager's expenditures on nonpecuniary benefits. This reduces the effective value of the firm to $V = \overline{V} - F$. If the owner-manager holds a fraction α of the shares of the firm, its utility will be described by the real function

$$U(\alpha V, F),$$

which is increasing and concave in both arguments. In this context, two main results are in order. First, given an optimal choice of F, utility to the owner-manager decreases as new equity is issued. Second, the effective value of the firm decreases. In fact, the decline in the value of the firm is entirely imposed on the owner-manager. This is reflected in the decrease of his/her utility.

For fixed α, the optimal value $F^*(\alpha)$ is obtained maximizing the utility

$$\max_{F} U[\alpha(\overline{V} - F), F].$$

In other words, $F^*(\alpha)$ must satisfy the first-order condition

$$-\alpha U_1 + U_2 = 0. \tag{3.1}$$

Let $\xi(\alpha)$ denote the optimal value of the utility, or

$$\xi(\alpha) \equiv U[\alpha(\overline{V} - F^*(\alpha)), F^*(\alpha)].$$

Using the first-order condition (3.1), it is clear that $\xi(\alpha)$ is a monotonic increasing function of α, since

$$d\xi(\alpha) = (-\alpha U_1 + U_2)dF^* + Vd\alpha = Vd\alpha.$$

This means that as α increases, the optimal utility of the owner-manager increases. Issuing equity is just the reverse process, reducing the value of α. Thus, the first result comes:

Proposition 3.1.1. *As new equity is issued, the utility to the owner-manager decreases.*

It was just stressed that the decrease in the utility comes from the fact that the owner-manager carries all the reduction in value of the firm when new equity is issued. Indeed, since

$$V = \overline{V} - F,$$

it follows that $dV = -dF$. In order to show that the value increases with α, it suffices to show that F decreases. This follows since $dF/d\alpha$ can be obtained differentiating the first-order condition (3.1) and using the envelope theorem. It follows that

$$\frac{d^2 U}{dF^2} \frac{dF}{d\alpha} = U_1.$$

By assumption $U_1 > 0$ and since these derivatives are calculated at the optimum,

$$\frac{d^2 U}{dF^2} < 0,$$

leading to

$$\frac{dF}{d\alpha} < 0.$$

Thus, this confirms the second result:

Proposition 3.1.2. *As new equity is issued, the effective value of the firm decreases.*

It is clear from the preceding formalism that the reason why the value of the firm decreases is that the optimal market value F^* of the nonpecuniary benefits increases. The managers would have an incentive to convince the outsiders that the value of the firm will remain at the level $V^* = \overline{V} - F^*$ and the fringe benefits will be kept at F^*. Jensen and Meckling (1976) point out that this suggestion is not credible if the outsiders are rational. Basically, they know that it would be optimal for the management to stay at V^* only if they hold the fraction α of the shares.

Under the assumption that $\overline{V}$ is fixed, the new shareholders know beforehand that managers will be tempted to increase their benefits, given that now they only bear a smaller fraction of the costs associated with F. That is why selling some shares will decrease the value of the firm to a level $V^\circ < V^*$, with benefits at a level $F^\circ > F^*$.[7] Knowing that, the new

shareholders in fact would not be willing to pay more than the fraction
of the new value $V°$ corresponding to their fraction of shares.

In order to solve this problem, the management may accept being
controlled by the outsiders. This can be done either by systematic auditing
(to see whether $F = F^*$), by formal control systems, by budget restrictions,
by incentive compensations to the management, or by the market for
corporate control.

In the next section, a situation will be described where the managers
are taken as not owning shares of the firm, in order to isolate the question
of incentive compensations.

3.1.2 Principal–Agent Problems

Managements are typically assumed to act in the interest of the
shareholders, but, especially when they do not own (or own just a few)
shares of the firm, there is no good reason for that to happen. In fact,
there are several natural sources of conflicts between the two parts. Some
examples are

1. Managers in general prefer to expend a lower level of effort than what
   the shareholders expect of them.
2. Managers are tempted to underinvest, either because they are typically
   risk averse in their strategy selection of investments or because of their
   short horizons. This last factor could lead them to reject profitable
   long-term projects that would not return an immediate profit.
3. Also, managers are more interested in ensuring their jobs than in supporting changes in the corporate control that might increase the value
   of the firm but might also affect their employment prospects.

This type of contractual relationship creates what is known in the literature as principal–agent problems. There is a principal, who offers a
contract, and an agent, who may accept or reject the contract to work for
the principal. In order to induce the desired behavior in managers, the
shareholders have to incur contracting costs. As Masulis (1988, Chapter 6,
p. 48) notes, the extension of the decision-making power of the management may be reflected in an important weight of the managerial compensation on the capital structure of firms.

The management contractual incentives regarding their level of effort
are discussed next.

Determining Optimal Fee Schedules
The first formalization of the problem of determining an optimal fee
schedule was made by Ross (1973). In this model the management takes
an *unobservable* action that determines the probability distribution of the

shareholders' payoff. The payment to the management is a function of the payoff, which is observable. The fee schedule is determined optimally by the shareholders in order to provide the incentives for the managers to choose the best possible actions when maximizing their utility. This maximization is constrained to providing managers a reservation expected utility.

Notice that if the actions of the management *are observable* and managers are risk averse, a first-best solution is attainable by making the fee very low, unless the optimal action (from the shareholders' viewpoint) is taken by the management. In other words, the payment schedule will share the risk associated with the managers' action optimally. If the actions are not observable, as in Ross's model, the expected utility for the shareholders will be lowered by their ignorance, since they will have to find a *costly* way to induce the managers to take an optimal action. The difference in the expected utility to the shareholders reflects the agency cost of monitoring the management through the payment schedule.

The problem is to define an optimal fee schedule f to the management such that it will be in the interest of the managers to take the actions desired by the shareholders.

Let a be the action chosen by the management, defined in a space $\mathcal{A}$ of feasible actions. Uncertainty is described by the set of states of nature Ω together with a probability distribution over the elements of Ω. As before, for $w \in \Omega$, the expectation of a random variable $x(w) \in R^{\Omega}$ on Ω is denoted by $E(x)$.

Let the result of action a be a payoff $\theta(a, w)$ in the state of nature $w \in \Omega$, which is assumed to be *unknown* beforehand to both management and shareholders. This payoff is thus a real valued function $\theta(a, w)$: $\mathcal{A} \times \Omega \rightarrow R$.

The fee f is assumed here to be a function *uniquely* of the payoff,[8] that is,

$$f \equiv f(\theta(a, w)).$$

Managers and shareholders are supposed to have their preferences represented respectively by the utility functions G and U. The management faces the problem of choosing an optimal action $a°$ as a function of a jointly optimal fee schedule f^* to be determined, such that

$$\max_{a \in A} E\{G[f^*(\theta(a, w))]\}, \tag{3.2}$$

constrained to a minimum level of expected utility k

$$E\{G[f^*(\theta(a°, w))]\} > k.$$

Hence, the optimal action taken by the managers depends on the established fee schedule f^*. It will be denoted by $a(f^*)$. On the other hand, the shareholders will have to choose the optimal fee schedule f^* so it will be the schedule f satisfying the following variational optimization:

$$\max_{f} E\{U[\theta(a(f), w) - f(\theta(a(f), w))]\} \tag{3.3}$$

subject to

$$E\{G[f(\theta(a^\circ, w))]\} > k.$$

The problem can be considerably simplified if one looks for a specific type of solution. Here, two kinds of fee schedules are proposed, following Ross's model.

1. A family of fee schedules can be achieved if managers and shareholders cooperate, maximizing a weighted sum of their expected utilities. In this case, f satisfies

$$\max_{f} E\{U[\theta - f] + \lambda G[f]\}.$$

where λ parameterizes the family, defining the weights of both utilities. This family of fees is said to be *Pareto-efficient*. When U and G are both monotonic and concave, the optimal fee schedule must maximize the argument of the expected value and therefore is defined implicitly by the equation

$$U'[\theta - f] = \lambda G'[f]. \tag{3.4}$$

2. An alternative approach to find a fee schedule is to assume that, at optimality, the utilities of managers and shareholders are positively and linearly related. That is to say, the optimal fee schedule must satisfy the *similarity condition*

$$U[\theta - f] = cG[f] + b, \tag{3.5}$$

for constants c and b such that $c > 0$. It is clear that both managers and shareholders have the same attitude toward risky payoffs, and hence this similarity condition ensures that the managers will always choose the act more desired by the shareholders.

Ross argues that (3.4) and (3.5) are simultaneously satisfied only if both utility functions U and G are in the linear risk tolerance class. This will imply that the optimal fee schedule f is a *linear* function of the payoff.

Furthermore, consider the three different conditions as defined before: Pareto efficiency, similarity, and linear fee schedule. Any two of them imply the third one. But these are particular forms of somehow *imposed* solutions. A relevant question is to know how the similarity condition or the Pareto efficiency condition relates to the solution of the more general problem described in (3.3).

In the original problem, there is the restriction that the expected utility of the managers should not be below a certain level. Besides, there is a constraint that the managers will act so as to optimize their own expected utility, which is expressed by the first-order condition

$$E\{G'[f(\theta)]f'(\theta)\theta_a\} = 0, \tag{3.6}$$

where θ_a denotes the derivative of θ with respect to a and $k = 0$. Then, the shareholders' problem is to maximize with respect to f the Lagrangean

$$\mathcal{L} = E\{U[\theta - f(\theta)] + \psi G'[f(\theta)]f'(\theta)\theta_a + \lambda G[f(\theta)]\},$$

where ψ and λ are the Lagrange multipliers associated respectively with the restrictions expressed in (3.6) and (3.3). Under some general conditions[9] the Euler-Lagrange equation characterizes optimality provided that

$$\frac{U'}{G'} = \lambda - \psi \frac{d}{d\theta}\left(\frac{\theta_a}{\theta_w}\right).$$

Comparing this solution with (3.4), it follows that in general the fee schedule will be Pareto efficient if either

1. $\psi = 0$, meaning that (3.6) is not binding and the fee schedules will be Pareto-efficient independently of the payoff function θ, or
2. The term $d(\theta_a/\theta_w)/dw$ is a function only of a.

For the optimal fee schedule to be Pareto efficient independently of the payoff function $\theta(a, w)$, the first of these two conditions has to be fulfilled, implying a linear fee schedule, as shown by Ross, and therefore linear risk tolerance utility functions U and G.

If $\psi \neq 0$, the fee schedule will be Pareto efficient only if condition 2 is satisfied—namely, if

$$\frac{d}{d\theta}\left(\frac{\theta_a}{\theta_w}\right) = \varphi(a)$$

where φ is an arbitrary function only of a. The solution for this differential equation is shown to be of the form

$$\theta(a, w) = h(z)$$

where $h : R \to R$ is an arbitrary real function and its argument z is of the form

$$z = we^{[\int^a \varphi(x)dx]} - \int e^{[\int^a \varphi(x)dx]}[-dw/dx - \theta(x)\varphi(x)]dx + K$$

defined up to the constant of integration K. Notice that this solution is independent of the properties of the utility functions U and G.

Most of the subsequent literature in this topic is centered on the case where the managers are averse to effort and the shareholders try to maximize the value of the firm (i.e., are risk neutral). For instance, Shavell (1979) shows that under these conditions a Pareto optimal fee schedule does not maximize the expected profits of the shareholders. This, once again, reflects the costs of monitoring the actions of the management.

In principle, the risk associated with the output is shared among the management and the stockholders. The way this is done strongly depends on the risk-aversion characteristics of both shareholders and managers, as discussed by Shavell. Even in the case of risk neutrality of the shareholders, the fee schedule cannot be fixed as a constant value because then the managers would have no incentive to overcome their aversion to effort. The payment schedule has to depend on the output, leading as before to a second-best solution.

It may be proved that the shareholders will use any indication of the level of effort of the management in the equilibrium fee schedule, in order to approach its first-best solution. Information, even if incomplete, thus has value. It is also clear that the less reliable the proxy for the managers' effort is, the worse off the shareholders will be (i.e., the more distant their solution is from the first-best).

In conclusion, the perfect knowledge of the action would destroy the agency costs associated with the monitoring of the management.

Executive Stock Options

An interesting alternative to help solving the principal–agent problem in the context of management's compensation is to offer a package including call options on shares of the firm. Such options are typically offered *at the money*—that is to say, at an exercise price coinciding with the current value of the shares (say, S). Recalling that the payoff of such options at time T is

$$\max[0, S_T - S],$$

this component in an executive compensation package will give the right incentive for the manager to care about S_T, the future value of the shares.

Among other advantages, it is clear that the introduction of such instruments as a payment device align the incentives of managers with those of the shareholders. In fact, the residual claim to shareholders, as expressed in (2.2), can be seen as an option on the value of the firm with an exercise price that coincides with the face value of debt. If the management is given options, that constrains the real value of the payment to the performance of the firm, as reflected in the market value of the stock.

A second advantage is that this type of instrument allows the reduction of the base pay of the management, thus reducing salary differences among different employees.

Finally, in this setting, the payment of the manager is at risk. At least, this component of the package may be worthless at time T, which justifies a real commitment with the goals of the firm.

3.1.3 Agency Costs of Debt

At the origin of the conflicts between stockholders and bondholders, there is the fact that the value of the firm V may be decomposed into the value of its debt (B) and the value of its equity (S), $V = S + B$. For a fixed V, it is clear that an increase in the value of the equity S can be made only at the expense of B.

Besides, debtholders have fixed claims with default risk as opposed to the limited liability of the residual claims to the stockholders. In other words, stockholders are left with the remaining value of the firm once the maturity of debt expires.

To illustrate the situation, suppose that the only bonds outstanding are zero-coupon bonds,[10] (i.e., bonds with a single face-value payment F at the expiration time T). If at that date the value of the firm is greater than the face value of debt, the bondholders will receive F, and the shares in the hands of the stockholders will have the value of the remaining $V - F$. If, on the other hand, $V < F$, the debtholders will get all V (which still is not enough to cover the face value of their claim), whereas the stockholders are left with nothing.

As first noted by Black and Scholes (1973), owning the equity of a firm is like having the right to buy the company paying the face value of the debt F to the bondholders, at the expiration time. At that moment T, such a right will be worth $V_T - F$ if $V_T > F$ or be worth zero otherwise. Therefore, the current value of the equity S_t must be given by the current value of such a right.

The current value of equity is then given as the value of a call option on the future value of the firm V_T with exercise price F. Within this view of the value of the equity, it is easier to determine the relevant factors that increase it, expropriating therefore the value to the bondholders. Using the results in Chapter 1, the value of the equity S_t at any time t decreases with the face value of the debt, F,

$$\partial_F S_t < 0.$$

The intuition is simple. The more the bondholders get at the end of the process, the less is left for the shareholders, decreasing the value of their right.

Also, it may be shown that S_t increases with

1. The value of the firm,

$$\partial_V S_t > 0.$$

This happens since the higher the value of the firm at time t, the higher is the expected value of $V_T - F$, the value of equity to the shareholders at the expiration date T. Also, the less likely it is that the final value is below the threshold K.

2. The riskless interest rate r,

$$\partial_r S_t > 0.$$

For a high interest rate, the present value of the face value of the debt decreases. This effect clearly increases the value of the equity.

3. The variance of the returns to the firm σ^2, or its volatility σ,

$$\partial_\sigma S_t > 0.$$

There is an intuitive explanation for this effect, as well. The higher this volatility, the higher the likelihood is that the value of the firm is either very high or very low at time T. But if it is very low, the stock-holders will not be able to cover the value of the debt, and therefore their expected gain is zero. Stockholders only gain if $V_T > K$, in fact, and by the argument just described, whenever $V_T - F$ is greater than zero, it is expected to be *much* greater for high variances than for low variances.

4. The time to liquidation $T - t$,

$$\partial_{T-t} S_t > 0.$$

This factor works in a very similar way to the variance. The longer it is, the more the value of the firm may vary. Most of the negative variations will not be considered in the value of the equity, because they are associated with final states with the same value zero. Hence, an increase in the time to expiration increases the value of the equity.

It has been explained that the bonds and stocks add up to the total value of the firm at any fixed time t. Hence, at any point in time, anything that increases the value of the equity will be done at the expense of the bondholders if the value of the firm is not to change. The preceding properties hint clearly which variables are relevant to this type of manipulation.

The Cost of Overinvestment

Galai and Masulis (1976) describe typical situations in which increases in the value of the equity are done at the expense of the bondholders. For instance, a riskier investment is certainly preferred by the stockholders to a less risky investment, other things being equal, since it would increase σ. The reason is that, given

$$\partial_\sigma S_t > 0,$$

the choice of the riskier project would increase the value of the equity and would lower the value of the bonds. Acquisitions of risky assets should be incorporated in this class of investment decision. It is clear that such unanticipated investment decisions will affect the market value of the debt and equity of the companies.

The cost of agency arises when the present value of the riskier investment is lower than the present value of the alternative investments. The natural choice, having in mind the total value of the firm (debt plus equity), should be the investment with the highest net present value. However, in a highly levered firm, the managers have the previously described incentive to choose the riskier project, even if this lowers the total value of the firm. This decrease in value is an agency cost that is usually termed the cost of overinvestment.

Coming back to the argument of Jensen and Meckling, if the debtholders know that the stockholders have the choice between investments with different risks, they will presume that the management will choose the riskier, and will be willing to pay a lower value for the bonds issued, increasing the cost of debt R_b. In such a case, the stockholders will not be able to expropriate the bondholders. The value of the firm will decrease since the firm is likely to take the riskier investment, but the agency cost would be transferred to the stockholders.

The Cost of Underinvestment

Myers (1977) shows how, even when the investment decision *does not affect the variability of the returns*, there is an opportunity wealth loss driven by the impact of debt in the investment decisions. His main argument follows from the fact that the value of a firm is given not only by the value of its assets in place but also by the present value of the opportunity to make future investments. To finance the investments, suppose that the firm can issue up to a certain amount I of equity. The rest must be raised issuing debt with a face value F at maturity. Given the uncertainty with respect to the return on the investments, only risky debt is considered.

The point is that managers tend to invest in states of the world in which they expect the returns to be enough to pay back the debtholders and still leave a positive residual claim for the shareholders. The higher the debt, the more selective the managers will be with their projects, reducing the opportunities of the investment and, hence, the value of the firm. Thus the present value of the firm is a decreasing function of the promised payment F to the bondholders.

Another implication of this idea is the definition of the optimal level of debt. In fact, the current value of debt should reflect the present value of what the bondholders expect to receive at maturity. If $F = 0$, such present value is clearly zero, as well. If F is very high, the present value of the debt will be low, since it will be less and less likely that F will be paid, as F increases at high levels[11]. There must be an optimal face value of debt F^* at which the present value of debt is maximized.

The Costs of Monitoring and Bonding

There are possible ways of limiting these conflicts, such as including various covenants to protect the interest of the debtholders and limiting the decisions of the management. Clearly, there are also costs associated with these procedures, such as the costs of writing such provisions and of enforcing them as well as the reduced profitability of the firms, due to the limitations imposed on the management. All such costs related to covenants are the so-called *monitoring costs*.

Additionally, it is in the interest of the stockholders that the monitoring activities are performed at the lowest cost, since they are the ones who bear such costs. Probably it would be to their advantage to disclose information in order to facilitate the work of control. For that information to be credible, its accuracy should be verified by an independent outside auditor. The cost of providing such information and contracting auditors is called the *bonding costs*.

Smith and Warner (1979) present a detailed analysis of bond covenants appearing in debt contracts, which are expected to reduce the agency monitoring and bonding costs. The various types of covenants are described according to the way in which they try to protect the bondholders.

The first are covenants imposing restrictions on the investment policy of the firm and therefore on its production. Among them, there are restrictions on investments and on the disposition of assets, restrictions on mergers to avoid the expropriation problems discussed previously, and restrictions on the transfer of title of pledged assets to the bondholders until the bonds are paid in full. The debt is said to be *secured* in this last case, and the way in which this form of contract protects the bondholders is by precluding the substitution of assets and controlling the incentives for stockholders to take projects reducing the value of the firm.

The second type are bond covenants restricting the payment of dividends. This may be a relevant issue, since the change of the dividend policy may be made at the expense of the investment policy on which the valuation of the bonds was based.

Costs may also be reduced through the introduction of covenants restricting subsequent financing policy. This is also relevant, since the firm may try to reduce the value of the outstanding debt by issuing additional debt of the same or higher priority. This would certainly affect the value of the outstanding bonds.

Finally, there may exist covenants modifying the pattern of the payoff to the bondholders. This is the case, for instance, with *convertible debt*, giving the debtholder the right to exchange the debentures for other securities of the company, to be specified by the provision, and within a period of time also to be specified. This lowers the incentives of the stockholders to expropriate the debtholders, since the debtholders will share most of the wealth transfer from bonds to stock.

Another type of covenant in this class is the *callability provision*, giving the firm the right to redeem the debentures before maturity at a stated price schedule. In this case, the stockholders will have the possibility to undertake certain low-risk but profitable projects that otherwise would not be taken, since they would primarily benefit the debtholders. It is, in fact, a costly solution for the problem of underinvestment discussed previously, and it may still increase the value of the firm.

3.1.4 Empirical Evidence

Following the ideas just presented, one could say that, in general, the larger the growth opportunities of investments for a firm, the larger are the potential problems of underinvestment associated with debt financing. Therefore, the lower should be the levered ratio of such firms. Conversely, the more restricted are the growth opportunities for a firm, the larger will be the problems of overinvestment, which leads such firms to present higher leverage ratios.

Most of the evidence clearly points to the existence of something like an optimal capital structure. Schwartz and Aronson (1967) found evidence that the average debt-to-book asset ratios differ from industry to industry. Also, they found a tendency of companies within each industry to cluster around these averages. Besides, strong evidence has been found that the leverage ratios within each industry tend to be related to factors that may be used as proxies for growth opportunities, such as R&D.

To confirm this type of relation, a study by Long and Malitz (1985) showed that the five most levered industries in the U.S. were very mature and quite asset-insensitive. On the other hand, the less levered industries were those that reveal a greater growth potential, implying high investments in R&D and advertising.

Other studies have used cross-sectional regression techniques to test whether the determinants of capital structure indeed affect the financial decisions. For instance, Bradley, Jarrell, and Kim (1984) found evidence that the average debt-to-book asset ratio is negatively related not only to the volatility of net results of the firm, but also to the advertising and R&D investments. Such findings are compatible with high costs of financial distress for growing firms.

More recently Barclay, Smith, and Watts (1995) have contributed to this body of evidence with a study of about 6,700 U.S. companies over a period of 30 years, presenting all sorts of debt-equity ratios. As suggested by the theory, the authors tried to relate the ratios with some proxy for growth opportunities. Thinking about a proxy, it is simple to realize that the more growth opportunities a firm with a given level of assets in place has, the higher should be the market value as compared to the book value. The proxy that Barclay, Smith, and Watts used then was simply the market-to-book value of the firm. Regressing the debt ratios on this proxy provided strong support for the relationship investigated. Companies with high market-to-book ratios have significantly lower leverage ratios than do companies with low market-to-book ratios.

Rajan and Zingales (1995) also found support for this relation in the capital structure of markets outside the U.S., providing further robustness. Examining data from Canada, France, Germany, Italy, Japan, the U.K., and the U.S., they found that leverage decreases as market-to-book ratio increases and also that leverage is higher if the ratio of fixed assets to total assets is higher.

Completely different in spirit, Parrino and Weisbach (1999) found further evidence that the incremental cost of debt is higher for firms that make larger investments. These authors used numerical techniques to estimate the impact of stockholders–bondholders conflicts in the investment decisions of 23 firms and examined to what extent these conflicts explain observed cross-sectional variations in the capital structure. Besides finding that the firms with the highest leverage (and also relatively higher cash flow volatility) are those that have the largest underinvestment problem, they also showed evidence of the costs of maturity of the debt. Firms with relatively short debt duration were shown to present almost no stockholder–bondholder distortion. This suits very well the prediction of the theory as presented previously and first suggested by Myers (1977).

In fact, the issue of debt maturity—which is deferred to a later chapter—is very relevant. Guedes and Oppler (1996) documented the determinants of the term to maturity of more than 7,000 bonds and notes issued between 1982 and 1993 in the U.S., and found that typically large firms with good credit ratings borrow at both short and long maturities. On the other hand, firms with speculative credit ratings borrow typically in the middle of the maturity spectrum. This is consistent with the theory that risky firms do not issue short-term debt in order to avoid inefficient liquidation, but are screened out of the long-term debt market because of the prospect of risky asset substitution.

3.1.5 Exercises

1. In the context of Subsection 3.1.1, what is the effect of an increase in α over the value of the firm V? Suppose outsiders receive voting rights. Assuming managers want to keep control, what effect will this have on α and V?

2. Prove that an outsider will not pay more than $(1-\alpha)$ times the value he expects the firm to have—that is, he will not pay the value $(1-\alpha)V^*$, but only $(1-\alpha)V^0$, for the fraction $(1-\alpha)$ of the shares.

3. Some authors argue that one way to control the conflicts of interests between managers and stockholders is to give stock options to managers. How can we explain this argument using the simple model of section 3.1.1? What other factors should be included in this analysis?

4. Explain condition (3.4) and show what happens to the optimal value $f^*[w(a^\circ, \theta)]$ when θ changes.

5. Show that the risk-sharing rule implied by condition $U'/G' = \lambda - \psi d(w_a/w_b)/d\theta$ is not Pareto-efficient when the agent is risk averse. Is it when the agent is risk neutral?

6. Prove that when both utility functions V and G have constant absolute risk averse coefficients, the optimal fee schedule $f(\cdot)$ is a linear function of the payoff.

7. How can the issuance of convertible debt and warrants contribute toward reducing the agency costs between stockholders and bondholders? What about call provisions in debt contracts?

8. Under what conditions can we say that the value of debtholders' position is the same as if they owned the company's assets and had given stockholders a call option with exercise price equal to the face value of debt? Using this result, show that as the face value of debt increases, the market value of the debt also increases, but by a smaller percentage.

9. Following the notations and assumptions of Myers (1977), show that management tends to underinvest and lead to an opportunity wealth loss when risky debt is considered.

10. How can the restrictions on dividends payment protect debtholders? What happens when the firm has plenty of cash?

3.2 Informational Asymmetries

The balance of debt and equity has been described within different contexts, such as the presence of taxes and agency problems. In this section an additional imperfection is considered—namely that the agents involved in capital structure decisions have different information about the firm.

Some managers in charge have much more information about the real value and potential of firms than other agents in the economy, such as the creditholders and shareholders. Explicitly, in all the models to be described, the following assumption is made:

Assumption 3.2.1. Managers have better information about the value of the firm than other agents in the economy.

Assuming also that managers act in the interest of the shareholders, their informational advantage may be used in order to increase the value of the firm whenever the use of their private information tells them that the firm is undervalued. That is, the managers are tempted to tell the market that the firm is undervalued. The aim of this section and the models presented herein is to discuss credible ways of passing on this type of information.

There are two main problems associated with asymmetry of information. The first is that if there is no flow of information, the market may fail to exist. The second is that information cannot be transferred directly.

Beginning with the last point, information cannot be directly transferred in a credible way. In principle, there would be a reward for exaggerating positive qualities. The uninformed agents, aware of that fact, will not rely on any information transmitted that way. In other words, if every manager claims positive qualities, no information is, in fact, transmitted. A necessary condition for the transfer of information to be credible is that it implies apparent losses for the informer, which in equilibrium are possibly offset by the advantage of passing the information.

The fact is that the informational flow is necessary for the market to survive. If such transfer of information does not exist, the market will value the average quality. This being the case, the supply of low-quality projects will be much higher than the supply of good projects, since the above-average projects will not be interested in participating in a market that has undervalued them. The true average is therefore lower than the average used by the market initially. Realizing this, the market revises its evaluation of the average quality at a lower level, taking away from the market the best projects still present. The process goes on, selecting at each time projects with lower-than-average quality and increasing the cost of capital to finance any project. With a high cost of capital, even the good projects, about which there is no great uncertainty, may not be financed.

Hence, without an indirect information transfer, venture capital markets may fail to exist.

Signaling becomes a crucial ingredient in a world with asymmetric information. In this context, firms are assumed to be of different types but will always wish to signal that they are of the best type. If firms of all types are led to use the same signaling strategy in all states, this signaling is said to be a *pooling* equilibrium. Otherwise, the equilibrium is said to be *separating*. Notice that a separating equilibrium does not necessarily distinguish among all the types. If that were the case, the equilibrium would be termed *fully separating*.

In this section, several models will be presented, according to which firms try to signal their values to the market indirectly through their debt levels, for instance. This is an alternative way to explain why firms look for an optimal debt level.

3.2.1 Managers' Signaling because of Fee Schedules

In the model of Ross (1977), the signal for the value of the firm is the total amount of debt issued with face value B. As discussed before, the signal must imply some cost for the management, supposedly offset by the benefits of signaling in equilibrium. Ross proposes a fee schedule including a punishment for the case of bankruptcy.

Two additional assumptions are required: the first to allow for explicit calculations of the cost of bankruptcy, and the second to clarify the kind of informational asymmetry incorporated.

Assumption 3.2.2. *The returns X of the firm are represented by a random variable uniformly distributed on $[0, k]$, where k characterizes the type of the firm and runs over the interval $[c, d]$.*

Assumption 3.2.1 here takes the specific form:

Assumption 3.2.3. *Managers–insiders know their own firm's k type.*

The model is defined within two points in time. Taking γ_0 and γ_1 as two real numbers, and V_0 as the time-0 value of the firm, the incentive schedule has two components: one for time 0 and another for time 1. The first one is proportional to the value of the firm at time 0, taken to present value at time 1. For a constant interest rate r, the component reads

$$M_0 = (1 + r)\gamma_0 V_0. \tag{3.7}$$

The second component is taken proportional to the *expected* return minus a penalty L in case of bankruptcy—that is, in case $X < B$,

$$M_1 = \gamma_1 E(X - L\mathbf{1}_{\{X<B\}}),$$

where $1_{\{X<B\}}$ denotes a random variable assuming the value 1 if $X < B$ and a value of 0 otherwise. The higher the debt, the higher the risk of bankruptcy, and therefore the more efficient the management should be to avoid the penalty.

If the type of the firm is known with certainty (say, $k = t$), the density of probability of the returns is constant and equal to $1/t$ in the interval $[0, t]$, and the value of the firm at time 1 is written

$$(1+r)V_\circ = \int_0^t x \frac{dx}{t} = \frac{t}{2},$$

which implies that

$$V_\circ = \frac{t}{2(1+r)}. \qquad (3.8)$$

If the essence of this approach is that the debt level B should be chosen so as to signal the type t through some function, say, $t = a(B)$, then the incentive schedule for the manager

$$M = M_\circ + M_1$$

must be seen by an outsider as

$$M = \frac{1}{2}\gamma_\circ a(B) + \gamma_1 \left[\frac{1}{2}t - L\frac{B}{t} \right]. \qquad (3.9)$$

To write M in the form (3.9), the expression (3.8) was substituted in equation (3.7) with $a(B)$ in the place of t and M_1 was rewritten using the fact that

$$E(X) = \int_0^t x \frac{dx}{t} = \frac{t}{2} \text{ and } E(1_{\{X<B\}}) = \int_0^B \frac{dx}{t} = \frac{B}{t},$$

with B taken to be less[12] than t.

The signal of the true t is therefore a function $a(B)$ at time 0. The manager chooses B so as to maximize its schedule M. The debt level B must therefore satisfy the first-order condition[13]

$$\frac{1}{2}\gamma_\circ a'(B) = \gamma_1 \frac{L}{t}. \qquad (3.10)$$

However, the management will also want the signal to be efficient, which is to say that the market perceives in equilibrium the correct type t through $a(B)$. Hence, the condition

$$a(B) = t \qquad (3.11)$$

must be *imposed.* Substituting (3.11) into (3.10) gives in differential form

$$a(B)da(B) = 2\frac{\gamma_1}{\gamma_\circ}LdB.$$

Integrating both sides, it follows that

$$\frac{1}{2}a(B)^2 = 2\frac{\gamma_1}{\gamma_\circ}LB + b, \tag{3.12}$$

which can be solved for the signaling function $a(B)$ up to the constant of integration b:

$$a(B) = 2\sqrt{\frac{\gamma_1 L}{\gamma_\circ}}\left[B + b\frac{\gamma_\circ}{2\gamma_1 L}\right]^{1/2}. \tag{3.13}$$

To find the constant b, a *boundary condition* is necessary. In the context of this model, such a condition follows from the fact that it does not pay to the lower type $k = c$ to signal, that is, $c = a(0)$, from what follows from either equation (3.12) or equation (3.13)

$$b = \frac{c^2}{2}.$$

Substitution of this value of b into (3.13) together with the equilibrium condition (3.11) gives

$$t = \sqrt{\frac{4\gamma_1 L}{\gamma_\circ}B + c^2}$$

or, equivalently,

$$B = \frac{\gamma_\circ}{4\gamma_1 L}\left[t^2 - c^2\right]. \tag{3.14}$$

For this signaling to be an equilibrium, it should satisfy two conditions:

1. It gives managers no incentive to signal a *false type* as long as the probability of bankruptcy is different from 1, and
2. It permits full discrimination of the types.

In equilibrium all types of agents other than c will pay a cost, since they will implicitly accept a positive probability of incurring a penalty.

The optimum level of debt is used to identify the class to which the firm belongs. Note that given the type of the firm, its value is directly given by equation (3.8), independently of its capital structure which is compatible with the MM framework.

What this model states is that, under asymmetric information, by changing B the management changes the *perceived* value of the firm to the uninformed investors. The fact that these economic agents are aware of this forces the optimal relation between t and B to be unique and given by (3.14).[14]

However, as noted by Kim (1989), this model has a weakness. It does not impose any penalty on bondholders or stockholders if the optimal debt level is exceeded. Hence, these agents may have an incentive to give a "side payment" to managers in order to adopt a higher debt ratio than the equilibrium one, which makes the signaling mechanism in Ross's model noncredible.

One more important criticism is discussed in the paper: Managers cannot deal in their own shares. Otherwise, they would have incentive to signal erroneously, enhancing the value of the firm, and then to cash in.

3.2.2 When Managers Are Also Investors

Leland and Pyle (1977) developed a model in the same signaling context as Ross, in which risk averse managers are also investors in the firm. Consider entrepreneurs starting a project with a random return $X = \overline{X} + \epsilon$, with $E(\epsilon) = 0$, needing a capital investment K. Here, these entrepreneurs, who are going to manage the project, are the only individuals who know the expected return $\overline{X} = E(X)$. At time 0 they sell a fraction $(1 - \alpha)$ of the project and retain a fraction α. The uninformed investors use this proportion as a signal of the value of the firm. Underlying this idea is, clearly, Assumption 3.2.1. As the management better knows the value of the firm, the fact that it holds a reasonable part of the equity is a good signal, whereas no participation will naturally be considered as a bad signal. As the managers are risk averse, they would like to diversify but cannot, since they have to hold on to their shares. That is their cost of signaling, and that is why the signal is credible. Managers of good projects are then easily identified with this procedure because their claim on the firm is worth more. That is why they can afford to signal in that way and hold onto a greater portion of the shares.

In this model, Assumption 3.2.1 that managers have superior information takes the simple form

Assumption 3.2.4. *Only the management knows the value of the expected return X.*

Uninformed investors will have to *infer* in equilibrium the expected return through a function of α, say, $X(\alpha)$. Consequently, the *perceived* value of the firm, say, a function $V(\alpha)$, will also depend on α. As in Ross's model,

Leland and Pyle work in a two-time framework. As in equation (3.8), the perceived value of the firm will here be given by

$$V(\alpha) = \frac{X(\alpha) - \lambda}{1 + r}, \tag{3.15}$$

where λ is a risk adjustment parameter and r is the risk-free interest rate.

At time 0, managers have their initial wealth W_o. Additionally they may issue risk-free debt in the amount of B and sell a fraction $(1 - \alpha)$ of the perceived value of the project. The value of such a fraction is worth $(1 - \alpha)[V(\alpha) - B]$ at time 0, since debt must be paid from the proceeds of the project. Thus, entrepreneurs initially have

$$W_o + B + (1 - \alpha)[V(\alpha) - B].$$

This amount is assumed to be invested in three different assets, namely the project, the market portfolio, and a risk-free asset. The decision variables will be the proportion α of the equity of the firm held by the entrepreneurs and the proportion β of the market portfolio held. The rest of their wealth (say, Y) will be invested in a risk-free asset. The optimal way to make this allocation is constrained by

$$W_o + B + (1 - \alpha)[V(\alpha) - B] = K + Y + \beta V_M,$$

where V_M is taken as the value of the market portfolio. This equation is the *budget constraint* faced by the management when deciding how to allocate its wealth. Using equation (3.15) it follows that

$$Y = W_o + B - K - \beta V_M + \frac{1 - \alpha}{1 + r}[X(\alpha) - \lambda - (1 + r)B]. \tag{3.16}$$

The objective of the managers is to maximize the expected utility of their random wealth at the end of the process (i.e., at time 1). If the return on the market portfolio is denoted by $\widetilde{M}$, the wealth of the management at that time is the random variable

$$\widetilde{W}_1 = \alpha[X - B(1 + r)] + \beta \widetilde{M} + (1 + r)Y.$$

Substituting the value of Y by the expression in (3.16) (that is, incorporating in the random wealth the budget constraint with respect to which the utility maximization must be subject), it follows that

$$\widetilde{W}_1 = \alpha[\overline{X} + \epsilon - X(\alpha) + \lambda] + \beta[\widetilde{M} - (1 + r)V_M]$$
$$+ (W_o - K)(1 + r) + (X(\alpha) - \lambda).$$

Assuming that the management has a utility function U, its problem becomes

$$\max_{(\alpha,\beta)\in[0,1]\times[0,1]} E[U(\widetilde{W}_1)], \qquad (3.17)$$

for which there will be a solution $\alpha^* \equiv \alpha^*(\overline{X})$ and $\beta^* \equiv \beta^*(\overline{X})$. As in other signaling models, in equilibrium the values of α^* and β^* must reveal the true expected return, that is to say, the equilibrium condition

$$\overline{X}[\alpha^*(\overline{X})] = \overline{X}$$

must be imposed on the solution of the problem. There are two necessary first-order conditions to be satisfied in order to solve (3.17): one with respect to α and the other with respect to β. Denoting by $X(\alpha)_\alpha$ the derivative $dX(\alpha)/d\alpha$, the first-order condition reads

$$(1 - \alpha)X(\alpha)_\alpha = -\frac{E[U'(\widetilde{W}_1)(\epsilon + \lambda)]}{E[U'(\widetilde{W}_1)]}, \qquad (3.18)$$

and the second is

$$E\{U'(\widetilde{W}_1)[\widetilde{M} - (1+r)V_M]\} = 0. \qquad (3.19)$$

Solving (3.19) for β and substituting this value of β into (3.18), one gets a differential equation for $X(\alpha)$ whose solution does not depend explicitly on β and is uniquely defined up to a constant of integration.

The following two important results are proved by Leland and Pyle:

Proposition 3.2.1 (Leland and Pyle, 1977). *$X(\alpha)$ is strictly increasing in α if and only if the management demand for equity is normal.*[15]

Proposition 3.2.2 (Leland and Pyle, 1977). *In equilibrium signaling, managers with normal demand have a value of α higher than the proportion they would invest if they could costlessly communicate the true value of $\overline{X}$.*

This last result may be seen as a welfare cost result. In fact, the cost of signaling reflected in the overparticipation of the management in the equity of the company may be used as a criterion to choose the constant of integration defining $X(\alpha)$ as the solution of the differential equation previously described. The constant will be chosen so as to minimize this signaling cost.

The relevant issue here is how these results relate to the debt policy followed by the firms. All other factors being fixed, including the amount invested by the management in equity, in most cases the level of debt increases with the proportion α of the equity owned by managers.

From Proposition 3.2.1, it follows that $X(\alpha)$ increases with debt; therefore equation (3.15) implies that the perceived value $V(\alpha)$ increases with the debt level B, just as in Ross's model.

Notice once again that the MM results are not really questioned here. As in Ross's model, V and B may be parameterized through the signaling variable α, in the context of the transfer of information. It is *not* a causal relationship that links V and B and therefore the MM propositions are preserved in all their purity, as they should be.

3.2.3 Signals Conditioned by Investment Opportunities

Another model that describes how informational advantages of the managers may affect the decision to issue stock or not is developed by Myers and Majluf (1984).

Supposing that there is an investment opportunity, management can try to raise internal funds to finance the investment or to raise external funds by issuing either debt or equity.

To issue equity is problematic. Taking into account the informational advantage of the management, having too many securities in the market leads the market players to suspect overpricing, and the prices of the securities fall, lowering the value of the company. Hence, there is a cost that the management will be willing to incur only if the benefits of the new investment are large enough to offset it.

As a consequence, a firm that needs to issue equity to invest will pass up some good investment projects with positive net present value. In this sense, it would be preferable to be able to be financed by internal funds, since there would be no opportunity cost. Thus, internal funds have an intrinsic value. If the management could costlessly communicate to the outsider investors that equity is being issued in order to raise funds to finance excellent investment from which the outsiders could well benefit, and not to expropriate them, the value of the internal funds would disappear. Also, the prices would not fall and the cost of signaling would not exist. However, such direct transfer of information is not credible, as aforementioned, and the only way of avoiding the costs of raising external funds is to have enough internal funds. Also, it follows from the model of Myers and Majluf that, on average, risky debt implies lower costs than equity. Hence, a hierarchy in the financing mechanism is established by this model in the sense that internal funds are preferred to external ones, and, among these, debt is preferred to equity issue.

Note that this hierarchy strongly contradicts the free cash flow hypothesis of Jensen (1986) according to which shareholders would appreciate low levels of cash and a high level of debt. Among other advantages, this strategy lowers the cost of monitoring the management. In contrast,

Myers and Majluf claim that it is good to have internal funds, so that profitable investments will not be passed up. Therefore, these two hypotheses
here described are direct competitors.[16]

To see how all these conclusions are derived, the model must be formalized. Let I be the required investment and S denote the *slack* of the
firm (i.e., large holdings of cash or marketable securities) or the ability to
issue default-risk-free debt.

If $S \geq I$, it will not be necessary to issue any equity at all in order to
finance the investment. The only interesting case happens when $S < I$,
where the required amount of equity to be issued is $E = I - S$.

As opposed to the other models previously discussed, this is a three-
date model with three distinct times—say, time 0, time 1, and time 2. Let
us introduce the following notation. At time 0, the possible value of the
assets of the firm at time 1 is described by a random variable $\widetilde{A}$. Similarly,
let $\widetilde{B}$ denote the possible net present value of the investment opportunity
at time 1.

At time 0, the information is symmetric. All the agents, managers and
market, have the same information—namely, the distributions of $\widetilde{A}$ and $\widetilde{B}$
and the value of S.

At time 1, the asymmetry of information between managers and outsider investors is specified. Assumption 3.2.1 takes the form

Assumption 3.2.5. *At time 1, the management knows the realizations of $\widetilde{A}$ and
$\widetilde{B}$, denoted respectively by a and b, which are unknown to the outsider investors.
Negative values of a and b are ruled out.*

At this stage, the only thing that the outsiders know is that the amount
of equity to be issued is $E = \max[0, I - S]$. Also, at time 1, let P be the
market value of the shares of old shareholders if the stock is not issued
and P' be the price of the same shares if it is issued. At time 2, finally, all
the information is disclosed.

Let V° be the value of the firm for the old shareholders. If the management, knowing the values of a and b, decides not to issue equity, then
the company is still owned by the same old shareholders with assets of
value a and slack S. Thus

$$V^\circ = a + S.$$

If, on the other hand, knowing the value of a and b, the management
decides to issue equity E, then the ownership of the company is shared
between the old and new shareholders. The total value of the company
will include the issued equity E and the net present value of the investment opportunity apart from the assets of value a and slack S. But the
old shareholders will have only a proportion $P'/(P' + E)$ of all of this.

Thus, in this case

$$V^\circ = \frac{P'}{P' + E}(E + S + a + b).$$

To explain the decision of the managers, the following assumption is required:

Assumption 3.2.6. *The management acts in the best interest of the old shareholders. Moreover, old shareholders are assumed to be passive—that is, they do not adjust their portfolios in response to the issue–invest decision of the firm.*

If that is so, the decision to issue new equity is taken only if the old shareholders are better off in such case—that is, only if

$$\frac{P'}{P' + E}(E + S + a + b) \geq a + S.$$

This inequality may be rewritten as

$$b \geq -E + \frac{E}{P'}(S + a) \tag{3.20}$$

and should naturally be restricted by Assumption 3.2.5 to the region $a \geq 0$, $b \geq 0$.

Hence, inequality (3.20) divides the domain of the joint probability distribution of $\tilde{A}$ and $\tilde{B}$ into two disjoint regions identified in Figure 3.1: a region M' in which all pairs (a, b) satisfy the inequality and the firm issues new equity and invests in the new project, and a region M in which no pair (a, b) satisfies the inequality and there is no investment. In the first region, the amount of equity issued is $E = I - S$, whereas in the second, it is zero.

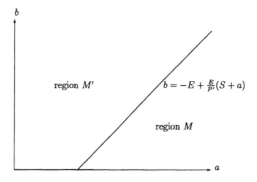

Figure 3.1. *The Regions of Investment and No-Investment Decisions According to Myers and Majluf's Model*

It is simple to see that the price P for the shares when $(a, b) \in M$ is greater than the price P' when $(a, b) \in M'$. The equilibrium prices should be given by[17]

$$P = S + E(\widetilde{A}|M) \tag{3.21}$$

and

$$P' = S + E(\widetilde{A} + \widetilde{B}|M').$$

For any $(a, b) \in M$, the inequality (3.20) is not satisfied and hence

$$b < -E + \frac{E}{P'}(S + a) \text{ or } a > P'(1 + b/E) - S.$$

Since $b/E \geq 0$ from Assumption 3.2.5, it follows that for any $(a, b) \in M$, $a > P' - S$. Thus $E(\widetilde{A}|M) > P' - S$ and (3.21) gives directly $P > P'$.

As advanced by Myers and Majluf themselves, in the case where the managers are also investors, the work of Leland and Pyle discussed already provides a natural extension of this model. In that case, the interest of the management in buying the new issues would not be a signal that the shares are overvalued, but rather that there is a good investment opportunity.

Up to now, only equity issue has been considered in this model. However, other forms of external funds could be raised, such as debt. To consider the relative benefits of issuing either debt or equity, it is necessary to describe the gains or losses to the old shareholders at disclosure of information. The amount of equity issued has the value $E = I - S$ at time 1 and is assumed to have a value $E + \Delta E$ at time 2. Here ΔE denotes the capital gain when information is revealed to the market.

Similarly, if debt is issued, the same argument holds with B replacing E and with ΔB in the place of ΔE. Capital gains may have both negative and positive values, reflecting the fact that both debt and equity considered here are risky securities.[18]

However, under the restrictive assumptions such as those in the paper of Galai and Masulis (1976), the values of ΔE and ΔB will have the same signal but $|\Delta E| > |\Delta B|$. Put differently, capital gains or losses are always less in absolute value when issuing debt than when issuing equity. This is because equity is riskier than debt.

The variation at time 2 of the additional payoff to the old shareholders from the fact of issuing and investing is seen from (3.20) to be $b - \Delta E$ in the case of equity and $b - \Delta B$ in the case of debt.

Hence, it is always in the interest of the old stockholders to issue debt rather than new stock. The opposite would happen only when $\Delta E < \Delta B$ and this, by the preceding arguments, implies that both ΔE and ΔB are negative. In other words, equity issue would be preferred to debt issue by stockholders only if there is a capital loss. But that is a horrible signal, so there would be no investors to buy the new stock.

Hence, the less risky the security, the better off are the old shareholders. From this point of view, internal funds are preferred to external funds and, among the latter type, debt dominates equity.

This hierarchy expresses what is usually known as the "pecking order" hypothesis about the preferences over different types of funds. This result can be seen as constructed from the fact that debt's and equity's different information sensitivities imply different adverse selection costs. The point is that the pecking order holds because debt is less sensitive to management's private information and hence is less costly to issue.[19]

Masulis (1988) reports a work[20] that provides counterexamples to the assumption that the pecking order hypothesis can be generalized from Myers and Majluf's model.

An alternative justification for issuing new stock is to assume some additional informational asymmetry on the parameters that value the options of issuing debt or equity. For instance, a large asymmetry of information regarding the variance rate may tempt the managers to issue equity, in the case that investors overestimate it, other things being equal. The management might do that to signal to the investors that the firm is safer than prospective debtholders might think, which would make the issue of debt very expensive.

3.2.4 Stock Repurchase as a Signal

As an almost inverse problem to the one just described, Vermaelen (1981,1984) studies the case of stock repurchase. In this case, the management would use its informational advantage to buy back shares of its company from the market. Intuitively, and following the same line of reasoning developed in the previous models, this would suggest to the market that securities are *underpriced*. Thus, after a stock repurchase announcement, one would expect the share prices to rise as a reaction.

It is interesting to notice that firms spend their cash and/or debt capacity to buy back stock. The sources for future investment may therefore be reduced and firms might be restricted to funds at the lowest levels of the pecking order (i.e., their better-valued stock). Hence, stock repurchases strongly contradict the pecking order theory.

If the management wants to signal that the stock is underpriced, there are two simultaneous signals to give. One is the price offered to buy back the stock, P_T, and the other is the number of shares to be repurchased, N_p.

Clearly, this process increases the debt-equity ratio. The issues to be discussed in this section are how stock repurchases affect the prices of bonds and stock, what the economic explanations for stock repurchases are, and what the implications for portfolio management are.

The model is defined in a framework with two points in time. At time 0 there is an asymmetry of information according to which the management has information that the market has not. At time 1, the information is disclosed through the purchase announcement. Let I denote the value of that information at time 1 and $\overline{I}$ denote its value at time 0.

The market infers the value of information through a function of the signals—say, $i(P_T, N_p)$. In equilibrium, this function must give the correct value of the information to the market; that is

$$i(P_T, N_p) = \overline{I}. \tag{3.22}$$

If P_o is the market price per share at time 0 and if there are N_o shares outstanding, the actual true price at time 0 for the shares should be

$$\overline{P} = P_o + \frac{\overline{I}}{N_o}.$$

An important assumption of this model is that

Assumption 3.2.7. *Managers do not buy or sell anything before $\overline{I}$ is revealed.*

The price at which the company buys will be greater than the true price (that is to say, $P_T > \overline{P}$), giving rise to a signaling cost per share of $P_T - \overline{P}$. Thus, the total signaling cost is

$$N_p(P_T - \overline{P}).$$

Who pays this cost is clearly the shareholders who do not tender—that is to say, the owners of the $N_o - N_p$ nontendered shares. Let M_o be the number of shares held by the management. Therefore, the signaling cost to the management is a fraction $M_o/(N_o - N_p)$ of the total cost,

$$\frac{M_o}{(N_o - N_p)} N_p(P_T - \overline{P}).$$

Denoting the fraction of shares repurchased by $F_p \equiv N_p/N_o$, and by $W[i(P_T, N_p)]$ the increasing[21] compensation from passing to the market the perceived value of information $i(P_T, N_p)$, the net benefit to the management is

$$C(P_T, N_p) = W[i(P_T, N_p)] - \frac{M_o}{(N_o - N_p)} N_p(P_T - \overline{P})$$

$$= W[i(P_T, N_p)] - \frac{M_o F_p}{(1 - F_p)} \left(P_T - P_o - \frac{\overline{I}}{N_o} \right). \tag{3.23}$$

Hence, the managerial problem is to maximize (3.23) with respect to P_T and N_p (or, equivalently, with respect to P_T and F_p), subject to equation (3.22).

Vermaelen (1984, footnote 1) argues that the use of a double signal leads to first-order conditions in the form of two differential equations with no closed-form solution. A way to overcome this problem is to fix one of the signals (say, the tender price P_T) and work out the equilibrium solution for F_p.

In this case, the perceived value of information is rewritten as a function only of F_p, say, $I(F_p)$, and the problem of the managers is

$$\max_{F_p} W[I(F_p)] - \frac{M_\circ}{(1 - F_p)} F_p \left(P_T - P_\circ - \frac{\overline{I}}{N_\circ} \right)$$

subject to $I(F_p) = \overline{I}$. This constraint is simply equation (3.22) rewritten in terms of the new perceived value function. From the first-order condition it follows that

$$\frac{dW}{dF_p} = 0 \Longrightarrow \frac{dW}{dI}\frac{dI}{dF_p} = -\frac{M_\circ \left(P_\circ + \frac{I(F_p)}{N_\circ} - P_T \right)}{(1 - F_p)^2}. \tag{3.24}$$

To solve this differential equation, the following assumption is made:

Assumption 3.2.8. *The marginal benefit of the perceived value is constant.*

Denoting the constant derivative dW/dI by w, then the differential equation in (3.24) becomes

$$\frac{M_\circ}{wN_\circ}\frac{dF_p}{(1 - F_p)^2} = -\frac{dI(F_p)}{N_\circ P_\circ + I(F_p) - N_\circ P_T}.$$

Integrating both sides and denoting $\frac{M_\circ}{N_\circ}$ by $m_\circ$ gives

$$-\frac{m_\circ}{w(1 - F_p)} = \ln[I(F_p) - N_\circ(P_T - P_\circ)] + b,$$

where b is a constant of integration. Solving for $I(F_p)$,

$$I(F_p) = N_\circ(P_T - P_\circ) + K \exp\left[-\frac{m_\circ}{w(1 - F_p)} \right],$$

where $K = e^{-b}$. Using as a boundary condition the fact that if the value of information is 0 there is no advantage in signaling (that is, if $I = 0$, then $F_p = 0$), it follows that K must satisfy

$$0 = N_\circ(P_T - P_\circ) + K \exp\left(-\frac{m_\circ}{w} \right)$$

or simply

$$K = -N_{\circ}(P_T - P_{\circ}) \exp\left(\frac{m_{\circ}}{w}\right).$$

Thus,

$$I(F_p) = N_{\circ}(P_T - P_{\circ}) - N_{\circ}(P_T - P_{\circ}) \exp\left(\frac{m_{\circ}}{w}\right) \exp\left[-\frac{m_{\circ}}{w(1 - F_p)}\right]$$

$$= N_{\circ}(P_T - P_{\circ})\left\{1 - \exp\left[-\frac{m_{\circ}F_p}{w(1 - F_p)}\right]\right\}. \tag{3.25}$$

Defining the *premium* π as the relative gain for sellers,

$$\pi \equiv \frac{(P_T - P_{\circ})}{P_{\circ}},$$

the *value of information* α can be represented by the "abnormal" return per share

$$\alpha \equiv \frac{I}{N_{\circ}P_{\circ}}.$$

Notice from equation (3.25) that if there were no need to signal (i.e., if $F_p = 0$), one would have $\alpha = 0$. Only when $F_p = 1$ is the premium exactly equal to the abnormal return per share. According to (3.25), the costs of signaling simplifies this premium to

$$\alpha = \pi\left\{1 - \exp\left[-\frac{m_{\circ}F_p}{w(1 - F_p)}\right]\right\}.$$

From this expression, it is simple to see that the premium π, the fraction of repurchased shares F_p, and the fraction of shares held by insiders $m_{\circ}$ are positively related to the value of information; that is, when any of those factors increases, α increases as well. In contrast, the value of information decreases with an increase in the marginal benefits w of the perceived value.

It has been argued that outside shareholders, who are assumed to control managerial compensation ex-post, can impose penalties on the insiders if they are hurt because of incorrect signaling. In this case, managers would have a natural incentive to tell the truth, and signals would be unnecessary. In this case, when information is transferred directly, as discussed previously the value of information will coincide with the premium

$$\alpha' = \pi.$$

An alternative framework would be to assume that the nontendering shareholders would be able to charge the insiders ex-post, so that they would bear all the costs and not simply the fraction $M_\circ/(N_\circ - N_p)$. The total net benefits in such a case would be

$$\overline{C}(F_p) = \overline{W}[I(F_p)] - N_p(P_T - \overline{P}),$$

and the first-order condition for the constrained maximization of this function leads to the differential equation

$$wdI(F_p) = -N_\circ(\overline{P} - P_T)dF_p.$$

Integrating this equation, it follows that the value of information is given by

$$\alpha'' = \pi[1 - \exp(-F_p/w)].$$

The most relevant point of this equation is that the insider-holdings variable $m_\circ$ no longer enters the equilibrium valuation. Insiders carry *all* the costs, not only the costs corresponding to their fraction $m_\circ$ of the shares.

It is an empirical issue to decide which of these three competing predictions for the value of information is correct. Only the market figures can tell whether stock repurchases reveal information, whether there are costless fully revealing mechanisms, or whether full ex-post settling up is possible. Some of these results are referred to at the end of the next section.

3.2.5 Empirical Evidence

The model by Myers and Majluf implies that equity is the least preferred way of raising investment funds. In particular, an issue of new equity should imply a decrease in the price of the shares. This follows from the simple observation that, when issuing equity, a firm sells part of its assets in place at the same time that it acquires for the old shareholders a share in the NPV of the new investment project. Not issuing equity to invest in a valuable project may be seen as a signal that the assets in place are undervalued. In fact, were that the case, the dilution suffered by the old shareholders when the firm issues equity may not be compensated by the gains of the investment project, in which case the firm would prefer not to issue equity. That signal would allow the market to recognize the situation, and the price of the shares would increase to readjust the market valuation of the assets in place.

The Myers and Majluf model therefore implies that an issue of equity should be interpreted by the market as a signal of overvaluation, thus leading to a share price drop. Some prior research, such as the paper by Smith (1986), indicates that issuing new equity on average conveys negative information about the firm, lowering the price of shares. This seems to confirm the ideas of Myers and Majluf, whose theory is often cited as the explanation for this effect.

However, the decision to issue equity should not be associated only with an overvaluation of assets in place. There may be the genuine case of a highly valuable project for which external funds are required through the issuance of equity. The latter reason would drive the share price up, whereas the former would drive it down. The effect of issuing equity may then be ambiguous in terms of its effect on the price of shares, and it actually becomes an empirical issue to define which effect dominates.

Indeed, after Smith's paper, studies such as Wruck (1989), Hertzel and Smith (1993), and Kato and Schallheim (1993) present some evidence of significant increases in stock price upon the announcement of private-equity issues. Thakor (1993) presents mixed evidence of positive and negative market reactions, with those reactions always remaining negative in the case where there is sufficient retained earnings to finance the project. This has raised some questions about the rationale underlying the Myers and Majluf model.

In fact, the model would also imply that the price drop would be greater for equity issues, less for convertible debt, and least for straight debt. In other words, the more the security issued depends on the value of the firm, the larger should be the price drop.[22] Empirical evidence does not support this. For example, Mikkelson and Partch (1986) find that when convertible debt is issued, the price drop in the shares is a decreasing function of the quality of debt. In a different way but confirming the lack of relationship between the value of the firm and the instrument price sensitivity, Eckbo (1986) shows that there is no evidence of correlation between the quality of straight debt and the market reaction.

However, several studies have also provided support for the pecking order theory of Myers and Majluf. Among others, Kester (1986), Rajan and Zingales (1995), and Titman and Wessels (1988) provide evidence that there is a strong negative relation between past profitability and leverage. Furthermore, Shyam-Sunder and Myers (1999) contribute to this body of research by comparing this negative relation between the leverage ratio and profits (or operating cash flows) to a simple target-adjustment model of capital structure according to the contracting costs. It turns out that the time series variance of debt ratios is much better explained by the preceding negative relation. This is, in general, taken as a confirmation that managers do not set target ratios.[23]

Regarding the signaling models such as the one presented previously for stock repurchase, it is an empirical issue to decide which of these three competing predictions for the value of information is closer to reality.

Vermaelen (1981,1984) provides evidence that on average the premium π is significantly higher than the value of information, which is inconsistent with the hypothesis of the existence of costless fully revealing mechanisms. Also, it is reported that the insider-holdings variable is statistically significant, which contradicts the hypothesis that full ex-post settling up is possible and confirms the initial assumption that stock repurchases reveal information.

Finally, it is important to stress that when firms announce a capital structure change, they usually raise money to invest and/or reveal inside information. Some discussion of the dynamic pecking order theory (proposed by Loughran and Ritter (1997)) should also be mentioned. Their basic idea is that firms tend to issue shares when they are overvalued and buy them back when they are undervalued. This means, although the firm has some long-run target leverage ratio, financial managers may once in a while deviate from this target for opportunistic reasons. For example, you may want to issue equity, even if you are below your target debt-equity ratio, because you believe your shares are undervalued. This type of opportunistic timing behavior is consistent with long-term event studies and makes it almost impossible to test or optimal capital structure theories.

3.2.6 Exercises

1. Consider the signaling model of Ross (1977). Explain what happens to the optimal decision of debt (3.14) if $\gamma_0 = 0$. And what happens if $\gamma_1 = 0$?
2. In the context of Leland and Pyle (1977), suppose that the expected utility of the manager is given by $E[U(W_1)] = G[E(W_1) - \frac{b}{2}\sigma_{W_1}^2]$, where G is an increasing function, $\sigma_{W_1}^2$ is the variance of the wealth At time 1, and the risk adjustment parameter λ is given by $\lambda = \frac{E[M]-(1+r)V_M}{\sigma_M^2} \text{cov}(\varepsilon, M)$. In this case, under what conditions does the level of debt increase with the proportion α of the equity owned by the managers?
3. Prove Proposition 3.2.2.
4. Instead of Assumption 3.2.6, assume that the management acts in the interest of all shareholders. How would that affect the investment decision of the management? If management acts in the interest of the new shareholders, what is the optimal equity issuance rule?
5. Myers and Majluf (1984) assume that there are no issuing costs and prove that $P' < P$. What happens to the investment decision of the management and to the conclusion that $P' < P$ in the presence of issuing costs?
6. Prove that in Section 3.2.4, P_T is always higher than $\overline{P}$.

4
Payout Policy

CORPORATE MANAGERS have to make two kinds of decisions. The first kind involves investment, as discussed in Chapter 1. The other type relates to the financing structure of the investments. Chapter 2 discussed the parameters of these decisions, with the wealth of shareholders in mind. Chapter 3 considered that managers may have other types of concerns than the wealth of shareholders. Agency problems were then introduced together with considerations of information asymmetry. The impact of these factors on the financing decision was discussed. A secondary, but still very important, issue in the financing decision is the payout policy that management follows in determining the size, pattern, and timing of cash distributions to shareholders over time. Some years ago, this chapter would have been called "Dividend Policy" instead of "Payout Policy." In fact, for most of the 20th century corporations used dividends as the main form of distributing excess cash to the equityholders. In the mid-80s a radical change of profile started to be seen, favoring the gradual increase of an alternative method, namely stock repurchases. As reported in Grullon and Michaely (2000), in 1998, for the first time in history, U.S. corporations distributed more cash in the form of repurchases than in dividends. For that reason, this chapter incorporates a broad discussion of share repurchases as an alternative to dividend policy.

There is no consensus in the marketplace on the need and importance of payout policies. On one hand, most managers and some academics pay careful attention to the payout policy, believing that it significantly affects the value of firms and, thus, the wealth of shareholders. The argument raised by Jensen (1986) calling for a reduction of free cash flow in order to cut agency problems is a clear example of that line of thought. On the other hand, some managers and academics are quite skeptical about the value added of a carefully chosen payout policy. The irrelevancy result of Modigliani and Miller to be presented here is a radical example of that line of reasoning.

The issue is not a pacific one. After years of research on this topic, which is very conveniently summarized in Allen and Michaely (1995) and in Lease et al. (2000), there is still room for a great many opinions. The purpose of this section is to examine the different determinants of the payout policies of corporations.

4.1 Dividend Policy

This chapter starts with a classic result of Miller and Modigliani (1961) that sets the benchmark for discussing payout policies in general. Although the result was established for dividends, there is nothing in the argument that impedes the application to other payout forms such as stock repurchases. The basic result is that, in a world of perfect certainty together with all the other perfections typical of Miller and Modigliani's economy, the dividend policy followed by a corporation does not affect its value. The introduction of some imperfections such as taxes is shown to be not very relevant, even when considering the different ways in which capital gains and dividends are taxed. This happens since the shareholders can always use mechanisms to transform their dividend gains into capital gains.

Finally, it will be seen that in a world with perfect information and rational expectations, the announcement of a dividend policy is inconsistent with the equilibrium associated with an optimal investment policy. One solution for this inconsistency is to admit to an asymmetry of information between the management and the stockholders.

4.1.1 Another Irrelevancy Proposition

In the world of Miller and Modigliani, as in Chapter 2, the market is idealized in the following way:

Assumption 4.1.1. The market is assumed to be perfect, in the sense that the number of economic agents is large enough and each of them is marginally irrelevant in setting the prices, there are no transaction costs (including information costs), and there are no tax differentials. Moreover, agents are supposed to have a rational behavior, preferring more to less, and being indifferent to the way their wealth increases. Additionally, there is perfect certainty with respect to the future investment schedule and profits of the corporations.

To begin with, consider a discrete time setting, with unitary intervals separating consecutive times. Let p_t denote the price of the share of a given firm at time t and let d_{t+1} denote the value at $t + 1$ of the dividend per share paid in the time interval between t and $t + 1$. In a world of certainty the absence of arbitrage possibilities implies that the rate of return on every share is equal across securities at every given time. For simplicity, it will be taken as constant over time, and simply denoted by r. Then

$$p_t = \frac{1}{1+r}(d_{t+1} + p_{t+1}). \tag{4.1}$$

Moreover, let n_t denote the number of outstanding shares in the interval $[t, t+1)$. If an additional number of shares m_{t+1} is issued at $t + 1$ at the ex-dividend closing price p_{t+1}, then

$$n_{t+1} = n_t + m_{t+1}$$

and the value of the firm at time t is given by $V_t = n_t p_t$. The total value at $t + 1$ of the dividends paid by the firm in the time interval $[t, t+1)$ is $D_{t+1} = n_t d_{t+1}$. Hence, multiplying (4.1) by n_t, the value of the firm may be rewritten as

$$V_t = \frac{1}{1+r}(D_{t+1} + n_t p_{t+1}) = \frac{1}{1+r}(D_{t+1} + V_{t+1} - m_{t+1} p_{t+1}). \tag{4.2}$$

From these expressions it can be seen that there are essentially three channels through which the dividend policy may affect the current value of a firm:

1. Through the dividends D_{t+1}.
2. Through the future value of the firm V_{t+1} either in the case where this term reflects the future dividend policy or in the case where D_t conveys information about the future value of the firm.
3. Through the necessity of raising new capital in the amount $m_{t+1} p_{t+1}$ to keep the investment plans at a given level, which might not be necessary for lower levels of current dividends.

Some of these factors generate forces in opposite directions. A decision such as raising capital through an issue of equity may lower the value of the company, whereas a different decision such as the increase of dividend payments should increase the value of the company. There is, in principle, a trade-off between these effects. The dividend decision of a company is precisely the definition of the terms that could be used in the implementation of a policy.

In a world of certainty, this problem can be solved in a simple way. Let the firm have a given investment schedule I_t and a net profit X_t from which the dividends D_t are paid. Hence, from its net profits, the company disposes only of $X_t - D_t$ to invest. The amount of capital raised externally must be the difference between what is needed to invest, I_t, and what is available, $X_t - D_t$. In other words,

$$m_t p_t = I_t - (X_t - D_t). \tag{4.3}$$

Then, for a fixed investment policy the following proposition states that the dividend policy does not affect the value of the firm:

Proposition 4.1.1 (MM3). *Under Assumption 4.1.1, for a given investment schedule, the value of the firm is independent of its dividend policy.*

Proof. Plugging (4.3) into (4.2), it follows that the value of the firm is given by

$$V_t = \frac{1}{1+r}[X_{t+1} - I_{t+1} + V_{t+1}], \tag{4.4}$$

which is independent of D. ∎

The substitution used in the proof is quite illustrative of how the dividend policy may change without affecting the value. Basically, an increase in dividends is *exactly* compensated by the issue of new equity, so that both effects cancel out.

To take into account the effect of the future values of the firm on the present value, it suffices to solve recursively (4.4) so as to get

$$V_t = \sum_{\tau=1}^{T} \frac{1}{(1+r)^\tau}[X_{t+\tau} - I_{t+\tau}] + \frac{1}{(1+r)^T} V_{t+T}.$$

Assuming that V is always finite and r is positive, the last term goes to zero as T tends to infinity. In that limit the value of the firm can then be given by

$$V_t = \sum_{\tau=1}^{\infty} \frac{1}{(1+r)^\tau}[X_{t+\tau} - I_{t+\tau}]. \tag{4.5}$$

4.1.2 Alternative Valuations

There are alternative interpretations of the valuation of a company. First, the value of a corporation may be seen as the sum of its discounted cash flows. Second, it may also be seen as the accumulated value generated by its investment opportunities. Finally, it may be looked upon as the discounted stream of dividends to be distributed to the shareholders. All of these alternatives, whenever formulated properly, are equivalent and lead to (4.5).

Discounted Cash Flow

According to the discounted cash flow approach, the value of the firm is given by the present value of the stream defined as the difference between the cash receipts and the cash outlays. But in the simple model here derived, this difference at any time $t + \tau$ is simply $[X_{t+\tau} - I_{t+\tau}]$. Hence the value of the firm at any time t is given as in (4.5).

Investment Opportunities

The value of a corporation based on the sum of the present value of wealth generated by its investment opportunities may be approached in the following way: Equation (4.5) may be rewritten as

$$
\begin{aligned}
V_t &= \sum_{\tau=1}^{\infty} \frac{X_{t+\tau}}{(1+r)^\tau} - \sum_{\tau=1}^{\infty} \frac{I_{t+\tau}}{(1+r)^\tau} \\
&= \sum_{\tau=1}^{\infty} \frac{X_t}{(1+r)^\tau} + \sum_{\tau=1}^{\infty} \frac{X_{t+\tau} - X_t}{(1+r)^\tau} - \sum_{\tau=1}^{\infty} \frac{I_{t+\tau}}{(1+r)^\tau} \\
&= \frac{X_t}{r} + \sum_{\tau=1}^{\infty} \frac{X_{t+\tau} - X_t}{(1+r)^\tau} - \sum_{\tau=1}^{\infty} \frac{I_{t+\tau}}{(1+r)^\tau}.
\end{aligned}
\tag{4.6}
$$

Thus, the value of a firm at time t is given by three components. The first term has the value of a perpetuity generated by a constant stream of the net profit received at time t, assumed to be repeated systematically in the future. The changes in the net profits at each period $t + \tau$, expressed in the second term, are seen as generated by the investment schedule $I_{t+\tau}$. The present value of the cost of this investment schedule is given by the third term.

Capitalizing Dividends

An alternative way to interpret the value of a firm is to see it as the present value of all the future dividends to be distributed to the shareholders, except for the amount of external resources required to keep the investment schedule. To see this, use expression (4.3) to rewrite the value of the firm as

$$
\begin{aligned}
V_t &= \sum_{\tau=1}^{\infty} \frac{1}{(1+r)^\tau} [X_{t+\tau} - I_{t+\tau}] = \sum_{\tau=1}^{\infty} \frac{1}{(1+r)^\tau} [D_{t+\tau} - m_{t+\tau} p_{t+\tau}] \\
&= \sum_{\tau=1}^{\infty} \frac{D_{t+\tau}}{(1+r)^\tau} - \sum_{\tau=1}^{\infty} \frac{m_{t+\tau} p_{t+\tau}}{(1+r)^\tau}.
\end{aligned}
\tag{4.7}
$$

This expression can easily be rewritten as $V_t = n_t p_t$, coming back to the original construction and consistently closing the circle of definitions. This is left as an exercise.

4.1.3 Growth Rates

In the previous section it was shown that the approach to evaluating a firm using the stream of earnings is independent of any assumption on the time shape of the dividend stream. However, both streams are somehow indirectly related, since they give rise to the same valuation formula for the firm.

In this section, the preceding evaluation formulas are adapted to illustrate how close the time shapes of the streams of dividends and value are. In order to do that, a specific constraint will be imposed on the stream of earnings, and from the equivalence of the valuation using dividends and earnings, the effect on the stream of dividends will be discussed.

Suppose that the investment schedule I_t is related to the net profit X_t through the relationship

$$I_t = k_i X_t;$$

that is, the investments are a constant fraction k_i of the earnings, and such investment provides a constant yield r^* per period. Then the value of X_t is

$$X_t = X_{t-1} + r^* I_{t-1} = X_{t-1}[1 + k_i r^*],$$

so that X_t grows at a rate kr^* per period. This means that

$$X_{t+\tau} = X_t[1 + k_i r^*]^\tau.$$

Assuming that $kr^* < r$, this also implies, by simple substitution in (4.5), that

$$V_t = X_{t+1} \frac{1 - k_i}{r - k_i r^*}, \tag{4.8}$$

and therefore the value of the firm grows at the same rate as do the net profits. But it was discussed in the previous section that the valuation of the firm could just as equally be made in terms of the stream of dividends. The question is determining the *effective* rate of growth of the dividends g imposed by the constraint that the value of the firm is given by the preceding expression.

To begin with, notice that by definition of g one has

$$d_{t+\tau} = d_t[1 + g]^\tau.$$

Let k_d be the fraction of the earnings retained in each period, such that the dividends paid are $D_t = X_t(1 - k_d)$. Note that, k_i being the fraction of the total earnings represented by the investment, the amount of external funds raised at any time t will be

$$(k_i - k_d)X_t.$$

Assuming that $g < r$, equation (4.1) for the share price together with $d_{t+\tau} = d_t[1+g]^\tau$ gives

$$p_t = \sum_{\tau=1}^{\infty} \frac{d_{t+\tau}}{(1+r)^\tau} = \frac{d_{t+1}}{r-g},$$

which is known as the *Gordon model* for the share price. Recalling that $D_{t+1} = n_t d_{t+1}$ and writing $V_t = n_t p_t$, one obtains

$$V_t = \frac{D_{t+1}}{r-g} = \frac{X_{t+1}(1-k_d)}{r-g}.$$

Equating this expression for V_t with equation (4.8), it follows that

$$g = r - \left(\frac{1-k_d}{1-k_i}\right)(r - k_i r^*).$$

Notice that, in the particular case of a firm that raises no external funds and is entirely financed with its earnings, it follows that $k_i = k_d$ and $g = k_i r^*$. In other words, the dividends grow at the same rate as do the net profits and as does the value of the firm.

4.1.4 Relaxing Certainty

Miller and Modigliani were able to show in their work that, even in the case of uncertainty, their proposition holds under the assumption of absence of arbitrage opportunities.

Assume that a firm starts at time $t = 0$ and has payoffs Γ_{tj} in state j at any point in time t, with $j = 1, 2, \ldots K$ denoting the possible states of nature at time t. As in MMI, assume that markets do not allow for arbitrage opportunities and also that markets are perfect, in the sense that there are no frictions of any type, taxes included.

As before, debtholders buy a debt contract issued by the firm giving them the claim to a face value F at time T. Let V_{Tj} denote the positive part of Γ_{Tj}, or $V_{Tj} \equiv [\Gamma_{Tj}]^+$. The payoff to a debt instrument in the j-th state of nature is thus

$$B_j(T) = \min\{F, V_{Tj}\}.$$

If K is the number of possible states of nature at time T, then, in the absence of arbitrage opportunities, there exists a strictly positive vector $\psi \in R^K$ such that the present value of the debt is

$$B = \sum_{j=1}^{K} \psi_j B_{Tj}.$$

A *dividend policy* for the firm consists of a random variable D_{Tj} satisfying

$$[\Gamma_{Tj} - F]^+ \geq D_{Tj} \geq 0.$$

The amount D_{Tj} is an outflow at time T to shareholders or, at least, to a certain class of shareholders. The equityholders, the true owners of the firm, have the right to receive what is left from the payoff of the firm once the creditholders and dividends are paid, provided that the remaining value is positive. In other words, the payoff to equityholders in state j is

$$S_{Tj} = [\Gamma_{Tj} - D_{Tj} - B_{Tj}]^+$$

implying that

$$V_{Tj} = S_{Tj} + D_{Tj} + B_{Tj}.$$

The present value of the firm is thus

$$V = \sum_{j=1}^{K} \psi_j [S_{Tj} + D_{Tj} + B_{Tj}] = \sum_{j=1}^{K} \psi_j V_{Tj} = \sum_{j=1}^{K} \psi_j [\Gamma_{Tj}]^+,$$

which is completely independent of the particular choice of dividend policy. Then, this proposition follows:

Proposition 4.1.2. *Under perfect markets and in the absence of arbitrage opportunities, the value of a firm is independent of the dividend policy.*

4.1.5 Dividends and Taxes

In their paper Miller and Modigliani pay some attention to market imperfections that might affect the validity of their conclusions. The most important of them, they argue, may be the existence of personal taxes that accord to capital gains substantial advantage compared to the way in which dividends are taxed.

This tax disadvantage of dividends would generate a "clientele effect" in the sense that most of the shares paying dividends would be held either by investors with no tax differentials or by investors who may have tax advantages from dividends, such as corporations.

Miller and Scholes (1978) argue that even in spite of some empirical evidence confirming the clientele effect—for example, Pettit (1977)—the difference in personal taxations of dividends and of capital gains should not create such a radical clientele effect. The reason is that investors do not really care about the level of their personal tax rate on dividend income, τ_d, not even when $\tau_d > \tau_g$, τ_g being the capital gain tax, because they can transform their dividends into capital gains at any time, and therefore excessive taxes can be avoided in practice.

This may be done simply by borrowing at the risk-free rate an amount for which the interest expense will equal the dividend income. Investing the amount borrowed at the same riskless rate, there is no increase in the risk of the wealth position. Since the riskless cash inflows exactly match *by construction* the required payment on debt, which is to be deducted from the dividend income, the total gains are in this way transferred from the dividend income to a capital gain, which may be deferred for tax purposes, at the tax rate τ_g.

Of course, proceeding in this way, investors incur some transaction costs, but what is also clear is that the tax disadvantage of dividends may in principle be reduced to almost nothing. At this point, it becomes essentially an empirical issue to verify what the implications of dividend policies are.

4.1.6 Empirical Evidence

Two basic factors are of interest when analyzing the effect of a dividend policy of a corporation. The first is how it affects the wealth of the investors; the second is how it affects the stock prices. These two effects will be described next.

Wealth of investors is affected by dividend policy. As described already, in general, the dividends are taxed at a rate τ_d, which is different from the rate at which the capital gains are taxed, τ_g. The question is to know whether a particular dividend policy affects the wealth of the investors depending on different structures of τ_d. The main ingredient of the analysis is that these taxes differ across individuals. For most corporations, for instance, $\tau_d < \tau_g$, whereas in the case of pension funds, or any tax-exempt institution, $\tau_d = \tau_g$. Personal investors, as has been discussed, have under current legislation $\tau_d > \tau_g$.

The consequence is that dividends may generate a negative wealth impact on personal investors. This happens, of course, if they hold shares of a company with an active dividend policy instead of holding shares of a firm that does not pay dividends at all. The clientele effect suggested by Modigliani and Miller therefore appears to avoid such negative wealth impacts. Evidence for its existence is provided in a paper by Pettit (1977).

Regarding the stock prices, there are two ways of testing their relation to dividend policy. The first is to regress the returns in terms of the risk and the dividend yield; the second is to study trade around the ex-dividend dates.

Regressing the Returns

The idea of regressing the returns is based on a CAPM-like formulation according to which, in the absence of taxes, investors would choose portfolios with mean-variance efficient returns. In the presence of taxes, the same type of reasoning would imply that the *after-tax return* should be mean-variance efficient.

Under the assumption of proportional individual tax rates and unlimited borrowing at the riskless tax rate r_f, Brennan (1973) derived the equilibrium relation for the return on the security i,

$$E(R_i) = r_f + \gamma_\circ \beta_i + \gamma_1 [d_i - r_f],$$

where d_i denotes the dividend yield D_i/P_i. Brennan could not reject the null hypothesis that $\gamma_1 = 0$. His test presents a lack of power that has two different sources. On the one hand there is a typical error in variables problem, since the regression is to be run on estimated values of β. On the other hand, when estimating the βs the procedure implies grouping securities in an ad hoc way[1]

Besides, the variable D/P should not be taken as a long-term expected dividend yield, because it may hide some omitted risk variable. In fact, a high ratio of D/P reflects a relatively small P. And P may be small because it reflects discounted future cash flows at very high rates (or, equivalently, high risk).

Short-term measures may therefore look more suitable. The data for such regression should be taken only around the ex-dividend day, which was not the case in Brennan's work. Litzenberger and Ramaswamy (1979) presented an extended version of Brennan's after-tax CAPM, taking into account data only in ex-dividend months.

A relevant limitation of Brennan's work is that dividend announcements are used to estimate the returns, ignoring the possible informational effect of these announcements. If there is, in fact, an informational value, the expected returns will be different from what they should be by the simple nature of the taxable effect.

To avoid this effect, Litzenberger and Ramaswamy compute the dividend yield according to what they define as the "level-revised monthly dividend yield." For any firm i it is calculated as $D_{i,t}/P_{i,t-1}$ if the ex-dividend month is t and the announcement is prior to t, or using the last regular dividend yield, going back as far as one year, otherwise.

In equilibrium, Litzenberger and Ramaswamy derived the relation

$$E(\tilde{R}_i) - r_f = a + b\beta_i + c[d_i - r_f],$$

which is equivalent to the model of Brennan when $a = 0$. To test this equation, Litzenberger and Ramaswamy run a cross-sectional GLS regression for each time t of

$$\tilde{R}_{it} - r_{ft} = \gamma_\circ + \gamma_1\beta_{it} + \gamma_2[d_{it} - r_{ft}] + \tilde{\epsilon}_{it},$$

obtaining estimates for the parameters γ for each time, and taking the final estimated value of the different γs as a time average of the cross-sectional estimates.

Litzenberger and Ramaswamy find a positive and significant value 0.236 for γ_2, indicating that for every dollar of dividends paid, investors require 0.236 in extra return. In other words, dividends seem to be undesired by the investors, since the higher the dividend to be paid, the higher is the return required by the investors.

Moreover, they also find empirical evidence supporting the existence of a clientele effect. Stockholders in high tax brackets tend to hold stocks with low dividend yields, while investors in low tax brackets do the opposite.

Following their line of reasoning, that dividend policy should not be relevant for the value of the firm, Miller and Scholes (1982) suggest that the results of Litzenberger and Ramaswamy are biased since their correction for the informational effect is not accurate enough.

Miller and Scholes basically replicate the reasoning of Litzenberger and Ramaswamy to show that the level-revised monthly dividend yield provides a lower estimate of the coefficient γ_2 in the dividend yield than if the pure dividends announced are used.

The point of Miller and Scholes is that there are other effects to be taken into account, such as the existence of firms that *announce* dividends but *suspend* their payment. Cutting dividends constitutes potential information about the future earnings of the firm, usually leading to negative returns. Hence, the level-revised monthly dividend yield would include this specific informational effect, associating these negative returns to the zero dividend yields and spuriously increasing the positive correlation between the two variables.

Discounting for this effect, Miller and Scholes find that the estimate of the relevant coefficient γ_2 is statistically insignificant. This is compatible with their theoretical explanation that the way dividends are taxed should not be a relevant issue, since dividend gains can be transferred to capital gains.

Trade around Ex-Dividend Dates

A second way of testing the relation between returns and dividends is by studying the trade around ex-dividend dates. The principle is that the levels of share prices and dividends are linked through a nonarbitrage relationship. The idea is that an individual holding a share would be indifferent between selling it before receiving dividends and selling it afterwards.

Let P_o be the price at which the share was bought and D the amount of dividends to perceive. If P_b is the price at which the share can be sold just before the payment of dividends and P_a is the price if the share is sold just afterwards, the gains for selling the share before and after the dividends are, respectively,

$$P_b - (P_b - P_o)\tau_g \tag{4.9}$$

and

$$P_a - (P_a - P_o)\tau_g + D(1 - \tau_d). \tag{4.10}$$

The nonarbitrage condition equalizes (4.9) and (4.10). Hence

$$P_b - (P_b - P_o)\tau_g = P_a - (P_a - P_o)\tau_g + D(1 - \tau_d)$$

or, equivalently,

$$\frac{P_b - P_a}{D} = \frac{1 - \tau_d}{1 - \tau_g}.$$

All variables are easily available, so that testing is feasible. Elton and Gruber (1970) provide the marginal tax rate τ_d of an average investor. Ranking groups of firms according to their dividend payouts, Elton and Gruber were able to provide evidence that increasing dividend yields are associated with decreasing implied marginal tax brackets, supporting therefore Miller and Modigliani's clientele hypothesis.

Notice that the whole argument just used here is based on the trade of investors who would trade for reasons that are unrelated to dividends. The price is actually set by investors deciding whether it is better to transact before or after the ex-dividend date. That is why the price in the ex-day incorporates information on the tax structure of the average investor. In this case, transaction costs are to be considered as fixed costs and should not be relevant for determining the equilibrium prices.

Kalay (1982) argues that the clientele effect is not perfect; That is, for a given firm there may be marginal investors who pay the marginal tax implied by the preceding model, as well as inframarginal short-term traders. The presence of such traders may lead to tax arbitrage around the ex-dividend day.

If such arbitrage trade exists, it must be positively related to the dividend yield and negatively related to the transaction costs.

Lakonishok and Vermaelen (1986) tested these implications and found that for cash dividends the trading volume increases significantly around the ex-dividend day. Moreover, the effect is greater the higher is the dividend yield. Consistent with the hypothesis, for nontaxable distributions, such as stock dividends, negative abnormal volume of trade was reported.

Regarding the transaction costs, these authors found a significant positive relation between the trading volume and the introduction of negotiated trading commissions. This evidence seems to clarify, at least in part, what is called the dividend puzzle—namely, to understand why firms insist on paying dividends if they are supposed to be irrelevant to the value of the firm. The answer seems to be that the payment of dividends has a natural market among the inframarginal investors who can make some tax-based arbitrage profit.

4.1.7 Exercises

1. If issuance costs are considered, how does the valuation equation (4.5) change?
2. Show that the value expressed in equation (4.7) may be written as $V_t = n_t p_t$.
3. If dividends are to increase at a growth rate of g, as in Section 4.1.3, what is the growth rate of P?
4. Section 4.1.3 assumes that investment opportunities generate a constant rate of growth of profits in perpetuity. What if the investment opportunities are not available in perpetuity but only over some finite interval of T periods? What can be said about the relationship between r and kr^* in both cases?
5. In the presence of debt financing, is the dividend's irrelevance proposition of Modigliani and Miller still valid?
6. Justify the relationship between Litzenberger and Ramaswamy's equation for the excess return and that of Brennan by showing that a is proportional to α.
7. Show that in the presence of short-term traders and transaction costs, the tax rate cannot be inferred from equation $\frac{P_b - P_a}{D} = \frac{1 - \tau_d}{1 - \tau g}$. (Notice that profits from short-term trades—that is, profits realized in less than 12 months—are taxed as ordinary income.)

4.2 Dividends and Information

4.2.1 The Informational Content of Dividends

It has been empirically well established[2] that a change in the dividend policy affects the share prices, sometimes in a drastic way. This very commonly raises the point that the dividend policy, in fact, seems to determine the value of the firm in an apparent opposition to the arguments raised by Miller and Modigliani (1961), in particular to their irrelevancy proposition.

These authors argue, however, that managers may use dividend changes to reflect a possible change in their own expectations about the future earnings of firms, due to inside information. Dividend changes could then be seen as a simple mechanism to adapt the market value to the new prospective of corporations' insiders. Accordingly, the market value of corporations would react to the announcement of dividend changes reflecting their informational content. What is not valid to argue is that the change in dividend policy causes the change in the value of the firm. This change was actually caused by the original private information known to the insiders.

Hence, the change in dividends is interpreted by the market as signaling a change in the management's view of the future earnings of the company. This point raises the issue of knowing exactly what this information is, whether it adds something to the information conveyed by the earnings announcement, and, still, why firms choose this way to transfer information.

To answer these and related questions, some models formalizing the signaling content of dividends were developed. They are all based on the assumption that managers have private information about the future prospects of the firms, and choose the level of dividends so as to signal their private information to the market. The model by Bhattacharya (1979) was the first to appear in this context. Assuming that managers have superior information about the quality of the projects they are involved in, Bhattacharya sees the commitment with a certain level of payout policy as a signal of that quality. In this model, if the payoff of the project is not sufficient to cover the committed payout, the firm will have to raise resources externally with the associated transaction costs. Accordingly, a firm with genuine high-quality projects will have lower expected transaction costs, while a firm with fewer good-quality projects will expect higher transaction costs. Therefore, a firm with high-quality projects can commit to a high dividend level more easily and with more credibility.

A second model in this vein comes from John and Williams (1985). In their model an equilibrium is characterized such that larger dividends are paid by firms expecting higher operating cash flows in the future.

Also, the level of dividends is related to the tax disadvantage relative to capital gains. In other words, the larger this disadvantage, the smaller should be the optimal dividend. Finally, John and Williams show that dividend variability should be smaller than operating cash flow variability.

In a similar spirit, Miller and Rock (1985) developed a simple two-period model to be described in the next two sections.

4.2.2 A Signaling Model

This is a two-period model with times $t = 0, 1, 2$. When studying the growth of the stream of dividends in section 4.1.3, it was assumed that there was a particular relation between the investment and earnings in the past period—namely, that they were proportional. Let the (random) future return at t be denoted by $\widetilde{X}_{t+1}$. A general function relating the future earnings at $t = 0$ and $t = 1$ to the investment at those points in time will be considered. Let this function be described by

$$\widetilde{X}_{t+1} = F(I_t) + \tilde{\epsilon}_{t+1}.$$

Here, the random $\tilde{\epsilon}$ is a white noise variable with $E_t(\tilde{\epsilon}_{t+j}) = 0$ for $j > 0$ and $E_t(\tilde{\epsilon}_{t+1}|\epsilon_t) = \gamma \epsilon_t$, where E_t denotes expectation at time t. As in the previous section, the investment I_t relates to the net earnings X_t in the sense that I_t plus the dividends D_t must equal the net earnings X_t plus the amount of additional funds raised externally, here denoted by B_t. This is the content of equation (4.3), here rewritten as

$$B_t + X_t = I_t + D_t.$$

Under the conditions of Miller and Modigliani's irrelevancy proposition, the decision problem of the firm, once the true values of X_1, B_1, and D_1 are revealed, reduces to the maximization of the value of the firm given in (4.4). In other words, it should maximize

$$V_1 = X_1 - I_1 + \frac{1}{1+r} E_1(\widetilde{X}_2|\epsilon_1) = X_1 - I_1 + \frac{1}{1+r}[F(I_1) + \gamma \epsilon_1].$$

If there is an internal solution for the optimal investment level (say, I_1^*), it must satisfy the first-order condition of a maximum,

$$F'(I_1^*) = 1 + r. \tag{4.11}$$

The value of the firm at its maximum is thus given by

$$V_1 = F(I_o) + \epsilon_1 - I_1^* + \frac{1}{1+r}[F(I_1^*) + \gamma \epsilon_1]. \tag{4.12}$$

This is the value of the firm once the dividends, earnings, and financing decisions are announced, provided that the optimal investment decision can be evaluated by everybody from the first-order condition in (4.11). But before these announcements, the traders develop their own expectations of the value of the firm, $E_\circ(V_1)$, conditioned by the information they have up to time 0. The difference between the value after the announcement and the expected value before the disclosure of information is the *unexpected value*, to be calculated as $V_1 - E_\circ(V_1)$.

The pre-announcement value is therefore

$$E_\circ(V_1) = E_\circ\big(\tilde{X}_1 - I_1\big) + \frac{1}{1+r}E_\circ[F(I_1)] = F(I_\circ) - I_1^* + \frac{1}{1+r}F(I_1^*),$$

where the last line follows from the fact that the agents know the optimal investment level from (4.11). Subtracting this equation from (4.12), it follows that the unexpected value is

$$V_1 - E_\circ(V_1) = \epsilon_1\left[1 + \frac{\gamma}{1+r}\right]. \tag{4.13}$$

As is clear from this simple calculation, the variation in the value of the firm (and therefore in the price of the shares) exists, because when computing $E_\circ(V_1)$ the value of X_1 is substituted for by its expected value, whereas V_1 is evaluated with the precise X_1.

Then, this effect can be seen as resulting from the announcement of earnings. From

$$X_t = I_t^* + (D_t - B_t), \tag{4.14}$$

note that disclosing X_t conveys exactly the same information as disclosing the *net dividends* $D_t - B_t$, since the optimal investment decision is given by the first-order condition in (4.11). Thus, this model predicts that the disclosure of earnings is equivalent to the disclosure of net dividends and any one of these announcements (or even a simultaneous announcement) provides the same price variation given here.

From this analysis it turns out that the pure dividend is not enough to forecast X_t exactly. It was shown that the *net* dividend could do that job, but not D_t. Given the announcement of the dividends, the level of external financing B_t is necessary in order to disclose the true value of X_t and therefore of V_t. Hence, there may be a *financing announcement effect* as well.

This line of reasoning suggests that the announcement of dividends must be followed by an announcement of either earnings or financing level, in order to fully reveal the true value of firms. Hence, this explains how dividends convey information to the market.

A Weakness of the Model

The model developed so far, however, does not yield a consistent equilibrium, since it provides the possibility of making a profit from the inside information that the optimal investment level is given by (4.11).

To see how simple it is to deviate from the original equilibrium, suppose that there is a certain fraction of shareholders (say, k) planning to sell their shares between the net dividends announcement and the earnings announcement. They could be induced to pay the management to increase the dividends and cut the investment level below the optimal level I_t^*.

In this case, the information conveyed by the net dividends is not equivalent to the information revealed by the earnings, since by construction the investment level is no longer fixed at the ideal level. But the shareholders who do not intend to sell do not know that. They think that the investment at time 1 is still I_1^*.

Notice that the difference between the net dividend paid and the expected net dividend is ϵ_1,

$$(D_1 - B_1) - E_\circ(D_1 - B_1) = X_1 - F(I_\circ) = \epsilon_1,$$

and then, from (4.13), for each unit in this difference the gain in value for the sellers is

$$k\left(1 + \frac{\gamma}{1+r}\right),$$

which is positive for $\gamma \geq 0$. To evaluate the losses to the fraction $1 - k$ of stayers, just use (4.14) in the expression for the value of the firm in (4.12) to get at $t = 1$

$$V_t = D_t - B_t + \frac{1}{1+r}[F(I_t^*) + \gamma\epsilon_t].$$

A change in the dividends of dD_t at the expense of a cut of the same magnitude in the investments generates a change in the value of the firm of magnitude dV_t,

$$V_t + dV_t = D_t + dD_t - B_t + \frac{1}{1+r}[F(I_t^* - dD_t) + \gamma\epsilon_t].$$

Subtracting this last equation from the former, it follows that

$$dV_t = dD_t + \frac{1}{1+r}[F(I_t^* - dD_t) - F(I_t^*)] = dD_t - \frac{1}{1+r}F'(I_t^*)dD_t$$

$$= \left[1 - \frac{F'(I_t^*)}{1+r}\right]dD_t = 0.$$

Hence, there is no loss for the stayers in this situation. From this simple derivation it is seen that the possible losses from the decrease in the investment level are exactly balanced by the benefit of a greater dividend. The conclusion is that there is no incentive for them to try to exercise any counterpressure regarding the incentives of potential sellers.

The model as it is does not sustain the optimal criterion for investment. For the signals to have a clear role, some of the mechanisms in this model must change.

4.2.3 A Consistent Signaling Model

The preceding lack of equilibrium has its root in the fact that sellers and stayers had different valuations for the firm. The firm, which is supposed to maximize the value to the stayers, could be induced to underinvest in order to benefit those shareholders who intend to sell.

As was shown, it is not convincing to argue that managers try to maximize the value of the stayers. That is the reason why that objective does not lead to an equilibrium. To be stable, an equilibrium must reflect the maximization of a linear combination of the two different values of the firm. The cost of such equilibrium will clearly be a certain level of underinvestment.

To simplify the notation, let D_t now denote the net dividend. Consider what happens at time $t = 1$. The value to the stayers, (say, V_t^1) is still given by (4.12),

$$V_t^1 = D_t + \frac{1}{1+r}[F(I_t) + \gamma\epsilon_t], \tag{4.15}$$

whereas the value to the sellers is the expectation of that expression conditioned by the knowledge of the past data plus the announced dividend,

$$V_t^2 = D_t + \frac{1}{1+r}E_\circ[F(I_t) + \gamma\tilde{\epsilon}_t].$$

The objective of the firm is described as to maximize a convex linear combination of V_t^1 and V_t^2—namely,

$$\alpha V_t^1 + (1-\alpha)V_t^2.$$

When there are no potential sellers $(k = 0)$, the correct function to maximize is V_t^1, and therefore α is taken to be $1 - k$. The optimization program that follows is

$$\max_{D_t, I_t}(1 - k)V_t^1 + kV_t^2$$

subject to the budget constraint $X_t = I_t + D_t$. Substituting this constraint in the maximization problem, the optimization becomes unidimensional. Moreover, noticing that

$$V_t^1 \equiv V_t^1(X_t, D_t)$$

and

$$V_t^2 \equiv V_t^2(D_t),$$

the problem becomes

$$\max_{D_t}(1 - k)V_t^1(X_t, D_t) + kV_t^2(D_t).$$

Notice that given X_t, this maximization tries to find an optimal D_t^*. The reverse mapping is $X_t(D_t)$, and if it is single-valued, the signal conveyed by the optimal level of dividends should be consistent in the sense that the valuation of the sellers should coincide with the valuation of the stayers,

$$V_t^1\big(X_t(D_t), D_t\big) = V_t^2(D_t).$$

The optimal dividend must satisfy the first-order condition obtained by substituting this consistency expression into the preceding objective function and differentiating with respect to D_t. Doing that, it follows that

$$k\partial_x V_t^1\big(X_t(D_t), D_t\big)X_t'(D_t) + \partial_d V_t^1\big(X_t(D_t), D_t\big) = 0.$$

As a boundary condition to solve this equation, it is assumed that the earnings X_t are bounded from below by $\underline{X}_t$. For a company at that level of earnings, it does not make any sense to signal anything. It is a situation in which the worst possible expectations of the sellers would be correct. Hence, such a firm would choose the optimal level I_t^* defined in (4.11). Therefore, the boundary condition is

$$X_t(\underline{X}_t - I_t^*) = \underline{X}_t,$$

which uniquely defines the solution to the preceding differential equation. Notice also that equation (4.15) can be used to write the differential equation in a more explicit way, since

$$V_t^1 = D_t + \frac{1}{1+r}[F(I_t^*) + \gamma\epsilon_t]$$

$$= D_t + \frac{1}{1+r}\{F(X_t - D_t) + \gamma[X_t - F(I_o)]\}.$$

Then

$$\partial_x V_t^1(X_t(D_t), D_t) = \frac{1}{1+r}[F'(X_t - D_t) + \gamma]$$

and

$$\partial_d V_t^1(X_t(D_t), D_t) = 1 - \frac{1}{1+r}F'(X_t - D_t).$$

Substituting these values into the differential equation, it follows that

$$k\frac{1}{1+r}[F' + \gamma]X' + 1 - \frac{F'}{1+r} = 0,$$

or still, isolating $X_t'(D_t)$,

$$X'(D) = \frac{F' - (1+r)}{k[F' + \gamma]}.$$

This equation has an important implication. If it is assumed that firms increase their dividends as their earnings increase,[3] this implies that $X'(D) \geq 0$ for all values of D.[4] If that is the case, the numerator in the preceding ratio must also be positive, implying that the level of investment, the argument of F', is below the optimal level I^* determined in the previous section.

4.2.4 Empirical Evidence

Several empirical observations of unexpected returns in the payment of dividends test the informational content of dividends. Before the work of Aharony and Swary (1980), a long and inconclusive debate had taken place. For instance, Pettit (1972,1976) and Watts (1973,1976) were not in accordance with respect to the value conveyed by information. In fact, both were using primarily monthly data but rather different methodologies.

The main dispute between these studies pivots on the correct distinction between the information conveyed by the earnings and that conveyed by the dividends. All of these studies used monthly data as well, suffering from the same problem as Brennan's study described previously, and making it more difficult to distinguish between the two informational effects. Three more recent papers have discussed unexpected returns using daily return data.

The first of them is a paper by Charest (1978), who was actually more interested in analyzing issues related to market efficiency. In this paper, significant abnormal returns are reported, on the order of 1%. However, given his main concern, no effort was made to separate the component due to the dividends from the one due to earnings.

Aharony and Swary (1980) consider only firms from which they have data on quarterly dividends and earnings per share, announcement dates, and daily rates of return.

These authors use a naive model of expectations, according to which the expected dividend of a firm j at the quarter q, $\widehat{D}_{jq}$, equals the dividend payment in the previous quarter, D_{jq-1}. Accordingly, a dividend announcement is said to be *favorable* if $D_{jq} > \widehat{D}_{jq}$ and *unfavorable* if $D_{jq} < \widehat{D}_{jq}$. Otherwise, the dividend is said to be *stable*. Confirming the known tendency of firms not to change their dividend policies, Aharony and Swary find that in their sample, in about 87% of the cases the dividends are stable.

In order to isolate the dividend effect from the earnings effect, only firms in which dividend announcement dates differ from the earnings announcement dates by at least 11 days are taken into account.

Using the naive expectation model, the sample data are divided into three groups: favorable, unfavorable, and stable dividends. Still, each of these groups is subdivided according to whether the dividends announcement preceded or followed the earnings announcement.

The abnormal returns are computed from a market model

$$\widetilde{R}_{jt} = \alpha_j + \beta_j \widetilde{R}_{mt} + \tilde{\epsilon}_{jt},$$

where $\widetilde{R}_{jt}$ is the return[5] of security j at day t, and α_j and β_j are constants, and $\widetilde{R}_{mt}$ reflects the mean return on the market[6] around time t. The residual $\tilde{\epsilon}_{jt}$ represents the abnormal return, the expected value of which is zero.

Notice that only moments in time within a distance of 11 days or less from the announcement of dividends at $t = 0$ are being considered. Hence, $-11 < t < 11$. The average abnormal return at time t is calculated averaging for each quarter q the estimated residual for all available securities in that quarter at a distance t of the announcement, and then taking the average of that over all the quarters.

The result is an average residual depending on t, AR_t. The null hypothesis is that AR_t is distributed around zero and has a t-distribution if suitably scaled.

The main results of Aharony and Swary are twofold. First, they show that in the case of stable dividends, there are no significant abnormal returns (AR), and in the case of changing dividends they find either positive abnormal returns of about 1% in the case of increasing dividends, or negative AR of about -3% when the dividends decrease.

Second, they find support for the semistrong form of the efficient capital market hypothesis in the sense that most of the stock market price adjustments—that is to say, most of the abnormal returns—happen at times 0 and -1. This means that almost all of the price adjustments occur in the space of two days around the announcement.

Following the same line of research, Asquith and Mullins (1983) are more interested in investigating the effect of dividends on shareholders' wealth. The negative wealth impacts may come either from the tax effects discussed already or from other costs associated with the payment of dividends, such as the costs of administering a dividend program and the costs of issuing equity to raise funds in order to pay the dividends. To balance these costs, on the positive side there is the value of the informational content of dividends.

As do Aharony and Swary, these authors use daily data to completely separate the effects of different announcements. The main difference between these two studies is that Asquith and Mullins take firms that did not pay dividends at least in the previous 10 years. This solves a basic problem common to all of the works analyzing the unexpected dividends, namely how to calculate the expected part. As described before, Aharony and Swary use a naive model of expectations. But other authors such as Fama and Babiak (1968) use more sophisticated models taking past payment of dividends into account. In the case of Asquith and Mullins, all such models collapse in the naive one, since it is as if all past dividends were zero and the increase in the dividends is the dividend itself.

Studying initial dividends has the advantage then of making the hypothesized informational effects clearer. Also, it should clarify the clientele effect, since before the first dividend, firms were only providing capital gains and afterwards there are also dividend gains at the expense of the former.

Another issue raised with this line of argument is that if initial dividends can be considered as unexpected, validating the naive expectation model, the same may not be true for subsequent dividends. The idea of these two authors is to relate the wealth effect to the magnitude of dividends, and to verify whether the same expectations model is valid for the subsequent increases in dividends.

The initial dividends generate a larger wealth effect than the subsequent changes in dividends. This is natural, since the initial value of the dividends is much higher than later variations. However, if the wealth effect is adjusted for the magnitude of the dividends' increase, Asquith and Mullins show that subsequent dividends generate higher or at least as-high wealth effects as did the original dividends.

This finding suggests that the investors have some ability to forecast dividends or, in other words, that the naive expectations model is not correct for the subsequent dividends, for, if it were, one would expect to observe the same results for subsequent dividends as for the initial ones.

This result refines the analysis of Aharony and Swary, but the main conclusions still remain. Using a similar procedure, Asquith and Mullins estimate the average excess return and make a similar test using the t-statistics. They find an average return of 3.7% with a t-statistic of 6.59—a much higher number than the 1% found by Charest and by Aharony and Swary. In essence, however, the informational content of the dividends is confirmed, as well as the semistrong form of the efficient capital market hypothesis—namely, that almost all the price adjustment was made in two days around the announcement date.

4.2.5 Exercises

1. Find the exact change in the value of the firm due to the financing announcement effect mentioned two paragraphs below equation (4.14).
2. Show that $X'(D)$ has to be positive in order to get to a solution to the following maximization problem:

$$\max_{D_t}(1 - k)V_t^1(D_t, X_t) + kV_t^1(X(D_t), D_t).$$

3. Show what happens to the optimal dividend level satisfying the first-order condition

$$k\frac{1}{1+r}[F' + \gamma]X' + 1 - \frac{F'}{1+r} = 0$$

when
    (a) The parameter γ changes, with all other factors fixed.
    (b) The parameter k changes, with all other factors fixed.
4. Find the optimal level of investment when the investment/production function is given by $F(I) = \ln I$.

4.3 Stock Repurchases

Instead of paying cash dividends, firms may prefer to distribute their excess cash flow to shareholders in the form of share repurchases. This is an alternative available for firms in the U.S., Canada, and the United Kingdom that has only recently started to become popular in some other European countries.

This section analyzes the recent trend showing unambiguously that share repurchases are taking the place of cash dividends as the main pay-out policy. The natural question arises of whether share repurchases are being used as a substitute for dividends.

This substitution hypothesis is perfectly compatible with the results analyzed in earlier sections and chapters. The work of Modigliani and Miller (1961), for instance, implies that in perfect capital markets share repurchases and dividend payments are perfect substitutes. In other words, under the MM assumptions and given the investment policy, the wealth of the shareholders does not depend on the method the firm chooses to distribute its residual cash. Also, the argument of Jensen (1986) that firms should not keep free cash flow to avoid agency problems does not depend on the chosen mechanism to distribute the residual cash. Similarly, most signaling models such as those of Bhattacharya (1979) and Miller and Rock (1985) assume an implicit equivalency between dividends and stock repurchases.

Whether the substitution hypothesis holds is an empirical issue. In order to discuss this point, the different types of reasons to buy back stock are compared to the reasons underlying the dividends payments. A related issue is to understand why firms failed to substitute repurchases for dividends earlier than they have. In order to answer these questions a careful analysis of the theory, of the evolution of the legal status, and of the empirical evidences is presented.

4.3.1 Trends in Payout Policies

For many years a puzzling fact intrigued people analyzing shares repurchases. The issue was why firms opted for dividends over share repurchases despite the clear tax advantages of the latter.

The first to report a remarkable change in the repurchase market in the 1980s were Bagwell and Shoven (1989). As described in Lease et al. (2000), in a short period of four years share repurchases grew from 12% to 40% of the total cash distribution. Although this tendency slowed in the early 90s, Grullon and Michaely (2000) report that in 1998, for the first time, for each dollar U.S. firms paid in dividends, a larger amount— 1.04 dollars, to be precise—was spent repurchasing stock.

Furthermore, Grullon and Michaely (2000) show that the increase in the buyback activity from the mid-80s to the end of the 90s has helped the total payout to increase. Curiously, they also show that the dividend payout ratio is negatively correlated with the payout ratio associated with share repurchase during that period. The dividend yield is reported to decline consistently in that period, from 3.86% to 1.48%, at the same time that share repurchase yield increased from 0.5% to 1.54%. Although at some periods in time, one may observe a reduction of the total cash distributions to the shareholders with respect to the market value of equity, these authors show that the total payout yield has shown relative stability over the past decade.

4.3.2 Reasons for Stock Repurchases

The reasons leading to the decision to repurchase stock may not be very different from those leading to the dividend initiative.

To start with, stock repurchase is an effective way for a firm to employ its free cash flow whenever better investment alternatives are not present. Just as in the case of dividend payments, this procedure allows the firm to reduce the cost of agency problems raised by the presence of free cash flows as argued by Jensen (1986).

A second reason for repurchasing stock is to exploit the asymmetry of information between the insiders and the market. Stock repurchases may be a very convenient mechanism to convey superior information to the market as illustrated by the model of Vermaelen studied in section 3.2.4. Ofer and Thakor (1987) present an integrated setting allowing signaling through either cash dividends or stock repurchase. More specifically, these authors considered that firms having both alternatives available will choose the cheapest way of signaling. In particular, when the difference in value between undervalued stock and the intrinsic value of the stock is small, a dividend payout will be sufficient. When this difference is more significant, a stock repurchase can signal that fact more efficiently. In an alternative model, Hausch and Seward (1993) show that if the managers of a high-quality firm are not too risk averse, given their investment projects, they prefer to signal the value of the firm through a stock repurchase. If their degree of risk aversion is above a certain threshold, however, the managers of a high-quality firm will prefer to signal the value of their firm through a certain cash dividend distribution. As seen in the previous section of this chapter, the information asymmetry between the insiders and the market may also be a good reason to pay dividends. The signaling model of Miller and Rock (1985) is an example.

Third, one may think of stock repurchase as a strategy for transferring wealth from debtholders to stockholders. This is very similar to the conflicts generated between these two parts when dividends are paid, in the sense that fewer resources are left to the firm in the case of liquidation.

In the fourth place, one may argue that, especially when financed with debt, stock repurchases may lead to an effective restructuring of the capital of the firm. In principle, such changes in structure are analogous in nature to those that would occur in the case of a debt-financed dividend payment.

All four reasons are as valid for stock repurchases as for the payment of dividends, although the magnitude of the effect of stock repurchases is typically greater than that of dividend payouts. One would be tempted to say that, apart from a scale issue, both methods are equivalent. In spite of these similarities, however, there are at least two important differences.

The first one lies in the different tax treatment of cash dividends and stock repurchases. Dividends are taxed as ordinary income, whereas the income from stock repurchases is taxed as a capital gain. Depending on how the law treats these two types of taxes, stockholders may prefer a stock repurchase to dividends. As reported in Lease et al. (2000), with the exception of the period between 1986 and 1993, U.S. law has systematically favored the tax treatment of capital gains as compared to ordinary income. There are, however, two distinct aspects to the tax issue. On one hand, taxes generate a natural "clientele effect." For example, capital gains are taxed based upon the difference between the tender price and the (historical) price at which the shares were bought. This creates a higher incentive for those who bought the shares at high prices to sell back the shares. For similar reasons, shareholders in low tax brackets have more incentive to sell back their shares than shareholders in higher tax brackets. On the other hand, capital gains are taxed only when those gains are realized. Therefore, assuming that the share prices increase after the share repurchase, this increment of value does not necessarily mean that a tax payment is immediate. Such payment may be deferred if the shareholders who did not tender their shares will keep them for a certain time. Thus, these two different dimensions imply that the effective tax to shareholders is, in general, lower in the case of share repurchases than in the case of cash dividend distributions, even when the law does not provide preferential treatment for capital gains, as was the case in the U.S. between 1986 and 1993.

The second important difference is that the stock repurchase does not affect all the stockholders equally, as occurs in the case of a dividend payment. In fact, stock repurchases entitle only those shareholders who choose to tender or sell back their shares to receive the cash distribution. Therefore, this mechanism affects the proportion of shareholders' holdings, implying a potential change in the ownership structure of the firm. This aspect will be covered in more detail in Chapter 6.

As discussed in Lease et al. (2000), the results of different surveys trying to determine the main reasons underlying the actual repurchases have not led to conclusions. Survey responses can suffer from typical problems such as strong biases and nonresponses.

4.3.3 Empirical Evidence

The typical image of a share repurchase is that of a fixed-price tender offer. In this case the firm offers to buy back a specified number of its outstanding shares at a specified price up to an expiration date. The average premium paid in the references cited in Lease et al. (2000) range from 16.7% in the study of Hertzel and Jain (1991) to 24% in Dann, Masulis, and Mayers (1991). Within the same set of references, the average fraction of firms' shares sought range from 14.8% in Hertzel and Jain (1991) to 18.8% in Comment and Jarrell (1991). The remaining shares have excess returns in the range of 10.1% to 18.5% in Dann (1981). Most of these authors conclude that tender offers increase share prices because they convey credible managerial signals to the market.

The most common form of share repurchase, however, is open-market repurchase. Here, the firm buys back a fraction of its outstanding shares at market prices over a long period of time. As compared to tender offers, open-market repurchases pay by construction low premiums, if any. Here, the fraction of the firm's outstanding share sought ranges from 5% in Vermaelen (1981) to 7%, the value that Lease et al. (2000) inferred from the paper by Comment and Jarrell (1991). Estimates of the wealth impact on the remaining shares range from 2.3% in Comment and Jarrell (1991) to 3.3% in Vermaelen (1981). The typical interpretation is that the signaling power of these operations is lower.

More recently, Dutch auction stock repurchase became a current alternative mechanism for buybacks. As one would expect, the premium paid is significantly lower than in the case of tender offers. Both in Comment and Jarrell (1991) and in Bagwell (1992) the premium is around 13%. The average percentage of shares sought is typically around 15.5%, a number very much in the range observed for usual tender offers. Not surprisingly, the wealth impact on the remaining shares—from 6.7% in Bagwell (1991) to 8.3% in Comment and Jarrell (1991)—is less than the impact in the case of tender offers. The fact that in an auction the prices are determined by the outsiders helps to argue that the informational content of these operations is inferior to the content of a tender offer, explaining the lower premiums.

Finally, when tender offers are directed toward a specific segment of shareholders, the premium paid is about 10% as reported in Bradley and Wakeman (1983). If the target of the offer is actually a single, large-block shareholder, the terms of the repurchase may be negotiated, leading to higher premia, as in Dann and DeAngelo (1983) and in Mikkelson and Ruback (1991). These are the only repurchases that reported consistently negative returns, from 4% to 6% around the announcements. The reason is that this form of repurchase is a defense mechanism against hostile takeovers, the cost of which is reflected in that way.

Grullon and Michaely (2000) provide some clarifying evidence on the relationship between dividends and stock repurchases that is consistent with the substitution hypothesis. First, they provide evidence that the growing share repurchase activity recently observed in the U.S. has been financed with potential increases in dividends. Using a simple model developed by Lintner (1956) to generate expected future dividend payments, they show that the difference between actual and expected dividends tends to be negatively correlated with resources spent in repurchases. This result strongly suggests support for the substitution hypothesis. Second, they find that the market reaction to a decrease in dividends is not significantly different from zero for firms involved in stock repurchases, which reinforces the idea underlying the substitution hypothesis.

5
Financial Contracting

THE PREVIOUS CHAPTERS explicitly relate the choice of the financial structure of a firm to its control structure. Whether decisions are taken by agents or by the principal is an issue that may lead to costs; the debt-equity choice of the firm was shown to be a relevant instrument in reducing the impact of such costs. The existence of asymmetries of information was shown to lead to similar implications.

To be more specific, the agency approach of capital structure explains that when control and ownership of a given firm are in different hands, there is the possibility of decisions from the controllers that are suboptimal with respect to the goal of maximizing the value for the shareholders. This happens simply because the two parts may have divergent incentives. In this context, the existence of debt contracts is shown to eliminate, or at least reduce, this type of agency cost.

Debt contracts in particular, but contracts in general, cannot specify all the possible future contingencies that decisions are based upon. In other words, contracts are usually incomplete. In the sequence of the discussion of agency problems, two influential papers, by Grossman and Hart (1986) and Hart and Moore (1990), discuss and develop stylized models for studying situations where contracting is constrained by the existence of important future variables that are difficult or impossible to describe initially and that, therefore, must be left out of the contract. These variables are described by Grossman, Hart, and Moore as ex-post observable for the parties in a given contract, but not observable for any third party, and thus they are not verifiable. Therefore, they are not enforceable, in the sense that the payoff of contracts cannot be written conditioned upon their observed value. This framework is known as the GHM approach.

The financial contracting literature has been developed starting from the GHM framework. It explicitly introduces wealth constraints, as opposed to the original GHM papers, in order to address the issues of financial structure and its relation to corporate control. In this context, financial structure is herein understood not simply as a mix of debt-equity, but rather as the set of characteristics of the different financial contracts that the firm is linked to. Under this perspective, *financial contracting* becomes an instrument for avoiding or reducing agency costs, leading to a definition of the control structure of the firms that optimizes the decision process for the possible states of nature to be revealed. This is the content of the first part of this chapter.

In the second part, a specification of the analytical setting is implemented in order to characterize debt contracts. The effect of some information asymmetry among the parties under contract is also introduced in order to explain the choice of debt duration and priority.

In spite of the success of incomplete contract theory in explaining some crucial aspects of financing contracts, Tirole (1999) points out that the explanatory potential of complete contracting is not exhausted at all. In particular, he stresses that the complete contract methodology may perfectly account for standard issues such as control and ownership, recalling a different approach not yet fully exploited for the understanding of the subjects here discussed.

5.1 Contracting and Allocation of Control

In this section a stylized approach to the problem of corporate governance is developed. This issue essentially involves the distribution of power among several players (managers, investors, creditors, and shareholders) who all have different interests in the performance of the firm.

In general, a contract regulates the relationship between two or more parties, such as by defining ex-ante the future implications of such a relationship for each of the parties, depending on what will occur. In other words, these implications depend on the states of nature to be revealed in the future.

Incomplete contracts are taken here as contracts that do not foresee all possible future contingencies with implications for each of the parties, either because it is not possible to do so, or because it is not convenient for those who wrote the contract. Given the possibility of future events that are not specified ex-ante by the contract, or events that simply cannot be specifiable, it becomes essential to define which part of the contract may be decided on behalf of the firm's interest. It is this issue of control allocation that Williamson (1988) Termed governance structure.

The financial structure of a firm actually helps to implicitly define a governance structure, not only by its composition of debt and equity but also through the specific contractual terms underlying the structure.

The choice of financial structure of firms has to be made in such a way as to maximize the return from future decisions, most of them investment decisions, but taking into particular account the governance structure that is induced.

As each firm is different from the others with respect to the distribution characteristics of the results, clearly each one will look for its own optimal financial structure. This establishes, from the outset, an important distinction from the usual agency theory, which implicitly assumes only one possible governance structure which is the same for every firm.

5.1.1 The Model

The relationship between incomplete financial contracts and the allocation of control in a firm may be discussed within a simple analytical context, as in the paper of Aghion and Bolton (1992). This section discusses their model, where a bilateral contract is considered between an entrepreneur having no initial wealth and an investor who has the resources to invest the amount K at $t = 0$. This is a model with three points in time characterizing the following dynamic setting:

At $t = 1$, the state of nature θ is revealed. This state may be either good (θ_g) with probability q or bad (θ_b) with probability $1 - q$. Finally, at $t = 2$, the result of the investment is obtained, expressed as a rate of return r. After the realization of the state of nature at $t = 1$ and before the maturity of the contract at $t = 2$, an action a is undertaken by one of the agents, either the investor or the entrepreneur. The decision about who takes the action is to be contracted at $t = 0$. The agent who chooses the action is said to be the one who owns the project or who retains control.

The action a and the state of nature θ are determining elements of the stochastic return r. An action is said to be optimal if it maximizes the expected wealth conditional to a given state of nature. Let a_g denote the optimal action under the state of nature θ_g and let a_b denote the optimal action under the state of nature θ_b.

The model follows the idea of Grossman and Hart (1986) that incomplete contracts are characterized by the fact that the state of nature is impossible or very costly to describe ex-ante and, therefore, the ex-ante contract cannot be contingent on the state θ. Unlike Grossman and Hart (1986), however, it is assumed here that at $t = 1$ there is a publicly verifiable signal $s \in \{0, 1\}$ that is correlated with the state of nature θ and that the contract may be contingent on s. One then defines the two conditional probabilities

$$\beta_g = \text{Prob}(s = 1 | \theta = \theta_g) > 1/2$$
$$\beta_b = \text{Prob}(s = 1 | \theta = \theta_b) < 1/2.$$

Note that $\beta_g = 1$ and $\beta_b = 0$ imply that the public signal s is a perfect proxy for θ. In other words, one may infer θ directly from the observable signal s, and thus the contract is no longer incomplete. For a contract to be incomplete, either β_g is at a certain distance from 1 or β_b is away from zero, or both situations occur. One may then use the sum of these two distances, namely,

$$d = |\beta_g - 1| + \beta_b, \tag{5.1}$$

as a measure of the degree of incompleteness of the contract.

The entrepreneur (E) and the investor (I) are assumed to be risk neutral in income and to have utility functions given, respectively, by

$$U_E(r, a) = g(r) + l(a, \theta)$$
$$U_I(r, a) = r - g(r),$$

where $l(a, \theta)$ is part of the total payoff of the entrepreneur that, although depending on the action undertaken and on the state of nature, is nonmonetary and not observable by third parties. Therefore, this term is taken as reflecting the *private benefits* for the entrepreneur.

It is also assumed that the stochastic return at $t = 2$ may take only two values: $r = 1$ or $r = 0$. As described previously, the stochastic return depends on both the state of nature θ and on the undertaken action a. Define y_j^i as

$$y_j^i = E\left[r | \theta = \theta_i; a = a_j\right].$$

In other words, y_j^i is the expected rate of return given that the state of nature is θ_i and the action undertaken is a_j. Under the same state of nature and action, let the private benefit to the entrepreneur be denoted by l_j^i. Then, for the project to be feasible from the point of view of the investor, one must have a positive net present value for the project,

$$q y_g^g + (1 - q) y_b^b > K.$$

Also, the optimality of a_g and a_b is assumed to be expressed as

$$y_g^g + l_g^g > y_b^g + l_b^g$$
$$y_b^b + l_b^b > y_g^b + l_g^b.$$

Finally, it is assumed that the entrepreneur is compensated with a positive monetary transfer schedule $g(r) = t(s, r)$, which is a function of the first-time-period public signal, revealing information about the state of nature and also the function of the return of the project at the end of the second period. Given that r can take only the values 0 and 1, with no loss of generality, this implies that the schedule $t(s, r)$ is composed of a fixed part and a variable part, proportional to r:

$$t(s, r) = t_s r + t'_s \geq 0, \tag{5.2}$$

where t_s and t'_s are constants. All residual returns go to the investor. Hence, if each one of the agents could choose the action to be taken maximizing his/her utilitiy, then the entrepreneur would maximize $t_s y^i_j + t'_s + l^i_j$ and the investor would maximize $(1 - t_s) y^i_j - t'_s$. The problem to be discussed within this model is the following: How does the structure presented induce the agents to settle an ex-ante agreement on who should decide which action should be taken after the state of nature is revealed? Is there room for renegotiation of the contract once the state of the world is revealed, but before the action is undertaken?

5.1.2 Entrepreneur Control

In this section, the case where the entrepreneur has full control is studied. This means that the entrepreneur chooses the action a. The action will therefore be chosen so as to maximize the entrepreneur's reward and will be given by

$$a^E(\theta_i, s) = \arg \max_{a_j} \{ t_s y^i_j + t'_s + l^i_j \},$$

for $i = g, b$ and $j = g, b$. In order to describe the nature of the different contracts that may arise in this context, we say that a contract is *efficient* if the action chosen is the optimal action for the realized state of nature. Also, we say that a contract is *feasible* if the investor expects to obtain at least as much as the amount invested, K.

First, consider the case where the private benefits (l) satisfy the inequalities $l^g_g > l^g_b$ and $l^b_b > l^b_g$. In that case, it is said that the private benefits (l) are comonotonic[1] with the total revenues $(y + l)$. It is fairly simple to show that, in this situation, a contract with a schedule $t(s, r)$ given by a constant t, independent of the signal perceived and of the return obtained, is efficient. Under the assumption of comonotonic private benefits,

$$t + l^g_g > t + l^g_b$$
$$t + l^b_b > t + l^b_g,$$

thus ensuring that the revelation of a good state $(i = g)$ implies $a^E = a_g$ and the revelation of a bad state $(i = b)$ implies $a^E = a_b$. In other words, the optimal choice of the entrepreneur coincides with the optimal choice for the project and one may say that entrepreneur control is efficient.

In this case, for the contract also to be feasible, the constant fee schedule $t \geq 0$ must be chosen such that $qy_g^g + (1 - q)y_b^b - t = K$. One such constant always exists given the assumption $qy_g^g + (1 - q)y_b^b > K$ and it follows

Proposition 5.1.1 (Aghion and Bolton). *If $l_g^g > l_b^g$ and $l_b^b > l_g^b$, then entrepreneur control is always efficient and feasible.*

A different treatment is required when the assumptions of the preceding result are not satisfied. Without loss of generality, assume that in state θ_b the inequality $l_b^b < l_g^b$ holds.

Under such a condition and depending on the fee schedule designed (namely, on t_s), the action chosen by the entrepreneur in certain states may not be the one that maximizes the value of the project. Therefore, there is room for renegotiation of the contract, in order to guarantee that there are no ex-post inefficiencies. It is also clear that all the gains from renegotiation revert to the entrepreneur.

Since the issue of renegotiating or not depends on the design of the fee schedule, one first looks for sufficient conditions that guarantee the absence of renegotiation and feasibility of the contract. In this case one would like the contract to induce the entrepreneur to choose action a_b in state θ_b. In other words, the fee schedule and the private benefits to the entrepreneur should relate as

$$t_s y_b^b + l_b^b \geq t_s y_g^b + l_g^b$$

or $t_s \geq (l_g^b - l_b^b)/(y_b^b - y_g^b)$. Let this lower bound be denoted by

$$\hat{t} \equiv \frac{l_g^b - l_b^b}{y_b^b - y_g^b}.$$

For the contract with $t_s = \hat{t}$ to be feasible, then it is required that the expected payoff to the investor be greater than K or, denoting by π_1 the expected payoff,

$$\pi_1 \equiv q(1 - \hat{t})y_g^g + (1 - q)(1 - \hat{t})y_b^b \geq K.$$

This case is feasible only if K is low enough as compared to the expected payoff (that is what the preceding condition means) and/or the fee schedule is high enough (that is the meaning of $t_s \geq \hat{t}$), transferring to the entrepreneur a relatively high part of the monetary proceedings of the project.

Consider now the case where $t_s < \hat{t}$ for $s = 0, 1$. In order to maximize the ex-ante expected payoff, the investor will only accept a contract with $t_s = 0$ whatever signal is observed. The schedule $t(r, s)$ in this contract becomes a simple fixed fee. This fact, together with the assumption that $l_b^b < l_g^b$, implies that the entrepreneur will always choose a_g, independently of the state of nature. Then, the ex-ante expected return to the investor is given by

$$\pi_2 = q y_g^g + (1 - q) y_g^b.$$

For the contract to be feasible, one requires that $\pi_2 \geq K$. In this situation, and given that $y_b^b > y_g^b$, there is an incentive to renegotiate. The investor is willing to pay up to $q y_g^g + (1 - q) y_b^b - \pi_2$ for the entrepreneur to choose action a_b in state θ_b. It turns out that this is an interesting offer to the entrepreneur who in this way increases its expected payoff. All the bargaining power being on the side of the entrepreneur, the ex-ante expected payoff to the investor remains π_2 after the renegotiation.

Finally, consider the case where the investor's expected payoff is maximized for an optimal schedule such that $t_s = \hat{t}$ for $s = 0$ and $t_s = 0$ for $s = 1$. Thus, if $s = 1$ and the state of nature is θ_b, the entrepreneur will be induced to choose the action a_g. It is then in the best interest of the investor to renegotiate the contract in order to invert the entrepreneur's choice. Thus, the ex-ante expected profit to the investor is

$$\pi_3 = q\left[\beta_g y_g^g + (1 - \beta_g) y_g^g (1 - \hat{t})\right] + (1 - q)\left[\beta_b y_g^b + (1 - \beta_b) y_b^b (1 - \hat{t})\right]$$

and for the contract to be feasible, one requires that $\pi_3 \geq K$. These three results are summarized in the following:

Proposition 5.1.2 (Aghion and Bolton). *Entrepreneur control is efficient and feasible if and only if* $\max(\pi_1, \pi_2, \pi_3) \geq K$.

Thus, for high values of K, entrepreneur control is not feasible.

5.1.3 Investor Control

This section analyses the extreme opposite of entrepreneur control. Here, the investor is assumed to be the one who decides on the action a, and every possible opportunistic behavior of the entrepreneur is avoided.

Similarly to what occurred in the previous section, when the action chosen by the investor is not the first-best, there is room for renegotiation. However, and unlike what happened before, if the entrepreneur is supposed to compensate the investor under the renegotiation, wealth constraints may not allow the renegotiation to take place.

An analogy with the previous section, however, should make it clear that if monetary benefits are comonotonic with total revenues, then the first-best choice can be achieved under investor control.

In fact, with the proportional schedule $t(s, r) = \bar{t}r$, the investor chooses the optimal action a_i in state θ_i. To see this, notice that the expected profit for the investor choosing action a_j in state θ_i is simply $\pi^i(a_j) = (1 - \bar{t})y_j^i$. Then, given the comonotonic property that makes $y_g^g > y_b^g$ and $y_b^b > y_g^b$, it follows that $\pi^i(a_j)$ is maximized when $i = j$. Therefore, the following result holds:

Proposition 5.1.3 (Aghion and Bolton). *If $y_g^g > y_b^g$ and $y_b^b > y_g^b$, then investor control is always efficient and feasible.*

If, however, monetary returns are not comonotonic with total returns, a renegotiation of the parameters at time $t = 1$ may allow for the first-best solution, but it requires a lower value of $\bar{t}$ for the entrepreneur.

Taking, without loss of generality, the case $y_g^g < y_b^g$, and assuming $t_s \leq 1$ and $t_s' = 0$,[2] it follows that the investor will not choose a_g in state θ_g since

$$(1 - t_s)y_g^g < (1 - t_s)y_b^g.$$

In order for the investor to make a different choice of action at date $t = 1$, it is necessary to have a renegotiation at that point in time that redefines the value of t_s in the fee schedule. Denoting this new value by $\hat{t}_s$, it must satisfy

$$(1 - \hat{t}_s)y_g^g \geq (1 - t_s)y_b^g$$

or

$$\hat{t}_s \leq 1 - (1 - t_s)\frac{y_b^g}{y_g^g}.$$

Clearly, it follows from this solution that either a large ratio y_b^g/y_g^g or a small t_s are sufficient conditions to get a negative $\hat{t}_s$, thus making a successful renegotiation impossible. This result may be condensed in the following:

Proposition 5.1.4 (Aghion and Bolton). *When monetary returns are not comonotonic with total returns, investor control is always efficient and feasible if and only if $\pi_4 = [qy_b^g + (1 - q)y_b^b](y_g^g/y_b^g) \geq K$.*

Here, π_4 denotes the expected payoff for the investor under renegotiation. The proof of this proposition is left as an exercise.

5.1.4 Contingent Control

In this section, it is established that when neither private benefits nor monetary returns are comonotonic with total returns, there may be contingent control allocations that strictly dominate both types of control discussed before. This means that depending on the realization of the first-period signal, either the entrepreneur or the investor has control.

Proposition 5.1.5 (Aghion and Bolton). *When neither monetary returns nor private benefits are comonotonic with total returns, there are values of K such that*

1. *Entrepreneur control is not feasible.*
2. *Investor control is not first-best efficient.*
3. *Both unilateral control allocations are dominated by the contingent control allocation defining a_b if $s = 0$ and a_g if $s = 1$ as the degree of incompleteness expressed in equation (5.1) goes to zero.*

5.1.5 Financing Contracts

Three types of control have been discussed: control of the entrepreneur, control of the investor, and contingent control. If one concludes that the investor control is the optimal one, then capital for the investment enters in exchange for the power of deciding which action to take after the state of nature is revealed. This could be seen as equivalent to giving voting rights to the investors, in the sense that they would have decision power (actually *all* the power) over the decisions to be made. This situation is analogous to the issuance of voting equity.

If, on the other hand, full control by the entrepreneur is preferred, the project should be financed in such a way that the investors receive no right about the choice of the action to be taken. Investors will benefit from the project as if they were nonvoting shareholders, holding equivalent rights to what is known as preferred stock.

Finally, it is true that for some values of K, as the contract becomes more complete, its optimal design becomes contingent upon the public signal revealing the state of nature. This captures an essential feature of debt contract instruments, which is a shift in control contingent upon the revelation of a public signal.

Financing projects with debt is a natural way of implementing contingent control allocations. The entrepreneur may retain the control contingent upon the ability to meet the required payments of the debt contract. This is a very specific contingency that characterizes debt contracts. Failure to fulfill these compromises implies that the control passes to the investor, who may choose the liquidation of the firm or the reorganization of the firm, meaning simply a restructuring of the claims. The fact that control passes from the entrepreneur to the investor is another specific property of the debt contracts. Although the model of Aghion and Bolton explains shifts in control, as noted by Hart (1995), it does not necessarily describe a contract with these standard properties of debt.

5.1.6 Exercises

1. Since r can take only the values 0 and 1, show that the schedule $t(s, r)$ can be written as in (5.2) with no loss of generality.
2. Analyzing the case where private benefits are not comonotonic with total revenues in Section 5.1.2, attention is restricted to compensating schemes such that $t'_s = 0$ and $t_s \leq 1$.
   (a) Show why t_s will not be greater than 1.
   (b) Show that $t'_s = 0$ is optimal compared to other situations with $t'_s > 0$.
3. Under entrepreneur control, show that the renegotiation of the contract whenever $t_s < \hat{t}$ for $s = 0, 1$ leads to an increase in the expected payoff of the entrepreneur.
4. Show that the expressions for π_1, π_2, π_3, and π_4 are those given in the text.
5. Prove Proposition 5.1.3.
6. Prove Proposition 5.1.4.

5.2 Debt Contract Design

This section is devoted to the characterization of a debt contract. An important feature of debt contracts has been explained before—namely, shifts in control. However, important aspects of these contracts have not been explained, such as a characterization of the type of control transference and the signal that triggers such a shift.

The setting to be described here builds on the work of Hart and Moore (1989,1995) and Bolton and Scharfstein (1990,1996), which can be seen as a specification of the model of Aghion and Bolton (1992).

5.2.1 Extending the Model

As before, all the agents are risk neutral and the risk-free rate is assumed to be zero. The time schedule refers to a two-period model and is characterized as follows: At time $t = 0$ an amount K is invested in the project. The entrepreneur, as before, is assumed to have no initial wealth. In this specification of the model, the state of nature is characterized by the cash flow at $t = 1$. It may be $\theta_g = x$ with probability q and $\theta_b = 0$ with probability $1 - q$. The cash flow is observable for both the investor and the entrepreneur, but not for any third party, and is thus not verifiable. Therefore, as before, a contract between the investor and the entrepreneur is incomplete.

The manager is assumed to have the ability to divert cash flow without the control of the investor. In that case a zero payoff would be declared at $t = 1$ when the actual payoff was x. If the declared cash flow at $t = 1$ is x, the contract states a payment of R_x to the creditholder and, with probability β_x, the right of the creditholder to liquidate a part of the assets that is worth L_x. If the cash flow is null, the values are, respectively, $R_o, \beta_o,$ and L_o.

Notice that taking $\beta_x = 0, \beta_o = 1,$ and $L_x = L_o,$ being equal to the value of the assets of the project at time $t = 1$, this reduces to a usual debt contract with face value $R_x < x$ and one-period maturity. The issue in designing a contract is to find the optimal values for the preceding parameters. Therefore, it is possible in this simple setting to analyze the conditions under which a debt contract would result as optimal.

In the second period, two things may happen. Either the manager continues the project or the project is liquidated, in the sense that it is separated from the manager. If the manager's activity continues, the cash flow at time $t = 2$ is y. In the case of no liquidation, the project thus has a net present value of $qx + y - K$.

The expected return to the firm is then written as

$$\pi_f = q[x - R_x + (1 - \beta_x)y] + (1 - q)[-R_o + (1 - \beta_o)y]. \tag{5.3}$$

On the other hand, the investor expects to get

$$\pi_i = q[R_x + \beta_x L_x] + (1 - q)[R_o + \beta_o L_o] - K. \tag{5.4}$$

Suppose for a moment that at time $t = 1$ the cash flow is x. The expected return to the firm would then be $x - R_x + (1 - \beta_x)y$, decomposed as follows: The cash flow x goes to the entrepreneur, who has to pay R_x to the investor. With probability β_x the project is liquidated at date $t = 1$, leading to a continuation value of zero, and with probability $1 - \beta_x$ the project continues until time $t = 2$, generating a cash flow y at that point. If, however, the manager hides from the outer investor the cash flow x, then only R_o will be paid at time $t = 1$, and liquidation occurs with probability β_o, leaving to the firm a possible payoff S, not necessarily zero, as before. This happens because the liquidation value L_o does not correspond to the true value of the assets in that state of nature. In that case the expected return to the firm is $x - R_o + \beta_o S + (1 - \beta_o)y$.

For the manager to be induced to pay the due R_x when the cash flow is x, one must therefore impose

$$x - R_x + (1 - \beta_x)y \geq x - R_o + \beta_o S + (1 - \beta_o)y. \tag{5.5}$$

Noticing that $R_o = \beta_x = 0$ is optimal in the sense that these values maximize the profit to the firm and facilitates the verification of (5.5), the preceding inequality reads

$$R_x \leq \beta_o(y - S).$$

Among all these possible values for R_x that ensure a trustworthy behavior from the manager of the project, any investor would maximize its expected return by choosing the greatest value. Thus, at the optimum, this restriction is binding. Substituting the optimal values of the parameters in expression (5.4) for the expected result of the investor, one gets

$$\pi_i = \beta_o[q(y - S) + (1 - q)L_o] - K. \tag{5.6}$$

Using the optimal values of the parameters, namely those minimizing the profit to the investor, in the profit of the firm (5.3), it follows that

$$\pi_f = (qx + y - K) - (1 - q)\beta_o(y - L_o). \tag{5.7}$$

This result can be interpreted as the net present value of the project in the absence of liquidation minus a cost due to contract incompleteness.

For the profit in (5.6) to be positive, ensuring the minimum condition of feasibility of the contract, one must have

$$1 \geq \beta_o \geq \frac{K}{q(y - S) + (1 - q)L_o},$$

where the first inequality comes from the fact that β_o is a probability and the second inequality comes from the condition $\pi_i \geq 0$. Notice that π_f is decreasing in β_o whereas π_i is monotonically increasing in that parameter. Maximizing the expected return to the firm conditioned to a positive expected return to the investor defines the optimal value of β_o as the lowest possible. Thus

$$\beta_o = \frac{K}{q(y - S) + (1 - q)L_o}.$$

Both S and L_o (and thus also β_o) are still to be specified. There is no need to specify L_x, since the main feature of the optimal contract just described is that there is no liquidation in the good state. Liquidation occurs only, if at all, in the case of a poor performance. In order to understand what determines S and L_o some additional assumptions are required.

It is assumed that the entrepreneur is not able to continue managing the project in the case of bankruptcy after a zero cash flow. This is the case of a *liquidity default*. In that case, the creditor may sell the position to a third party who obtains at $t = 2$ a cash flow αy, with $\alpha \in [0, 1]$, meaning that the incoming manager cannot get better results out of the assets than the manager who left the firm.

In the case of bankruptcy after a nonzero cash flow, the original manager will negotiate the buyback of the firm with the creditholder, sharing the second-period return y. In that situation, $S = y/2$. This is the case of a *strategic default*.

It is also assumed that, in the case of liquidity default, the buyer of the assets incurs an informational cost $c \in [0, \bar{c}]$. This cost is modeled as a uniformly distributed random variable. Therefore, by a negotiating process similar to the preceding, the remaining value of the assets, αy, is equally divided between the creditor and the buyer. The buyer then negotiates only if $c \leq \alpha y/2$. Thus, assuming that $\alpha y/2 \leq \bar{c}$, the probability that this happens is

$$\Pr\left(c \leq \frac{\alpha y}{2}\right) = \frac{\alpha y}{2\bar{c}}.$$

Therefore, the expected value of the liquidation payoff in the case of a zero cash flow at $t = 1$ is

$$L_\circ = \frac{\alpha^2 y^2}{4\bar{c}},$$

and the optimal $\beta_\circ$ reads

$$\beta_\circ = \frac{K}{q\frac{y}{2} + (1 - q)\frac{\alpha^2 y^2}{4\bar{c}}}. \tag{5.8}$$

It follows[3] that the optimal value of $\beta_\circ$ decreases as q increases. Thus, the probability of liquidation of assets decreases as the probability of positive cash flow increases. Thus, the inefficiency due to contract incompleteness, expressed in (5.7) as $(1 - q)\beta_\circ(y - L_\circ)$, is lower for higher q, or, in other words, with lower risk of bankruptcy.

Also, the optimal value of $\beta_\circ$ decreases as α increases. This simply means that the closer the performance of the new manager is to achieving y at $t = 2$, the less damage is created by the reorganization procedure.

5.2.2 The Case of Many Creditholders

Bolton and Scharfstein (1996) bring to this discussion a related issue: The crucial element is the number, nature, and type of creditors—in other words, whether credit is private or public, whether it is granted by banks or obtained by issuing bonds in the marketplace, and also the nature of the governance structure among the creditors.

In this setting assume that at time $t = 0$ the amount K is invested to acquire the assets A and B. These are the assets that constitute the investment project. If there are two creditors, assume that each of the assets A and B provides collateral for each of them. Denoting by y^A and y^B the cash flows for assets A and B, as managed separately, one defines $\Delta = y - y^A - y^B$, which is assumed to be positive. This means that the cash flow generated by both assets is assumed to be greater than the sum of the cash flow generated by each of the assets individually. It is then possible to show that the expected value of liquidation at time $t = 1$ is given by

$$\overline{L}_{o} = \frac{\alpha^2 y^2}{4\overline{c}} - \frac{\alpha^2 \Delta^2}{36\overline{c}} < \frac{\alpha^2 y^2}{4\overline{c}} = L_{o}.$$

In other words, in the case of two creditors, the expected value of liquidation when there is a zero cash flow at $t = 1$ is lower than the value expected with only one creditor. Moreover, in the state with probability q,

$$S = \frac{y}{2} - \frac{\Delta}{6},$$

leading to an optimal value of β_{o} with a denominator given by

$$q\left(\frac{y}{2} - \frac{\Delta}{6}\right) + (1 - q)\left(\frac{\alpha^2 y^2}{4\overline{c}} - \frac{\alpha^2 \Delta^2}{36\overline{c}}\right),$$

which can be greater or less than the similar value found before with only one creditor. In fact, as asked in the exercises, it is simple to see that the creditors are paid more in the case of strategic default, but are paid less in the case of liquidity default. This shows that two creditors prevent strategic defaults more efficiently than does one single creditor, but implies more costly financial distress.

From equation (5.7), the inefficiency of liquidation is proportional to $\beta_{o}(y - L_{o})$, and this term is influenced by the number of creditors in two different ways: first, through the expected value of L_{o}, which is always greater with one single creditor; and second, through the critical value of β_{o}, which may go either way, since the effects on S and on L_{o} are in opposite directions.

Several conclusions may be derived from this stylized modeling. First, it is in the interest of the firm to increase the number of creditors when the risk of bankruptcy is low. When this risk is higher, actually the best way to reduce β_{o} is to increase L_{o}, thus reducing the number of debtholders. When this risk is low, the most efficient way to reduce β_{o} is to reduce S

or, in other words, the contractual advantage to the manager from reorganization, thus increasing the number of creditors.

Second, it is in the interest of the firm to increase the number of creditors when the complementarity of activities is reduced. This means that Δ will be reduced. By reducing Δ, notice that the decrease in S is much more significant than the similar effect in $L_\circ$.

Finally, it is in the interest of the firm to increase the number of creditors whenever α is small. This can be seen from the fact that the expected value of liquidation at $t = 1$ increases as α increases, and does so faster when there is only one creditor.

5.2.3 The Choice of the Duration

A very important aspect of debt contracting is the duration of the contracts. Some models take this aspect of the contract into account explicitly. The long-term debt avoids liquidation in the favorable state, when firms do not have sufficient resources to pay the short-term debt. On the other hand, short-term debt avoids strategic default or, in other words, the entrepreneur's incentive to go bankrupt in order to appropriate from the benefits of renegotiation. The way short-term debt avoids this is through the threat of short-term liquidation of the firm. For such a threat to be credible, one assumes that liquidation implies a loss in value as compared to the continuation of the firm. In other words, liquidation is assumed to be efficient ex-post at $t = 1$ to the short-term creditholder.

A model developed by Diamond (1991, 1993) illustrates in a very simple way the differences between short-term and long-term debt financing. The model is based on information asymmetry and credit rating.

Regaining the notation of Aghion and Bolton, consider an entrepreneur with a two-period project who needs funds for an initial investment $K = 1$. The project may be of one of two types: good or bad. At time $t = 2$ a good project has a payoff $X > 0$, whereas a bad project pays that amount with a probability π, and pays zero with probability $1 - \pi$. Let θ denote the type of project, θ_g referring to a good project and θ_b referring to a bad project. The quality of the project is known to the entrepreneur but not to the investor. Given a project, as of date $t = 0$ the investor assigns a probability f that $\theta = \theta_g$. This probability is referred to as a *credit rating* and reflects the lender's information about the project. It follows that, as of time 0, the probability q that a borrower pays the loan at date $t = 2$ is given by

$$q \equiv f + \pi(1 - f) = \pi + f(1 - \pi). \tag{5.9}$$

At time $t = 1$ information about the project becomes available to the investor. This new information is not verifiable, so it makes no sense to write contracts contingent upon that information, since they cannot be enforced. However, the investors update their beliefs about the quality of the project and the credit rating will be either upgraded or downgraded. Under this revision of the credit rating, let f^u denote the probability that $\theta = \theta_g$ given an upgrade and let f^d denote the probability that $\theta = \theta_g$ given a downgrade. In that case, the probability that an entrepreneur who receives a downgrade repays at time $t = 2$ is

$$q^d = \pi + f^d(1 - \pi) > f^d. \tag{5.10}$$

Moreover, it is here assumed that

$$f^d < f < f^u,$$

meaning that the probability that the project is good is greater given an upgrade than given a downgrade. Furthermore, the simplifying assumption $f^u = 1$ is also made. Thus, given an upgrade at date $t = 1$, it is certain that the project is good. However, it is not certain that all projects of good quality are upgraded. There is room for one such project to be downgraded. Let e denote the probability of such an event.

All projects are also assumed to produce a nonassignable control rent C if the management has control at time $t = 2$. Also, if at time $t = 1$ the manager defaults on short-term debt, lenders then have the right to remove the management from control, selling the assets for a liquidation value $L < K = 1$. All projects may be liquidated at that point in time, under those conditions. If the project is liquidated, the entrepreneur is prevented from consumption of his/her present or future cash flows and control rents. In this case, an optimal contract is a debt contract enforced by the right to liquidate the project if the debt is not repaid in full.

Just as in the case of the borrowers, lenders are assumed be risk neutral. Moreover, lenders have alternative investments at $t = 0$ that provide a return R at $t = 2$. The condition $L < X/R$ ensures that a good project yields a higher return when not liquidated.

A project may be financed with either long-term or short-term debt. In the context of this model, long-term debt refers to a contract issued at $t = 0$ with no refinancing at date $t = 1$ and maturing at $t = 2$. If one such instrument provides $K = 1$ at time $t = 0$ with face value $\rho \leq X$, the lender expects to receive at maturity $\rho[\pi + f(1 - \pi)] = R^2$. Notice that if $\rho > X$, a borrower with credit rating f will not be able to provide the lender with the required rate of return R^2. Now, if the project is upgraded at time $t = 1$, the market value of the debt contract at that point in time becomes $V_l^u = \rho/R$. Similarly, if the project is downgraded, the market value of debt at time $t = 1$ becomes $V_l^d = q^d \rho/R$.

Short-term debt, on the other hand, is debt financed at $t = 0$ with face value r_1 and maturity at time $t = 1$. If short-term borrowers are upgraded at $t = 1$, their debt contract at that point in time is worth $V_s^u = r_1$ and they may refinance their project by issuing a new short-term debt contract with maturity at $t = 2$ and face value $r_1 R$ that will be paid with certainty and guarantees a return of R per unit invested by the lender. If short-term borrowers are downgraded, however, in principle they may refinance their debt with a new short-term contract only if $q^d X/R > r_1$, since X is the maximum that a borrower can pay at $t = 2$. If that is the case, at $t = 1$ the market value of the short-term debt issued at $t = 0$ would be $V_s^d = r_1$ if the borrower pays, possibly through the refinancement mechanism. But what happens if $q^d X/R < r_1$? In that case there is still room for a refinancement provided that the liquidation value L is less than the expected value to the lender from a refinancement, $q^d X/R$. Under a downgrading, the time $t = 1$ value of the short-term debt is thus

$$V_s^d = \min\left[r_1, \max(L, q^d X/R)\right].$$

The face value of short-term debt is established such as to provide the lenders with an expected return of R per period. It then follows that

$$r_1 = \frac{R - [1 - (1 - e)f]V_s^d}{(1 - e)f}. \tag{5.11}$$

Given this model, the point is to characterize under what conditions short-term or long-term maturities will be offered. The maturity preferred by the entrepreneurs of good projects will be the only one offered to all borrowers. This happens because if any other maturity is offered, it reveals a project of bad quality and lenders will not be willing to finance it.

The following result implies that, in the absence of liquidation given a downgrade, the entrepreneurs of good projects prefer short-term debt:

Lemma 5.2.1 (Diamond, 1991). *Comparing two debt contracts issued at $t = 0$, neither of which involves liquidation on a downgrade at $t = 1$, the one with the higher value at that point in time given a downgrade, V^d, is preferred by the entrepreneurs of good projects.*

Proof. The expected payoff to the entrepreneurs of good projects from debt not yielding liquidation is

$$e\left(X + C - \frac{RV^d}{q^d}\right) + (1 - e)(X + C - r_1 R).$$

Using expression (5.11) this payoff is rewritten as

$$X + C - \frac{R^2}{f} + RV^d e\left(\frac{1}{f^d} - \frac{1}{q^d}\right).$$

Given (5.10) this expression for the payoff is clearly an increasing function of V^d. ∎

This implies that when there is no liquidation after a downgrade, short-term debt is preferred. The idea behind this result is simple. If there is no risk of liquidation, in order to reduce their expected financing costs, borrowers of the good type, who are less likely than average to be downgraded, prefer to extract larger payments from those who are downgraded. However, if there is the possibility of liquidation, the increase in the payment extracted from those who get a downgrade incorporates, for the good entrepreneurs, the risk of losing control rents. In that case the following result characterizes the trade-off incurred:

Lemma 5.2.2 (Diamond, 1991). *Consider a debt structure that does not imply liquidation and leads to a value of debt V^d, given a downgrade. Compare it with an alternative structure that implies liquidation. Entrepreneurs of good projects prefer the latter if and only if the control rent $C < \widehat{C}$, where the upper bound is given by*

$$\widehat{C} = \frac{LR}{f^d} - X - RV^d \left(\frac{1}{f^d} - \frac{1}{q^d} \right) > 0.$$

It follows that a sufficient condition for the good entrepreneur to prefer liquidation is that $C = 0$, representing the absence of control rents. It is also sufficient for the good entrepreneur to prefer liquidation if that state does not provide sufficiently high control rents C to the entrepreneur compared to the proceeds L to the investor or

$$\frac{q^d X + f^d C}{R} \leq L. \tag{5.12}$$

The following result uses the preceding lemmas to show how the credit rating of the borrower determines the choice between short-term and long-term debt:

Proposition 5.2.1 (Diamond, 1991). *If $C = 0$, all entrepreneurs of good projects prefer short-term debt, independently of their credit rating f. If $C > 0$, entrepreneurs of good projects prefer short-term debt to long-term debt only if their credit rating f is above a bound S given by*

$$S = \frac{\pi[R^2 - LR + f^d(C + X - R^2)]}{(1 - \pi)[LR - f^d(C + X)]}.$$

Otherwise, long-term debt is preferred.

It follows from this result that a sufficient condition for all borrowers of good projects to prefer long-term debt is that $S \geq 1$ or

$$f^d \geq \frac{LR - R^2\pi}{C + X - R^2\pi}.$$

The intuition for these results is simple. First, notice that long-term debt never leads to liquidation at time $t = 1$, because lenders do not hold control rights at that point. Having the possibility to choose between liquidation or not, the combination of the previous two lemmas ensures that, in order to prefer long-term debt, the control rent C must be greater than $\widehat{C}$ (or, in other words, that the liquidation value is not close enough to the efficient value).

The analysis of Diamond (1991) focused on the case of one project and one investor, characterizing the preference for either short-term or long-term debt. Another possibility is that the project may be financed by different investors with different claims. In this spirit, Berglöf and Von Thadden (1994) explain why a firm's short-term and long-term debt should be allocated to different lenders. The profit of the project is assumed to be verifiable, but the effort of the entrepreneur is not.

Assuming the existence of two investors, the model developed by Berglöf and Von Thadden (1994) implies in general that the optimal financial structure leads to the issuance of three different types of contract: equity, long-term debt, and short-term debt using the assets as collateral. Debt and equity are different claims on the verifiable profit of the project.

It follows that, if both maturities are to be issued, then it is optimal to have one investor holding short-term debt and another one holding long-term debt. The basic idea is that if both investors hold long-term debt, the situation is too soft to the entrepreneur, since there is no threat of liquidation at $t = 1$. In contrast, if one of the investors holds only short-term debt and the firm defaults at $t = 1$, this lender may have no incentive to wait for $t = 2$ and will be eager to liquidate the firm. This situation may force the entrepreneur to make some concessions and gives him/her the right incentive to avoid default. Under this reasoning, it is clear that equity may be an acceptable substitute for long-term debt, provided short-term debt has been issued.

Other conclusions follow from this model. First, for reduced levels of investment, only long-term debt is issued. Also, for a high enough investment level (K), long-term debt is not issued. Second, the amount financed through short-term debt increases with the level of total investment, K, and decreases with the profitability of the project, which is assumed to be negatively correlated with K.

The model of Diamond (1991) can be generalized to accommodate the simultaneous issue of short-term and long-term debt. A maturity mix allows the entrepreneurs of good projects to benefit from the good news at $t = 1$ that they anticipate. However, there is the risk of liquidation. An adequate maturity mix balances this trade-off. The first step in the analysis of the optimal mix is to characterize the preference for liquidation for both the entrepreneurs and lenders given a downgrade at time $t = 1$.

From the point of view of short-term lenders, the condition to liquidate is that the future value obtained through the liquidation, LR, is greater than what they expect from continuation, $q^d X$:

$$LR \geq q^d X.$$

Using the expression for q^d in (5.10), this inequality also reads

$$f^d < \frac{LR - \pi X}{X - \pi X} \equiv \lambda.$$

From the side of the entrepreneurs of good projects, however, debt structure should be chosen in order to maximize the expected cash flows, including control rents and the payment to lenders. Taking $V^d = q^d X / R$ in Lemma 5.2.2, one establishes that the entrepreneur prefers liquidation if and only if the control rent to be lost is low enough:

$$C \leq \frac{LR}{f^d} - \frac{Xq^d}{f^d}.$$

Use of (5.10) in the inequality implies that preference for liquidation is equivalent to having

$$f^d \leq \frac{LR - \pi X}{X + C - \pi X} \equiv \beta.$$

For any positive control rent C, notice that $\lambda \geq \beta$. These results are summarized in the following:

Lemma 5.2.3 (Diamond, 1991). *Given a downgrade, entrepreneurs of good projects prefer liquidation to refinancing with face value X if and only if $f^d \leq \beta$. Lenders with short-term debt liquidate if and only if $f^d \leq \lambda$.*

It follows that for $f^d \in [\beta, \lambda]$, lenders liquidate too often if there is only short-term debt. For those values of the credit rating given a downgrade, an alternative structure mixing long-term and short-term debt could be optimal in the sense that liquidation when occurring would maximize the wealth of both borrower and lender.

Assume that the fraction of the initial investment $K = 1$ financed through short-term debt is $\alpha \in [0, 1]$. Therefore, the long-term debt finances $1 - \alpha$. In this case, the face value of the long-term debt is

$$\rho = (1 - \alpha)\frac{R^2}{q},$$

where q is given in (5.9). In the case of the short-term debt, and assuming that it is refinanced at time $t = 1$, after a downgrade of credit rating the face value will be

$$r^d = \alpha\frac{R^2}{q^d}.$$

In order for the entrepreneur of a good project not to lose the control rights to the lender, short-term debt at time $t = 1$ must be riskless. In other words, it must be easily refinanced at date $t = 1$. For debt to be refinanced at date $t = 1$, it is necessary that the sum of both face values be less than the total amount X generated by the project at $t = 2$:

$$X \geq \rho + r^d = R^2\left(\frac{1}{q^d} - \frac{1}{q}\right)\alpha + \frac{R^2}{q}. \tag{5.13}$$

The right-hand side of (5.13) is the equation of rising straight line. In order to profit from the benefits of the short-term debt, entrepreneurs prefer a mix satisfying the preceding constraint that maximizes the proportion of short-term debt. The largest value of α satisfying the constraint is thus

$$\alpha = \frac{(Xq - R^2)q^d}{R^2(q - q^d)} = \frac{\{X[\pi + f(1 - \pi)] - R^2\}[\pi + f^d(1 - \pi)]}{R^2(f - f^d)(1 - \pi)} > 0.$$

Notice that, since $\alpha \in [0, 1]$, whenever the solution of the preceding equation is greater than 1, the proportion of short-term debt should be taken as 1. Then, the following holds:

Proposition 5.2.2 (Diamond, 1991). *If $f^d \in [\beta, \lambda]$, then an optimal maturity mix is given by a proportion α^* of short-term debt and a proportion $(1 - \alpha^*)$ of long-term debt, where $\alpha^* = \min(\alpha, 1)$.*

Borrowers with better credit ratings will choose a higher fraction of short-term debt. Just as in Proposition 5.2.1, shorter average maturity is preferred by good entrepreneurs because it yields a higher sensitivity of financing to new information, without leading to liquidation.

5.2.4 The Effect of Seniority

In general, not only maturity but also priority must be studied in the design of optimal debt contracts. In the model presented so far, the amount paid at maturity is either X or zero, leaving little role for differing priority, as Diamond (1991) points out. An extension of this model is presented in Diamond (1993) that allows for such considerations.

Consider that in the context of simultaneous emission of short-term and long-term debt, Y denotes the largest payment at $t = 2$ that the manager of a good project may promise to a new short-term investor at $t = 1$. Denoting by r_2 the face value of the short-term debt issued at date $t = 1$, it follows that $r_2 \leq Y \leq X$.

As before, in case of default at the intermediate date $t = 1$, the old investor has the alternative of liquidating the project, selling the assets by L, and destroying the control rent C or claiming the cash flow at $t = 2$. Entrepreneur and the old short-term investor can also renegotiate the terms characterizing the initial debt contract—namely, Y, r_1, and ρ.

If the long-term debt contract includes a covenant that does not allow debt that is senior to it, but places no other restrictions, then $Y \leq X - \rho$. Alternatively, making $r_2 \geq X - \rho$ dilutes the existing long-term debt.

Denote by f_1 the value of credit rating at $t = 1$. Let q_1 denote the probability as of $t = 1$ that the project succeeds at $t = 2$, providing a return X, given a credit rating f_1. Define the numbers

$$\hat{q}_1 = \min\{r_1/Y, L/X\} \text{ and } q_1' = \frac{r_1}{X - \rho}.$$

Then the following holds:

Lemma 5.2.4 (Diamond, 1993). *There is liquidation at time $t = 1$ if and only if $q_1 < \hat{q}_1$. For $q_1 \geq \hat{q}_1$ there will be no liquidation and the maturing debt is fully repaid. Moreover, if $q_1 \in [\hat{q}_1, q_1']$, the total payment at $t = 2$ is X, and for $q_1 > q_1'$ the payment will be $\rho + r_1/q_1$.*

Being risk neutral, an entrepreneur of a good project will choose a debt structure that maximizes the expected return to the project. An entrepreneur of a good project receives at $t = 2$ a payoff denoted by $\Psi(f_1)$ corresponding to the amount $X + C$ minus whatever is paid to the lenders. The objective of the entrepreneur is thus to solve for Y, r_1, and ρ minimizing

$$\min_{Y, r_1, \rho} \Theta \equiv X + C - \Psi(f_1).$$

This optimization is carried out constrained by the fact that lenders require from the resulting debt structure an expected payment at time $t = 2$ that compensates their investment, given their cost of capital.

Diamond (1993) shows that the optimal value of Y is X, thus implying that long-term debt is junior with respect to the short-term debt issued at $t = 1$. This is summarized in the following:

Proposition 5.2.3 (Diamond, 1993). *Optimality of a mix of both maturities implies that short-term debt is senior and long-term debt is junior. Long-term debt allows new issues of debt that dilute its value or are senior to it at $t = 1$ and $Y = X$.*

Diamond (1991,1993) is centered on the fact that contracts are incomplete and, also, on the asymmetry of information between investors and entrepreneurs who wish to borrow money. In a different context, assuming symmetric information, Hart and Moore (1995) model the optimal design of a public company's security structure. As the company is public, it allows for the introduction of the traditional agency approach. Managers are no longer entrepreneurs and make choices according to their own interests, not necessarily coincident with the goal of maximizing the value of the firm.

The financial structure to be optimally designed here is understood as a mix of equity and short-term and long-term debt. Such a structure is chosen at date $t = 0$, given an investment at $t = 1$ providing returns at $t = 2$. Also, Hart and Moore (1995) assume that the firm's going-concern value exceeds its liquidation value, and that the earnings at $t = 1$ are not sufficient to refinance short-term debt internally. In this context, the optimal level of short-term debt is easily shown to be zero.

Therefore, the focus is on the role of long-term debt as a reliable mechanism for controlling the ability of management to finance future investments. In fact, companies that are highly indebted are shown to have more difficulties raising capital, since new security holders will have lower priority than the old creditors. In this case, given a project with a positive net present value, the firm may not find resources to finance it. Companies with high levels of debt may then face the problem of *underinvestment*, losing value because of that fact. Companies with low levels of debt do not face that problem and find ways to fund investment projects more easily. In particular, they may find it easy to finance projects with negative net present value, thus reducing the value of the firm. This problem is known as *overinvestment*.

Given the trade-off faced by the investors, Hart and Moore (1995) derive the optimal ratio of debt-equity and show that, under some circumstances, it may be optimal to issue other types of securities than simply long-term debt and equity. Sometimes it is optimal to issue debt instruments with different seniorities possibly incorporating covenants that allow dilution of each class.

Finally, they show that their characterization of optimal financing structure is compatible with the well established facts that profitability and financial leverage are negatively correlated and also that increases in leverage raise the market value.

5.2.5 *Exercises*

1. Show that in the optimal debt contract, the probability β_o defined in (5.8) decreases as q increases as stated in the text.
2. Show that two creditors are paid more in the case of strategic default than one creditor, but are paid less in the case of liquidity default.
3. Prove equation (5.11).
4. Prove that inequality (5.12) provides a sufficient condition for the good entrepreneur to prefer the debt structure that leads to liquidation under the conditions of the lemma to which it refers.
5. This exercise illustrates the case of Lemma 5.2.1 in the model of Diamond (1991). Take $L = R = 1, \pi = \frac{1}{2}, X = 1\frac{3}{4}, C = 0, f = \frac{1}{2}$, and $f^d = \frac{1}{3}$.
   (a) What are the face values of a short-term and a long-term debt contract?
   (b) Show that in this example there will be no liquidation.
   (c) What is the payoff of a good project financed with long-term debt?
   (d) What is the probability that a good project receives a down-grade at $t = 1$?
   (e) What is the payoff of a good project financed with short-term debt?
6. This exercise illustrates the case of Lemma 5.2.2 in the model of Diamond (1991). Keep everything from the previous exercise except that here $X = 1.4$ and $C = 0.35$. Show that in this case, if the project is financed with short-term debt, it will be liquidated in the case of a downgrade at $t = 1$. Show also that this leads the entrepreneur of a good project to prefer long-term to short-term debt. Finally, show that this conclusion is reversed if the initial credit rating is $f = \frac{3}{4}$ instead of the initial $\frac{1}{2}$.

PART III
Capital Restructuring

6

Going Public

A PRIVATE FIRM is a firm with no shares being transacted in a public equity market. There are two alternative ways in which a firm such as this may raise additional equity capital. The first is by selling shares to a venture capitalist, maintaining the private nature of the firm. The second is by raising the required additional capital in a public equity market, in which case the firm is said to *go public*. An initial public offering (IPO) is the first effort by a private firm to go public, by issuing shares.

An initial public offering may be the best way to refinance a firm from different points of view. It is possible that some people having considerable wealth invested in the enterprise wish to add liquidity to their investments and also want to diversify their portfolios. To take the company public is a simple way to reach that goal compared to selling shares back to the company. A different view is that raising funds through an IPO instead of being financed by a bank or through venture capitalists may add more value to the firm. In fact, depending on the circumstances, the equity market may be a more efficient mechanism to raise large sums of external capital.

The way an IPO is operated involves four main agents. The first is the issuing firm, which is going public. In order to sell its shares, this firm needs the help of some institution in the financial market. Such an institution, with a more knowledge of the market and its demands, is better positioned than the issuing firm to price the new issue and becomes responsible for the credibility of the final offering price. This role is played by an investment bank. Once the price is established, the firms need to find intermediaries (*underwriters*) to introduce the shares in the market. Most of the time, the investment bank is also one of the underwriters. The final agents to be considered are the investors in the market who will buy (or not buy) the new issue.

The first part of this chapter presents a model[1] that describes in a stylized way the going-public decision. The model is directed toward understanding why and under what circumstances firms go public, rather than undertake their projects using private equity financing.

Once the decision to go public is made, an interesting fact is that the IPOs are systematically underpriced *on average*.[2] In other words, the offering price is typically inferior to the market price of the shares *after* the IPO. This has been empirically verified,[3] and different models based on information asymmetry have been developed to explain this phenomenon.[4] These models and some further implications of the existence of asymmetric information are presented in the second part of this chapter.

6.1 The Going Public Decision

6.1.1 The Model

Consider a risk-neutral entrepreneur with a one-period project who needs funds for an initial investment. The funds may be obtained through one of two alternatives: either through a private placement of equity with an investor, or through selling shares to numerous investors in the new-issues market. The entrepreneur is assumed to hold a number of shares m and, in the case of a public offer of shares, would be willing to sell n shares, thus diluting the ownership of the firm.

The project may be one of two types: good or bad. Let θ denote the type of project, θ_g referring to a good project and θ_b referring to a bad project. The quality of the project is known to the entrepreneur but not to the investor. At a cost c, outsiders can evaluate the quality of the project. Let e denote the outside evaluation of the project, e_g referring to a good evaluation and e_b referring to a bad evaluation. It is assumed that

$$\Pr(e_g|\theta_g) = 1 \text{ and } \Pr(e_g|\theta_b) = y \in (0, 1).$$

The project pays off at date $t = 1$. The amount paid depends on the quality of the project and on the amount k invested. The cash flow at $t = 1$ is assumed to be

$$X_\theta(k) = \gamma_\theta k + \tilde{\varepsilon} \text{ for } k < K \text{ and } X_\theta(k) = \gamma_\theta K + \tilde{\varepsilon} \text{ for } k \geq K$$

where $\tilde{\varepsilon}$ is a random variable distributed with mean zero and variance σ_ε^2. Therefore, no entrepreneur will choose an investment level above the upper bound K. Also, it is assumed that $\gamma_g > \gamma_b$, where γ_g denotes γ_θ when $\theta = \theta_g$ and γ_b denotes γ_θ when $\theta = \theta_b$. For convenience, let V_G and V_B denote the entrepreneur's expected cash flow of the firm at the full investment level $k = K$. In other words, $V_G = \gamma_g K$ and $V_B = \gamma_b K$.

Since the entrepreneur is risk neutral, his/her objective is to maximize the expected cash flow accruing to him/her at date $t = 1$.

If the investment of the entrepreneur is to be financed by a venture capitalist, assume that this investor would have enough wealth to fund the project in full. If the offered terms are sufficiently favorable, the investor will thus take a large stake in the firm. It is assumed that the wealth not invested in the project is invested in the risk-free asset. Let $\widetilde{W}$ denote the wealth of this venture capitalist, who is assumed to be risk averse with utility function

$$U(\widetilde{W}) = \mu_W - \rho\sigma_W^2, \tag{6.1}$$

where μ_W is the expected wealth and σ_W^2 is its variance. The parameter ρ is the investor's risk aversion coefficient. The venture capitalist's objective is thus to maximize his/her utility at time $t = 1$.

The venture capitalist may or may not look for information about the project according to the following: Depending on the value of the cost c and of the precision of the evaluation technology (characterized by y in an earlier equation), the investor is offered one of two possible contracts: an unconditional price contract, with no costly evaluation of the firm from his/her side, or a contract with information production, the price for each share depending on the outcome of the costly valuation. Given an offer, the venture capitalist may decide either to invest or to reject the offer. This implies that investment is made only if equity is offered at a sufficiently attractive price that leads to an expected utility of wealth at $t = 1$ that is at least as rewarding as investing in the risk-free asset.

If the decision of the entrepreneur is to go public, the distribution of shares will be assumed to be extremely diluted. Therefore, the investors will be taken as being risk neutral. Again, any amount of the investors' wealth not invested in the offer is assumed to be invested in the risk-free asset. Investors can thus either (a) ignore the public offering and invest all their wealth in the risk-free asset, (b) bid for shares without any information, or (c) get information and invest in the offer in case of a good evaluation or invest in the risk-free asset in case of a bad evaluation.

Given an offer with m, n, and the share price p, let α be the proportion of investors who choose to become informed among those who decide to invest in the public offer. In other words, if an investor decides to participate, the probability that he/she incurs the cost of information is α. The equilibrium value of this probability depends on the parameters m, n, and p characterizing the offer, but also on c and on σ_ε^2. A fraction $(1 - \alpha)$ of the participants will bid uninformed.

6.1.2 The Equilibrium

Initially a different analysis is made for each of the two alternative solutions available to the entrepreneur: either private or public financing. At the end, the optimal solutions for each alternative are compared and an overall assessment of the optimal strategy to the entrepreneur as of date $t = 0$ is characterized.

Private Financing

If the entrepreneur opts for private financing, he/she must not only choose the kind of contract, but also decide upon the price and the number of shares to offer. The investor may only accept or reject the given offer. Although the venture capitalist evaluation may be observable by both the entrepreneur and the investor, it is assumed that it is not verifiable and thus cannot be contracted upon.

Let ϕ be the venture capitalist's prior probability assessment of $\theta = \theta_g$. Then, using Bayes' rule, $\Pr(\theta_g | e_b) = 0$ and

$$\Pr(\theta_g | e_g) = \frac{\phi}{\phi + y(1 - \phi)} > \phi.$$

Now, let $V_e \equiv E(\gamma_\theta K | e)$ denote the venture capitalist's expected cash flow to the project at the full investment level, conditioned to his/her evaluation, and let $\sigma_e^2 \equiv \mathrm{var}(\gamma_\theta K | e)$ denote the conditional variance of its deterministic part. Similarly, denote by $V_u \equiv E(\gamma_\theta K | \phi)$ and by $\sigma_u^2 \equiv \mathrm{var}(\gamma_\theta K | \phi)$ the unconditional expected cash flow and its respective variance. Under a bad evaluation and since $\Pr(\theta_g | e_b) = 0$, it follows that $V_b = V_B$ and the information-based uncertainty is characterized by $\sigma_b^2 = 0$. Also, let s denote the lowest share of the firm's equity that the venture capitalist will accept in return for investing K.

If the venture capitalist is offered a contract with information production, his/her lowest acceptable share of the firm's equity will depend on the evaluation and will be labeled s_e. Since these lowest acceptable shares must leave the venture capitalist indifferent between investing and keeping the money at the risk-free rate (here assumed to be zero, for simplicity), it happens that s_g and s_b must satisfy

$$K + c = s_g V_g - \rho s_g^2 (\sigma_g^2 + \sigma_\varepsilon^2) \qquad (6.2)$$

$$K + c = s_b V_b - \rho s_b^2 \sigma_\varepsilon^2. \qquad (6.3)$$

If the offered contract is an unconditional-price contract, however, the lowest acceptable share s_u arising from utility maximization must satisfy

$$s_u V_u - \rho s_u^2 (\sigma_u^2 + \sigma_\varepsilon^2) = K.$$

From the side of the entrepreneur, the choice of contract to be offered depends on the analysis of this behavior. If the project is of good quality, $\theta = \theta_g$, the entrepreneur chooses to offer the information-production contract if $s_g < s_u$, and chooses the unconditional-price contract otherwise. The first type of contract, with information production, minimizes the extent of pooling with type θ_b, yielding a price advantage. The disadvantage is that the venture capitalist incurs the informational cost c, which is ultimately borne by the entrepreneur through a lower price. Therefore, the preference of the entrepreneur for this type of contract holds as long as these costs are not too high. Chemmanur and Fulghieri (1999) characterize that critical value for c, denoted by c_p. Similarly, the larger the risk aversion of the venture capitalist, the higher the premium that must be paid for the amount invested. This means also that there is a critical value of the risk aversion coefficient, denoted by ρ_p.

On the other hand, if $\theta = \theta_b$, the entrepreneur has all the incentive to maximize his/her pooling with the type θ_g. However, when circumstances are such that this means offering an information-production contract, the expected share to be offered will be

$$ys_g + (1 - y)s_b.$$

If, under these circumstances, the entrepreneur had offered an unconditional-price contract, its bad type would had been revealed. Let s_B denote the lowest share that must be offered to the investor in that eventuality. Then, to offer an information-production contract is advantageous only if $ys_g + (1 - y)s_b < s_B$. Thus, when $\theta = \theta_b$, an unconditional-price contract is offered only when this condition is satisfied. These results are summarized in the following:

Proposition 6.1.1 (Chemmanur and Fulghieri). *If $\rho < \rho_p$ and $c < c_p$, then the equilibrium in the case where the firm chooses private equity financing involves both types of entrepreneurs offering the venture capitalist a financing contract with information production, and the venture capitalist accepts the contract.*

The fact that the investor is assumed to be risk averse allows us to analyze the impact of different factors on the fraction s of the project's equity that has to be offered. First, the larger is the capital invested (K), the larger is the fraction of the venture capitalist's wealth tied to the project. Given his/her risk aversion, it follows that the larger is K, the larger will be the fraction s.

Second, the investor's risk aversion requires a larger share s, the greater is the ex-ante variability in the time $t = 1$ cash flow to the project.

Third, since the coefficient ρ is the direct measure of his/her risk aversion, a similar argument is made as ρ increases. The larger is ρ, the larger should be s.

Finally, as the cost to obtain information increases, the offered share s must also increase in order to compensate the investor for becoming informed. These comparative statics results are presented in

Proposition 6.1.2 (Chemmanur and Fulghieri). *The fraction of equity that has to be offered to the investor in return for the required financing is (a) increasing in the capital intensity of the firm K, (b) increasing in the uncertainty in the firm's investment technology σ_ε^2, (c) increasing in the cost c of evaluating the firm, and (d) increasing in the investor's risk aversion coefficient ρ.*

Public Financing

In the case of public financing, the entrepreneur chooses the number n of shares to be issued at a price p, diluting his/her original stake in the firm. Therefore, his/her goal is to maximize the amount raised, minimizing the number of shares.

If the project is a good one, the entrepreneur feels confident that the required capital K will be raised setting a number of shares n_H and a price p_H, since investors' evaluation will be $e = e_g$. These variables are thus chosen satisfying

$$n_H p_H = K.$$

If the project is a bad one and the entrepreneur tries to mimic the behavior of a good project, only a fraction y among the informed investors will make an erroneously good evaluation and buy shares. Let N denote the total number of investors. Since α denotes the probability that an investor becomes informed, the fraction x of the n_H shares that is expected to be actually sold satisfies

$$x n_H = N[(1 - \alpha) + \alpha y].$$

Denoting by $\beta \in (0, 1]$ the probability that a project with $\theta = \theta_b$ pools with the good projects by issuing n_H shares, each at the price p_H, then the probability that an uninformed investor sees the project as good is

$$\pi = \Pr(\theta_g | n_H, p_H) = \frac{\phi}{\phi + \beta(1 - \phi)}.$$

A necessary condition for a pooling equilibrium to hold is that an uninformed investor does not pay more for a share than its expected value. It then follows that

$$p_H \leq \pi \frac{V_G}{m + n_H} + (1 - \pi) \frac{x V_B}{m + x n_H}. \tag{6.4}$$

Another aspect of this pooling equilibrium is that those investors who seek information should expect a positive net value from avoiding a bid for shares in a bad project. In other words, the cost c must be less than the benefit from gathering information:

$$c \leq (1 - \pi)(1 - y)\left[p_H - \frac{xV_B}{m + xn_H}\right]. \tag{6.5}$$

Regarding the way in which the proportion α of investors who become informed is determined, consider the extreme case where most of the investors are uninformed. In that case, the cost for an entrepreneur of a bad project to pool is low, and high prices will be charged. On the opposite side, if most investors become informed, an entrepreneur of a bad project has no incentive to mimic the behavior of a good project, and there is less incentive for the investors to look for information. In equilibrium, a fraction α is determined such that the entrepreneur of a bad project is indifferent between issuing xn_H shares at price p_H and issuing n_L shares at price p_L, with $n_L > n_H$ and $p_L < p_H$ or

$$\frac{m}{m + n_L}V_B = \frac{m}{m + xn_H}xV_B. \tag{6.6}$$

Clearly, the number n_L of shares and the price p_L are chosen such that

$$n_L p_L = K \text{ and } p_L = \frac{V_B}{m + n_L}.$$

Finally, consider the probability β that an entrepreneur of a bad project sets the price at the level p_H. This probability is settled in equilibrium in such a way that investors are indifferent between being informed or not. In other words, the values of α and β are determined in equilibrium to be such as to satisfy the equalities in (6.4), (6.5), and (6.6). Moreover, the equilibrium characterizing this fraction of informed investors will exist, provided that the errors committed in evaluating are sufficiently unlikely and the costs of becoming informed are not too high. In other words, equilibrium will always exist if y is bounded from above by some value (say, $y < \bar{y}$) and if there is a similar bound for the costs c (say, $c < c_s$). These results are summarized in Proposition 6.1.3.

Proposition 6.1.3 (Chemmanur and Fulghieri). *There is an equilibrium in the case where the firm chooses to go public involving the following: If $\theta = \theta_g$, the firm issues n_H shares, each at the price p_H, raising a total amount K for the investment; if $\theta = \theta_b$, with a probability $\beta \in (0, 1]$, it pools with the good projects by issuing n_H shares, each at the price p_H, of which only a number xn_H are bought by investors in equilibrium $(0 < x < 1)$, thus raising only the amount xK; with probability $(1 - \beta)$, it separates from the good projects by issuing n_L shares, each at the price p_L, with $n_L > n_H$ and $p_L < p_H$, thus raising the entire amount*

K required for the investment. On the other hand, a fraction α of the investors in the IPO produce information, bidding for a share if and only if they get a good evaluation; the remaining fraction $(1 - \alpha)$ *engage in uninformed bidding. Such an equilibrium will always exist if* $c < c_s$ *and* $y < \bar{y}$*. In other words, equilibrium exists if the outsiders' cost of evaluating the firm is not too high and if evaluations' errors do not occur too often.*

Let p_H^* denote the equilibrium value of the offer price, satisfying the previous equations. In terms of comparative statics, as the cost of becoming informed increases, the larger is the number of bad projects behaving as good projects and the smaller is the equilibrium value of π. It follows that the equilibrium price p_H^* decreases. A similar argument can be made as the probability y of a wrong evaluation by the outsiders increases. In both cases the equilibrium price p_H^* becomes a noisier indicator of the true value of the project for the investors.

Consider now the impact of an increase in K, the required capital. As K increases, the cost of mimicking the behavior of a good project increases in the sense that there is always a fraction of investors who evaluate the project correctly. If the costs are higher, the probability that a bad project mimics a good project decreases, resulting in a larger equilibrium value of π and thus a higher equilibrium price p_H^*. These results are described next.

Proposition 6.1.4 (Chemmanur and Fulghieri). *The equilibrium pooling price* p_H^* *is (a) decreasing in* c*, the outsiders' cost of information production, (b) decreasing in* y*, the error probability in the outsiders' evaluation, and (c) increasing in* K*, the capital intensity of the firm.*

The Choice between Private and Public Financing
Comparing the two basic propositions characterizing the behavior of the agents in a public and a private offer, some conclusions are in order. Regarding the venture capitalist, it was seen that his/her risk aversion does not allow him/her to invest if his/her stake in the firm is not big enough. The condition $\rho < \rho_p$ reflects this fact. However, for low enough risk aversion (say, $\rho < \rho_M$ with $\rho_M < \rho_p$), there is an initial number of shares, m_o, such that for $m > m_o$ the venture capitalist will invest, provided that the costs of being informed are not too high. Let the upper bound in these costs be denoted by c_B. In that case, the firm will have to choose between a public and a private offer. It follows that if the evaluation costs are below a certain threshold value c_A satisfying $c_A < c_s$, then the firm is better off by going public. This result is summarized as follows:

Proposition 6.1.5 (Chemmanur and Fulghieri). *Let* $\rho < \rho_M$ *and* $m > m_o$*. Then there is a threshold* c_A *such that (a) if* $c < c_A$*, then the firm finances its project* *by going public, and (b) if $c_A < c < c_B$, then the firm finances its project using private equity financing in equilibrium.*

The advantage of private equity is that the entrepreneur may save a large amount in the aggregate evaluation cost. A single investor, however, is less diversified and requires a higher premium. Equilibrium characterizes this trade-off.

Now, if the firm is young—and, therefore, unknown—the evaluation costs are much higher and the benefits from going private are likely to outweigh the disadvantage of giving a higher return to the venture capitalist. However, as the firm ages, the opposite happens. The cost of evaluation diminishes, affecting the parameters of the decision and making the public equity market more attractive.

This analysis comparing an earlier or later financing decision, together with the preceding propositions, has some implications.

As stated in Proposition 6.1.2, the larger is K, the lower is the price at which shares may be sold to the venture capitalist. At the same time, as discussed in Proposition 6.1.4, the larger is the pooling price per share sold by good projects in the public equity market. Thus, the threshold value c_A for the evaluation costs increases, so that firms with great capital intensity will go public earlier.

A similar reasoning is possible regarding the variance σ_ε^2. As this variance increases, the cash flow at time $t = 1$ becomes more uncertain. The venture capitalists will then require a higher return on their investment, thus lowering the price per share at which they would invest. Therefore, the firm is driven to go public earlier, the higher the value of this variance.

A third result of the same nature follows if there is a technological shock such that the productivity of good projects in a certain industry increases. In this model, this means simply that γ_g increases, thereby increasing V_G. If a firm in this industry chooses to go public, the benefits to investors from information increases, yielding a higher value of π and a larger equilibrium price per share p_H^*. Consistently, the cutoff value c_A increases and, as before, firms prefer to go to the public equity market earlier.

These results reduce to the following.

Proposition 6.1.6 (Chemmanur and Fulghieri). (a) *Firms that have great capital intensity K go public earlier,* (b) *firms characterized by a great uncertainty in their cash flows at $t = 1$ go public earlier,* and (c) *if there is a productivity shock in an industry such that γ_g increases, the firms in that industry will go public earlier.*

The last part of this proposition provides an explanation for why firms in industries where there has been sudden technological impact tend to go public almost simultaneously. Markets where this happens are known as "hot issue markets."

6.1.3 Empirical Evidence

The model describing the decision to go public has several empirical and policy implications. This section presents reported empirical evidence sustaining some of those implications.

For example, it is clear from the model that the higher the evaluation cost, the less likely it is that firms go public. In many European countries the number of financial institutions engaged in producing information about companies is significantly lower than in the United States. Consistent with the model, on average, companies in these European countries should go public much later than in the United States. Pagano, Panetta, and Zingales (1998) report that the average age of Italian companies going public between 1982 and 1991 was 33.4 years. When compared to the American average of 6.7 years for venture-backed firms and 11 years for non–venture-backed firms reported in Lerner (1994), for example, this is quite a significant difference.

Similar findings for the average going-public age of companies in other European countries can be found in Rydqvist and Hogholm (1994).

6.1.4 Exercises

1. Writing n_H as a function of π, $n_H(\pi)$, show that c_s in Proposition 6.1.3 is given by

$$c_s = (1 - \phi)(1 - y)\left[\frac{1}{\bar{n}_H} - \frac{\gamma_B - 1}{m}\right]K$$

with $\bar{n}_H = n_H(\phi)$.

2. Assume that the venture capitalist is risk neutral and can extract from the entrepreneur a fraction ξ of the NPV of the project. Rewrite the optimization problem for the venture capitalist and the equations determining the fractional shares that should substitute for (6.2) and (6.3) after the bargain occurring in the sequence of the joint observation of the evaluation.

6.2 Underpricing and Information Asymmetries

As described in this chapter's introduction, once the decision of going public is made, a remarkable fact is that the IPOs are systematically underpriced on average. There are essentially four possible explanations for the underpricing of IPOs. The first explanation is that underpricing can be originated by an overreaction or a speculative bubble. In this case, speculative investors who could not get allocations of the oversubscribed new issues at the offering prices would try to get them in the aftermarket, temporarily pushing the value of the shares well above their true value. This reflects a nonrational behavior and hence loses interest from the modeling point of view. Besides, as discussed in Ritter (1984), there is no evidence to support the implications of a speculative bubble.

An alternative explanation could be the fact that underwriters are risk averse. Underpricing would serve as a way of reducing the probability of ending up with an unsuccessful issue and its associated losses. If this argument were true, there would be a reaction from the issuers that would tend to oppose this underpricing bias. The explanation does not take into account this trade-off or why this reaction does not work.

Also, to what extent the explanation is correct depends very much on the type of underwriting contract employed in the IPO. As described in Smith (1986), there are typically two forms—namely, the best-effort and the firm-commitment contracts. One would expect underpricing to be relevant in a firm-commitment offering. In this kind of offering, the issuing firm and the investment bank agree on the price and quantity for the firm's issuance of equity. If there is excess demand, the underwriter rations the shares among the investors. If there is excess supply, the investment bank pays the firm for the surplus shares and disposes of them at market prices. Unfortunately, the empirical evidence[5] is that best-effort contracts under which the underwriter acts only as a marketing agent for the firm tend to be far more underpriced than firm-commitment public offerings.

A third explanation would be the existence of a monopoly power for the underwriters, especially in the case of small or start-up issuing firms. Reputable investment banks do not usually accept underwriting common stock of such firms, leaving to smaller investment banks the exercise of some bargaining power over the issuers. The underwriters will then tend to underprice the securities and ration them to their regular customers. There are some problems with this approach, however. The first is the lack of explanation for why large banks refuse to underwrite some IPOs. The second is that such a fact is not enough to justify the bargaining power of smaller banks, since there may be competition among them for such IPOs. Finally, the whole argument assumes irrationality from the issuers. Besides, Tiniç (1988) presents evidence against the fact that rationing to the underwriters favors customers.

The final and most relevant explanation is that this effect may be due to asymmetric information. Different types of asymmetries may be present together with some reputational and legal issues. Some models taking these points into account are discussed shortly.

In what follows, contributions of different authors concerning information asymmetries are analyzed. Baron (1982) discussed these asymmetries between the issuers and the underwriters; Rock (1986) was centered

on the asymmetry between investors; Beatty and Ritter (1986) were concerned with the effect of reputational issues related to the investment
banks, while in the same vein, Carter and Manaster (1990) focused on the
reputation of the underwriters; finally, Tiniç (1988) brought to the discussion the relevancy of information asymmetries when facing legal issues as
a factor in the explanation of the underpricing phenomena.

6.2.1 Asymmetry between Issuers and Underwriters

To explain the underpricing of IPOs, Baron (1982) assumes that the
investment bank is better informed about investors' demand than the issuing firm. The bank should then be compensated for its superior information, being allowed to offer the new issue at easier conditions—namely, at
a lower price.

That bankers prefer to make an offering at a lower price than the
issuing firm can be formalized as follows: Let θ be the state of the world at
the moment of the public offering. Since the demand for shares depends
on θ, let $x(\theta)$ denote the capital raised by the IPO. The price per share
being p_o, let the fee schedule paid to the investment bank be denoted by
$S(x(\theta), p_o)$. Both the issuing firm and the investment bank are assumed
to have utility functions respectively denoted by U and V.

It is further assumed that the investment bank has access to a signal
ϕ about θ. Let Θ be the density of probability of θ and $a(\theta)$ denote the
effort developed by the investment banker to put the new issues in the
market.

Hence, the optimal price per share and fee schedule will be defined
by maximizing the program

$$\max_{S(x, p_o)} \int U[x - S(x, p_o)]\Theta(\theta)d\theta$$

subject to

$$\int \int V[S(x, p_o), a]\Theta(\theta|\phi)\Theta(\phi)d\theta d\phi \geq \Pi,$$

where Π is the minimum level of utility necessary to ensure the participation of the investment banker. For any given signal ϕ, the optimal price
level and optimal banker's effort are determined by maximizing the preceding integral over the states of nature,

$$[a(\phi), p_o(\phi)] = \text{argmax} \int V[S(x, p_o), a]\Theta(\theta|\phi)d\theta.$$

In conditions of *symmetric* information, the prices preferred by the underwriter and by the issuing firm, respectively p_u and p_f, are given by

$$p_u = \text{argmax} \int V[S(x, p_o), a]\Theta(\theta|\phi)d\theta$$

and

$$p_f = \text{argmax} \int U[x - S(x, p_o)]\Theta(\theta|\phi)d\theta.$$

Under such conditions it is possible to prove that if U'/U'' and V'/V'' are linear functions and a is an increasing function of the shares' price, then $p_f > p_u$.

In a situation of asymmetric information, however, the choice of the issuing firm is between pricing the issue itself with all the related risks, and paying a fee to the bank plus the implicit cost of underpricing in order to ensure a correct placement of the issue in the market. Baron (1982) shows that the last alternative works to the advantage of both.

However, Muscarella and Vetsuypens (1989) found empirical evidence destroying Baron's argument. When issues are self-underwritten, the initial returns are statistically higher than when the issuing firms did not serve as the lead manager of their own offerings. In the latter case, the offer is less underpriced.

6.2.2 Asymmetry between Investors

Rock (1986) uses a different asymmetry of information to explain the observed underpricing. He assumes that both underwriters and companies are uninformed,[6] but that some of the investors in the market are informed.

The uninformed investors do not have a criterion to decide if an IPO is underpriced or not, so they will go either for all of them or for none. The informed investors, on the other hand, will go only for the underpriced issues, since they can distinguish between the two types.

Underpricing follows naturally in this context, in order to keep the uninformed investors interested in the new issues. The condition for that to occur is that their expected return is nonnegative. In other words, their negative returns *must be at least compensated* by some positive returns from underpriced shares. If there is not enough underpricing in the market, such compensation will not be achieved and the uninformed investors will not participate in the IPO and there will be only informed traders. In such a case, only the underpriced shares will be sold. And even in that case, only those shares that are sufficiently underpriced to compensate the cost of being informed will be sold.

Suppose that the cost of information is c per investor, the price per share in the public offer is p_o, and the true value per share is a random variable v, to which is associated a density of probability $f(v)$. Let n be the total number of shares offered, N be the total number of informed investors, and α be the fraction of shares allocated to them. To formalize this model simply, it will be assumed, as in Beatty and Ritter (1986), that N is endogenous.

Clearly, if $p_o > v$, there will be only uninformed investors interested, whereas if $p_o < v$, both kinds of investors will appear. The equilibrium condition for p_o must be that investors make zero profit on average. For the uninformed this means that the expected losses must equal the expected gains:

$$\int_0^{p_o} n(p_o - v)f(v)dv = (1 - \alpha) \int_{p_o}^{\infty} n(v - p_o)f(v)dv. \qquad (6.7)$$

For the average profit of the informed investors to be equally zero, we must further impose that their total cost of information equals their expected profit:

$$Nc = \alpha \int_{p_o}^{\infty} n(v - p_o)f(v)dv. \qquad (6.8)$$

Substituting this last equation in (6.7), one has

$$\int_0^{p_o} n(p_o - v)f(v)dv = \int_{p_o}^{\infty} n(v - p_o)f(v)dv - Nc$$

or

$$Nc = n \int_0^{\infty} (v - p_o)f(v)dv.$$

This result also reads

$$E(v) - p_o = \frac{Nc}{n} > 0. \qquad (6.9)$$

In other words, the IPOs are underpriced on average according to this model. One can interpret this result as the equilibrium solution to the trade-off between the utility of the IPO for the issuing firm and the adequate incentive for participation of the two types of investors.

Another important issue incorporated by Rock in his model is the role of rationing. As stated before, the uninformed will lose interest in the IPOs if the offerings are not sufficiently underpriced. If issues are underpriced, both types of investors will be interested, increasing the demand. If the demand is great enough—or for low enough prices—there may be an oversubscription, in which case the underwriter rations the available shares. Depending on how this process is made (in particular, if it is a proportional rationing), as the price decreases more uninformed investors become interested in the issue, and the probability of obtaining desirable shares diminishes, counteracting the expected stimulus on the uninformed demand.

The important thing to remember from the rationing process is that uninformed investment increases with a price reduction. Hence, the task facing the issuer is to trade the guaranteed payment by lowering the price against the expected proceeds from that offering.

6.2.3 *Reputation of Bankers and Uncertainty*

Beatty and Ritter (1986) raise an important issue regarding the role of the investment banker in enforcing the underpricing equilibrium. In fact, the issuing firm needs the banker as a reputable certifier of information to make its offering credible to the market. Bankers bring credibility simply because they are repeatedly in the market and, hence, must protect their reputations. If, on average, an investment banker does not underprice enough, the average initial return will be too low and the uninformed investors will do no more business with that underwriter. If, on the contrary, the offerings are too underpriced, potential future issuers will not go for its services. This kind of trade-off justifies the presence of the investment banker in order to assure everybody that the issues will be reasonably underpriced.

In Rock's model there are informed and uninformed investors. One of the reasons pointed out for the existence of underpricing is the uncertainty of the uninformed investors about the true value of the issue before the offering. Following this reasoning, these two authors also propose and give empirical evidence that the expected underpricing increases with the ex-ante uncertainty about v, the true value of each share, expressed as its volatility.

The intuition behind this idea can be seen alternatively as follows: The decision to pay to become informed may be thought of as a call option giving the right to buy the new issue if its value v exceeds the strike price $p_\circ$. Accordingly, the cost of information c can be seen as the price of such an option. The value of the option must increase with the volatility of the true value v of the new issue. How much the decision of becoming informed is worth may be measured by the amount of underpricing. The conclusion therefore is that underpricing must increase with the volatility of v.

To see how this simple idea can be formalized, it suffices to put equations (6.8) and (6.9) together to get

$$p_\circ = E(v) - \alpha(p_\circ) \int_{p_\circ}^{\infty} (v - p_\circ) f(v) dv. \tag{6.10}$$

Here it is assumed that α is a function of $p_\circ$. Therefore, $p_\circ$ is a solution of the preceding complicated equation. It depends on two things only, namely, the function α and the density of probability $f(v)$—or its moments. In particular, its second moment is by definition the square of the volatility of the true value v of the new issue. Let this variance be denoted by σ_v^2. The statement to be formalized is simply that

$$\frac{\partial p_\circ}{\partial \sigma_v} < 0.$$

Beatty and Ritter (1986) do not really prove this result. What they do is to find a particular function α and a density of probability $f(v)$ simple enough, so that equation (6.10) can be explicitly solved and the result can be shown for their specific choice. Their basic result is that the average underpricing is greater for issues with greater price uncertainty and is very much in the spirit of Baron (1982).

In Baron's work the underwriters had an informational advantage over the issuers whereas in Beatty and Ritter's the advantage is mainly reputational in a context of unequally informed investors. Either explanation seems to work in the same direction, the underpricing resulting from these two different ways of fighting uncertainty.

The role of the banker's reputation can be extended if it is realized that there is a range of possible reputations. This segments the market of IPOs and creates a "clientele" for each type of banker. In this vein, a paper by Carter and Manaster (1990) claims that IPOs with a large participation of informed investors are more underpriced and are associated with low-rank bankers.

The range of possible reputations in the market goes from highly ranked investment bankers to fringe underwriters. The prestige of an underwriter is associated with the marketing of low-risk IPOs—that is to say, offerings about which the uncertainty is minimum and, hence, with small underpricing.

Since investors have scarce resources to invest in information, they will tend to invest in the most uncertain investments. In other words, they tend to pay for information about IPOs of large uncertainty and with high expected underpricing—those underwritten by lower-reputation investment banks. Thus, the underwriter's reputation may reveal the expected level of participation of the informed investors.

The formalization of these ideas follows the model of Rock. If all the investors have access to the true volatility σ_v, equations (6.7) and (6.8) become the conditional expectations

$$\int_0^{p_o} n(p_o - v)f(v|\sigma_v)dv = (1 - \alpha)\int_{p_o}^{\infty} n(v - p_o)f(v|\sigma_v)dv$$

and

$$Nc = \alpha \int_{p_o}^{\infty} n(v - p_o)f(v|\sigma_v)dv,$$

and it follows as before that as the proportion of informed investors (α) rises, the offer price p_o must fall in order to maintain the equilibrium. In other words,

$$\frac{\partial \alpha}{\partial p_o} < 0$$

or the larger the participation of informed investors in an IPO, the higher will be the underpricing. On the other hand, if we take the result of Beatty and Ritter that

$$\frac{\partial p_\circ}{\partial \sigma_v} < 0$$

and assume that $\alpha \equiv \alpha[p_\circ(\sigma_v)]$, it follows that

$$d\alpha = \frac{\partial \alpha}{\partial p_\circ} \frac{\partial p_\circ}{\partial \sigma_v} d\sigma_v > 0.$$

In other words, the participation of informed investors in an IPO increases with the degree of uncertainty.

However, if the degree of uncertainty is not observable, the investors should decide whether to become informed or not through the reputation of the investment banks. Let $g_i(\sigma_v)$ be the density of probability of the volatility σ_v associated with underwriter i. In this case, the original equilibrium equations (6.7) and (6.8) become for each banker i

$$\int_0^{+\infty} \int_0^{p_\circ} n(p_\circ - v) f(v|\sigma_v) g_i(\sigma_v) dv d\sigma_v$$

$$= (1 - \alpha) \int_0^{+\infty} \int_{p_\circ}^{\infty} n(v - p_\circ) f(v|\sigma_v) g_i(\sigma_v) dv d\sigma_v$$

and

$$Nc = \alpha \int_0^{+\infty} \int_{p_\circ}^{\infty} n(v - p_\circ) f(v|\sigma_v) g_i(\sigma_v) dv d\sigma_v.$$

Underwriter i is defined to be more prestigious than underwriter j if, for all values of a,

$$\int_0^a [g_i(\sigma_v) - g_j(\sigma_v)] d\sigma_v \geq 0$$

and, for at least one value of a,

$$\int_0^a [g_i(\sigma_v) - g_j(\sigma_v)] d\sigma_v > 0.$$

This is analogous to first-order stochastic dominance. With this definition of prestige and the two preceding equilibrium equations, it follows that there will be less investment in information for IPOs brought out by highly reputable underwriters.

6.2.4 How Underwriters Become Informed

Baron's model fails probably because of its simplicity. To explain underpricing only in terms of informational asymmetry between the banker and the issuer is clearly not enough, as discussed in previous sections.

As pointed out by Rock, asymmetry between investors seems to be a fairly attractive explanation. Nevertheless, as the extensions of Rock's model by Beatty and Ritter and Carter and Manaster suggest, the banker may have a special strength in the underpricing process through its reputation. In this section a work by Benveniste and Spindt (1989) is discussed, in which a banker in a situation of informational disadvantage can use its reputation to induce investors to reveal their information. This model provides, so to say, an "integrated" view of the models described already.

The basic difficulty facing an underwriter is that investors have no incentive to reveal positive information before the stock is sold. In order to show how this incentive may exist in the market and how it may contribute to the pricing process of an IPO, Benveniste and Spindt (1989) modeled the premarket as an auction conducted by the underwriter, in which investors understand how their indications of interest affect the offer price and the stock allotments they receive. By choosing a suitable rule associating the investor's indications to the offering price and to the issue's allocation, the underwriter can induce the investors to reveal their information.

The argument is based on the fact that the underwriter can discriminate between regular and occasional investors, so that the shares will be rationed in favor of the regulars, as suggested in Rock (1986), for example, giving the underwriter a lever—namely, the threat to reduce an investor's allocation priority in the future—that can be used to induce the regular investors to provide good information in the premarket.

Suppose that there are H regular investors, of which h give good information. Assume that A is the price to be established if all information is good (i.e., if $h = H$). Also assume that if $h \neq H$, the deviation from A is proportional to the number of bad informers:

$$p_h = A - [H - h]\xi.$$

Here, ξ is taken as a fixed number that may be seen as a measure of how fast the price p_h tends to price A as the number h of regular investors with good information approaches the total number H of regular investors. These two convergence processes do not occur at the same rate. The rates of convergence are proportional and the number ξ measures this proportionality. For an additional investor with good information, we have

$$p_{h+1} = A - [H - h]\xi + \xi = p_h + \xi.$$

In this sense ξ is also a measure of the marginal impact of the good information of regular investors on the expected price of the issue.

To add the effect of noisy information from occasional investors, the price will be written

$$p_{h,\lambda} = A - [H - h]\xi + \lambda,$$

where λ is a random variable of zero mean. It is also assumed that all informed investors have the same preferences and equal demands q, exhausting the issue of n shares, such that $Hq = n$. The information of the investors is independent and there is a probability ζ for each regular investor that his/her information is good. Hence the probability that there are h good regular informers is

$$\pi_h = \binom{H}{h} \zeta^h (1 - \zeta)^{H-h}.$$

From the viewpoint of a regular investor with good information, however, the (conditional) probability of state h is

$$\pi_h'(\text{good}) = \binom{H-1}{h-1} \zeta^{h-1} (1 - \zeta)^{H-h},$$

whereas for a regular investor with bad information, his/her (conditional) probability of the same state is

$$\pi_h'(\text{bad}) = \binom{H-1}{h} \zeta^h (1 - \zeta)^{H-h-1} \equiv \pi_h'.$$

Therefore, it is clear that $\pi_h'(\text{good}) = \pi_{h-1}'(\text{bad}) = \pi_{h-1}'$. Then the reservation price in the premarket for a regular investor with good information is

$$p_g = \sum_{h=1}^{H} \pi_h'(\text{good}) p_h = \sum_{h=1}^{H} \pi_{h-1}' p_h = \sum_{h=0}^{H-1} \pi_h' p_{h+1},$$

whereas for those with bad information, the reservation price will be simply

$$p_b = \sum_{h=0}^{H-1} \pi_h' p_h.$$

It is easily seen that $\xi = p_g - p_b$, reflecting the value of a regular's information relevant to the aftermarket price of the stock.

Taking the volume of premarket orders at face value, most IPOs are oversubscribed. Therefore, investors tend to overstate their true interest, expecting to be allocated only a fraction of their indicated interest. From these indications the underwriter is assumed to infer either good or bad information to be used in pricing the IPO.

Let $p_\circ(h)$ denote the offer price at state h, and let $q_{g,h}$ and $q_{b,h}$ be the numbers of shares allocated to investors who indicate, respectively, good and bad in state h. The $n - q_{g,h} - q_{b,h}$ shares left are assumed to be sold in the aftermarket at full information price.

The incentive conditions for a regular investor with good information not to lie are as follows: The expected profit when the investor does not lie must be greater than when he/she does lie; that is,

$$\sum_{h=0}^{H-1} \pi'_h [p_{h+1} - p_\circ(h+1)] q_{g,h+1} \geq \sum_{h=0}^{H-1} \pi'_h [p_h - p_\circ(h) + \xi] q_{b,h}. \qquad (6.11)$$

Also, investors must be assured of nonnegative expected profits, or $p_h \geq p_\circ(h)$. The expected proceeds in state h will then be

$$p_h n - [p_h - p_\circ(h)][h q_{g,h} + (H - h) q_{b,h}].$$

Let $\tilde{n}$ denote the number of shares sold in the premarket. Then, the program to be maximized by the underwriter is

$$\max_{p_\circ(h), q_{g,h}, q_{b,h}} \sum_{h=0}^{H} \pi_h \{ p_h n - [p_h - p_\circ(h)][h q_{g,h} + (H - h) q_{b,h}] \}$$

subject to (6.11) and

$$\tilde{n} \leq h q_{g,h-1} + (H - h) q_{b,h},$$
$$p_\circ(h) \leq p_h,$$
$$0 \leq q_{g,h} \leq q,$$
$$0 \leq q_{b,h} \leq q,$$

for all h. Solving this problem, it can be shown that $q_{g,h} = q$ for every h, that $p_h = p_\circ(h)$ as far as $hq < \tilde{n}$, and that otherwise underpricing occurs. Also, the expected proceeds are

$$\sum_{h=0}^{H} \pi_h \left[p_h n - \frac{\xi \zeta}{1 - \zeta} \max(\tilde{n} - hq, 0) \right]$$

and the expected underpricing is

$$\sum_{h=0}^{H-1} \pi'_h [p_{h+1} - p_\circ(h+1)] = \frac{\xi}{q} \sum_{h=0}^{H-1} \pi'_h \max \left(\frac{\tilde{n} - hq}{H - h}, 0 \right).$$

The intuition behind this result is compelling. Expected underpricing arises to provide incentives for regulars to reveal good information.

Some empirical implications follow as the conclusion that underpricing is directly related to the ex-ante marginal value of private information ξ and to the level of presales $\tilde{n}$. Also, because the level of profit is determined by the allocation to regulars who declare "bad," underpricing is minimized if priority is given to orders from investors who indicate good information.

Taking into account that an underwriter is repeatedly selling IPOs in the market, developing a reputation and, therefore, a regular clientele, the underwriter may hold the threat that if an investor refuses to purchase the issue at hand, he/she will be denied the profits accruing to regular investors in the future.

Let L represent the present value of expected future profits to a regular investor, derived from expectations about the underpricing of future issues. Introducing the value of future participations in IPOs into the analysis allows the underwriter to expect investors to purchase shares of the current issue even if by doing so they incur a loss. The clear constraint is that the loss does not exceed the present value of the future expected profits or, for any h,

$$[p_\circ(h) - p_h]q_{b,h} \leq L.$$

Adding this constraint to the preceding optimization program provides unconditionally dominating proceeds for the IPO.

6.2.5 Legal Liabilities

Tiniç (1988) proposes the alternative hypothesis that underpricing may work as an insurance against legal liability for both the issuing firm and the investment banker.

To begin with, it must be recognized that underwriters face considerable difficulties in estimating the true value of the shares in IPOs. Because the issue is new, there is little or no publicly available information about the firms (specifically about the true quality of their management) that decide to go for such an offering.

Nevertheless, it will still be easier for underwriters than for investors to look for that information. Therefore, the investor may have to rely on the information provided by the investment bankers.

Doing this job, the underwriter puts its reputation at risk. The issuing firm also has incentives to see that information is produced so that its issue is correctly priced. While the consequences of an underpriced offering are obvious, as stated previously, the real consequences of an overpriced issue have not yet been fully discussed. It is conceivable that in such a case the gains would be overwhelmed by potential legal liabilities and/or higher risk premiums that the market may demand for future securities of the same issuer.

Indeed, the Securities Act of 1933 mandates investment bankers to conduct due-diligence investigations to avoid liability not only for false or misleading information but also for material omission in the registration statement. To recover damages, a purchaser of an IPO can sue any signatory of the registration statement, any director or partner in the issuing firm, and every investment banker who is associated with the offering.

The expected costs of legal liability can be very high as the meaning of *due-diligence investigations* is not precise. Hence it is very easy to be sued since any nondisclosed piece of information, even one that seems inconsequential, may ex-post facto be judged a material omission in a legal action.

Since both the issuers and investment bankers are vulnerable, it would seem natural to jointly purchase an insurance policy against such damages. However, the premium may be prohibitive because of the typical moral hazard problem: Once they are protected, they have incentives to shirk their responsibilities to produce reliable information about the firm, increasing the probability of lawsuits and the expected losses of the insurer.

Instead, underpricing of the offering may provide the issuer and the underwriter with protection against potential legal liabilities more efficiently.

To present the relationship between p_o and the expected legal liability at any time t, let p_t be the market price of the shares at time t and assume that the density of probability of a lawsuit is a decreasing function φ of the argument p_t/p_o. Moreover, let L_t denote the legal liability at time t and let the dollar value of the potential damages be an increasing function γ of the difference $p_o - p_t$. Hence

$$E(L_t) = \int_0^\infty \varphi(x)\gamma[p_o(1 - x)]dx,$$

and since $\gamma' > 0$, we can conclude that for any fixed t, the expected liability $E(L_t)$ increases with the offering price. Therefore, this legal consideration is also a driving force toward underpricing.

Tiniç also provides empirical evidence of this fact, showing that IPOs issued after the 1933 Act exhibit initial excess returns on the order of 11.06%, which is relatively large compared to the 5.17% among IPOs brought to the market in the pre-SEC era.

6.2.6 Empirical Evidence

There are several hypotheses leading to explanations for the underpricing of IPOs. All are based on information asymmetry and on the way agents who look for information discriminate between those who have it. In fact, in some models, underwriters discriminate between investors, whereas in others, investors discriminate between underwriters.

The argument in Rock (1986) is that informed investors only bid for stock in issues they know to be underpriced, thus creating an adverse selection problem to issuers, who are led to underprice. In Benveniste and Spindt (1989) underpricing compensates the valuable information revealed by the demand of informed investors.

Hanley and Wilhelm (1995) use confidential allocation data for a limited number of IPO investors in the United States and show that institutional investors receive the same approximate proportion of shares in overpriced and underpriced issues. Assuming that institutions are proxies for informed investors, Hanley and Wilhelm interpret their results to imply that informed investors are forced by the underwriters to bid on overpriced issues, thus supporting the model of Benveniste and Spindt and rejecting Rock's underlying idea.

However, Field (1997) provides evidence that the level of institutional investment in IPOs, measured approximately one semester after the offering, is highly variable. In particular, Field shows that IPOs with the smallest institutional investments tend to have the poorest long-run returns. These findings seem to be at odds with those of Hanley and Wilhelm.

Although interesting, the content of these works may lead to very ambiguous alternative interpretations. For example, the assumption on which the conclusions are based, that institutional investors have superior information, may simply not be true. In that case, the result of Hanley and Wilhelm might simply reflect that fact, precluding any conclusion with respect to Rock's or to Benveniste and Spindt's view too. Field's study reflects the same ambiguity regarding the proxy for information as well, since she examines only postissue holdings. Therefore, an interpretation of her evidence in terms of the quality of ex-ante information may raise some doubts.

In order to verify the extent to which allocations reflect differences of information between investors, the relationship between actual allocations and unconstrained demand must be studied. If such a relationship is not taken into account, the allocation data may be taken as reflecting the underlying demand, which may be misleading. Data to analyze this problem are available only in some specific markets. Using private data from 28 Finnish IPOs, Keloharju (1997) shows that institutional investors place significantly larger orders than do retail investors. The argument raised by Chowdhry and Sherman (1996) that informed investors place larger orders than do uninformed investors, even when they have the same wealth level, leads to the conclusion that the institutional investors are a good proxy for informed investors.

In a similar vein, Lee, Taylor, and Walter (1999) show that in the Singaporean IPO market large investors tend preferentially to request participation in IPOs with higher initial returns, which is consistent with the fact that these investors are better informed. These types of work allow us to come back to the papers of Hanley and Wilhelm (1995) and Field (1997), and try to draw conclusions about the relationship between the observed behavior of investors and the information differential.

Still, the difference between these two works remains to be explained. Krigman, Shaw, and Womack (1999) provide evidence that the practice of flipping (immediately selling IPO allocations back to the market) makes such differences compatible. Institutional investors may buy equally underpriced and overpriced issues, as described by Hanley and Wilhelm. Based on their superior information, for institutional investors flipping is a rational response to underwriters' mispricing. In this spirit, heavily flipped IPOs are shown to significantly underperform less flipped issues over future holding periods. In that case, the result reported in Field (1997), that institutional investors' holdings in IPOs one semester after the offering are highly variable, comes as no surprise.

Underpricing appears as an equilibrium compensation for both the lack of information and the effort to find it. However, Ritter (1991) gives empirical evidence that the underpricing of IPOs is a short-run phenomenon. In the long-run the issues are, in fact, overpriced on average. This is consistent with a pattern in which investors are periodically overoptimistic about the earnings potential of young growth companies, and firms take advantage of these windows of opportunity.

This empirical evidence resurrects the hypothesis of speculative bubbles. The idea is that just after the offering, the demand for the new issues would be irrationally high and the supply would not be enough to contain the rise of prices. Once the situation is normalized, the prices would come down to their "natural" level.

Lee, Taylor, and Walter (1996) analyze this issue in the Singaporean IPO market and are not able to support the fad or speculative bubble argument. Market efficiency fits their results better.

Krigman, Shaw, and Womack (1999) relate long-run performance with first-day performance. In particular, they provide evidence that initial returns predict subsequent long-run (one-year) returns. IPOs that outperform on the first day will be outperforming one year later, on average. Similarly, those IPOs that underperform on the first day will also be underperforming after one year. Exceptions to this rule are the extrahot issues, which provide the worst future performance.

These results are, once again, understood given the existence of flipping by the best informed investors in the IPO. The authors show that flipping is predictable and, therefore, that the underwriters' mispricing is intentional.

6.2.7 Exercises

1. Why should we expect underpricing to be more relevant in a firm-commitment offering than in a best-effort contract?
2. In his model, Baron assumes that the investment bank has access to a signal ϕ about θ, which is the unknown state of nature at the moment of the public offering. Give an interpretation of ϕ.
3. In a situation of asymmetric information, when the bank has superior information to that of the firm, the first-best solution is not attainable. Why?
4. Show that the probability of an uninformed investor receiving an allocation of an underpriced issue (π) is less than or equal to the probability of receiving an allocation of an overpriced issue (π').
5. Rock's work assumes a type of rationing that could be associated with a firm-commitment offering. If we suppose instead a best-effort underwriting, is there still a downward pressure on the offering price?
6. When there are informed and uninformed investors, it is said that as the proportion of informed investors (α) rises, the offer price (p_0) must fall to maintain the equilibrium. Explain why.
7. In the context of Carter and Manaster, it is concluded that low-uncertainty firms would benefit by making that fact available to the public. Why?
8. Explain the incentive condition for a regular investor not to lie in the model of Benveniste and Spindt.
9. Explain the equation of the expected proceeds in state h,

$$p_h n - [p_h - p_0(h)][hq_{g,h} + (H - h)q_{b,h}].$$

10. It is stated that if we take into account that an underwriter is repeatedly selling IPOs, we expect the proceeds for the IPOs to be higher. Why?
11. The results of Benveniste and Spindt are consistent with the empirical evidence that, on average, best-effort offerings are more underpriced than firm-commitment offerings. Explain why.

7

Going Private

THE TERM *going private* refers to revising the capital structure so that a publicly held corporation is totally or partially transformed into a private corporation. In other words, the stock of a public corporation (or a significant part of it) is acquired by a small number of investors and is no longer traded. This is just the reverse of the going public process.

A first restructuring process of this nature, the repurchase of stock, was already analyzed in Section 3.2.4. The ideas underlying a stock repurchase are discussed in the first part of this chapter, in the context of its impact on the capital structure of a firm.

Going private transactions are very often *leveraged buyouts* (*LBOs*), characterized by the fact that the cash offers, either from outsiders or not, are highly financed with debt. It is common that the group of small investors is dominated by managers of the purchased firm, in which case the operation is termed a *management buyout* (*MBO*). These operations are discussed in the second part of this chapter.

7.1 Stock Repurchases

In a stock repurchase there is distribution of excess cash and an increase of leverage, and the company gets rid of pessimistic shareholders. Buybacks may be thought of as an antitakeover device just as in the targeted repurchase discussed already.

In the theoretical signaling model developed by Vermaelen (1984) and described in Section 3.2.4, stock repurchases are taken by the managers as a signaling device to inform the market that the shares are undervalued.

Let N_o and P_o be the number of shares and the price per share before the announcement of the repurchase at a price P_T; let N_E and P_E be the number of remaining shares and the price per share after the expiration. Then, in an efficient capital market,

$$N_E P_E = N_\circ P_\circ - P_T(N_\circ - N_E) + I,$$

where I denotes the total change in the value of the shares. As pointed out before,[1] the value of transferring information to the market is related to I and therefore to the *abnormal return* $\alpha = I/N_\circ P_\circ$.

Hence, stock repurchases can be seen as a mechanism to avoid takeovers at a relatively low offer premium. It has been argued that takeovers may benefit the shareholders, but the point here is that noninsider shareholders probably prefer no takeover to a takeover at a low-bid premium when their shares are undervalued.

To support this view of the stock repurchase mechanism, Vermaelen (1984) compares the number of buybacks and the number of takeovers in the market in different years and finds that the two sequences are fairly correlated. This is interpreted as suggestive evidence that takeover threats increase repurchase incentives.[2]

In spite of their advantages, buybacks do not occur in Europe because they are too regulated. Here are four arguments for the regulations:

- The first argument is that buybacks are restricted to protect creditors. Stock repurchases reduce the capital base of the company and increase riskiness of creditors. In fact, what happens is that the book value of the equity decreases much more than does its market value. There is an intrinsic value to revealing information to the market, which on average raises the market price of the shares. Vermaelen (1981), among others, reports abnormal returns[3] on the order of 15%. Therefore, this argument against buybacks does not hold.
- Another argument is that if, in a buyback, insiders do not sell and the firm buys shares at a price lower than the true market price,[4] the outsider shareholder is being expropriated. This could occur once in a company's life, but it would never happen again, because the market would defend itself by increasing the stock price upon the announcement of other repurchases to reflect the likely value increase. Hence, under the assumption of market efficiency, if such an expropriation were to occur once, the market would learn from that experience and would adapt to that fact, and the share price would rise above the tender price so that a repeated expropriation would not take place.

In a paper by Lakonishok and Vermaelen (1990), the hypothesis is tested that the market does not fully adjust to the signal provided by the repurchase and thereby underestimates the true value of the shares. This is equivalent to the market inefficiency just described, and it implies a reduction in the signaling cost to the managers/insiders at the expense of the tendering shareholders. If such an inefficiency exists, a profitable trading rule would be to buy securities after the expiration of the share repurchase and hold them.

Over a two-year period, Lakonishok and Vermaelen found that this trading rule beats the value-weighted index by 12% per year (23.11% over two years or 1.05% per month). Correcting this result for size and beta, the abnormal return falls to 0.40% per month, but is still significantly positive. This effect is shown[5] to be due to small firms, which is consistent with findings in Vermaelen (1981). The pattern for large firms is on average of abnormal returns positive prior to the repurchase, and not significantly different from zero after the repurchase. Hence, inefficiencies of the market, if they exist, are associated with small firms. This evidence does not, therefore, support the argument against the existence of share repurchases.

- A third argument against buybacks is that they are antitakeover devices and therefore not in the long-run interest of shareholders. If the argument holds, prices should fall after the announcement, which runs contrary to the evidence. Actually, an antitakeover device protects shareholders from having their shares bought at a price that is too low, as discussed already.
- A fourth argument is that buybacks reduce government tax revenues since capital gains are taxed at a lower level than dividends. This argument supposes that firms lower their dividends if buybacks are allowed. There is no such evidence. In fact, firms are reluctant to cut dividends, as seen in Chapter 4. Hence there is, in principle, no reason for the tax revenue to governments to decrease. It follows that this argument does not hold either.

As we refute the basic criticism of the buyback process, its relevance in corporate restructuring becomes clear. The buyback is a signaling device of the true value of the firms and simultaneously a healthy antitakeover device.

7.2 Leveraged Buyouts

7.2.1 The Mechanism of Leveraged Buyouts

An LBO operation usually goes through four stages. The first one concerns fund raising to finance the LBO. In the first step, the original group of investors, typically led by some top managers, enters with a small percentage of the required amount, constituting the equity base of the new firm. A large majority of the capital is raised in secured bank loans as borrowings against the company's assets. The remaining capital is raised by issuing senior and junior debt in private placements or junk bonds. There are important aspects to notice from this financing procedure. First, LBOs do not involve public outside equity. Second, financing choices reflect a specific selection of the entire debt structure. In particular, the case of MBOs is characterized by the fact that the debt structure is chosen by the incumbent management, with private information. These are solid reasons for Diamond (1991, 1993) to claim that LBOs are a fertile field for studying the implications of his model about the seniority of debt structure presented in Section 5.2.4.

Once the required cash is raised, the second step is to buy the outstanding shares of the company. This second stage of the operation may be performed in one of two ways: either by purchasing the assets (thus constituting a new, privately held firm) or by buying all of the outstanding shares.

Changes in the management are implemented next, in order to increase profits and cash flows. This third step is achieved by reorganizing or consolidating strategies and processes. It is necessary in order to satisfy the service of debt and to justify the investment made in the LBO process.

Finally, the investors who made the LBO may decide to take the company public again through a public equity offering, "reverting" the LBO. This is understandable from the point of view of the existing stockholders who seek liquidity, once the company emerges stronger and the goals of the investors are achieved.

One of the reasons why LBOs became so common is that these transactions require little equity capital. Just as in any tender offer, the shareholders are willing to sell their shares in an LBO at a premium. Although in a merger or a takeover, the premium may be justified by possible strategic synergies, in the case of an LBO this is not clear. After all, there is only one firm involved.

Because of its leveraged nature, one of an LBO's most evident sources of value is the tax advantage generated by debt. Lowenstein (1985), for instance, argues that most of the premium paid to former shareholders is financed from tax savings. Kaplan (1989b) argues, however, that these tax benefits, being predictable, are appropriable by the prebuyout shareholders.

Another related source of value is the reduction of agency costs between management and shareholders, especially in the case of MBOs. Since most previous shareholders have no more holdings in the firm after such a restructuring, managers become owners and therefore identify their goals with the maximization of the firm's value in a costless way. Also, because buyers are typically insiders and the debt-equity rate increases, gains in an LBO are thought to come at the expense of bondholders and of the (few) noninsider shareholders left. The relative importance of each of these factors is an empirical issue to be examined shortly.

Jensen (1989) argues that high leverage, concentrated equity owner-ship by managers, and monitoring by an LBO sponsor firm work together to reduce incentive problems faced by more traditional organizations, adding value especially in slow-growth sectors of the economy. In par-ticular, an increased equity ownership of managers in the organization strengthens incentives for the management to create shareholder value. Additionally, debt service obligations reduce the overinvestment problem associated with "free cash flows." Finally, the control exercised by non-management insiders, such as the LBO sponsor firm, tends to increase monitoring. These arguments led Jensen to argue that LBOs and LBO-like organizations could supplant the more typical public corporation in mature industries. Although supported by other authors,[6] this view is con-troversial. Rappaport (1990), for instance, argues that these organizations are inherently transitory. The basis of his argument is that a highly lever-aged capital structure and a concentrated equity ownership do not give enough flexibility for an organization to face changing economic condi-tions and competitive pressures. LBO organizations may be forced to go public in a later stage for reasons such as demand for capital, liquidity desires, or risk-sharing incentives. This argument coincides with the wave of reverse LBOs that has been observed in the market since the 90s, as reported in Weston, Siu, and Johnson (2001).

7.2.2 A Model for MBOs

Elitzur et al. (1998) develop a model in which managers who retain a significant share of the firm's common stock perform an LBO such that they increase their share while reducing their wealth invested in the firm, thus allowing for a more diversified portfolio of investments.

Let R_t denote the reported net income at time t, and let B_t be the level of investments budgeted. The management bonus being $k(R_t - B_t)$, the firm's net cash flow is perceived as $\Lambda_t(R_t, B_t, k)$. If there are N out-standing shares, the price of each one at time $t = 0$ is

$$P_\circ = \frac{1}{N} \sum_{t=1}^{\infty} \rho_t \Lambda_t(R_t, B_t, k),$$

where ρ_t is the market discount factor for time t cash flow. The manage-ment is assumed to have a proportion $w_\circ$ of the shares in the public firm, or a total amount of $n_\circ = w_\circ N$ shares. Moreover, let e denote the effort level of the managers with unit cost μ. Managers are assumed to have H_t invested in projects outside the firm and ΔH_t denotes the change in the value of such outside holdings. Let their effort in these outside activities be denoted by e^{out}. Similarly, the effort in the originally considered firm is denoted by e^{pu} if the company is public and e^{pr} if the company goes private. The expected wealth of a manager if the company remains public is

$$W^{\text{pu}} = \sum_{t=1}^{\infty} \rho_t \big[k(R_t - B_t) - \mu e^{\text{pu}} + \Delta H_t - \mu e^{\text{out}} \big] + n_{\text{o}} P_{\text{o}} + H_{\text{o}}.$$

Substituting the value for P_{o} gives

$$W^{\text{pu}} = \sum_{t=1}^{\infty} \rho_t \big[k(R_t - B_t) - \mu e^{\text{pu}} + \Delta H_t - \mu e^{\text{out}} + w_{\text{o}} \Lambda_t \big] + H_{\text{o}}.$$

If the company goes private, an amount of debt D is issued to finance the transaction at a price $P_{\text{o}} + \phi$ per share. Let I_t denote the interest charge on this new debt. The value of total equity will thus be $N(P_{\text{o}} + \phi)$. Let λ be defined as the debt-equity ratio, satisfying

$$D = \lambda N (P_{\text{o}} + \phi).$$

The number of shares bought is clearly $D/(P_{\text{o}} + \phi) = \lambda N$. The position of the management holding initially $w_{\text{o}} N$ is worth $w_{\text{o}} N (P_{\text{o}} + \phi)$ at the time of the offer. Let w_1 denote the new proportion of shares held by the management after the offer. Therefore, after a going-private transaction the management will hold $w_1 N (1 - \lambda)$ shares, each one at the value $P_{\text{o}} + \phi$. The change in value is thus

$$w_{\text{o}} N (P_{\text{o}} + \phi) - w_1 N (1 - \lambda)(P_{\text{o}} + \phi) = N(P_{\text{o}} + \phi)[w_{\text{o}} - w_1 (1 - \lambda)].$$

Denoting for simplicity the manager's only compensation under private ownership at time t by

$$w_1 (\text{NCF}_t - I_t),$$

where NCF denotes the net cash flow, the expected wealth of the management under a going-private transaction is

$$W^{\text{pr}} = \sum_{t=1}^{\infty} \rho_t \big[w_1 (\text{NCF}_t - I_t) - \mu e^{\text{pr}} + \Delta H_t - \mu e^{\text{out}} \big]$$
$$+ N(P_{\text{o}} + \phi)[w_{\text{o}} - w_1 (1 - \lambda)] + H_{\text{o}}.$$

Assuming that the management is risk neutral, going private makes sense if it is possible to choose λ, w_1, and e^{pr} such that W^{pr} will be greater than W^{pu}. This optimization, however, must be made under a number of constraints. First, the total effort level made by the management must not be above a certain upper bound X. Second, and more important, the outside shareholders in the privatized firm must have the right incentives to participate in this game. In fact, outsiders who participate in the buyout incur monitoring costs, denoted by η. They own a proportion $1 - w_1$ of the shares in the new private company, so their expected wealth is

$$W^o = \sum_{t=1}^{\infty} \rho_t [(1 - w_1)(\text{NCF}_t - I_t) - \eta_t] - N(P_o + \phi)(1 - w_1)(1 - \lambda).$$

Thus, the management's problem is to choose the values of the parameters λ, w_1, η_t and e^{pr} such that maximize simultaneously W^{pr} and W^0 subject to having $W^0 > 0$. Then, the management should compare with their optimal expected wealth if they remain public. Formally, a management buyout occurs if

$$\max W^{\text{pr}} \geq \max W^{\text{pu}} \tag{7.1}$$

under the respective constraints. Let M_t denote the level of monitoring. In particular, the expected wealth to the management under an MBO results from the maximization problem

$$\max_{\lambda, w_1, e^{\text{pr}}} W^{\text{pr}}$$

subject to

$$W^o > 0$$

$$\eta_t = \eta_t(M_t^*) \text{ where } M_t^* \in \arg\max_{M_t} W^o$$

$$X = e^{\text{pr}} + e^{\text{out}}.$$

The optimal level of monitoring results from the optimization of W^o. The first-order condition reads

$$(1 - w_1)[\text{NCF}_t'(M_t) - I_t'(M_t)] - \eta_t'(M_t) = 0$$

where $\text{NCF}_t' > 0$ and $I_t' < 0$, leading to the first result:

Lemma 7.2.1 (Elitzur et al.). *Outsiders monitor the manager to the point at which the incremental cost of monitoring equals the incremental benefit of monitoring, where the incremental benefit of monitoring is the sum of greater net operating cash flows and lower interest rates on the new debt.*

Using the implicit function theorem, the preceding first-order condition allows us to write at the optimal level of monitoring,

$$\frac{dM_t}{dw_1}\bigg|_{M_t=M_t^*} < 0,$$

leading to

Proposition 7.2.1 (Elitzur et al.). *Optimal monitoring is negatively correlated with the percentage of stock held by management in the newly privatized company. With greater stock ownership, the interests of the manager and the new outside owners are more closely aligned, and the marginal benefits of monitoring are not as large.*

A simple corollary follows from the fact that

$$\frac{d\eta_t}{dw_1}\bigg|_{M_t=M_t^*} = \eta_t'(M_t)\frac{dM_t}{dw_1}\bigg|_{M_t=M_t^*} < 0$$

or

Corollary 7.2.1 (Elitzur et al.). *Monitoring costs in the postbuyout company are negatively correlated with management's share in the equity of the privatized firm.*

Once the problem of optimal monitoring is characterized, it is possible to characterize the optimization problem of the management under an MBO in a more integrated form. Substituting the outsider equity investor constraint in the management objective function W^{pr}, and using the envelope theorem to suppress the optimal monitoring choice, the management problem becomes

$$\max_{\lambda, w_1, e^{\text{pr}}} W^{\text{pr}} = \sum_{t=1}^{\infty} \rho_t \left[(\text{NCF}_t - I_t) - \eta_t - \mu e^{\text{pr}} + \Delta H_t - \mu e^{\text{out}} \right] \qquad (7.2)$$

subject to

$$\eta_t = \eta_t(M_t^*) \text{ where } M_t^* \in \arg\max_{M_t} W^o$$

$$X = e^{\text{pr}} + e^{\text{out}}.$$

Let $r(e^{\text{out}})$ be the cost of opportunity to the management of funds left in the firm. These costs depend on the level of effort spent in the outside activities of the management. The characterization of the optimal debt level to the management is obtained from the first-order condition with respect to λ that reads

$$\sum_{t=1}^{\infty} \rho_t \left\{ -I_t'(\lambda) + r(e^{\text{out}})(P_\circ + \phi) N w_1 [1 + r(e^{\text{out}})]^{t-1} \right\} + N(P_\circ + \phi) = 0.$$

This result is interpreted as follows:

Proposition 7.2.2 (Elitzur et al.). *The manager will choose to finance the buyout with an amount of debt that balances the present value of the net losses from changing the proportion of debt financing against the amount paid to stockholders to make the firm private. The net losses are composed of the present value of the increased interest payments due to the increased debt plus the opportunity cost of funds left in the firm.*

The optimal proportion of shares in the hands of management after an MBO is similarly determined by the first-order condition with respect to w_1:

$$\sum_{t=1}^{\infty} \rho_t \left\{ \eta_t'(w_1) - r(e^{\mathrm{out}})(P_\circ + \phi)N(1 - \lambda)[1 + r(e^{\mathrm{out}})]^{t-1} \right\} = 0,$$

which can be read in the following way:

Proposition 7.2.3 (Elitzur et al.). *The manager will choose to take as much stock in the postbuyout firm as required to balance the reduction in monitoring costs from his/her increased share of the firm's stock against his/her opportunity cost of leaving funds in the firm.*

Regarding the level of effort that a manager will want to expend in the privatized firm in order to maximize his/her wealth, the first-order condition leads to the following conclusion:

Proposition 7.2.4 (Elitzur et al.). *A manager will increase his/her efforts in the management of the postbuyout company until the gains in the company's net cash flows from such efforts equal the opportunity costs to the manager of such increased efforts in forgone return.*

In other words, the amount of effort is determined by balancing the value created in the privatized firm against the opportunities lost by not investing elsewhere.

Turning to the relationship between the optimal level of monitoring and the optimal effort developed by the management, using the implicit function theorem, the model leads to the following derivative at the optimal point:

$$\frac{de^{\mathrm{pr}}}{dM_t^*} > 0.$$

Therefore

Proposition 7.2.5 (Elitzur et al.). *Increased monitoring increases management's efforts in managing the postbuyout firm.*

As seen from this result, and consistent with the agency literature, monitoring by outside shareholders influences the level of effort
expended by the management. Within this model, this is an endogenous
result and it holds even when taking into account the value to the manager of his/her effort in other activities.

Having characterized the optimal strategy and its consequences when
the management undergoes an MBO, one may compare the optimal level
of effort in the public company with that of a company that goes private.
Let A denote the net investment or disinvestment made by insider owners
in the MBO process. By maximizing W^{pu}, the authors show from comparison of the first-order conditions that the manager's effort increases after
the company goes private if

$$\text{NCF}'_t(e^{pr}) + r'(e^{out})A[1 + r(e^{out})]^{t-1} > kR'_t(e^{pu}) + w_o\Lambda'(e^{pu}).$$

The left-hand side represents the marginal impact of increased manager's
effort in the net cash flows together with the reduction of the manager's
opportunity cost of effort due to a change in their investment in the new
privatized firm. The right-hand side reflects the marginal benefit of the
effort expended in a public company that originated in the change of the
manager's bonus and the wealth obtained from his/her equity investment
in the firm.

Thus,

Proposition 7.2.6 (Elitzur et al.). *The manager's efforts in the private company
will be higher than the manager's efforts in a public company if the incremental
wealth effects of such efforts are higher for the manager's rebalanced portfolio.*

7.2.3 Empirical Evidence

Empirical research has been unanimous in describing a positive premium
for public stockholders of around 50% over their market price one or
two months before the announcement of LBOs. These results have been
present since the earliest papers such as DeAngelo, DeAngelo, and Rice
(1984) and Lowenstein (1985). In particular, the latter pointed out that
the more bids involved, the higher the premium would be, strongly sug-
gesting the creation of an auction system that would motivate multiple
bids. Later empirical papers, such as Kaplan (1989a), Muscarella and Vetsuypens (1990), and Travlos and Cornett (1993), confirmed the existence
of large premiums and abnormal announcement returns to prebuyout
shareholders.

Much of the empirical literature focused on the sources of wealth
generated by the going-private transactions. The empirical work of Kaplan
(1989b), in particular, was centered on the tax benefits. Performing

regression analyses, Kaplan showed that the returns to the prebuyout shareholders are positively and significantly related to tax benefits from LBOs. The returns to the postbuyout shareholders, however, are not. They were shown to be positively related to operating income subsequent to the transaction. This result was seen by Kaplan as evidence that the tax benefits are mostly captured by the prebuyout shareholders. Besides, the hypothesis that returns to the shareholders are at the expense of bondholders is rejected.

These results corroborate those of Lehn and Poulsen (1988), who also found that returns to the prebuyout shareholders are positively related to pre-LBO tax liability to equity ratios, providing evidence of the relevance of tax benefits in LBOs.

Travlos and Cornett (1993) show that in LBOs, the effects induced by the change in the capital structure are insufficient to explain the abnormal returns observed when the buyouts are announced. This contradicts the tax benefits argument, but is perhaps explained by the temporary nature of at least some part of the new debt. In line with these explanations were the findings of Muscarella and Vetsuypens (1990). In a sample of 72 reverse LBOs, the average debt to value ratio was 90% at the LBO, 78% before reverting the LBO, and 60% after the reversion.

Roden and Lewellen (1995) test traditional theories of capital structure. Within a sample of 107 LBOs from 1981 to 1990, they show that just over 60% of the capital was senior secured debt financed by banks. Next comes about 25% of unsecured subordinated long-term debt, followed in the end by a small proportion of preferred stock (4%) and common equity (7%).

The LBOs were described as some sort of concentration of ownership and control. Managers become owners of the firm, aligning their goals with those of maximizing the firm's value. However, Baker, Jensen, and Murphy (1988) show that actual executive compensation is very often insufficient to provide optimal incentives for managers. However, even if that is true, there is still room for reduction of agency costs in a different way, in particular following Jensen's free cash flow hypothesis. Increasing debt commits future cash flows, reducing managerial discretion in the allocation of free cash flow.

Lehn and Poulsen (1989) indirectly test Jensen's hypothesis through the direct relationship between the nondistributed cash flow to equity ratio and the premium paid to prebuyout shareholders. This relationship is shown to be highly significant. The likelihood of going private is also shown to be directly related to the cash flow to equity value ratio. Although Lehn and Poulsen are frequently cited as providing evidence supporting the applicability of Jensen's free cash flow hypothesis to going-private transactions, a paper by Kieschnick (1998) reexamines the data in

Lehn and Poulsen to arrive at quite different inferences. First, Kieschnick finds that neither the level of a public corporation's pretransaction free cash flows nor its prior growth rate are significant determinants of its probability of going private. Second, Kieschnick finds that the significant determinants of the premiums paid to go private are a firm's size and its potential for reducing taxes, rather than its pretransaction level of free cash flows. And finally, analyzing the 1980–83 subsample of Lehn and Poulsen reveals that firms that went private during the 1984–87 period demonstrate a greater incidence of prior takeover interest, lower prior tax burdens, and slower prior growth than firms that went private during the 1980–83 period—all of which supports Kaplan and Stein's (1993) overheated buyout market hypothesis.

Regarding the control structure of LBOs, Kaplan (1989a) shows that the management postbuyout ownership increases by about three times the prebuyout values. Muscarella and Vetsuypens (1990) report data confirming that management ownership remains high after reverting LBOs.

Muscarella and Vetsuypens (1990) also analyze the operating performance in their sample of reversed LBOs. More than two-thirds of the firms disclosed at least one restructuring activity undertaken since the LBO. This fact is suggested to represent a significant change in strategy that would not have been implemented had the LBO not occurred. This restructuring in the activities of the companies is argued to be at the root of the substantial improvement observed in the operational results. Kaplan (1989a) and Smith (1990) also provide evidence of improved operational results following LBOs.

Holthausen and Larcker (1996) analyzed a sample of 90 reversed LBOs between 1983 and 1988. Their study relates changes in accounting performance to incentive variables. During the first four years following the reversed LBOs, firms outperform their industries, although their performance decreases during that time interval. The authors observed that performance decreases as the management's ownership decreases, and found no evidence of a relationship between performance and leverage level. Capital expenditure increased following the LBO, compatible with Rappaport's (1990) argument that LBO firms are cash-constrained.

Travlos and Cornett (1993), on the other hand, show that the abnormal return to prebuyout shareholders and the price-earnings ratio of the firm relative to its sector are negatively correlated at a significant level. If low P/E ratios are associated with high agency costs, then the lower the ratio, the greater the gains to be obtained from an LBO. This interpretation may be wrong, however, for the simple reason that a low P/E ratio may mean nothing but lower growth opportunities.

Finally, there is the issue of whether the gains of the prebuyout shareholders come at the expense of the prebuyout bondholders.

Travlos and Cornett (1993) report significant losses at the statistical level for bondholders and preferred stockholders at the time of the LBO announcement. These losses are small, however, when compared to the gains to the prebuyout shareholder, thus failing to provide a satisfactory explanation.

7.2.4 Exercises

1. Following the suggestions in the text, show that the manager's optimization problem is the one given in (7.2).
2. In the context of the model presented, show that the relation between $r(e^{\text{out}})$ and w_1 is negative. Give the intuition for this fact.
3. Empirical evidence is consistent in finding large positive premiums for public shareholders and also finding that these gains are substantially sustained. Explain some of the sources of such large gains.

8
Mergers and Acquisitions

CORPORATIONS ARE INVOLVED in a range of activities including expanding, shrinking, and otherwise restructuring asset and ownership structures. The study of corporate restructuring is devoted to understanding what the underlying forces driving these changes are.

In general, corporate activities are defined and implemented by corporations' managements. Corporate restructuring, in particular, is aimed at obtaining or keeping (depending on the case) the control of corporations—that is to say, the right to determine the top-level managers of resources.

Some authors[1] see the market for corporate control as a market in which alternative management teams compete for such rights. This differs from the traditional view, according to which financiers and activist stockholders, having different interests, try to control corporations in order to achieve an optimal utilization of the resources according to their respective points of view.

As opposed to this idea, if competing managements are the main players of this game, it transforms the stockholders from active participants into simple potential sellers of shares or, in other words, simple market pawns to be used in the competing management's game strategy.

In this perspective, the fight for corporate control constrains the utilization of resources by the management to closely follow shareholders' wealth maximization and, at the same time, provides the mechanism through which synergies available from combining or reorganizing control and management of corporate resources are realized.

Some typical activities related to control restructuring are briefly described in this introduction and will be studied later in greater detail.

For example, one way to expand a corporation is to *merge* it with another. A *merger* is any transaction that joins two or more economic units into a single one. Another way of expanding is to make a *tender offer*. In such an operation, one party is seeking to control the other corporation and asks the stockholders of the target firm to tender their shares of stock. When a company gains control over another without the approval of the target's management, the takeover is said to be *hostile*. One of the most common consequences of a hostile takeover is the total or partial replacement of the management. Ways of avoiding this have become important and are known as antitakeover devices. Typically, when there is a threat of a hostile takeover, the management may look for an alternative offer from a more desirable partner, a so-called *white knight*.

Other antitakeover devices exist. Usually they consist of changes in the corporate bylaws to make an acquisition of the company more difficult or more expensive. Such changes may need the approval of the target's stockholders. There is some evidence, to be discussed,[2] that takeovers are usually good for the stockholders, but this is essentially an empirical issue. Takeovers may be not so good for the management of the target corporation, and depending on the real power of the management, these antitakeover devices may or may not come into play. Examples will be discussed shortly. The existence of antitakeover devices may also suggest that takeovers are good for bidders and bad for targets. The question of who profits more from a takeover will be discussed in the next section in some detail.

Besides mergers, tender offers, and antitakeover amendments, there are other forms of corporate control to be discussed, such as *proxy contests*, in which an outside group seeks to obtain representation on the board of directors. Such procedures are usually taken as actions against the existing management. Also to be considered are premium buybacks, called *greenmail*, where a firm purchases its own stock, at a premium, from investors who might otherwise seek to acquire the firm or else to initiate a proxy fight to oust the present management.

Finally, there is the possibility of *divestitures*, such as a *spinoff* in which the corporation is separated into two companies having the same proportion of ownership in both for each stockholder. The controls of both are independent and they may follow different policies. A *split-off* is a similar operation in the sense that a second company is created, but in this case only some of the stockholders receive stock in the new company in exchange for the main company's stock. Hence, the ownership is also split. In an *equity carve-out* a part of the company is sold to outsiders.

8.1 Tender Offers and the Free-Rider Problem

In this section the mechanisms of tender offers are examined. Before going into the empirical evidence, some theoretical ideas and models are discussed. Most of the models have important empirical implications. The empirical evidence is presented afterwards.

This part is devoted to modeling the forces inducing and opposing the realization of takeovers. Issues such as the free-rider problem and the patterns of stock ownership, which influence the outcome of takeovers, are considered.

8.1.1 Largely Diffused Ownership

A first model of takeovers is the one by Grossman and Hart (1990), who introduce the free-rider problem. Their idea is to formalize the way in which shareholders free-ride on the bidder potential improvements to the corporation, reducing the bidder's potential profits to zero and thus making takeovers unattractive.

Let A denote the space of possible activities of the management, and $f(a)$ be the market value of the shares described as a function of some $a \in A$. The function f describes to a certain extent the ability of the current management under which the maximum possible profit is

$$\max_{a \in A} f(a) = f(a^*).$$

Suppose now that a raider wishes to take over the firm and announces a tender price $p > f(a^*)$ at which he/she will buy all available shares. His/her abilities are supposed to be different from the current management and he/she is supposed to be able to improve the profits by an amount of Z. In this case, the expected market value is denoted by

$$v = \max_{a \in A} f(a) + Z,$$

where $Z > 0$. Assume that v and Z are known to all the shareholders. Clearly, if $v > p > f(a^*)$, the offer looks attractive to the shareholders and to the raider. However, in a diffusely held firm, such an attempt at control will not succeed. Here is an important assumption to reach this conclusion:

Assumption 8.1.1. *The ownership of the firm is largely diffused in the sense that there are a large number of shareholders, each of them holding a very small proportion of the outstanding shares.*

Therefore, given a tender offer, the impact of each shareholder's tender decision is negligible in the final result. Under rational expectations, it turns out that the outcome of the bid is not stochastic. That is to say, the only successful bids are those expected to be successful with a probability of 1 and all other bids will not happen. This is so, since given a tender offer with $p < v$, any shareholder who knows that the offer will succeed prefers to make v instead of getting only p. Knowing that his/her decision has no impact on the outcome of the bid, each shareholder will be better off not tendering (thus receiving p) than tendering and receiving v. Therefore, no one tenders, and the bid does not succeed. The alternative would be to tender at $p \geq v$, but such conditions are clearly uninteresting to the bidder since his/her profit is reduced at least to zero.

Takeovers do exist, however. A way to explain them in this context is through different valuations due to information asymmetries, for instance. In such a case the shareholders would use, say, $v_s \neq v$ instead of v, and the bid could be successful at the tender price v_s at which the shareholders would be indifferent between tendering and not tendering. If the cost of the raid is c, the raider's profit in this case would be

$$\Pi_r = v - v_s - c. \tag{8.1}$$

Another way of handling a takeover is to make the valuation of the bidder artificially higher than the valuation of the shareholders. This is possible if the shareholders are willing to *dilute* their own rights in order to stimulate the raider[3] and penalize the current management. This idea is compatible with the common belief that a corporation that is not being run in the interest of its shareholders will be vulnerable to a takeover bid. This attitude immediately generates $v_s \neq v$. The degree of dilution may be measured by a factor ϕ defined as $\phi = v - v_s$. Hence, by the preceding arguments, the tender price must not be smaller than v_s. Also, if the current management provides a market value of q, shareholders will not be interested in tendering for less than q. Therefore, to maximize the raider's profit,

$$p = \max(v_s, q) = \max(v - \phi, q)$$

with equation (8.1) substituted for by

$$\Pi_r = v - p - c = \min(\phi, v - q) - c.$$

The choice of the *current* management's action a_o giving rise to the market value $q = f(a_o)$ depends, therefore, on the level of dilution ϕ.

Suppose that the manager has a utility $U(q)$ from the market value q in the event of no raid and has zero utility if the raid occurs. The realizations of v and c being random to the manager, let them be denoted by $\tilde{v}$ and $\tilde{c}$, and let the probability of a raid be denoted by

$$\varphi(\phi, q) \equiv \Pr[\min(\phi, \tilde{v} - q) > \tilde{c}].$$

Hence the manager's expected utility from market value q is

$$W(q) = U(q)[1 - \varphi(\phi, q)].$$

If $\tilde{v}$ and $\tilde{c}$ were nonstochastic, raids would occur with a probability of either 0 or 1, and since $\varphi(\phi, q)$ is a decreasing function of q, the manager would choose q large enough so that no raid occurs. Randomness of these variables is thus essential to conclude that, in general, raids may occur.

The second relevant problem in the context of this model is to know how it is that the shareholders choose their optimal value of the dilution factor. This can be understood by writing the expected return to the shareholders as a function of ϕ:

$$r(\phi) = q[1 - \varphi(\phi, q)] + E[\max(\tilde{v} - \phi, q) | \min(\phi, \tilde{v} - q) > c]\varphi(\phi, q).$$

The effects of an increase in ϕ are ambiguous. On the one hand, the tender price decreases, which is bad for the shareholders. On the other hand, both the probability of a raid and the current market value q increase, which is good.

Grossman and Hart go on to show that if shareholders know the cost of a takeover bid, then by setting $\phi > c$ they can compensate the raider for these costs and that it is optimal for them to fully exploit the threat of raids. Hence, in a model where all the shareholders are atomistic, the free-rider problem is solved, and takeovers may be explained through the dilution device.

Another way to overcome the free-rider problem in a universe of atomistic shareholders is to make two-tier offers, as argued first by Dunn and Spatt (1984). A two-tier offer consists of two parts. In the first, a cash tender offer for a limited number of shares is made at a premium. If the bidder obtains controlling interest in the target through this first stage, in a second stage a merger plan takes effect.

There are three crucial parameters in this schedule. One is the price level of the first part of the bid. The second is the (lower) price level of the other part of the bid, when the bidder takes control of the corporation. The third relevant factor is the fraction of shares that are paid the higher price.

Bradley and Kim (1985) as well as Comment and Jarrell (1987) explore the issue of whether a bidder can force the shareholders to tender in an unsatisfactory offer, through a prisoner's–dilemma–like game. The idea is simple. Each shareholder has to decide whether or not to tender in the first part of the offer at a reasonable price. The trade-off is clear: To tender ensures a moderate outcome, whereas not to tender risks the worst outcome, where shares are bought at the lower price in the event that the other shareholders do tender and the offer is successful.

The optimal solution for each of the shareholders would be available only if most of them resist the tender offer so that the offer fails. If they are unable to guarantee the implementation of such a strategy, the threat of a later dilution effect by offering a lower price in the second part of the offer forces each shareholder to tender.

Notice that the analogy with the prisoner's dilemma is not complete. On the one hand, shareholders are free to cooperate among themselves, and on the other hand, two-tier bidders may face competition from other bidders.

Bradley and Kim (1985) argue that tender will occur even in situations that leave the target worse off than initially. Shareholders will be better off if the current managers compete with the bidder for control, or if there are several bidders competing, they argue.

8.1.2 The Role of a Large Shareholder

In the former model the bidder is an outsider who makes a profit at the expense of the shareholders, who agree with the takeover in order to punish the existing management. It is known,[4] however, that large blockholders serve as an internal control on the managerial behavior and play an important role in takeovers. This provides an alternative defensive mechanism against bad management, through the possibility of proxy fights or tender offers from the large shareholders.

An extension of the former model seems to be in order, substituting for Assumption 8.1.1 with

Assumption 8.1.2. *There is one large minority shareholder who owns a given proportion of the shares, and there is a fringe of atomistic shareholders.*

This idea was formalized by Shleifer and Vishny (1986). Hereinafter the large shareholder will be referred to as L. Let α be the proportion of the shares owned by L. Since he/she is a minority, $0 < \alpha < \frac{1}{2}$. Also, let Z denote the random increase in the discounted market value generated by the substitution of an inefficient management.

Assume that the increase in value comes from the fact that L has privileged access to a new technology. Let I denote the probability of drawing a positive improvement value Z from a probability distribution $F(Z)$ with support on $(0, Z_{\max}]$. In this case, I can be thought of as research intensity. This probability (or research intensity) comes at a cost $c(I)$ satisfying $c' > 0$ and $c'' > 0$. Under these conditions, the bidder will move to make an offer if he/she can purchase $\frac{1}{2} - \alpha$ of the shares. The expected market value under the existing management being q, the tender price must be higher than q, say,

$$p = q + \pi,$$

where π must satisfy the condition

$$\frac{1}{2}Z - (0.5 - \alpha)\pi - c \geq 0, \tag{8.2}$$

such that the bid is profitable for the raider. For the small shareholders the expected benefit from a bid is

$$E[Z|0.5Z - (0.5 - \alpha)\pi - c \geq 0]$$

and therefore, to tender is the best strategy if

$$\pi - E[Z|Z - (1 - 2\alpha)\pi - 2c \geq 0] \geq 0. \tag{8.3}$$

The role of L is to define the tender price by choosing the value of π that minimizes the left-hand side of (8.3). The optimal value clearly depends on α. Let it be denoted by $\pi^*(\alpha)$. Notice that $\pi^*(\alpha)$ is just the expected value of an improvement, conditional on the takeover being profitable.

Shleifer and Vishny show that $\pi^*(\alpha)$ is unique and is a decreasing function of α. Notice that $\alpha = 0$ replicates the case of diffuse ownership discussed already. In this case, equation (8.2) implies that $Z > \pi$ is a necessary condition for a takeover to succeed. But under that condition no one tenders, reproducing the result of Grossman and Hart (1990).

Defining $Z^c(\alpha)$ as the cutoff value of Z that makes L indifferent between taking over and not (that is to say, the smallest value of Z satisfying (8.2) with $\pi \equiv \pi^*(\alpha)$), they show that $Z^c(\alpha)$ is a strictly decreasing function. Also, $I^*(\alpha)$, the optimal probability of drawing a positive value of Z, increases with α, the proportion of shares held by L.

In other words, the higher the proportion of shares held by L, the more he/she is willing to pay (for research, say) to increase the chances of getting a positive Z having a takeover in view, and the lower is the premium he/she is willing to pay to the other shareholders. Also, the lower is the improvement value of the profits that makes him/her indifferent to the takeover, and hence the more probable the takeover is. This result is quite intuitive, since the larger L is, the easier it will be for him/her to get control. This is so because he/she will have to buy fewer shares to get the 50%, which gives him/her more bargaining power in that trade, allowing him/her to pay a lower price. That is why π decreases with α.

To see how an increase in α affects the market value of the firm, notice that this market value may be written as

$$V(\alpha, q) = q + I^*(\alpha)\{1 - F[Z^c(\alpha)]\}E[Z|Z \geq Z^c(\alpha)].$$

This formula tells us that the value of the firm increases from the original value q by an amount that is proportional to the product of three factors: (1) the optimal probability of drawing a positive value of Z, (2) the expected value of increase in discounted market value generated by the substitution of an inefficient management, provided that it is above a certain minimum threshold that makes the investment worthwhile, $E[Z|Z \geq Z^c(\alpha)]$, and (3) the probability that such an increase in profits is above that threshold, $1 - F[Z^c(\alpha)]$.

Notice that all three of these terms depend on α, the fraction of the firm owned by the large shareholder L. The product of these three terms is the difference between the value q of the firm under the current management and the expected future value under the change of management. Thus, this product may be viewed as the expected conditional (on α) increase in value of the firm under change.

Shleifer and Vishny show that $\{1 - F[Z^c(\alpha)]\}E[Z|Z \geq Z^c(\alpha)]$ is increasing in α. It then follows that an increase in α, the proportion of shares held by L, results in an increase of the market value of the firm as well, leading to their first proposition:

Proposition 8.1.1 (Shleifer and Vishny, 1986). *An increase in the proportion of shares held by L results in a decrease in the takeover premium but an increase in the market value of the firm.*

Finally, it is also proved that an increase in the costs c have the opposite effect. That is to say, the premium rises, but the market value of the firm decreases. An increase in the costs has the same result as a decrease in the proportion of shares held by L.

Up to this point it has been assumed, among other things, that the large shareholder can improve the market values by the amount Z. Usually this requires the implementation of a new policy and, therefore, the change of the existing management. Moreover, it has also been implicitly assumed that the replacement of the management would be made as a consequence of a takeover that would give L the majority of the shares.

There are, however, other ways to change the management and implement the new policy—for instance, a *proxy fight*. In this case, the proportion of shares owned by L does not change. Supposing that the cost of a proxy fight is c_p, with $c_p < c$, his/her profit is

$$\alpha Z - c_p.$$

The fact that L can profit from Z on his/her own shares, means that if he/she makes a tender offer (at a higher cost) there will be an expropriation of the potential increment of wealth of the other shareholders.[5] Hence, under the conditions described, there should be no tender offers. The fact that tender offers exist may reflect high costs of proxy fights or simply that they are not effective means of obtaining the full value of the improvements.

An alternative means of management participation is through friendly negotiations, a process known as *jawboning*. Negotiation means compromise, and in this case it is assumed that L cannot impose the radical change of policy that he/she would like to see implemented, but only a partial one. The result is that the market value will not increase by Z but by a smaller amount—say, βZ, where $0 < \beta < 1$. The profits of L are then given by $\alpha \beta Z$. If, additionally, it is assumed that proxy fights are not allowed, a tender offer will be preferred to the friendly negotiations if

$$0.5Z - (0.5 - \alpha)\pi - c \geq \alpha \beta Z > 0$$

or

$$Z \geq \frac{0.5 - \alpha}{0.5 - \alpha\beta}\pi + \frac{1}{0.5 - \alpha\beta}c.$$

If the cost c of tendering is sufficiently large and β is large enough, it is possible that the preceding inequality is not satisfied and jawboning may occur. In any case, this practice is to be used whenever Z is not big enough or, in other words, for less-valuable improvements of the market values.

These results also suggest that large blocks are unlikely to be dissipated. In fact, since the value of the firm increases with α, it follows that if L sells some of his/her shares, the remaining shares will be worth less and the probability of a value-increasing takeover will be diminished. But this result could possibly tempt L to improve his/her gain by simply buying more shares. Unfortunately, this would not be possible, since the fringe shareholders would free-ride on that market value. That is to say, none of them would sell their shares (expecting some of the others to do it), so that they would also benefit from the value increase of the shares.

8.1.3 Uncertain Outcome of a Takeover

It was said that L chooses the value of π minimizing the left-hand side of (8.3). This value leaves the shareholders indifferent between tendering and not tendering. In such a case, it has been assumed that they tender their shares. A further step is to assume, as did Hirshleifer and Titman (1990), the following:

Assumption 8.1.3. *The decision of the shareholders is random.*

That is to say, there is a probability $P(\pi)$ that the bid is accepted. The reason for this probability to depend on π is the following: In a situation of uncertainty a high-gain bidder has an incentive to bid higher to ensure success. Doing so, he/she signals high gains and the shareholders who notice that do not tender, expecting to free-ride on those market values. For that reason low-gain bidders insist on making a low bid, in order to ensure the success of their bid. Therefore, shareholders infer that Z must be positively correlated with the bid, and they may more easily accept the low bids. However, it is not certain that this will happen, since high-Z bidders should be deterred from bidding low. The way to construct the probability $P(\pi)$ is to ensure that equilibrium is reached in which the bid is fully revealing with $\pi = Z$.

Let $\omega = 0.5 - \alpha$ and the cost $c = 0$. For a given $P(\pi)$, the goal of the bidder is to maximize his/her expected gain $G(\pi) = [0.5Z - (0.5 - \alpha)\pi]P(\pi)$:

$$\max_{\pi} G(\pi) = \max_{\pi}[0.5Z - (0.5 - \alpha)\pi]P(\pi)$$

$$= \max_{\pi}[\alpha Z + (Z - \pi)\omega]P(\pi).$$

The first-order condition is

$$\frac{\partial G}{\partial \pi} = P'(\pi)[\alpha Z + (Z - \pi)\omega] - P\omega = 0. \tag{8.4}$$

On the other hand, the situation of uncertainty under which the shareholders were in doubt between tendering and not tendering occurs when π satisfies $\pi = E(Z|\pi)$. In that case, the probability that shareholders tender is assumed to be $P(\pi)$. If π is below the solution of this equation, the probability of tender is zero, whereas if it is above, that probability becomes one. Equilibrium will occur at the situation of uncertainty. Clearly, for the shareholders it is ideal to tender with a probability $P(\pi)$ that supports a fully revealing equilibrium or, in other words, in such a way it forces the bidder to offer a bid $\pi = Z$. Such equilibrium is shown to exist in Hirshleifer and Titman (1990) and P is obtained by substituting $\pi = Z$ in equation (8.4). This leads to

$$\frac{P'}{P} = \frac{\omega}{\alpha \pi} \Rightarrow P(\pi) = k\pi^{\omega/\alpha}.$$

If there is a value Z_{max} of Z above which the shareholders tender with certainty, then $P(Z_{max}) = 1$ and it follows that

$$P(\pi) = (\pi/Z_{max})^{\omega/\alpha}. \tag{8.5}$$

Notice that if α is zero, the situation goes back to the one considered by Grossman and Hart. In fact, making $\alpha = 0$ and $\pi = Z$ simultaneously in (8.4), it follows that $P(\pi) = 0$. In other words, the bid will be unsuccessful with a probability of one, again reflecting the free-rider problem.

The net expected profit of the bidder should be positive. Hence,

$$\alpha Z P(\pi) - c = \alpha \pi (\pi/Z_{max})^{\omega/\alpha} - c = \alpha \pi^{\frac{1}{2\alpha}} Z_{max}^{-\omega/\alpha} - c \geq 0.$$

Since in equilibrium $\pi = Z$, the smaller bid will still have a positive expected profit, which is to say, the value of π satisfying the preceding equality will be the cutoff value Z^c. Hence, Z^c is the solution of

$$\alpha (Z^c)^{\frac{1}{2\alpha}} Z_{max}^{-\omega/\alpha} - c = 0$$

or

$$Z^c = (c/\alpha)^{2\alpha} Z_{max}^{2\omega}.$$

Hence, this value of Z^c is the critical value below which no offer is made. These results may be summarized in the following way: In the tender offer described, there is an equilibrium where there is a bid if $\pi \geq Z^c$, and there is no bid if $\pi < Z^c$. The tender offer will be successful with probability $P(\pi) = (\pi/Z_{max})^{\omega/\alpha}$ and the value of the bid, when it happens, is π.

This model has several empirical implications. For instance, from (8.5) it is seen that the probability of success of an offer increases both with the bid premium π and with the holdings of the bidder in the target α.

Another important implication is that the average bid premium declines with the size of the bidder's initial holdings, and increases with the number of shares needed to obtain control.

8.1.4 The Optimal Size of α before a Takeover

Until now, the number of shares held by L has been considered as given. However, according to the preceding reasoning, the proportion α is likely to affect the probability that a takeover is successful. Hence, it is a strategic variable, the optimal value of which can be established before a takeover attempt. This problem was formalized by Jegadeesh and Chowdhry (1994), assuming that the initial shareholdings is an endogenous variable to be determined so as to maximize the value of the firm, an assumption that replaces Assumption 8.1.2.

It is assumed that the bidder buys a fraction α of the shares in the open market at a current market price of zero. The value of α will be taken as a signal of his/her motivation to take the control. In his/her attempt to acquire a controlling interest, the bidder can purchase up to α_{max} shares in the open market, where $\alpha_{max} < 0.5$, and the actual number of shares $\alpha \in [0, \alpha_{max}]$ that the bidder acquires in the open market is determined endogenously.

The risk-neutral shareholder will not tender unless the bid is at least as large as the expected improvements of the profits, where both the bidder's toehold and the bid are considered as a signal; that is,

$$\pi \geq E(Z|\alpha, \pi).$$

This equation expresses the so-called *free-rider condition.* The value of the bid for the bidder is therefore[6]

$$G(\pi, \alpha; Z) = P(\pi)[0.5Z - (0.5 - \alpha)\pi], \tag{8.6}$$

and his/her problem is to maximize this value,

$$\max_{\pi, \alpha} G(\pi, \alpha; Z) \text{ subject to } \pi \geq E(Z|\alpha, \pi).$$

To obtain insightful results, two additional assumption are made:

Assumption 8.1.4. *The probability of a successful bid is increasing and concave in* π.

This assumption has several implications. The first is that G is a concave function in π. To see this, it is enough to differentiate equation (8.6) twice. In fact,

$$\frac{\partial G}{\partial \pi} = P'(\pi)[0.5Z - (0.5 - \alpha)\pi] - (0.5 - \alpha)P(\pi) \tag{8.7}$$

and

$$\frac{\partial^2 G}{\partial \pi^2} = P''(\pi)[0.5Z - (0.5 - \alpha)\pi] - 2(0.5 - \alpha)P'(\pi). \tag{8.8}$$

Since $0.5Z - (0.5 - \alpha)\pi$ is positive and $\alpha < 0.5$, the assumption ensures that (8.8) is negative and hence the value G is concave in π.

A second property is that, defining $\hat{\pi}(\alpha, Z)$ as the value of π that maximizes $G(\pi, \alpha; Z)$, it follows that $\hat{\pi}(\alpha, Z)$ increases with α. In fact, it is enough to notice that $\hat{\pi}$ must satisfy the first-order condition, making (8.7) equal to zero, or, in other words, it must satisfy

$$P'(\hat{\pi}(\alpha, Z))[0.5Z - (0.5 - \alpha)\hat{\pi}(\alpha, Z)] = (0.5 - \alpha)P(\hat{\pi}(\alpha, Z)).$$

Differentiating the preceding expression with respect to α, it follows that

$$\frac{\partial \hat{\pi}}{\partial \alpha} = -\frac{P(\hat{\pi}) + P'(\hat{\pi})\hat{\pi}}{P''(\hat{\pi})[0.5Z - (0.5 - \alpha)\hat{\pi}] - 2(0.5 - \alpha)P'(\hat{\pi})}.$$

It is easily verified that both numerator and denominator are negative, and hence the result that $\hat{\pi}$ increases with α follows.

Finally, the value of the bid $G(\pi, \alpha; Z)$ is increasing with Z. This is simply verified by derivating (8.6) with respect to Z. This gives $0.5P(\pi)$, which is clearly positive.

Taking α_{max} as defined before, a second assumption is made:

Assumption 8.1.5. *The constraint imposed by the free-rider condition is binding for all bidder types.*

Formally,

$$Z > \hat{\pi}(\alpha_{max}, Z) > \hat{\pi}(\alpha, Z).$$

This assumption implies that, in the absence of the free-rider constraint, all bidder types would prefer to bid less than their value of Z, and would prefer to bid as low as $\hat{\pi}(Z, \alpha)$. In their work, Jegadeesh and Chowdhry establish two preliminary results that are useful for analyzing one such equilibrium.

Their first result states that, in the absence of the free-rider constraint, the value of bidding high is increasing in the bidder's type Z. This result means that, for any initial value of α, the benefit derived from bidding low is the same regardless of the valuation of the bidder. Bidding low clearly reduces the cost of purchasing the shares. However, it also reduces the probability of success. The reduced probability of success hurts the high bidder more, since he/she has more to gain from the takeover. Therefore, the net benefit of bidding low is higher to the bidder with lower Z.

The second result says that, in the absence of the free-rider constraint, the cost of choosing any level of initial α is identical for the bidder regardless of his/her value of Z. The intuition behind this result is as follows: The cost of choosing a lower level of initial α is that after the bid, the additional shares required in order to have control will be more expensive. However, this expected cost does not depend on the value of Z.

The type of equilibrium obtained in this bid is discussed in detail by Jegadeesh and Chowdhry. There will be no pooling equilibrium—that is, an equilibrium in which α has no value as a signal and $\hat{\pi}$ is equal for all the bidders.

To see why such an equilibrium would not hold, suppose there are two bidders, with different values of Z—say, Z_L and Z_H with $Z_L < Z_H$. Assume that the unconditional expected value of Z is $E(Z) = Z_M$, such that $Z_L < Z_M < Z_H$.

Since in a pooling equilibrium the minimum value of the bid has to be the expected value of Z in order to avoid the free-rider problem and α plays no signaling role, every bidder will choose to bid Z_M with α_m in hand.

This equilibrium does not hold because the bidder with Z_L is bidding above his/her valuation. His/her strategy to escape from that situation is to bid Z_L with a lower value of α (say, α') to be chosen such that the other bidder does not have an incentive to mimic him/her. That is to say, α' must satisfy

$$G(Z_L, \alpha'; Z_H) = G(Z_M, \alpha_m; Z_H).$$

It may be shown that in such a situation the low-valuation bidder is strictly better off, which is to say

$$G(Z_L, \alpha'; Z_L) > G(Z_M, \alpha_m; Z_L)$$

and hence the pooling equilibrium does not survive.[7] Moreover, the new equilibrium is stable and easily extended to any finite number of bidders, as Jegadeesh and Chowdhry (1994) point out.

The cost of moving to a lower value α' is the same for all types (result 2), whereas the benefit of bidding a lower Z value is higher for the lower types (result 1). This breaks the pooling equilibrium, since the lower type has an incentive to credibly communicate that his/her valuation is lower by choosing a lower value of α.

The basic empirical implication of this model, which strongly contrasts with the earlier approaches, is that the bid premium should increase with α. It is interesting to notice that at the root of this difference from the other two models is the competition between bidders. The bargaining power given by large α decreases in the presence of competitors. Hence, the incentive for big values of α disappears and, in competition, bidders tend to have lower values for α.

Within this model, this result is obtained by the following mechanism: With different valuations by two bidders, neither of them acquires as many shares as he could in the market prior to the tender offer, even if the market price is lower than what he would be willing to pay. In this way, they credibly signal their type, and bid a lower amount in the tender offer.

8.1.5 Exercises

The next four exercises are related to Grossman and Hart (1990).

1. Show that if the bidder owns some shares of the targeted firm, it is still profitable to bid when $p \geq v$.
2. Show that when $v - \phi < p < q$, there are two rational equilibria.
3. Explain in detail the intuition behind the effect of an increase of ϕ over r.
4. Prove that if $\tilde{v}$ is stochastic and c is deterministic, raids may occur.
5. When there is a large shareholder, explain and show what happens to the following variables as the large shareholder becomes larger:
   - (a) The tender offer, $\pi(\alpha)$.
   - (b) The cutoff value of Z, $Z^c(\alpha)$.
   - (c) The market value of the firm, $V(\alpha, q)$.

   Assume now that $c = 0$ and let $F(Z)$ be the uniform distribution on $[0, 1]$. Solve for the values of $\pi(\alpha)$ and the cutoff value $Z^c(\alpha)$. Verify the relationships derived earlier in the exercise.
6. If we assume that shareholders are willing to dilute their own rights, how does the probability of accepting the bid change when the outcome of a takeover is uncertain. (Assume that the amount of dilution has a fixed component a and a proportional component b.)
7. Prove results 1 and 2 of Jegadeesh and Chowdhry, which were discussed previously.
8. In the discussion of a pooling equilibrium in the context of Jegadeesh and Chowdhry (1994), assume that $\alpha_m = 0.3$ and that there are two types of bidders with $Z_L = 40$ and $Z_H = 80$. Assume further that 60% are of the high-Z type and that $P(\pi) = \ln(\pi)$. Conditional on this information, show that there is no pooling equilibrium.
9. Compare the results obtained by Jegadeesh and Chowdhry and by Shleifer and Vishny regarding the bid premium as a function of α.

8.2 Merger Bids

In all the models previously described, a bid was made to the shareholders in order to obtain a certain fraction of shares. The main difference between these discussed tender offers and merger bids is that in the latter case, bids are directed to the management. In this section, competition between bidders is first examined. The issue of the ideal means of payment is then introduced to analyze how cash payment becomes a preemptive instrument in the competition between bidders. Finally, the issue of how management resists a hostile takeover by an alternative management is discussed.

8.2.1 *Competition between Bidders*

The first model to be described here along these lines is the one by Fishman (1988) in which there are two bidders (say, bidder 1 and bidder 2), who make successive bids until only one remains. The remaining bid is accepted by the target, provided that its value is greater than or equal to the value v, which is assumed to be reasonable by the target. Otherwise, there is no takeover. Here, v is taken as the current market value of the target, assuming that there is no takeover.

Let bidder 1 be the first to make an offer. The costs c_i for $i = 1, 2$ of the bid are the costs to the bidders of private observation of their own valuations $v_i, i = 1, 2$. Furthermore, it is assumed that the valuations are random variables such that $E(\tilde{v}_i) < v$. This means that bidders never make a bid without first observing whether the realization of their valuation is above v. If p is the initial offer made by bidder 1, it must be such that $v \le p \le v_1$ and at the same time makes competition unattractive to bidder 2. In other words, the expected payoff from competing to bidder 2 should be nonpositive.

The payoffs can be expressed simply in terms of a variable d that takes the value 0 if bidder 2 does not compete and takes 1 otherwise. For any two random realizations of v_1 and v_2 the payoff for bidder 1 is

$$\Pi_1(v_1, v_2, p, d) = v_1 - (1 - d)p - d \min[\max(p, v_2), v_1] - c_1 \qquad (8.9)$$

and for bidder 2 is

$$\Pi_2(v_1, v_2, p, d) = d[(v_2 - \min(v_2, v_1) - c_2]. \qquad (8.10)$$

Bidder 2 does not have access to v_1 as bidder 1 does not know v_2. But both of them know the densities of probabilities $f_i(v_i)$, which are assumed to be strictly positive in a closed interval $[l, h]$ and zero elsewhere. It is clear that if p is very large, it will discourage bidder 2 from making a higher bid. If it is not too costly, the ideal for bidder 1 is to find the threshold above which bidder 2 will not even incur the cost of being informed of his/her valuation v_2. Denoting this threshold by r, it must be such that the expected payoff of bidder 2 conditional on $v_1 \ge r$ is zero:

$$\frac{\int_r^h E_{v_2} \Pi_2(v_1, \tilde{v}_2, p, 1) f_1(v_1) dv_1}{\int_r^h f_1(v_1) dv_1} = 0.$$

For any bid v' higher than r, the expected payoff of bidder 2 will be negative. On the other hand, bidder 1 will be able to preempt only if $v_1 > r$. In the event that $v_1 \le r$, his/her best alternative is to offer v.

Therefore, if he/she preempts, the gain he/she gets for doing so at an offer price p' is

$$E_{v_2} \Pi_1(v_1, \tilde{v}_2, p', 0) - E_{v_2} \Pi_1(v_1, \tilde{v}_2, v, 1) = E_{v_2} \min[\max(v, \tilde{v}_2), v_1] - p'.$$

Let the highest price that bidder 1 is willing to pay be denoted by $\bar{p}(v_1)$. It has to be such that the preceding gain is still positive. Noticing that the gain is decreasing in p', it follows that

$$\bar{p}(v_1) = E_{v_2} \min[\max(v, \tilde{v}_2), v_1].$$

It can be shown that it is an equilibrium to bidder 1 to offer $\bar{p}(r)$ if $v_1 \geq r$ and v otherwise, whereas for bidder 2 it is an equilibrium not to bid in the first case and to bid in the second. It is a signaling equilibrium, although it is not fully revealing.

This model implies several things. It is clear that the expected payoff of bidder 1 increases with the cost c_2, since it is easier to preempt the entry of bidder 2 (r decreases). If the first bid can be lower, the expected payoff of the target's shareholders will also be lower. Hence it is in the interest of the target to lower the costs in order to improve competition among the bidders. However, there is a trade-off there, since if the costs of bidder 2 are too low, bidder 1 is discouraged from participating at all, eliminating the competition among the bidders.

A second implication of this model is that the expected payoff to the target conditional on observing a high initial bid is greater than the profit conditional on observing a low initial bid.

Another interesting effect is related to takeover regulations. If the law lowers the costs to competing bidders (through *disclosure* regulations, for instance), the expected payoffs of targets and second bidders would increase for the reasons mentioned before and the expected payoff of first bidders would decrease. Under these circumstances, competition among bidders is enforced and a higher frequency of multiple-bidder contests must be observed.

In all the models discussed until now in this section, it has been implicitly assumed that payment in a takeover would be made in cash. However, there are alternative means of payments such as stock.

8.2.2 Choosing the Means of Payment

In a model developed by Hansen (1987), payment is made either in cash or in stock of the merged corporation. The basis of the mechanism that makes management and bidder prefer one or the other (either cash or stock) is asymmetry of information.

The acquirer owns a firm of value x, which is known to both the acquirer and the target's management. The target firm is worth v to itself, but has a value $w(v) \geq v$ to the acquirer. The value of a merger will therefore be $x + v$. The asymmetry enters assuming that the bidder does not know the value of the firm v, but the current management does. Then, the target will never accept an offer below that value in a cash trade. This creates an adverse selection problem, against which the acquirer can protect himself/herself, defining his/her optimal strategy not on unconditional expected profit, but on expected profit conditional on the offer being accepted.

The acquirer takes v as a random variable with support on the closed interval $[v_l, v_h]$. For a cash offer C, the expected profit of the raider is an expectation conditional on the acceptance of the offer—that is to say, conditional on $v_l < v < C$. If $f(v)$ denotes the density of probability of v,

$$E(\Pi_r | C) = \int_{v_l}^{C} [w(v) - C] f(v) \, dv.$$

Denoting by $F(v)$ the distribution of v and by $E(w|C)$ the expected value of the target to the acquirer conditional on sale,

$$E(w|C) = \frac{1}{F(C)} \int_{v_l}^{C} w(v) f(v) \, dv,$$

the expected conditional wealth gain can be rewritten as

$$E(\Pi_r | C) = F(C)[E(w|C) - C].$$

The optimal cash offer C must satisfy the first-order condition

$$w(C) - C - \frac{F(C)}{f(C)} = 0$$

together with the obvious restrictions of positive expected profit

$$E(\Pi_r | C) \geq 0$$

and $v_l \leq C \leq v_h$. If $E(\Pi_r | C) < 0$, which is to say when $C > E(w|C)$, or if the solution is at v_l, no cash trade will take place.

But if the bidder offers stock of the merged firm (say, a proportion β), trade may still occur. From the point of view of the acquirer, such a trade is in the interest of the target with certainty if the final value held by the owners of the target is greater than or equal to v for whatever current value $v \in [v_l, v_h]$. It will be in the interest of the target with probability $F(v^*)$ if the same inequality holds for any $v \in [v_l, v^*]$. If the management of the target knows the function w, this means that with probability $F(v^*)$ trade is good for the target if

$$\beta[x + w(v)] \geq v \ \forall v \in [v_l, v^*]$$

or

$$\beta \geq \frac{v}{x + w(v)} \ \forall v \in [v_l, v^*], \tag{8.11}$$

which is equivalent to

$$\beta \geq \max_v \frac{v}{x + w(v)}.$$

Making Hansen's additional assumption that

$$\frac{dw}{dv} < \frac{x + w(v)}{v}$$

the preceding condition becomes simply

$$\beta[x + w(v^*)] \geq v^*.$$

More easily, the acquirer will be interested only if the value held by him/her after the transaction is greater than the current value. In other words,

$$(1 - \beta)[x + E(w|v^*)] \geq x. \tag{8.12}$$

These two conditions hold simultaneously if

$$\frac{E(w|v^*)}{\beta} - E(w|v^*) \geq x \geq \frac{v^*}{\beta} - w(v^*),$$

implying that

$$x \leq \frac{w(v^*) - v^*}{v^* - E(w|v^*)} E(w|v^*).$$

In a stock offer the expected wealth of the acquirer will be

$$F(v^*)(1 - \beta)[E(w|v^*) + x] + [1 - F(v^*)]x. \tag{8.13}$$

The optimal β for the acquirer is found by maximizing the preceding expression. It is possible to show that $F(v^*)$, the probability of success of a stock trade at optimal β, is decreasing in x. As we notice that v^* is defined through the maximization of (8.13), this last result is achieved by implicitly evaluating the derivative of v^* with respect to x from the first-order condition and using the second-order one to show that $dv^*/dx < 0$.

The conditions under which cash or stock trades with a given probability are possible are, therefore, established. Of course, it is possible that they are simultaneous. In such a case, for each feasible cash offer there will be a stock offer with the same probability of success that will be preferred by the acquirer. To see this, notice that the expected wealth of the acquirer after a cash offer C equals

$$F(C)[E(w|C) - C] + x. \tag{8.14}$$

Constructing a stock offer with β given by

$$\beta^* = \frac{C}{x + w(C)},$$

it is known from (8.11) that it will have the same probability of success $F(C)$ as a cash offer of value C. The acquirer's expected wealth in this case will be

$$F(C)(1 - \beta^*)[E(w|C) + x] + [1 - F(C)]x.$$

It is a simple algebraic exercise to check that this expression is greater than the one in (8.14). Therefore, in the situation described up to now in this model, no cash offers will occur, and only stock trade is possible.

Although stock trade dominates the scene, an essential outcome of the model is the fact that the acquirer's expected gain from the optimal stock offer decreases with x. The expected profit can be written by subtracting the original wealth x from the expected wealth in (8.13), giving

$$E(\Pi_r|\beta) = F(v^*)\{E(w|v^*) - \beta[E(w|v^*) + x]\},$$

with the optimal β satisfying

$$\beta = \frac{v^*}{x + w(v^*)}.$$

The preceding statement is easily verified differentiating the expected profit with respect to x and checking that this derivative is negative. Hence, stock offers in the simple context described here are always preferred by the acquirer to cash offers, but their advantages are decreasing with the acquirer's size.

This result was shown by Hansen and used to formulate some considerations on how to offset the dominance of stock offers, making the choice between stock and cash trade nontrivial.

The first observation regards the fact that cash and stock transactions are differently taxed. This may generate a net benefit from using cash transactions, supposedly independent of the acquirer's size x. Now, it is known that the expected profit under stock offers, even if it decreases with x, is always above the expected profit of a cash transaction. The argument in favor of cash offers is that the net benefit from cash transactions may equalize the expected profits at a certain size x^*, so cash offers are preferred by acquirers with $x > x^*$.

The second way to allow for cash trade in this model is to introduce more information asymmetry on the side of the acquirer. Assume that the value of the acquiring company is known only by the acquirer. The target is supposed to infer the true x in equilibrium through the offer made by the acquirer. Therefore, in this signaling equilibrium, the target takes the value of the acquirer as a function of β, $x \equiv x(\beta)$.

In this situation, the acquirer may be tempted to cheat with a lower β, signaling a higher value of x. But since the relationship

$$\beta = \frac{v^*}{x(\beta) + w(v^*)}$$

would still have to hold, this would decrease the probability of success of the offer and the acquirer's expected gain, as discussed before. In other words, there is a cost in that not so many states of the target can be acquired. In this new equilibrium, the optimal β must be the one that compensates benefits and costs. Of course, these costs will be higher for lower values of x. In other words, the higher x is, the more difficult it will be for the acquirer to try to be overvalued. Equilibrium will, in fact, require it to be undervalued for high enough x. In general, the optimal β will be different from the optimal β when the acquirer's value is publicly known.

The target, however, knowing these two effects well, will work out the function $x(\beta)$ that gives the correct value of x. In other words, the target knows x through a value of β that would not have been optimal had he/she possessed that information from the beginning. Hence, the expected profit for the acquirer will be lower than in a situation in which x is publicly known.

Hence, the basic conclusion is that bidders may prefer to offer cash instead of stock when its value is high, which is to say, if their equity is undervalued. Recalling equation (8.12), this means that β would be evaluated as

$$\beta = 1 - \frac{\bar{x}}{\bar{x} + E(w|v^*)}$$

with $\bar{x} < x$, which is higher than

$$1 - \frac{x}{x + E(w|v^*)}$$

since this function is decreasing with x. A higher β represents more wealth that the acquirer is offering to give up, and, depending upon how large this difference is, he/she might prefer a cash offer. This result is quite intuitive, since one always prefers to buy undervalued issues, not to sell them.

8.2.3 Cash as a Preemptive Instrument with Many Bidders

In the paper of Hansen, there is only one acquirer for the target. Fishman (1989) developed a model for choice of means of payment that allows more potential acquirers. In this model it is possible to see how the presence of competing bidders may affect the choice of the means of payment differently.

His idea was to extend his model of preempting bids discussed before, making the choice of the means of payment a reinforcing preemptive device.

The model is basically Fishman's earlier model, but the profit of the bidders will depend on an additional variable $\theta \in \{1, 0\}$ describing the chosen means of payment (1 for cash and 0 for issuing debt). In the event of a debt offer, p will denote its face value.

Since the value of a debt offer is state contingent, it is assumed that the target costlessly observes a private signal s that conveys information on both bidders' valuations. It is supposed that s may assume only two possible values, s^+ and s^-, referring respectively to a "good" and a "bad" state of the world, with probabilities γ and $1 - \gamma$. The valuations of the bidders will also depend on the state of the world that they infer. In other words, it is as if the density functions f_i depended on s. The value of any variable of interest will be labeled with a "+" if it is conditional on $s = s^+$ and with a "−" if conditional on $s = s^-$. For instance, it is assumed that $v_i^+ > v_i^-$. That is to say, for any bidder the valuation is higher in the good state of the world. Hence, the assumption that any bidder 1's offer face value is between v and v_1 may read

$$v \leq p \leq v_1^+.$$

In particular, a debt offer with face value p is worth $\min\{v_i^+, p\} \geq v$ if $s = s^+$ and $\min\{v_i^-, p\} < v$ if $s = s^-$. Thus, the target will accept the offer if $s = s^+$ and will reject it if $s = s^-$.

The main difference between a debt and a cash offer is that the value of the cash offer does not depend on the state of the world. Thus, cash offers cannot induce the target to make an efficient acceptance/rejection decision.

The profit itself will depend, directly and indirectly, on the state of the world. Introducing a variable δ that equals 1 when $s = s^+$ and 0 when $s = s^-$, the profits in (8.9) and (8.10) are replaced by

$$\Pi_1(v_1, v_2, \delta, p, \theta, d) = [\theta + (1 - \theta)\delta]v_1 - [\theta(1 - \delta) + \delta(1 - d)]p$$
$$- d\delta \min[\max(p, v_2), v_1] - c_1$$
$$\Pi_2(v_1, v_2, \delta, p, \theta, d) = d\{\delta[v_2 - \min(v_2, v_1)] - c_2\} \qquad (8.15)$$

for bidder 1 and bidder 2, respectively.

As before, bidder 1 tries to find the threshold r for the firm value above which bidder 2 will have zero profit. In other words, r is implicitly defined through

$$\frac{\int_r^h E_{v_2} \Pi_2(v_1, \tilde{v}_2, \delta, p, \theta, 1) f_1(v_1) dv_1}{\int_r^h f_1(v_1) dv_1} = 0.$$

For any bid v' higher than r, the expected payoff of bidder 2 will be negative. On the other hand, bidder 1 will be able to preempt only if $v_1 > r$. Therefore, the expected gain of preempting at an offer price p', other things constant, is

$$E\Pi_1(v_1, \tilde{v}_2, \delta, p', \theta, 0) - E\Pi_1(v_1, \tilde{v}_2, \delta, p', \theta, 1)$$
$$= \gamma\{E_{v_2} \min[\max(p', \tilde{v}_2^+), v_1^+] - p'\}.$$

This expression is clearly increasing in v_1. Hence, high-valuing first bidders stand to lose more in an auction and thus have a greater incentive to deter competition.

On the other hand, the expected gain of making a debt offer compared to a cash offer at face value p', other things constant, is

$$E\Pi_1(v_1, \tilde{v}_2, \delta, p', 0, d) - E\Pi_1(v_1, \tilde{v}_2, \delta, p', 1, d) = (1 - \gamma)[p' - v_1^-].$$

This gain is decreasing in v_1. From these two results it appears that first bidders will tend to preempt with cash whenever they have a high valuation for the target, and will possibly make a debt offer if they do not intend to preempt. This fact, however, does not strictly prevent low-valuing first bidders from preempting with a debt offer, but their offers will be restricted by their low valuations.

Now, let us cross these two pieces of information. Let $p_d(v_1)$ denote the highest face value of an offer that bidder 1 is willing to make in order to preempt. It has to be such that the preceding gain of preempting is zero. As we notice that the gain is decreasing in p', it follows that

$$p_d(v_1) = E \min[\max(v, \tilde{v}_2^+), v_1^+].$$

As for a cash offer, its maximum value $p_c(v_1)$ is defined by a zero expected profit from both preempting and paying in cash, which is to say, $p_c(v_1)$ must satisfy

$$\gamma\{E_{v_2} \min[\max(p_c(v_1), \tilde{v}_2^+), v_1^+] - p_c(v_1)\} = (1 - \gamma)[p_c(v_1) - v_1^-]$$

or

$$p_c(v_1) = \gamma E_{v_2} \min[\max(v, \tilde{v}_2^+), v_1^+] + (1 - \gamma)v_1^-.$$

It is possible to show that there exists a perfect sequential equilibrium such that the optimal strategy of bidder 1 is to make a debt offer of value v if he/she cannot preempt (which is to say, if $v \leq v_1 \leq r$) or to make a cash offer with value $p_c(r)$ if preemption is possible (in other words, if $v_1 > r$).

The optimal strategy of bidder 2, on the other hand, will be to compete if bidder 1 made a debt offer with face value lower than $p_d(r)$ or if he/she made a cash offer of value lower than $p_c(r)$. If bidder 1's cash offer equals (or is greater than) $p_c(r)$, bidder 2 does not compete.

Hence, it is clear that in the context of this model, the only reason why bidder 1 would use a cash offer would be to preempt bidder 2 from going into an auction process and to decide the takeover in his/her favor at the first offer. The preemptive mechanism works only if the first offer is large enough, and this will happen only if bidder 1 infers a high target value. Here, a cash offer is therefore a signal of high value of the target as opposed to Hansen's model, in which cash offers signal undervalued bidder's equity. The essential difference between the two situations is that in Fishman's model, there is competition (or potential competition) between bidders that destroys the "natural" results of the one bidder—one target case discussed by Hansen.

8.2.4 The Choice of Takeover Methods

When describing the different mechanisms of change of control of a corporation in the beginning of this section, a difference was made between friendly and unfriendly takeovers. Most of the models discussed up to this point do not treat this subject or just touch upon it in a superficial way, such as the one by Shleifer and Vishny (1986).

A paper by Harris and Raviv (1988) goes into greater depth in exploring the determinants of corporate takeover methods and their outcomes and price effects.

In their model there are three types of agent: the incumbent management, a rival management, and a large number of atomistic shareholders. To finance the $1 investment required, the incumbent may issue common stock and (nonvoting) debt. It is assumed that the only effect of debt is to increase the fraction of votes controlled by one of the contenders. Since debt reduces the value of the incumbent's control, in the absence of a takeover threat there will be no debt.

It is assumed that the management currently in control has one of two possible levels of ability (say, 1 and 2), with probabilities k and $(1-k)$, respectively. The present value of cash flows Y depends only on the ability of the management; its two possible values are denoted, respectively, Y_1 and Y_2, with $Y_1 > Y_2$.

The expected value of the firm is

$$Y_I = kY_1 + (1-k)Y_2.$$

The incumbent is supposed to have all its wealth W_I invested in the firm. Thus the fraction of the firm owned by the incumbent is

$$\alpha = \frac{W_I^*}{Y_I} \text{ with } W_I^* = W_I + Y_I - 1.$$

What happens when there is a takeover threat? This model assumes that there are benefits to being in control of the firm in addition to those that originate in net cash flows. In the event that there is a rival management trying to take over, the incumbent, to the extent that he/she owns stock in the firm, should not be opposed to the takeover if he/she believes that the rival has a higher ability. Benefits from control, however, provide contenders with incentives to vote for themselves regardless of their beliefs.

When the rival appears, the incumbent may choose, as an antitakeover device, to issue debt in exchange for equity, with the entire exchange being completed before the rival purchases equity. The value of the equity for a debt level D and controlling management of ability $i = 1, 2$ is denoted by $E_i(D)$, and it is assumed that $E_1 > E_2$ and E is decreasing with D. Then the incumbent's share of the equity becomes

$$\alpha_I(D) = \alpha Y(D)/E(D)$$

where $Y(D)$ denotes the value of the firm when the face value of the debt is D. Under Harris and Raviv's assumptions given the ability of the incumbent management, the value of the firm is not affected by the debt level. In other words, the dependence of Y on D appears only because the debt level affects the determination of who controls the firm. It follows that $\alpha_I(0) = \alpha$.

Also, assuming that the rival management invests its wealth W_R in the firm's stock, and given that the incumbent already has α_I, his/her share will be

$$\alpha_R(D) = \min\{W_R/E(D), 1 - \alpha_I(D)\},$$

and the passive investors will retain the rest:

$$\alpha_P(D) = 1 - \alpha_R(D) - \alpha_I(D).$$

The goal of the incumbent is to maximize the value of his/her shares plus the expected benefits of control. Denoting by $K(D)$ the benefits of control to the incumbent given a debt level D, the incumbent's problem is to choose D in such a way as to maximize

$$\alpha Y(D) + K(D). \tag{8.16}$$

Given the resulting distribution of ownership $(\alpha_P, \alpha_R, \alpha_I)$, the incumbent's share of the votes in any control contest consists of his/her own votes plus a fraction q_1 or q_2 of the passive votes, depending on his/her ability i, where $q_1 > q_2$. Here, q_i is the exogenous fraction of the passive shareholders voting for the incumbent, given his/her ability is i.

Hence, if the incumbent is of ability i, he/she will have $\alpha_I + q_i \alpha_P$ votes. It is clear that this number depends on the debt level. But on the other hand, the outcome of the takeover attempt depends on the number of votes on the side of the incumbent and therefore on the debt level choice.

For instance, a *successful tender offer* occurs in a situation in which the incumbent (even if of higher ability) will not get 50% of the votes. Formally, a tender offer is successful if D is chosen so as to satisfy

$$\alpha_I(D) + q_2 \alpha_P(D) \geq \frac{1}{2}. \tag{8.17}$$

If the management decides not to resist the tender offer, it will choose the value of D that maximizes (8.16) but is subject to (8.17), defining in this way the optimal debt level D^s. Since the only reason (assumed in this model) to issue debt is to avoid takeovers, it is not difficult to argue that $D^s = 0$.

An *unsuccessful tender offer* occurs for levels of debt D such that this number of votes for the incumbent is greater than 0.5 even if the incumbent is of low ability. In such a case, the rival will not take the control of the target. That is to say, the incumbent's maximization problem is

$$\max_{D \geq 0} \alpha Y(D) + K(D)$$

subject to

$$\alpha_I(D) + q_1\alpha_P(D) < \frac{1}{2}.$$

The authors easily show that the optimal debt level D^u that solves the preceding problem is 0 if

$$\alpha + q_2[1 - \alpha - W_R/Y_I] \geq \frac{1}{2},$$

is given by the solution of

$$W_I^*/E(D^u) + q_2[1 - (W_I^* + W_R)/E(D^u)] = \frac{1}{2}$$

if $W_I^* \geq W_R$, or otherwise by the solution of

$$\frac{W_I^*}{E(D^u)} = \frac{1}{2}.$$

Finally, a proxy fight is a situation in which the incumbent gets more than 50% of the votes only if it is of type 1. The optimal debt level D^p for this case is, therefore, the solution of

$$\max_{D \geq 0} \alpha Y(D) + K(D)$$

subject to

$$\alpha_I(D) + q_1\alpha_P(D) \geq \frac{1}{2}$$

and

$$\alpha_I(D) + q_2\alpha_P(D) < \frac{1}{2}.$$

In this case, the optimal debt level D^p that solves the preceding problem is 0 if

$$\alpha + q_1[1 - \alpha - W_R/Y_P] \geq \frac{1}{2},$$

where $Y(P)$ is now the value of the firm when the debt level is such that a proxy fight occurs. This level of debt D^p leads to a value of equity $E(D^p)$. Hence, D^p must satisfy

$$\alpha Y_P/E(D^p) + q_1[1 - (\alpha Y_P + W_R)/E(D^p)] = \frac{1}{2}$$

if $\alpha Y_P > W_R$. Otherwise, proxy fights cannot occur.

These values of optimal debt levels can be substituted in (8.16) to see what the preferred strategy of the incumbent will be. It follows that if the incumbent can keep control without issuing debt (the case in an unsuccessful tender offer), this alternative is preferred to a proxy fight. Similarly, if a proxy fight is feasible, the incumbent prefers this case to a successful tender offer.

Empirical implications can be derived from the preceding results regarding the average behavior of the stock price of target firms:

- It does not change in an unsuccessful tender offer and increases in a successful tender offer.
- It increases more in a successful proxy fight than in an unsuccessful proxy fight.
- It increases more in a successful tender offer than in a successful proxy fight.
- It increases more in an unsuccessful proxy fight than in an unsuccessful tender offer.

Regarding capital structure changes, it follows from the model that on average

- Takeover targets increase their debt levels.
- Targets of successful tender offers issue less debt than other targets.
- If the majority of passive investors vote for the incumbent when he/she is, in fact, of higher ability, then targets of unsuccessful tender offers issue more debt than targets of proxy fights.
- When the rival is successful in a proxy fight, debt issue is greater than when he/she is unsuccessful.

Therefore, the result of this model is a theory that relates capital structure changes to the type, outcome, and price effects of takeover activities.

8.2.5 Empirical Evidence

Up to now only theoretical models of mergers and tender offers have been discussed so we can understand their mechanisms and try to develop some intuition about what the expected outcome would be.

But mergers and tender offers do exist in real life. The purpose of this section is to compare what the market has to say with the set of possible theoretical explanations for different phenomena worked out already.

In fact, some of the models arrive at contradictory conclusions, as stressed in the previous section. For instance, Jegadeesh and Chowdhry claim that the premium per share in a takeover should decrease with the toehold of the bidder, whereas Shleifer and Vishny assure us that the opposite effect occurs. Also, Fishman states that bidders prefer cash trade in order to preempt other offers, whereas Hansen claims that whenever such trade occurs, it is for a completely different reason—namely, that the bidder's own equity is undervalued.

It is for the market to say who is right or, in other words, to provide evidence about which of the underlying theoretical hypotheses are dominant. Unfortunately, such empirical evidence is not entirely unambiguous, and some issues are left open. Also, many empirical results open the way to other possible explanations not explored in the models just discussed. For instance, an issue that has not been examined is whether these transactions are more profitable for bidders or for the target.

According to Jensen and Ruback (1983), in tender offers target shareholders earn returns of 30% on average while the bidders earn only 4%. In the case of mergers, these numbers are, respectively, 20% and 0.

Two questions immediately arise from these empirical numbers. The first is why the gains to the bidders are so small compared to those of the targets' shareholders, and the second is why returns are higher in tender offers.

Returns to bidders may be lower than returns to targets for many reasons:

- There may be competition among the bidders. As discussed in the theoretical models, this fact may induce bidders to pay higher premiums, thereby decreasing their gains and increasing the returns of the targets.
- Bidders are usually much larger than targets. Hence, bidders' returns are perhaps smaller than targets' returns, but their total gains may be much greater in dollars.
- The return to the bidder may be low around the time of acquisition. But in a sufficiently large time scale between the announcement and the acquisition, this may be different, since the stock prices are supposed to change due to the announcement.
- Management may behave opportunistically, being driven, not by the shareholder value, but, rather, by other goals such as diversification and growth.
- Management may be incompetent in acquiring other firms—for instance, overpaying for targets because they overestimate their own restructuring abilities.
- Markets are informationally inefficient, which is to say, merger announcements incorporate information effects. In this case, one would make an acquisition because there would be private information that the stock is undervalued, for instance.

On the other hand, tender offers provide higher returns to targets than do mergers for two reasons:

- Tender offers are less friendly than mergers. Hence, in mergers changes in the management are less likely and wealth gains are expected to be smaller. In spite of the fact that mergers and jawbonings are different things, this is roughly the same reasoning used by Shleifer and Vishny.
- In mergers, target shareholders are usually paid by the shares of the bidder, while in tender offers, they are paid with cash.

The last reason, the choice of payment method, may be important on three grounds:

1. *Taxes:* Transactions in cash are taxed. Therefore, the target shareholders demand a higher premium in order to be compensated for that apparent disadvantage. Among others, Hansen (1987) formally analyzed this hypothesis in his model discussed before, and Hayn (1989) has shown empirical evidence of this fact. However, Franks, Harris, and Mayer (1988) report higher premiums for cash offers in the U.K. before the introduction of law taxing capital gains. Thus, while this kind of consideration may help in understanding the choice of means of payment, it does not provide a complete explanation.

2. *Signaling:* This is the underlying argument of both Hansen (1987) and Fishman (1989). The bidder's choice to pay in cash may simply mean either that he/she knows the high potential synergetic value of the acquisition or that he/she thinks his/her own shares are undervalued.[8] In both cases, to pay in cash is an optimistic signal to the market that the bidder expects the value of the target.

3. *Agency costs:* This argument is due to Jensen (1986). It states that to pay in cash creates value because it eliminates free cash flows that otherwise could be spent on unprofitable projects.

Hence there are two different effects that may increase the target shareholders' returns: a *tender offer effect* and a *cash effect*. Empirical works controlling for these two factors in acquisitions lead to ambiguous conclusions. Franks, Harris, and Myer (1988) conclude that the first effect dominates the second, but Huang and Walking (1987) seem to arrive at the conclusion that the method of acquisition does not have any marginal explanatory power.

Up to now, all this discussion has been generated on the basis of two questions—namely, why are the gains to the bidders so small compared to the gains to the target's shareholders and why are returns higher in tender offers and smaller in mergers. A number of reasons were outlined already, most of which are plausibly good explanations for the empirical evidence. Other indirect reasons for the observed returns exist—almost all of them somehow related to the arguments just given. Among them are industry factors, regulation, and the ownership structure.

Regarding the industry factors, the existing literature does not provide many papers that study acquisitions in a specific sector. The general idea is that mergers driven by diversification generate lower returns than other acquisitions. However, studies reported in Vermaelen (1992) present lower returns than those expected according to Jensen and Ruback, for both bidders and targets for mergers in the U.S. banking industry. A justification already discussed that seems to fit this case particularly well is that the managements are not driven by the shareholder value, but rather by other goals such as diversification and growth.

Regulation of takeover activities can affect the returns in two ways: either by disclosing information, giving incentive to competition, as in Fishman (1988,1989), and therefore increasing the returns of the targets as discussed before, or by the protection of minorities among the shareholders.

However, empirical evidence is reported in Vermaelen (1992) that neither reason can be responsible for large damages. In fact, apparently in the U.S. the returns to targets increased and the returns to bidders decreased after the introduction of the Williams Act in 1968. However, the same thing happened in the U.K. at the same time, without any change in the disclosure regulations. Also, in Comment and Jarrell (1987), it is found that shareholders in two-tier bids, a situation in which minorities are not protected, are no worse off than in regular bids. Actually, the shareholders are less likely to tender in stage 1 of a two-tier offer than they are in an any-or-all offer. This is clearly inconsistent with the argument of Bradley and Kim (1985), according to which two-tier tender offers would overcome the free-rider problem.

A last factor to consider is the ownership structure. In other words, how are the returns affected by the percentage of shares held by institutional investors, by the management of the target, and by the bidder prior to the takeover?

- Institutional investors are more likely to tender than the target's management or the bidders because they are exempted from taxes. Hence bidders offer lower premiums. Empirical evidence reported in Vermaelen (1992) shows that target returns are negatively related to the fraction of shares held by institutional investors.
- Regarding the management of the target, the larger its ownership, the larger will be the gains of the target's shareholders at the announcement and the smaller will be the bidder's gain.
- The participation of the bidder in the ownership structure (toeholds) has ambiguous theoretical effects that have been extensively discussed

in the theoretical section. In fact, the larger the toehold, the larger will be the incentive for takeover (which is good for the target's shareholders), the larger will be the probability of takeovers (reducing the surprise effect and therefore potential gains for the target's shareholders), the larger will be the bargaining power for bidders (increasing the returns to bidders), and the smaller will be the change in the current management (implying lower returns, as discussed before).

Empirical evidence in Stultz, Walking, and Song (1990) regarding this point shows a significant negative relationship between targets' returns and bidder toeholds as well as a positive relationship between bidders' returns and the toeholds. Such evidence reinforces one of the theoretical implications pointed out earlier, namely the one related to the bargaining power of the bidders. However, this contradicts the consequences of the theoretical model of Shleifer and Vishny (1986).

Having analyzed the factors related to the returns of takeovers, it is still left to conjecture about the sources of such gains. There are three main sources suggested. The first regards the tax benefits, according to Hayn (1989), the second is the informational inefficiency of the market as discussed already, and the final one is related to the development of a market power, clearly associated with the industry factor discussed before.

Finally, there are in the market several antitakeover devices. It is also important to see how such measures affect the returns of the target's shareholders. From the discussion of the model by Harris and Raviv (1988), it is expected that antitakeover devices in general harm the target shareholders, which is to say, the value of the corporations. There are two types of measures—namely, those approved by the shareholders and those decided by the management.

In the first category there are

- *Supermajority provisions.* These must be approved by 2/3 or even up to 90% of the outstanding stock. Prices fall around 3% at the announcement of these provisions.
- *Fair price amendments.* These are similar to provisions but only concern two-tier tender offers. Prices fall by an insignificant 0.73%.
- *Dual class recapitalizations.* Equity is restructured in two different classes with different voting rights. The decline of prices at the announcement is insignificant and of the order of 0.93%.

Among the measures decided by the management, there are

- *Suits against the bidder.* If the management does not succeed, the target's shareholders' returns increase; otherwise, they decrease.
- *Poison pills.* A target's shareholders are given the right to purchase or sell additional shares to the company at attractive prices when there is an

offer for control. The price of the target's shares falls at the announcement of a poison pill.

- *Targeted repurchases (greenmail).* A major outsider shareholder (a potential bidder) is bought out by the company at a high premium. The price declines significantly. The premium plays the role of a payment for its investment and associated monitoring activity.

8.2.6 Exercises

1. Explain why the signaling equilibrium suggested by Fishman (1988) is not fully revealing. If v_1 could be privately observed by bidder 2, how would that change the signaling equilibrium?

2. Show what happens to the expected payoff of the target in equilibrium, if preemptive bidding is allowed/not allowed.

3. In the model of Hansen (1987), let v be uniformly distributed over $(0, 100)$ and take $w(v) = 1.5v$. Show that no mutually beneficial cash trade exists, but that a stock deal will work if $x < 150$.

4. Given asymmetric information in the model of Hansen (1987), show that for every feasible cash offer there exists a stock offer that is preferred by the acquirer.

5. Show and explain why, in the model of Hansen (1987), the acquirer's expected gain from the optimal stock offer decreases with the value of its own firm (x).

6. Hansen's model (1987) predicts that the target share price decreases if the offer is accepted. Why?

7. In the model of Fishman (1989), if competing bidders can choose the means of payment, explain why, once in an auction, there is no incentive to offer cash.

8. Show that, in the model of Fishman (1989), the face value needed to signal that v_1 is at or above any given level is lower with cash compared to debt.

9. In the context of the model of Fishman (1989), what is the effect of an increase of c_2 in the equilibrium?

10. Show that the incumbent and the rival managements will always want to vote for themselves regardless of their private signals.

PART IV
Appendices

Appendix A
Optimization Principles

A.1 Unconstrained Optimization

Consider a real function $f(x_1, \ldots, x_n)$. If this function has a local maximizer or a local minimizer in $x^* \in R^n$, then

$$\frac{\partial f(x^*)}{\partial x_i} = 0 \quad \text{for every } i = 1, \ldots, n.$$

However, this is only a necessary condition for a local maximum or a local minimum, because saddle points also satisfy this condition. Therefore, it is necessary to have a sufficient condition for the existence of either a local maximum or a local minimum. This implies using the second-order conditions in x^*. It follows that

Proposition A.1.1. *Let the real function $f(x_1, \ldots, x_n)$ be twice continuously differentiable and let $\frac{\partial f(x^*)}{\partial x_i} = 0$ for every $i = 1, \ldots, n$. If x^* is a local maximizer (minimizer), then the $D^2 f(x^*)$ matrix is seminegative (semipositive) definite.*

Note that in the univariate case, this is equivalent to saying that, if the second derivative in x^* is negative (positive), then x^* is a local maximizer (minimizer).

The maximum and minimum identified by the use of this proposition are not necessarily global ones. In order to determine if the maximum or minimum given by Proposition 1 are not only local but global ones, one must first define concave and convex functions.

Definition A.1.1. *Let the real function $f(x_1, \ldots, x_n)$ be defined in a convex set $S \subset R^n$. The function $f(x_1, \ldots, x_n)$ is concave if*

$$f(\alpha x + (1 - \alpha)x') \geq \alpha f(x) + (1 - \alpha)f(x).$$

If this inequality holds strictly, the function is said to be strictly concave.

Definition A.1.2. *Let the real function* $f(x_1, \ldots, x_n)$ *be defined in a convex set* $S \subset R^n$. *The function* $f(x_1, \ldots, x_n)$ *is convex if*

$$f(\alpha x + (1 - \alpha)x') \leq \alpha f(x) + (1 - \alpha)f(x).$$

If this inequality holds strictly, the function is said to be strictly convex.

This means that, in the multivariate case, if the function is concave (convex), the matrix $D^2 f(x)$ is seminegative (semipositive) definite in its domain. In the univariate case, this simply means that if the function is concave (convex), its second derivative is nonpositive (nonnegative).

This leads to the following proposition:

Proposition A.1.2. *In a concave (convex) real function of* R^n, *any point* x^* *in which* $\frac{\partial f(x^*)}{\partial x_i} = 0$ *for every* $i = 1, \ldots, n$ *is a global maximizer (minimizer) of* $f(x_1, \ldots, x_n)$. *If the function is strictly concave (convex), the global maximizer (minimizer) is also unique.*

A.2 Constrained Optimization

The optimization problem can be subject, however, to a set of constraints on the values of the function's arguments. One can generally define such a type of problem as

$$\max f(x_1, \ldots, x_n)$$

subject to $(x_1, \ldots, x_n) \in A$.

Two variations will be herein considered for this type of problem: when constraints are all equalities and when constraints include inequalities.

A.2.1 Equality Constraints

An optimization problem with equality restrictions is generally presented as follows:

$$\max f(x_1, \ldots, x_n)$$

subject to

$$g_1(x_1, \ldots, x_n) = b_1$$
$$\vdots$$
$$g_M(x_1, \ldots, x_n) = b_M.$$

As before, f is a function defined in R^N, as well as $g_1, \ldots, g_M$, and the set of all points in R^N satisfying all the constraints is called the constraint set and is denoted as

$$A = \left\{ x \in R^N : g_m(x_1, \ldots, x_N) = b_m \text{ for } m = 1, \ldots, M \right\}.$$

In this problem if $M > N$, there will be no points satisfying all the constraints. (Assume that the M restrictions are independent.) Therefore, usually $M \leq N$.

In order to solve this problem, assume that both f and $g_1, \ldots, g_M$ are twice continuously differentiable. Consider that the Jacobian of the restrictions has characteristic M. Define $X = \{x_1, \ldots, x_{N-M}\}$ and write the other M variables as a function of X, $h_i(X)$, for $i = 1, \ldots, M$. Therefore, one can rewrite the problem as

$$\max_{\{X\}} \mathcal{L}(X) = f(X, h_1(X), \ldots, h_M(X)),$$

which becomes an unconstrained optimization problem.

The necessary condition for a maximum or a minimum is, again, to have all partial derivatives equal to zero. In this case,

$$\frac{\partial \mathcal{L}}{\partial x_i} = \frac{\partial f}{\partial x_i} + \frac{\partial f}{\partial h_1}\frac{\partial h_1}{\partial x_i} + \cdots + \frac{\partial f}{\partial h_M}\frac{\partial h_M}{\partial x_i} = 0, \quad \text{for } i = 1, \ldots, N - M,$$

which in matrix notation can be written as

$$\frac{\partial \mathcal{L}}{\partial X} = \frac{\partial f}{\partial X} + \frac{\partial f}{\partial Y}\frac{\partial h}{\partial X} = 0, \tag{A.1}$$

where $Y = \{x_{N-M+1}, \ldots, x_N\}$. Applying the implicit function theorem, it follows that

$$\frac{\partial h}{\partial X} = -\left(\frac{\partial g}{\partial h}\right)^{-1}\left(\frac{\partial g}{\partial X}\right).$$

Plugging this expression into Equation (A.1), one gets

$$\frac{\partial \mathcal{L}}{\partial x} = \frac{\partial f}{\partial x} - \lambda\frac{\partial g}{\partial x} = 0,$$

for the original N variables. Returning to the original notation, this reads

$$\frac{\partial \mathcal{L}}{\partial x_i} = \frac{\partial f}{\partial x_i} - \lambda_1\frac{\partial g_1}{\partial x_i} - \cdots - \lambda_M\frac{\partial g_M}{\partial x_i} = 0, \quad \text{for } i = 1, \ldots, N. \tag{A.2}$$

Therefore, one can define a problem where one maximizes

$$\mathcal{L}(x_1, \ldots, x_N, \lambda_1, \ldots, \lambda_M) = f(x_1, \ldots, x_N) + \sum_{i=1}^{M} \lambda_i (b_i - g_i(x_1, \ldots, x_N)).$$

This function is called the *Lagrangian function* and λ_i is called the Lagrange multiplier. This function, when the restrictions are binding, has the same value as the original value function $f(x_1, \ldots, x_n)$. Therefore, in the optimum, they will have the same value.

In this problem, the first-order conditions are simply

$$\begin{cases} \frac{\partial \mathcal{L}}{\partial x_i} = \frac{\partial f}{\partial x_i} - \lambda_1 \frac{\partial g_1}{\partial x_1} - \cdots - \lambda_M \frac{\partial g_M}{\partial x_M} = 0, & \text{for } i = 1, \ldots, N \\ \frac{\partial \mathcal{L}}{\partial \lambda_k} = b_k - g_k(x_1, \ldots, x_N) = 0, & \text{for } k = 1, \ldots, M. \end{cases} \quad \text{(A.3)}$$

As in the unconstrained optimization problem, these are just necessary conditions. In order to have sufficient conditions that will identify if the point is a maximum or minimum, one must inspect the second derivatives of the Lagrangian. This leads to the following proposition:

Proposition A.2.1. *Let $(x^*, \lambda^*) \in (R^N, R^M)$ satisfy the first-order conditions for an optimum. If x^* is a local maximizer (minimizer), then the matrix $D^2\mathcal{L}(x^*, \lambda^*)$ is seminegative (semipositive) definite.*

This second-order condition only identifies a maximum, it does not differentiate between a local and a global maximizer. In order to identify a global maximizer, one must first define quasi-concave functions.

Definition A.2.1. *Let the real function $f(x_1, \ldots, x_n)$ be defined in a convex set $S \subset R^n$. Then $f(x_1, \ldots, x_n)$ is a quasi-concave function if its upper contour sets $\{x \in S : f(x_1, \ldots, x_n) \geq t\}$ are convex sets. If the upper contour sets are strictly convex sets, the function is said to be strictly quasi-concave.*

This leads to the following proposition:

Proposition A.2.2. *Suppose that the constraint set A is a convex set and the value function $f(x_1, \ldots, x_n)$ is quasi-concave. Then the maximizer is a global one. If the function is strictly quasi-concave, the global maximizer is also unique.*

To give an economic interpretation of the Lagrange multipliers, consider the change in the value of the Lagrangian function in the optimum when the values b_j in each restriction change. This reads

$$\frac{\partial \mathcal{L}^*}{\partial bj} = \sum_{i=1}^{N} \left[\left(\frac{\partial f}{\partial x_i} - \sum_{k=1}^{M} \lambda_k \frac{\partial g_k}{\partial x_i} \right) \frac{\partial x_i}{\partial b_j} \right] + \sum_{k=1}^{M} (b_k - g_k) \frac{\partial \lambda_k}{\partial b_j} + \lambda_j,$$

$$\text{for } j = 1, \ldots, M.$$

Using the first-order conditions given in (A.3) implies that

$$\frac{\partial \mathcal{L}^*}{\partial bj} = \lambda_j, \quad \text{for } j = 1, \ldots, M.$$

As referred to in the optimum, the value of the Lagrangian is the same as the value of the value function. Therefore $\frac{\partial \mathcal{L}^*}{\partial bj} = \frac{\partial f}{\partial bj} = \lambda_j$. This result leads to the following definition:

Definition A.2.2. *In the optimum, the value λ_j^* of the Lagrange multiplier in the j-th restriction represents the increase in the value function if one increases the slack in that restriction. Therefore, it is often referred to as the shadow price or the shadow value of the constraint.*

For instance, if one considers each restriction in an optimization problem to describe the use of a given resource, the Lagrangian multiplier reflects the value of the use of an extra unit of that resource.

A.2.2 Inequality Constraints

An optimization problem with equality restrictions is generally presented as follows:

$$\max f(x_1, \ldots, x_n)$$

subject to

$$g_1(x_1, \ldots, x_n) \le b_1$$
$$\vdots$$
$$g_M(x_1, \ldots, x_n) \le b_M.$$

As before, f is a function defined in R^N, as well as $g_1, \ldots, g_M$, and the set of all points in R^N satisfying all the constraints is, again, called a constraint set and is denoted as

$$A = \left\{ x \in R^N : g_m(x_1, \ldots, x_N) \le b_m \text{ for } m = 1, \ldots, M \right\}.$$

The way to solve this problem is again to represent the Lagrangian function of this problem:

$$\mathcal{L}(x_1, \ldots, x_N, \lambda_1, \ldots, \lambda_M) = f(x_1, \ldots, x_N) + \sum_{i=1}^{M} \lambda_i(b_i - g_i(x_1, \ldots, x_N)).$$

However, since the restrictions are not described by a set of equalities, the first-order conditions presented in the previous case no longer fully characterize the necessary conditions of optimization. The following result does this job, providing a set of necessary conditions (known as *Kuhn-Tucker conditions*) for an optimum:

Proposition A.2.3. *Consider the maximization problem just presented. If this function $\mathcal{L}$ has an optimum at $x^* \in A$, then*

Condition A.2.1.

1. $\frac{\partial \mathcal{L}}{\partial x_i} = \frac{\partial f}{\partial x_i} - \lambda_1 \frac{\partial g_1}{\partial x_1} - \cdots - \lambda_M \frac{\partial g_M}{\partial x_M} = 0$, *for* $i = 1, \ldots, N$;
2. $g_j(x_1, \ldots, x_n) \leq b_j, \lambda_j \geq 0$, *for* $j = 1, \ldots, M$;
3. $\lambda_j[b_j - g_j(x_1, \ldots, x_n)] = 0$.

The first statement corresponds to the usual optimization condition that all partial derivatives must equal zero. The second says that for x^* to be an optimum, the constraints must be satisfied and the shadow prices must be nonnegative. The last statement, called the *complementary-slackness condition*, says that if restriction j is nonbinding, then the shadow price must be zero. The interpretation for the Lagrange multipliers given in Definition A.2.2 justifies this condition. If the restriction j is nonbinding, if one increases the slack for that restriction, it will continue to be nonbinding. Therefore the effect of an increase in b_j will not affect the value function in the optimum. Consequently, the shadow price of that restriction is zero.

Again, these are just necessary conditions for an optimum. To ensure that a point satisfying the Kuhn-Tucker conditions is a maximum or a minimum, Proposition A.2.1 must be used. In order to evaluate if the point is a global optimum, one must then use Proposition A.2.2.

Appendix B
Notions of Game Theory

B.1 Introduction

Most developments in the corporate finance literature over the past 20 years have dealt with situations where there are *asymmetries of information* between economic agents. In the most common of examples one can think of, the case of a firm issuing securities, insiders in the firm (the *informed party*) know the true quality of the firm's projects, while outside investors (the *uninformed party*) do not; the latter know only that the firm belongs to one of different possible *types* (say, a "good" firm or a "bad" firm). The issue is then to understand under what conditions the informed party can take actions or send *signals* that somehow convey their type in a *credible* way to the uninformed party. In this appendix we survey briefly some of the tools available to analyze such situations, which fall under the heading of *games of incomplete information*.

We restrict our focus to what we will henceforth call the *Spence/Riley methodology*. Although in recent times more full-fledged game-theoretic artillery has been developed to analyze games of incomplete information, this framework remains essential to understanding most of the seminal models presented in this book, and is still used in research papers today. In the first section, we assemble the general setup and proceed to present an important equilibrium concept, the *informational equilibrium* of Riley (1979). We use examples from this book whenever possible and discuss the main features (including some drawbacks) associated with this equilibrium concept. The second section deals with *mechanism design* (which here can be seen mainly as a tool that simplifies analysis considerably) and its most closely associated result, the *revelation principle* of Myerson (1979). The style adopted here is discursive and intended above all to give the reader fertile ground on which a more rigorous treatment of the material can grow.

We assume the reader is familiar with basic game-theoretic notions, both from complete information games (e.g., Nash equilibrium, subgame

233

perfection) and from (static) incomplete information games (pooling and separating strategies, Bayesian Nash equilibrium). Gibbons (1992) and Rasmusen (1994) are very good undergraduate-level sources, while a thorough and rigorous treatment of the theory is available in Osborne and Rubinstein (1994). Finally, technically inclined readers are sent to the excellent Fudenberg and Tirole (1991).

B.2 Informational Equilibrium

Riley (1979) provided one of the first consistent frameworks to analyze this problem, and this section follows loosely his approach and notation. The setup is as follows: Suppose that there exist two agents (a seller and a buyer), who will engage in a transaction over one unit of a commodity. The seller actually belongs to a heterogenous group of agents, differentiated among themselves by some unobservable characteristic (which we call a type); this characteristic dictates the value of the asset for the buyer. Each seller can, however, engage in some (presumably costly) "selling activity" or action (which we call a signal) that is indeed observable. Let $y \in Y$ represent such signals, $\theta \in \Theta$ represent the type (i.e., the seller's private information), and P the price of the asset. We represent seller's preferences as $U(\theta, y, P)$ and the valuation for the buyer as $V(\theta, y)$.[1]

The idea behind this structure is always to find out an equilibrium in which sellers send a signal that meaningfully communicates their type to the buyer. Three relationships will be important in this equilibrium: first, the seller's choice of signal given his/her type, which we call *signal function* and denote $y^*(\theta)$; second, the buyer's inference about the seller's type given his/her action, the *inference function*, which we denote by $\theta^*(y)$; and finally, the buyer's valuation of the asset given the observed signal, or *pricing function*, denoted $P^*(y)$. We now proceed to a formal definition of equilibrium:

*An **informational Equilibrium** (Riley, 1979) is a pair $\{y^*(\theta), P^*(y)\}$ such that*

(i) $y^*(\theta) = \arg \max_y U(\theta, y, P^*(y))$
(ii) $P^*(y) = V(\theta, y^*(\theta))$.

That is, the seller chooses the signal that maximizes his/her utility given his/her type, and the buyer values the asset at fair price, according to inferences about the seller's type made after observing the signal.

Many models fit this general structure. The canonical example is Spence's (1974) analysis of education choice, where θ is the true ability of a worker, y represents the latter's level of education, and $P^*(y)$ represents the wage schedule offered by a company to the worker according to the latter's education (i.e., signal). The worker selects his/her level of education (i.e., maximizes his/her utility) facing a certain wage schedule. Using an example closer to home, in Leland and Pyle (1977), θ is the firm's expected return $E(X)$; y is the insider's holdings α; $P(y)$ represents the value of the firm as perceived by outside investors $V(\alpha)$; and so on. The entrepreneur selects his/her level of holdings by maximizing his/her expected utility and taking into account investors' market pricing functions.

We call pricing functions $P^*(y)$ that respect condition *(ii) informationally consistent.* The existence of (a family of) such functions was established by Riley, under certain assumptions, the most important of which is the *Spence-Mirrlees condition:*

Under the preceding setup, we say that $U(\theta, y, P)$ satisfies the Spence-Mirrlees condition (also frequently called single crossing property) if

$$\frac{\partial}{\partial \theta} \left[\frac{\frac{\partial U}{\partial y}}{\frac{\partial U}{\partial P}} \right] \quad \textit{is monotonic,}$$

That is, if the indifference curves of each type of seller cross only once in the (y, P) space.

The term inside brackets represents, keeping utility level constant, how much the seller is willing to trade between the (costly) signal y and the (beneficial) price P. A single crossing implies that this opportunity cost is monotonically related to the seller's type; *The idea is that better types should be willing to signal more for the same level of increase in price.* Putting it yet another way, it is should be relatively easier for the good types to signal. In Spence's model, for instance, it is easier for higher-ability workers to obtain education; in Leland and Pyle's, it is less costly for managers of good firms to retain equity stakes precisely because their firms are more valuable.

The importance of the assumption should not be understated. This property guarantees that $y^*(\theta)$ will be a function (a one-to-one mapping), because each type will select a single (different) point on the pricing function of the buyer. This in turn allows for $\theta^*(y)$, the inference function, to be well-defined; otherwise the buyer could not infer from the observed signal the type of the seller. In short, it is this property that guarantees a unique relationship between the level of signal and type.

At this point, it is useful to remind the reader of the main issue at hand here—whether signaling can work as an information transmission mechanism that avoids market breakdown (Akerlof, 1970). The benchmark case is obviously the one of *full information.* Conditional on type, the seller chooses the level of signal that maximizes utility: Equilibrium is reached, as usual, at the tangency point between the seller's indifference curve and the underlying constraint he/she is facing, the buyer's pricing function. Different types sell different assets that are valued accordingly by buyers; we achieve *first best.*

In the asymmetric information case, problems arise whenever "bad" types might want to disguise (i.e., send the same signal) as "good" types (say, low-ability workers want to disguise themselves as high-ability workers, if the latter receive better salaries). For a separating equilibrium to exist, some loss of efficiency will probably take place, and we are driven away from the first best: We have a case of *costly separation.* Better types must raise their levels of signal up to the point where it is no longer in the interest of worse types to pool; better types thus pay in equilibrium a signaling cost that allows the buyer to distinguish them from worse types. In Leland and Pyle (1977), for instance, the manager of a good firm is less diversified relative to the first best, while in Ross (1977), managers of better firms face a higher probability of bankruptcy (and hence a higher probability of incurring the monetary penalty).

Here we see again the importance of the Spence-Mirrlees condition: The equilibrium makes sense because (since it is relatively more costly for worse types to signal), this signaling is *credible.* Back to Leland and Pyle, it doesn't make sense to a manager of a bad firm to hold high stakes in his/her company (i.e., pool with the better types), since he/she would pay the diversification cost *and* hold a stake in a lower-valued firm. Note, however, that there can exist cases of *costless separation*—situations where the preferences of the sellers are such that asymmetric information is not really a problem: Worse types do not find it in their interest to pool and separation occurs naturally. As an example, in a two-type version of Ross's (1977) model, both the good and the bad firms issue amounts of debt such that no penalty is incurred in equilibrium (i.e., the probability of incurring the penalty is zero for both firms).

Several important remarks are in order. First, it is useful to check conditions on the *welfare of limiting types.* Suppose that $\theta \in [\underline{\Theta}, \overline{\Theta}]$. At a given informational equilibrium $\{y^*(\theta), P^*(y)\}$, it must be the case that

$$U\big(y(\bar{\theta}), \bar{\theta}, P^*(y)\big) \geq U(y(\underline{\theta}), \bar{\theta}, P^*(y)),$$

that is, *the best type does not want to be disguised as the worst type.* This would be the case if the cost of signaling was so high that the best type would prefer not to signal at all! In Ross (1977), if the penalty L is very small, the equilibrium level of debt given by the signaling function $D(t)$ is very high, implying that the probability of bankruptcy is very high for the best type. It can then be the case that the best type would prefer not to signal.

A second important remark concerns the following: In general, there will exist a family of signaling schedules $\theta^*(y)$ that are plausible in equilibrium (and, as a consequence, a family outcome $P^*(y)$ of pricing functions), since most of the times $\theta^*(y)$ is obtained by solving a differential equation.[2] To obtain a particular solution to this equation, we must therefore add a boundary condition. Suppose $y \in [0, \infty)$. The condition usually chosen is that $y^*(\underline{\theta}) = 0$ (such that $\theta^*(0) = \underline{\theta}$); that is, the worst type does not signal.

The rationale behind this choice is that it makes no sense for the worst type to incur an unnecessary cost; we call this particular solution the *Riley outcome*. Note that if the worst type would incur signaling costs, it would only imply that the better types would have to increase their respective signals, without affecting the ordering of types or the amount of information transmitted to the buyer. (The latter is already discriminating between types anyway.) Choosing the Riley outcome therefore amounts to minimizing adverse selection costs across the economy. Not surprisingly, the corresponding buyer's price function is called the *Pareto dominating price function*. In most of the models we saw in Chapters 3 and 4, the choice of the Riley outcome is clearly visible.

In spite of its importance, this methodology has also some drawbacks, most of which can be related to the fact that it does not correspond to a proper description of a game in extensive form. It is not clear, for instance, how we guarantee that the Riley outcome will be in fact achieved as the equilibrium of the game. Suppose you are outside the Riley outcome, in a Pareto inefficient pricing function $\widehat{P}^*(y)$; there is no built-in mechanism to take us to the Riley outcome, since a (say) intermediate-type firm has no incentive to lower its signal (thereby lowering its signaling cost to the efficient level) because it would be mistaken for an inferior-quality firm! There is no strategic description in this approach of what kind of process could lead to the Pareto optimal result that is assumed in the solution of these models. In general, questions of *multiplicity of equilibria* constitute a serious problem once a more rigorous approach is used.

Another issue concerns the existence of implicit assumptions on the underlying *signal space*. Suppose exogenous restrictions are placed in the set of possible signals (e.g., Ross's managers cannot leverage by more than a certain amount). It might then be the case that the proposed equilibrium breaks down, because several of the better types get "squeezed" in the sense that they are forced to select the same signal—which then becomes uninformative for the buyer. Thus the exact nature of equilibrium one is dealing with again comes into question.

B.3 The Revelation Principle

Suppose you have a game of incomplete information, such as an auction. There are many possible ways in which the seller of the object can design the auction in order to maximize his/her revenue. The analysis of this issue, as well as others along these lines, belongs to the realm of *mechanism design*. A mechanism can be seen simply as a set of rules that specifies how decisions are taken in the economy, as a function of the information known by agents (e.g., first-price versus second-price auctions). The idea is that, in situations where a "principal" is dealing with privately informed "agents," the former must select a set of rules that best suits his/her objectives, while at the same time recognizing the need for giving appropriate incentives to agents (so that the latter are willing to share truthfully their information).

While the set of all possible mechanisms one can think of is probably very big, it turns out that Myerson (1979), among others, derived a very important result—named the *revelation principle*—in games of incomplete information: Given an equilibrium of an original or indirect game, that equilibrium can always be represented as the equilibrium of a *revelation or direct game* where the actions of the players are simply to submit claims about their type; furthermore, this equilibrium is always *truth telling*—that is, each player submits its own true type. We call such games *direct mechanisms*; direct mechanisms where truth telling is an equilibrium are called *incentive compatible*.

We now formalize the result, in the context of the setup presented before. We propose the following revelation game: (*i*) Each seller submits a claim or report $\tilde{\theta}$ about its true type θ. (*ii*) Payoffs are allocated (and each seller receives a price) based on that claim. Denote the resulting outcome as

$$\{\hat{y}(\tilde{\theta}), \widehat{P}(\tilde{\theta})\},$$

where we require additionally that $\widehat{P}(\tilde{\theta}) \equiv \widehat{P}(y(\tilde{\theta})) = V(\tilde{\theta}, y(\tilde{\theta}))$. We state the following without proof:

Theorem (revelation principle). *Any informational equilibrium* $\{y^*(\theta), P^*(y)\}$ *can be represented by a truth-telling equilibrium of the revelation game, in the sense that*

$$\{y^*(\theta), P^*(y)\} = \{\hat{y}(\theta), \widehat{P}(\theta)\}$$

if $\{\hat{y}(\theta), \widehat{P}(\theta)\}$ *it respects the* incentive compatibility constraints

$$\theta \in \arg\max_{\tilde{\theta}} U[\hat{y}(\tilde{\theta}), \theta, \widehat{P}(\tilde{\theta})], \qquad \forall \theta \in \Theta.$$

That is, for a given type, saying the truth is maximizing over all possible claims, for the allocation provided for each possible claim $\tilde{\theta}$, and this must be true for all types. We call such equilibrium $\{\hat{y}(\theta), \widehat{P}(\theta)\}$ implementable.

Here is a word about the way the truth-telling equilibrium is constructed. Payoffs in the direct game are obtained by (*i*) replacing the player's report (about their type) into the *equilibrium strategies of the indirect game* and then (*ii*) substituting the resulting actions (i.e., the signals) from these strategies into the payoff functions of the indirect game. This point is important in understanding the intuition behind the result. Suppose the indirect/original game had an equilibrium $y^*(\theta)$. The optimal strategy of type θ_i, say, is to play strategy $y^*(\theta_i)$.[3] Now a central planner comes about and says, "Make claims about your type; then I will play the equilibrium strategies of the original game and attribute to you the resulting payoffs." From this, it is obvious that it is in the best interest of the players to tell the truth, because this way they ensure that the central planner will play the strategy that is optimal for them.

The revelation principle is an extremely useful tool, since it allows us to look only at incentive compatible equilibria when analyzing the game. There is no loss in generality from doing this, since we know that all equilibria of the indirect game can be represented as truth-telling equilibria of the direct game—and the latter is much easier to analyze: The strategy space is just the space of all possible types. The incentive compatibility constraints (also called *truth-telling constraints* or *nonmimicry constraints*) are, for the two-type case,

$$U\big[\hat{y}(\theta_1), \theta_1, \widehat{P}(\theta_1)\big] \geq U\big[\hat{y}(\theta_0), \theta_1, \widehat{P}(\theta_0)\big]$$

$$U\big[\hat{y}(\theta_0), \theta_0, \widehat{P}(\theta_0)\big] \geq U\big[\hat{y}(\theta_1), \theta_0, \widehat{P}(\theta_1)\big].$$

Suppose $\theta_0 < \theta_1$ represents the bad type. Usually we impose the incentive compatibility constraint for θ_0 to be an equality, because in a separating equilibrium the bad type will choose exactly the same level of utility that leaves him/her on the tangency point between his/her indifference curve and the buyer's pricing function. This is a mere consequence of the single crossing property and of the fact that are good types that will be paying the signaling cost in equilibrium.

The Riley outcome can be enforced if we assume that the worst type maximizes his/her utility (so that he/she will probably not signal). The full program to solve is then

$$U[\circ, \theta_0, \circ] = \max_{y, p} U\big[y^*(\theta_0), \theta_0, P^*(\theta_0)\big]$$

such that

$$U[\hat{y}(\theta_1), \theta_1, \widehat{P}(\theta_1)] \geq U[\hat{y}(\theta_0), \theta_1, \widehat{P}(\theta_0)]$$

$$P^*(\theta_0) = V\{\theta_0, y^*(\theta_0)\}.$$

This problem is much easier to analyze than the original Riley signaling problem discussed previously. The last condition is often called the *competitive-rationality condition*.

Several remarks and words of caution are in order. First, the setup used here is not by all means the most general one, but is only meant to give a feeling of the result. Ideally one should pursue a proper definition of the strategies, actions, and payoffs of the game under consideration, and the revelation principle can be applied to a whole variety of incomplete information games (e.g., Myerson (1986)). Second, even if we start by analyzing the direct game and manage to obtain the corresponding equilibrium, we might not be sure of what is the indirect game that implements it: the same equilibrium strategies could have been the outcome of different indirect games. In this sense, there is an issue of indetermination when dealing with the revelation principle. Third, we dealt here with a small number of types; denote the latter n. Incentive compatibility constraints are, however, as many in number as $n \cdot (n - 1)$, which adds considerable complexity to the problem once a large number of types are considered. With a continuum of types, things might demand more than a little effort from our devoted reader who is thinking of venturing into this area of research.

Appendix C
Suggested Solutions

C.1 Valuation

C.1.1 Valuation under Certainty

1. It suffices to differentiate twice $U(x, X - x)$ with respect to x to get

$$\frac{dU}{dx} = U_1 - U_2$$

$$\frac{d^2U}{dx^2} = U_{11} - 2U_{12} + U_{22} < 0,$$

where the inequality comes from the assumption that U is strictly concave. Thus $U_1 - U_2$ is always decreasing in x. If it is negative from the beginning at $x = 0$, it follows that optimal x is zero, the first result; if it is positive until the maximum possible value $x = X$, then it is at that level that maximum feasible utility is attained. Otherwise the solution comes from the simple first-order condition.

2. By the assumption that $d^2U/dx^2 < 0$ it follows that at the maximum x_o^* we have $U_{11} - 2U_{12} + U_{22} < 0$. Since in the iso-utility curve $y(x)$ we must have a constant value $U(x, y) = u$ for all pairs (x, y), taking first and second total differentials with respect to x gives

$$0 = U_1 + U_2 y' \Rightarrow 0 = U_{11} + 2U_{12}y' + U_{22}y'^2 + U_2 y''.$$

Recalling that $U_2 > 0$ and that at the optimal point in this context $y' = 1$, the result follows.

3. Differentiate the expression $y_p(x)$ to get $y'_p(x) = -[1 + \varphi(X - x)]$. Positiveness of $\varphi(I)$ ensures that $y'_p < 0$. The assumption that $\varphi(I)$ is decreasing ensures that $y''_p < 0$.

241

4. It suffices to differentiate twice $y(x)$ with respect to ϵ to get

$$\frac{dy(x)}{d\epsilon} = \varphi(\epsilon) - r$$

$$\frac{d^2y(x)}{d\epsilon^2} = \varphi'(\epsilon) < 0.$$

Hence, if $r \geq \varphi(0)$, the function $y(x)$ will be decreasing as ϵ increases and the maximum of $y(x)$ is attained for $\epsilon = 0$. Otherwise the optimal investment level ϵ is obtained by the first-order condition $\frac{dy(x)}{d\epsilon} = 0$, leading to the desired result.

5. Maximizing $y(x)$ for given x leads to a result independent of x. Thus, take $x = 0$ to get the future wealth as $Y + X(1+r) + \int_0^{\epsilon^*} [\varphi(I) - r]dI$. If future wealth is maximized, the presence of financial markets implies that also current wealth is maximized, since there is only a multiplicative discounting factor of $(1 + r)$ relating both.

6. The expression for $y_f(x)$ is obtained by substitution of $\delta = \epsilon^* - (X - x)$ in the expression for $y(x)$ with the optimal ϵ^*:

$$y_f(x) = Y + (X - x) + \int_0^{\epsilon^*} \varphi(I)dI - \delta r$$

$$= Y + (X - x)(1 + r) + \int_0^{\epsilon^*} [\varphi(I) - r]dI.$$

7. The proof that $y_p \geq y_o$ is already in the text. We are left to show that $y_f \geq y_p$.

First, let $r \geq \varphi(0)$. Then $r > \varphi(I), \forall I \geq 0$, and

$$\int_0^{X-x} [r - \varphi(I)]dI \geq 0 \Rightarrow (X - x)r \geq \int_0^{X-x} \varphi(I)dI$$

$$y_f(x) = Y + (X - x)(1 + r)$$

$$\geq Y + (X - x) + \int_0^{X-x} \varphi(I)dI = y_p(x).$$

Now take $r \leq \varphi(0)$. Then writing

$$y_f(x) = Y + (X - x) + \int_0^{\epsilon^*} [\varphi(I) - r]dI + \int_0^{X-x} rdI,$$

notice that

$$y_f(x) - y_p(x) = \int_0^{\epsilon^*} [\varphi(I) - r]dI + \int_0^{X-x} rdI - \int_0^{X-x} \varphi(I)dI$$

$$= \int_{X-x}^{\epsilon^*} [\varphi(I) - r]dI.$$

Since ϵ^* is defined such as $\varphi(\epsilon^*) = r$, and $\varphi' \leq 0$, the Preceding integral is always positive and the result is proved.

8. As defined in the text, NPV$(\varphi) = \frac{\Delta}{1+r}$, with $\Delta = 0$, for $r \geq \varphi(0)$ and $\Delta = \int_0^{\varphi^{-1}(r)} [\varphi(I) - r] dI$ for $\varphi(0) \geq r$. The problem of the agent is given by

$$\max U(x, y),$$

$$\text{s.t. } y = Y + (X - x)(1 + r) + \int_0^\epsilon [\varphi(I) - r] dI.$$

If $\Delta > 0$, agents will invest in the project since it will expand the region of admissible consumptions. On the other hand, agents only invest in the project if $\Delta > 0$, since otherwise the region of admissible consumptions would be smaller.

9. Each agent will face a utility maximizing problem subject to the consumption possibilities set. For $i = 1, 2$ this reads

$$\max_{x, y, e} U^i(x^i, y^i)$$

$$\text{s.t. } y^i = Y^i + \int_0^e [1 + \varphi(I)] dI - r[\delta].$$

The restriction can be rewritten as

$$y^i = X^i + Y^i - (1 + r)x^i + \int_0^e (-10 + r) dI - r(e - X^i).$$

The problem of agent A is

$$\max_{x, y, e} (x^A)^2 y^A$$

$$\text{s.t. } y = X + Y - (1 + r)x + \int_0^e (-10 + r) dI - r(e - X).$$

The Lagrangian is written as

$$\mathcal{L} = x^2 y + \lambda \left[y - 100 - 48.46 + x(1 + r) - \int_0^e (-10 + r) dI + r(e - 100) \right]$$

and the first-order conditions are

$$\begin{cases} \frac{\partial \mathcal{L}}{\partial x} = 0 \\ \frac{\partial \mathcal{L}}{\partial y} = 0 \\ \frac{\partial \mathcal{L}}{\partial e} = 0 \\ \frac{\partial \mathcal{L}}{\partial \lambda} = 0 \end{cases} \iff \begin{cases} 2x^A y^A = \lambda(1 + r) \\ x_A^2 = \lambda \\ e^A = 10 - r \\ y^A = 100 + 48.46 - (1 + r)x^A \\ \qquad + \int_0^e (-10 + r) dI - r(e - X). \end{cases}$$

From the first-order conditions it immediately follows that each agent's investment is independent of x and y and is given by $e^A = 10 - r$. Working out the equations we can get the present and future consumption levels. They are, respectively,

$$x^A = \frac{2}{3}\left[100 + \frac{48.46}{1+r} + \frac{10-r}{2}\right]$$

$$y^A = \frac{1}{3}(1+r)\left[100 + \frac{48.46}{1+r} + \frac{10-r}{2}\right].$$

Consider now agent B. The problem that agent B must solve is the following:

$$\max_{x,\,y,\,e} x^B (y^B)^2$$

$$s.a. \ y^B = 100 + 48.4(1+r)x^B + \int_0^e (-10+r)dI - r(e-100).$$

The result follows very close to the one for agent A. Once again the investment level does not depend on x and y and is given by $e^B = 10 - r$. The values for present and future consumption will be, respectively,

$$x^B = \frac{1}{3}\left[100 + \frac{48.46}{1+r} + \frac{10-r}{2}\right]$$

$$y^B = \frac{2}{3}(1+r)\left[100 + \frac{48.46}{1+r} + \frac{10-r}{2}\right].$$

In equilibrium

$$x^A + x^B + e^A + e^B = X^A + X^B. \tag{C.1}$$

Finally, when $r = 0.2$ we obtain

$$x^A = 120.1(6)$$

$$x^B = 60.08(3)$$

$$e^A = e^B = 9.8$$

and equation (C.1) is verified.

C.1.2 Valuation under Uncertainty

1. Let Γ_j denote the vector of future payoffs of asset j, and let V_j denote its initial value. If all the components of Γ_j are strictly positive, then V_j is also strictly positive because ψ is strictly positive, by assumption. On the other hand, if all the components of Γ_j are positive and one is strictly positive, then V_j is also strictly positive for the same reason.

If, on the other hand, the components of Γ_j are nonpositive, then V_j is also nonpositive because ψ is strictly positive. Therefore, there are no arbitrage opportunities.

2. Take the result

$$\text{var}(\Gamma'\theta^*) = \text{cov}(\Gamma'\theta^*, \Gamma'\theta^*).$$

Dividing by $(V'\theta^*)^2$ and multiplying by δ, we arrive at

$$\frac{\delta \,\text{var}(\Gamma'\theta^*)}{(V'\theta^*)^2} = \frac{\delta \,\text{cov}(\Gamma'\theta^*, \Gamma'\theta^*)}{(V'\theta^*)^2}.$$

Given $\delta = \Gamma'\theta^*$ and $R^* = \Gamma'\theta^*/V'\theta^*$, the equation simplifies to

$$\delta \,\text{var}(R^*) = \frac{\Gamma'\theta^*}{V'\theta^*} \,\text{cov}(R^*, \delta)$$

$$\Leftrightarrow$$

$$\delta = \frac{R^*}{\text{var}(R^*)} \frac{\text{cov}(R^*, \delta)}{E(\delta)} E(\delta).$$

From equation (1.16),

$$\delta = -\frac{R^*}{\text{var}(R^*)}[E(R^*) - R^0]E(\delta).$$

Equating these last two equations and knowing that

$$\frac{\text{cov}(R^*, \delta)}{\text{var}(R^*)} \,\text{cov}(R^*, R^\theta) = \text{cov}(\delta, R^\theta),$$

the result follows.

3. Notice that $\delta = \Gamma'\theta^*$ defines a system with N variables and S equations. If $N < S$, there are fewer variables than equations. In this case, when the number of linearly independent equations is bigger than N, there is no solution to the system (i.e., we cannot find a portfolio satisfying $\delta = \Gamma'\theta^*$). On the other hand, if $N \geq S$ we can be sure that the system has a solution. When the number of linearly independent equations is equal to N, the solution is unique; on the other hand, when the number of linearly independent equations is smaller than N, the system has multiple solutions. Therefore, we can conclude that $N \geq S$ is a sufficient but not a necessary condition for the existence of the portfolio satisfying $\delta = \Gamma'\theta$.

4. The consumption problem of each agent in this economy is given by

$$\max_{x,\,y,\,\epsilon,\,\delta} V = EU(x, y)$$

$$s.t. \ x + \epsilon = X + \delta$$

$$y = Y + F_\theta(\epsilon) - (1 + r)\delta.$$

Substituting the restrictions on the objective function, the problem can be written as

$$\max_{\epsilon, \delta} EU(-\epsilon + X + \delta, Y + F_\theta(\epsilon) - (1+r)\delta).$$

The first-order conditions of this problem are

$$\frac{\partial V}{\partial \epsilon} = -E\left[\frac{\partial U}{\partial x}\right] + E\left[\frac{\partial U}{\partial y}\frac{\partial F}{\partial \epsilon}\right] = 0$$

$$\frac{\partial V}{\partial \delta} = E\left[\frac{\partial U}{\partial x}\right] - E\left[\frac{\partial U}{\partial y}(1+r)\right] = 0.$$

Now, solving only for the "production/investment frontier," for all states simultaneously we have

$$\max_\epsilon y(\epsilon)$$

$$s.t. \ x + \epsilon = X + \delta$$

$$y(\epsilon) = Y + F_\theta(\epsilon) - (1+r)\delta.$$

As this problem can be written as $\max_\epsilon Y + F_\theta(\epsilon) - (1+r)(x + \epsilon - X)$, the solution is given by

$$\frac{\partial F}{\partial \epsilon}(\epsilon^*, \theta) = 1 + r. \qquad (C.2)$$

Condition (C.2) cannot hold simultaneously for all θ, unless $\frac{\partial F}{\partial \epsilon}$ is independent of θ (trivial uncertainty). If $\frac{\partial F}{\partial \epsilon}$ depends on θ, we must weight the future outcomes. Let $q(\theta)$ be the vector of weights. The new problem is given by

$$\max_\epsilon q(\theta)'y(\epsilon)$$

$$s.t. \ x + \epsilon = X + \delta$$

$$y(\epsilon) = Y + F_\theta(\epsilon) - (1+r)\delta.$$

Substituting the restrictions on the function that is being maximized, the problem can be written as

$$\max_\epsilon q(\theta)'[Y + F_\theta(\epsilon) - (1+r)(x + \epsilon - X)].$$

The solution is given by

$$q(\theta_1)\frac{\partial F}{\partial \epsilon}(\epsilon^*, \theta_1) + q(\theta_2)\frac{\partial F}{\partial \epsilon}(\epsilon^*, \theta_2) = 1 + r. \qquad (C.3)$$

We can rewrite the first-order conditions for the consumption problem as

$$(1 + r) \begin{bmatrix} p \frac{\partial U}{\partial y}(x, y(\theta_1)) \\ + (1 - p) \frac{\partial U}{\partial y}(x, y(\theta_2)) \end{bmatrix}$$
$$= \begin{bmatrix} p \frac{\partial F}{\partial \epsilon}(\epsilon, \theta_1) \frac{\partial U}{\partial y}(x, y(\theta_1)) \\ + (1 - p) \frac{\partial F}{\partial \epsilon}(\epsilon, \theta_2) \frac{\partial U}{\partial y}(x, y(\theta_2)) \end{bmatrix}. \tag{C.4}$$

We can observe that equations (C.3) and (C.4) are exactly the same if we define $q(\theta)$ as the state-price vectors:

$$q(\theta_i) = p_i \frac{\partial U}{\partial y}(x, y(\theta_i)), \quad i = 1, 2.$$

So, provided that there is a unique state-price vector (and this happens because we have two states of nature and two independent assets), we have the independence result. In this case, the optimal production decision is determined independently of individuals' subjective preferences that define their consumption decisions because, once we know the state-prices, we can solve equation (C.3) for ϵ^* with no knowledge of $U(x, y)$, x^*, or y^*. We can also conclude that the level of investment is independent of the endowments (X and Y).

5. (a) When there are no arbitrage opportunities in a complete market, we know that $\psi = \Gamma^{-1} V$. Then

$$\begin{pmatrix} \psi_1 \\ \psi_2 \end{pmatrix} = \begin{bmatrix} 1.01 & 1.01 \\ 10 & 5 \end{bmatrix}^{-1} \begin{pmatrix} 1 \\ 6.7 \end{pmatrix} = \begin{pmatrix} 0.35 \\ 0.64 \end{pmatrix}.$$

(b) We must compute $V_2 = -2 * 0.35 + 4 * 0.64 = 1.86$. $\text{NPV}_1 = 6.7 - 5 = 1.7$, and $\text{NPV}_2 = 1.86 - 2 = -0.14$. Agents in this economy would invest (buy) only in project 1.

6. (a) This is a complete market problem if and only if $D \neq U$.

(b) The proof of this exercise is divided into two steps. In the first place, we want to prove that $D < R < U \Rightarrow$ arbitrage-free market. Define

$$\varphi_1 = \frac{U - R}{R(U - D)}$$

$$\varphi_2 = 1 - \varphi_1 = \frac{R - D}{R(U - D)}.$$

It is easy to check that $\varphi_1 D + \varphi_2 U = 1$ and $\varphi_1 R + \varphi_2 R = 1$. So, as $D < R < U$, there is a vector $\varphi = (\varphi_1, \varphi_2)$ of strictly positive components such that $V = \Gamma\varphi$, where $V^T = [1, 1]$ and

$$\Gamma = \begin{bmatrix} D & U \\ R & R \end{bmatrix}.$$

Applying to Proposition 1.2.1, one concludes that the market is arbitrage-free. Now, we must prove the other direction of the implication—that is, an arbitrage-free market $\Rightarrow D < R < U$. By contradiction, assume that $U \leq R$. If we buy one unit of the risk-free asset and short sell one unit of the risky asset, the initial cost of our portfolio is zero and the final cost is never negative (i.e., there is an arbitrage opportunity). The same procedure applies if $R \leq D$.

7. (a) The consumption/investment problem of agent A in this economy is given by

$$\max_{\{x,\, y,\, \theta\}} V = x^{0.5} + \frac{1}{3}y_1^{0.5} + \frac{1}{3}y_2^{0.5} + \frac{1}{3}y_3^{0.5}$$

$$s.t. \ x = 5 + 100\theta_1 + 85\theta_2$$

$$y_1 = 1 + 101\theta_1 + 60\theta_2$$

$$y_2 = 1 + 101\theta_1 + 120\theta_2$$

$$y_3 = 1 + 101\theta_1 + 95\theta_2.$$

Substituting the restrictions in the objective function, the problem can be written as

$$\max_{\theta}(5 + 100\theta_1 + 85\theta_2)^{0.5} + \frac{1}{3}(1 + 101\theta_1 + 60\theta_2)^{0.5}$$

$$+ \frac{1}{3}(1 + 101\theta_1 + 120\theta_2)^{0.5} + \frac{1}{3}(1 + 101\theta_1 + 95\theta_2)^{0.5}.$$

The first-order conditions are

$$\begin{cases} \dfrac{85}{(5-100\theta_1-85\theta_2)^{0.5}} = \dfrac{60}{(1+101\theta_1+60\theta_2)^{0.5}} * \dfrac{1}{3} + \dfrac{120}{(1+101\theta_1+120\theta_2)^{0.5}} * \dfrac{1}{3} \\ \qquad\qquad + \dfrac{95}{(1+101\theta_1+95\theta_2)^{0.5}} * \dfrac{1}{3} \\[2ex] \dfrac{100}{(5-100\theta_1-85\theta_2)^{0.5}} = \dfrac{101}{(1+101\theta_1+60\theta_2)^{0.5}} * \dfrac{1}{3} + \dfrac{101}{(1+101\theta_1+120\theta_2)^{0.5}} * \dfrac{1}{3} \\ \qquad\qquad + \dfrac{101}{(1+101\theta_1+95\theta_2)^{0.5}} * \dfrac{1}{3}. \end{cases}$$

The solution of this system gives the optimal portfolio for agent A.

$$\theta_1 = -0.026754$$

$$\theta_2 = 0.056179$$

Solving an analogous problem for agent B, we obtain his/her optimal portfolio, which is given by

$$\theta_1 = -0.046304$$

$$\theta_2 = 0.075044.$$

(b) This market is incomplete, so there are several state-prices in this economy. Rewriting the first-order conditions, we get

$$
\begin{cases}
85 = \frac{60(5-100\theta_1-85\theta_2)^{0.5}}{(1+101\theta_1+60\theta_2)^{0.5}} * \frac{1}{3} + \frac{120(5-100\theta_1-85\theta_2)^{0.5}}{(1+101\theta_1+120\theta_2)^{0.5}} * \frac{1}{3} \\
\quad + \frac{95(5-100\theta_1-85\theta_2)^{0.5}}{(1+101\theta_1+95\theta_2)^{0.5}} * \frac{1}{3} \\
100 = \frac{101(5-100\theta_1-85\theta_2)^{0.5}}{(1+101\theta_1+60\theta_2)^{0.5}} * \frac{1}{3} + \frac{101(5-100\theta_1-85\theta_2)^{0.5}}{(1+101\theta_1+120\theta_2)^{0.5}} * \frac{1}{3} \\
\quad + \frac{101(5-100\theta_1-85\theta_2)^{0.5}}{(1+101\theta_1+95\theta_2)^{0.5}} * \frac{1}{3}
\end{cases}
$$

and we can identify the state-prices for agent A as

$$
\begin{cases}
\psi_1 = \frac{(5-100\theta_1-85\theta_2)^{0.5}}{(1+101\theta_1+60\theta_2)^{0.5}} * \frac{1}{3} \\
\psi_2 = \frac{(5-100\theta_1-85\theta_2)^{0.5}}{(1+101\theta_1+120\theta_2)^{0.5}} * \frac{1}{3} \\
\psi_3 = \frac{(5-100\theta_1-85\theta_2)^{0.5}}{(1+101\theta_1+95\theta_2)^{0.5}} * \frac{1}{3}.
\end{cases}
$$

Substituting for the optimal value of the portfolio, we have

$$
\begin{cases}
\psi_1 = .43946 \\
\psi_2 = .25287 \\
\psi_3 = .29775.
\end{cases}
$$

Doing the same for agent B, we have

$$
\begin{cases}
\psi_1 = .44482 \\
\psi_2 = .26039 \\
\psi_3 = .28486.
\end{cases}
$$

(c) Now we have a complete market, because there are three assets, with nonlinearly dependent payoffs, and three states of nature. The state-prices of this economy are uniquely determined and given by the solution of the following system:

$$
\begin{cases}
85 = 60\psi_1 + 120\psi_2 + 95\psi_3 \\
100 = 101\psi_1 + 101\psi_2 + 101\psi_3 \\
38.02 = 50\psi_1 + 70\psi_2 + 30\psi_3
\end{cases}
\Leftrightarrow
\begin{cases}
\psi_1 \approx 0.3 \\
\psi_2 \approx 0.06 \\
\psi_3 \approx 0.63.
\end{cases}
$$

C.1.3 Valuation of Flexibility

1. If

$$C > \frac{1}{1+r}\left[\frac{(1+r)S_0 - S_2}{S_1 - S_2}C_1 + \frac{S_1 - (1+r)S_0}{S_1 - S_2}C_2\right],$$

we can have a sure profit having a short position in the option, buying $\frac{C_1-C_2}{S_1-S_2}$ units of the security and investing $\frac{C_2S_1-C_1S_2}{(1+r)(S_1-S_2)}$ at the risk-free rate. Otherwise, if

$$C < \frac{1}{1+r}\left[\frac{(1+r)S_0 - S_2}{S_1 - S_2}C_1 + \frac{S_1 - (1+r)S_0}{S_1 - S_2}C_2\right],$$

we should buy the option, short-sell $\frac{C_1-C_2}{S_1-S_2}$ units of the security, and borrow $\frac{C_2S_1-C_1S_2}{(1+r)(S_1-S_2)}$ at the risk-free rate. With each of these strategies we would obtain arbitrage profits.

2. No, at least we need two assets with nonlinearly dependent returns in order to replicate any possible payoff of the option at maturity.

3. For fixed expected return ε, to characterize the sensitivity of π to changes in the volatility amounts to calculating

$$\frac{d\pi}{d\sigma} = \frac{\partial\pi}{\partial U}\frac{dU}{d\sigma} + \frac{\partial\pi}{\partial D}\frac{dD}{d\sigma} = -\frac{\pi}{U-D}\sqrt{\frac{1-p}{p}} + \frac{1-\pi}{U-D}\sqrt{\frac{p}{1-p}}$$

$$= \frac{p-\pi}{(U-D)\sqrt{p(1-p)}}.$$

Therefore, when σ changes, π can either increase or decrease depending on π being higher or smaller than p.

4. From exercise 5 of the previous section we know that the vector of state-prices is $\psi = [0.35; 0.64]$.

   (a) Without the option to defer the decision of investment, the NPV of project 1 is 1.7. But with this option, $\text{NPV}^* = 5 * 0.35 = 1.75$. As $\text{NPV}^* > \text{NPV}$, it is better not to invest today.

   (b) With the option to cancel project 2, $\widehat{V}_2 = 4 * 0.64 = 2.56$. As $\widehat{V}_2$ is greater than the investment needed, it is a good strategy to invest in that project.

C.2 Optimal Capital Structure

C.2.1 The MM Propositions

1. (a) In this situation the firm will pay the face value of the debt in any state of nature; that is, there will be no bankruptcy. Then

$$E(B) = 5$$
$$B = F/R \approx 4.95.$$

Notice that $\sum \psi_j = \frac{1}{R}$, leading to $R \approx 1.0101$. We also need to compute

$$S^\tau = \sum \psi_j S_j^\tau = 1.614$$
$$E(S^\tau) = \sum p_j S_j^\tau = 1.8$$
$$V_u^\tau = (1-\tau) \sum \psi_j V_j = 4.584$$
$$E(V_u^\tau) = (1-\tau) \sum p_j V_j = 4.8.$$

Proposition MMI states that $V_l^\tau = V_u^\tau + \tau B$. We know that $V_l^\tau = S^\tau + B = 6.564$ and that $V_u^\tau + \tau B = 4.584 + 0.4 * 4.95 = 6.564$. The statement is verified.

Proposition MM2 states that when there is no bankruptcy,

$$R_s^\tau = R_s^u + \left(R_s^u - R\right)\frac{B}{S^\tau}(1-\tau) = 1.1152.$$

On the other hand, $R_s^\tau = E(S^\tau)/S^\tau = 1.1152$ and MM2 is checked. The weighted average of the costs of debt and equity is simply

$$\overline{R}^\tau = 1.1152\frac{1.614}{1.614 + 4.95} + 1.0101\frac{4.95}{1.614 + 4.95} = 1.0359.$$

(b) Some computation leads us to the values $B = 6.49$, $S^\tau = 0.69$, and $V_l^\tau = 7.18$. We also need to compute

$$R_s^u \approx 1.04712$$
$$R_d \approx 1.02722$$
$$\theta^\tau \approx 0.46$$
$$E(\theta^\tau) \approx 0.5(3).$$

Then, $R_s^\tau \approx 1.15942$.

(c) The weighted average of the costs of debt and equity is

$$\overline{R}^\tau = 1.15942\frac{0.69}{0.69 + 6.49} + 1.02722\frac{6.49}{0.69 + 6.49} = 1.0399.$$

As expected, $\overline{R}^\tau$ increases, reflecting more risk in the firm.

2. Suppose first that $V_l > V_u$. An individual with a proportion α of shares of the levered firm will receive $\alpha(V_j - B_j)$ in each state of nature. An alternative portfolio is to sell these shares receiving αS_l and to borrow αB. These resources could be used to buy $\alpha\frac{S_l+B}{S_u}$ shares of the unlevered firm. In each state of nature the return with this position is $\alpha\frac{S_l+B}{S_u}V_j - \alpha B_j$, which dominates the return of the first portfolio if

$$\alpha\frac{S_l + B}{S_u}V_j - \alpha B_j > \alpha(V_j - B_j)$$

$$\Leftrightarrow$$

$$\alpha V_j\left(\frac{V_l}{V_u} - 1\right) > 0.$$

As we assumed that $V_l > V_u$, there exists an arbitrage opportunity. Suppose now that $V_l < V_u$. An individual with a proportion α of shares of the unlevered firm will receive αV_j in each state of nature. An alternative portfolio is to sell these shares, receiving αS_u, and buy shares and bonds of the levered firm with weights $\frac{S_l}{S_l+B}$ in stocks and $\frac{B}{S_l+B}$ in bonds. Then the investor has a fraction $\frac{\alpha S_u}{S_l+B}$ of the net profits of the levered company: $\frac{\alpha S_u}{S_l+B}(V_j - B_j)$. It also has a fraction $\frac{\alpha S_u}{S_l+B}$ of debt, implying income $\frac{\alpha S_u}{S_l+B}B_j$. Hence, the total outcome of the second portfolio is $\frac{\alpha S_u}{S_l+B}V_j$, which dominates the first one if

$$\frac{\alpha S_u}{S_l + B}V_j > \alpha V_j$$

$$\Leftrightarrow$$

$$\alpha V_j\left(\frac{V_u}{V_l} - 1\right) > 0.$$

This is true by assumption. It is proved that if $V_u \neq V_l$, one can explore arbitrage opportunities.

3. Modigliani and Miller demonstrate that arbitrage profits could arise for individuals able to do "home-made" leverage from unlevered undervalued firms or to undo leverage of undervalued levered firms. Suppose there are two firms. Firm u is financed only with common stock and firm l has some debt. Then, $V_u = S_u$ and $V_l = S_l + B$. The return to

the stockholders of firm u is $X(1 - \tau)$ and the return to the stockholders of firm l is $(X - rB)(1 - \tau)$. Here we prove only MM1 with taxes. To prove MM1 without taxes, it suffices to take $\tau = 0$ in what follows.

If $V_l > V_u + \tau B$, an individual with a proportion α of the shares of firm l could sell them, making αS_l dollars, and also borrow $\alpha B(1 - \tau)$ at rate r. With these resources he/she will buy a proportion $\frac{\alpha(S_l + B(1 - \tau))}{S_u}$ of the shares of firm u. If he/she did not do this operation, he/she would have returns $\alpha(1 - \tau)(X - rB)$. The gain for using the strategy is

$$\frac{\alpha(S_l + B(1 - \tau))}{S_u} X(1 - \tau) - \alpha B(1 - \tau)r - \alpha(1 - \tau)(X - rB)$$

$$= \alpha(1 - \tau) X \frac{S_l + B(1 - \tau) - S_u}{S_u}.$$

Therefore, if $V_l > V_u + \tau B$, the gain of this strategy is positive and there is an arbitrage opportunity. To eliminate arbitrage opportunities, one must have that $V_l \le V_u + \tau B$.

Suppose now that $V_l < V_u + \tau B$. An individual with a proportion α of the shares of firm u could sell them, making αS_u dollars. These resources could be used to buy shares and bonds of firm l in the same proportion as S_l and B are to $S_l + B(1 - \tau)$. The return with this position minus the return of the initial position is

$$\frac{\alpha S_u}{(S_l + B(1 - \tau))}(X - rB)(1 - \tau) + \frac{\alpha S_u(1 - \tau)}{(S_l + B(1 - \tau))}rB - \alpha X(1 - \tau)$$

$$= \alpha(1 - \tau) X \frac{S_u - S_l - B(1 - \tau)}{(S_l + B(1 - \tau))}.$$

To eliminate any arbitrage opportunities, this gain should be zero or negative—that is, $V_u + \tau B \le V_l$. Hence, it follows that $V_u + \tau B = V_l$.

4. Suppose first $V_l > V_u$. An individual with a proportion α of the shares of the levered firm has the uncertain income $\alpha(X - rB_l)$. An alternative portfolio is to sell these shares, receiving αS_l, and to borrow αB_l at the interest rate $\bar{r}$. These resources could be used to buy $\alpha \frac{S_l + B_l}{S_u}$ shares of the unlevered firm. The return of this position is

$$\alpha \frac{S_l + B_l}{S_u} X - \alpha \bar{r} B_l$$

and it will dominate the first one if

$$\alpha \frac{S_l + B_l}{S_u} X - \alpha \bar{r} B_l > \alpha(X - rB_l)$$

$$\Leftrightarrow \alpha \frac{X}{V_u}(V_l - V_u) + \alpha B_l(r - \bar{r}) > 0.$$

If $V_u > V_l$, an individual with a proportion α of the shares of the unlevered firm can sell these shares, making αS_u. These resources could be used to buy shares of the levered firm in the total value $\alpha S_u \frac{S_l}{V_l}$ and to lend the remaining, $\alpha S_u \frac{B_l}{V_l}$, at the interest rate $\underline{r}$. The income of this portfolio is

$$\alpha \frac{S_u}{V_l}(X - rB_l) + \alpha \frac{S_u}{V_l} B_l \underline{r} \Leftrightarrow \alpha \frac{S_u}{V_l} X - \alpha \frac{S_u}{V_l} B_l(r - \underline{r})$$

and it will dominate the first one if

$$\alpha \frac{S_u}{V_l} X - \alpha \frac{S_u}{V_l} B_l(r - \underline{r}) > \alpha X \Leftrightarrow \alpha X \left(\frac{S_u}{V_l} - 1 \right) - \alpha \frac{S_u}{V_l} B_l(r - \underline{r}) > 0.$$

If we assume that $\underline{r} = r - \epsilon$, and $\bar{r} = r + \epsilon$, there will be no arbitrage opportunities if

$$V_u \left(1 - \frac{\epsilon B_l}{X} \right) \leq V_l \leq V_u \left(1 + \frac{\epsilon B_l}{X} \right).$$

5. If $V_u > V_l$, an individual with a proportion α of the shares of the unlevered firm can sell them, receiving $\alpha S_u - T$. With this resources he/she will buy shares and bonds of the levered firm, paying again the fixed cost T, and this will leave him/her with only $\alpha S_u - 2T$ to invest. He/she will get a proportion $\frac{\alpha S_u - 2T}{V_l}$ of the shares of the leveraged firm and a proportion $\frac{\alpha S_u - 2T}{V_l}$ of the bonds of the firm. The return of this portfolio is

$$\frac{\alpha S_u - 2T}{V_l}(X - rB_l + rB_l) = \frac{X}{V_l}(\alpha S_u - 2T).$$

To eliminate any arbitrage portfolio, we must have that

$$\frac{X}{V_l}(\alpha S_u - 2T) \leq \alpha X \Leftrightarrow V_u \leq V_l + 2T/\alpha.$$

If $V_l > V_u$, an individual with a proportion α of the shares of the levered firm can sell them, receiving $\alpha S_l - T$, and borrow αB_l at the interest rate r. He/she will buy a proportion

$$\frac{\alpha S_l + \alpha B_l - 2T}{S_u}$$

of the shares of the unlevered firm. The return with this new position is $\frac{\alpha S_l + \alpha B_l - 2T}{S_u} X - \alpha r B_l$, which compared with the return $\alpha(X - rB_l)$ yields a gain $\alpha \frac{X}{V_u}(V_l - V_u - 2T/\alpha)$. Then, to eliminate any arbitrage opportunity, it follows that $V_l \leq V_u + 2T/\alpha$. Finally, considering both conditions, there will be no arbitrage opportunities if

$$V_u - \frac{2T}{\alpha} \leq V_l \leq V_u + \frac{2T}{\alpha}.$$

C.2.2 Personal and Corporate Taxation

1. An individual with a proportion α of the levered firm has an uncertain return of

$$\alpha(X - rB)(1 - \tau_c)(1 - \tau_S).$$

However, this can be replicated buying a fraction α of the unlevered firm, which yields $\alpha X(1 - \tau_c)(1 - \tau_S)$, and borrowing $\alpha B \frac{(1-\tau_c)(1-\tau_S)}{(1-\tau_b)}$. As these alternative strategies give the same return, their initial cost must be the same:

$$\alpha S_l = \alpha S_u + \alpha B \frac{(1 - \tau_c)(1 - \tau_S)}{(1 - \tau_b)}$$

$$\Leftrightarrow$$

$$V_l = V_u + B\left[1 - \frac{(1 - \tau_c)(1 - \tau_S)}{(1 - \tau_b)}\right].$$

2. Firms at the top rate should use debt financing until they have enough tax deductions to drive their marginal tax rate to the lower market equilibrium corporate tax rate. Firms with a lower marginal tax rate should use equity financing.

C.3 Implications for Capital Structure

C.3.1 The Role of Agency Costs

1. According to Section 3.1.1, $V = \overline{V} - F(\alpha)$ where $\overline{V}$ is the value of the firm, $F(\alpha)$ are the fringe benefits consumed by managers, α is the managers' fraction of the firm, and V is the effective value of the firm. Then, $dV = -\frac{\partial F}{\partial \alpha}d\alpha > 0$ since $\partial F/\partial \alpha < 0$. Hence, we can say that a decrease in α makes the value of the firm fall.

   If outsiders receive voting rights, and we assume that managers want to keep control of the firm, α can only be as low as 0.5. This restriction on α limits the decrease in the value of the firm.

2. See Jensen and Meckling (1976), page 318.

3. Conflicts of interest generate agency problems between managers and stockholders because ownership is separated from control. Such agency costs can be reduced by giving stock options to managers. In this case the expected payoff to stock options increases with the stock price variance, and options provide the manager with incentives to invest in projects that increase the riskiness of the firm's cash flows. Options thus help to control managers' incentives to take too little risk. Stock options also help to control the underleverage problem. Higher leverage becomes more attractive to the manager since it increases the variance of the equity and thus the value of the options.

Applying the model of Section 3.1.1, to give stock options to managers is equivalent to an increase in α, leading to an increase in the firm's value.

Other factors to be considered are (i) the effects of the options exercise by managers since the firm must issue new shares and (ii) as managers choose riskier projects, there may be a transfer of wealth from bondholders to stockholders.

4. Equation (3.4) can be rewritten as

$$\frac{U'[w - f(w)]}{U'[w' - f(w')]} = \frac{G'[f(w)]}{G'[f(w')]}$$

where w and w' characterize the payoffs of the firm for two distinct states of nature. This way, the marginal rates of substitution of income between the different states of nature are equal for the two agents and risk is shared optimally. In fact, if effort is completely observed, a first best solution is obtainable.

To see what happens to the optimal value $f^*[w(a^0, \theta)]$ when θ changes, we start differentiating the optimal condition with respect to θ,

$$U'[w(a, \theta) - f(w(a, \theta))] = \lambda G'[f(w(a, \theta))]$$

$$U''\left[\frac{dw(\cdot)}{d\theta} - \frac{df(\cdot)}{d\theta}\right] = \lambda G''\frac{df(\cdot)}{d\theta}$$

$$U''\left[\frac{dw(\cdot)}{d\theta} - \frac{df(\cdot)}{d\theta}\right] = \frac{U'}{G'}G''\frac{df(\cdot)}{d\theta},$$

where this last equation was obtained using condition (3.4). Rearranging terms, and knowing that the absolute risk averse coefficient of agent i is $R_a^i = -U''/U'$, we arrive at the condition

$$\frac{df(\cdot)}{d\theta} = \frac{R_a^P}{R_a^P + R_a^A}\frac{dw(\cdot)}{d\theta},$$

where R_a^P is the absolute risk averse coefficient of the principal (stockholder) and R_a^A is the absolute risk averse coefficient of the agent (manager). This equation shows how the management fee changes with different payoffs implied by different states of nature. When both managers and stockholders are risk averse, they will share risk optimally according to this equation. When the stockholder is risk neutral, the fee paid to managers is constant and the stockholders will bear all the risk. When the manager is risk neutral, the stockholder will receive a fixed rent and the agent will bear all the risk. This is what Shavell (1979) proves.

5. When the agent is risk averse, we can show that the risk sharing implied by this condition is not Pareto efficient. Take the case of when the principal is risk neutral. Pareto efficient risk sharing induces complete insurance to the agent (as stated in the previous exercise). But if the fee is fixed, the agent will choose the most favorable level of effort for him/her, that is, zero. To make him/her put forth some effort, the fee must depend on the total payoff. As the payoff is uncertain, this cannot be an optimal rule of risk sharing. When the agent is risk neutral, the optimum is obtained by giving him/her an amount equal to the total payoff minus a fixed income to the principal. Since the manager receives all benefits of his/her actions, his/her choices will be optimal. This is also what Shavell (1979) says.

6. Let $U = -(1/\delta)e^{-\delta(w-f)}$ and $G = -(1/\alpha)e^{-\alpha f}$. These functions have constant absolute risk averse coefficients equal to δ and α, respectively. Then, using condition (3.4),

$$U'[w - f] = \lambda G'[f],$$

we have

$$e^{-\delta(w-f)} = \lambda e^{-\alpha f} \Leftrightarrow -\delta(w - f) = \ln \lambda - \alpha f,$$

implying that

$$f = \frac{\delta}{\alpha + \delta} w + \frac{\ln \lambda}{\alpha + \delta}.$$

7. A convertible bond is one that gives the holder the right to exchange the bond for the firm's common stock. Convertibles can be used to control the asset substitution problem—that is, the stockholders' incentive to have the firm take some unprofitable high-variance projects. Risk-increasing activities raise the value of the conversion option and thus reduce the gain to stockholders from taking high-risk projects by transferring part of the gains to convertible bondholders. Green (1984) shows that the issuance of convertibles and warrants lowers agency costs in a similar way.

Another way to indirectly reduce agency costs is to use a call provision on debt, which has the effect of realigning shareholder incentives toward maximization of the total value of the firm. Call provisions can be used to reduce agency costs of debt due to, for example, the risk incentive problem. This possibility was identified by Galai and Masulis (1976) using the Black-Scholes (1973) option pricing model. The risk incentive problem refers to situations in which stockholders can expropriate wealth from bondholders by increasing the risk of the firm. Because the value of the call provision to the equityholders declines as the value of the firm decreases, stockholders have less incentive to shift to high-variance, low-value projects after the debt is issued. Other reasons can be found in Thatcher (1985).

8. We can say that $B = S - C$, where B is debt, S means total assets, and C is the call value if (1) a company has common stock and bonds outstanding and its only assets are shares of common stock of a second company, (2) the bonds are pure discount bonds with no coupon and give the holder the right to a fixed amount of money, if the firm can pay it, at a given maturity, T, (3) the company cannot pay any dividends until the bonds are paid off, and (4) the company plans to sell all the stock at the end of T, pay off the bondholders if possible, and pay any remaining money to the stockholders. Under these conditions, the bondholders own the company's assets and have given options to the stockholders to buy the assets back. (Based on Black and Scholes, 1973)

Now, we want to prove that $0 \leq \partial B / \partial K < 1$, where K is the face value of the debt. From $B = S - C(K)$, we have $\partial B / \partial K = -\partial C / \partial K = e^{-r_f t} N(d_2)$, where this last equality is stated in Galai and Masulis (1976). The expression $e^{-r_f t} N(d_2)$ is always positive since it is an interest rate multiplied by a probability and these are always positive. At the same time, it also takes a value smaller than 1 since the maximum value that $N(d_2)$ can reach is 1 and it comes divided by $e^{-r_f t}$, which is higher than 1.

Black and Scholes (1973) justify this fact since "an increase in the corporation's debt, keeping the total value of corporation constant, will increase the probability of default and will thus reduce the market value of its bonds." However, as pointed by Jensen and Meckling (1976) among others, the pricing option model of Black and Scholes takes as exogenous the value of the underlying asset, S, and does not apply when the value of the firm is a function of the debt-equity ratio. Then, this implication drawn from the option pricing model is only suggestive.

9. If the firm is all equity-financed, the investment rule at $t = 1$ of the management is $V(s) \geq I$ and the value of the firm, V, is

$$V = \int_{s_a}^{\infty} q(s)[V(s) - I]ds$$

if $s \geq s_a$, and zero otherwise, where $q(s)$ is the uniform density function over the states $s \in [0, s']$ and s_a is the break-even state in which $V(s) = I$. If risky debt is considered and it matures after the firm's investment decision is taken, then outstanding debt will change the firm's investment decision in some states. If P is the promised payment to bondholders, then the investment is taken only if $V(s) \geq P + I$. If $V(s) < I + P$, then the market value of the equity is less than the investment, I. If s_a is the break-even state in which $V(s) = I$ and s_b is the break-even state in which $V(s) = I + P$, then the resulting loss in value is given by

$$\int_{s_b}^{\infty} q(s)[V(s) - I]ds - \int_{s_a}^{\infty} q(s)[V(s) - I]ds = \int_{s_a}^{s_b} q(s)[V(s) - I]ds.$$

Positive net present values are thereby forgone in states $s_1 \in [s_a, s_b]$.

10. Bond covenants restricting the payment of dividends exist because debt holders may fear a sudden cash outflow from the firm to shareholders. At the same time, they can protect against suboptimal investment decisions induced by risky debt. As Myers (1977) shows, firms financed with risky debt will pass up valuable investment opportunities that could make a positive net contribution to the market value of the firm. Then, since dividend and investment policies are interdependent, the specification of a maximum on dividends imposes a minimum on the fraction of earnings retained in the firm. When the firm has plenty of cash, it can either invest the cash or distribute dividends if they are not restricted. Then, the firm's investment decisions are unchanged. But if dividends are restricted, the firm must invest in something. If there are projects with a positive net present value, they will be undertaken and the value of the firm is maximized. In this case, dividends' restrictions lead the firm to accept good projects that, otherwise, it would not do in the presence of risky debt.

Some authors note that a policy of paying dividends increases the frequency with which the corporation's managers go to the capital markets to obtain new equity. This policy subjects the firm more frequently to intensive capital market monitoring and discipline, which lowers agency costs.

Myers (1977) also argues that the standard bond covenant restricting dividends is only a partial solution since

(a) There are still monitoring costs since there are many other ways to transfer capital to the firm's owners. As Jensen and Meckling point out, when managers also own the firm, transfers can take the form of fringe benefits.
(b) The investment incentives are not exactly right. Shareholders may still prefer risky assets to safe ones and transfer wealth from bondholders to stockholders.
(c) The dividend restriction may force the firm to keep cash on hand or even undertake projects with a negative net present value.

C.3.2 Informational Asymmetries

1. Ross (1977) proves that debt can be used as a signal to the market when the management maximizes their incentive return, which is a function of debt. He shows that the optimal face value of debt is given by $B = \frac{\gamma_0}{4\gamma_1 L}[t^2 - c^2]$. If $\gamma_1 = 0$, managers will maximize only time 0 value. Since they share no consequences of the next period's performance, they will not care about the probability penalty. Then, the optimal level of debt is ∞ to all firms and debt cannot be used as a signal to distinguish between firms. If $\gamma_0 = 0$, managers don't care about a firm's valuation at time 0 when they were to decide about the sign to the market. In this case, applying equation (3.9), the optimal level of debt is zero to all firms. In summary, in order to use debt as a sign to the market, the incentive return the manager maximizes must consider at least two periods. Otherwise, the model will fail to be a signaling model.
2. See page 377 of Leland and Pyle (1977).
3. See page 386 of Leland and Pyle (1977).
4. If managers act in the interest of all shareholders, they will decide to invest if $E + S + a + b \geq E + S + a \Leftrightarrow b \geq 0$. This rule simply says that management will accept all positive-NPV projects, maximizing the value of the firm.

   If managers act in the interest of the new shareholders, deciding to issue or not, they will solve the equation

$$\left(1 - \frac{P'}{P'+E}\right)[E + S + a + b] \geq E$$
$$\Leftrightarrow$$
$$b \geq P' - (S + a).$$

This condition is less restrictive than the one considered in Myers and Majluf (1984).

5. See footnote 12, page 203, of Myers and Majluf (1984).
6. See Appendix, page 181, of Vermaelen (1984).

C.4 Payout Policy

C.4.1 Dividend Policy

1. In a world of certainty, the amount of capital raised externally $(m_{t+1}p_{t+1} - IC)$ must be the difference between what is needed to invest and what the firm has available—that is,

$$m_{t+1}p_{t+1} - IC = I_{t+1} - [X_{t+1} - D_{t+1}].$$

Then, by substitution in the equation that gives the value of the firm,

$$V_t = \frac{1}{1+\rho}[D_{t+1} + V_{t+1} - m_{t+1}p_{t+1}],$$

we will get

$$V_t = \frac{1}{1+\rho}[X_{t+1} - I_{t+1} + V_{t+1} - IC].$$

Making a systematic substitution of this last equation in itself, we get

$$V_t = \sum_{\tau=0}^{T} \frac{[X_{t+\tau} - I_{t+\tau}]}{(1+\rho)^{\tau+1}} - IC\frac{1 - (1/(1+\rho)^{T+1})}{1 - 1/(1+\rho)}\frac{1}{1+\rho} + \frac{1}{(1+\rho)^T}V_{T+t}.$$

Assuming that T goes to infinity, the last term goes to zero and we have the final equation,

$$V_t = \sum_{\tau=0}^{\infty} \frac{[X_{t+\tau} - I_{t+\tau}]}{(1+\rho)^{\tau+1}} - \frac{IC}{\rho}.$$

2. From the definitions, use $D_{t+\tau} = n_{t+\tau-1}d_{t+\tau}$ and $m_{t+\tau} = n_{t+\tau} - n_{t+\tau-1}$. As we recall that $p_{t+\tau} = (1+\rho)p_{t+\tau-1} - d_{t+\tau}$, the expression for V_t becomes

$$V_t = \sum_{\tau=1}^{\infty} \frac{1}{(1+\rho)^\tau}[D_{t+\tau} - m_{t+\tau}p_{t+\tau}]$$

$$= \sum_{\tau=1}^{\infty} \frac{n_{t+\tau-1}d_{t+\tau} - (n_{t+\tau} - n_{t+\tau-1})[(1+\rho)p_{t+\tau-1} - d_{t+\tau}]}{(1+\rho)^\tau}$$

$$= \sum_{\tau=1}^{\infty} \frac{n_{t+\tau-1}p_{t+\tau-1}}{(1+\rho)^{\tau-1}} - \sum_{\tau=1}^{\infty} \frac{n_{t+\tau}[(1+\rho)p_{t+\tau-1} - d_{t+\tau}]}{(1+\rho)^\tau}$$

$$= \sum_{\tau=0}^{\infty} \frac{n_{t+\tau}p_{t+\tau}}{(1+\rho)^\tau} - \sum_{\tau=1}^{\infty} \frac{n_{t+\tau}p_{t+\tau}}{(1+\rho)^\tau} = n_t p_t.$$

3. It follows from

$$p_t = \sum_{\tau=1}^{\infty} \frac{d_{t+\tau}}{(1+\rho)^{\tau}} = \sum_{\tau=1}^{\infty} \frac{d_t(1+g)^{\tau}}{(1+\rho)^{\tau}}$$

that

$$p_{t+n} = \sum_{\tau=1}^{\infty} \frac{d_{t+\tau+n}}{(1+\rho)^{\tau}}$$

$$= \sum_{\tau=1}^{\infty} \frac{d_t(1+g)^{\tau+n}}{(1+\rho)^{\tau}} = (1+g)^n \sum_{\tau=1}^{\infty} \frac{d_t(1+g)^{\tau}}{(1+\rho)^{\tau}};$$

that is,

$$p_{t+n} = (1+g)^n p_t.$$

4. In this case, the value of the firm is given by

$$V_t = X_{t+1} \frac{(1-k)}{\rho - k_i \rho^*} \left[1 - \left(\frac{1 + k_i \rho^*}{1 + \rho} \right)^T \right].$$

When investment opportunities generate a constant rate of growth of profits in perpetuity, for the value of the firm to be finite we need to impose the condition $\rho > k_i \rho^*$, which means that the rate of growth of the firm must be less than the market rate of discount. When investment is finite, the equation of valorization of the firm holds even if $\rho < k_i \rho^*$. In the first case, we cannot accept that a firm always grows at a higher rate than the market, but we can accept that for only a finite number of periods.

5. In an uncertain world, firms can be financed by retained earnings, stock issues, and also debt issues. However, the introduction of debt will not change the dividends' irrelevance proposition. Considering debt issues, the total value of the firm is the total market value of debt plus equity $(B_t + n_t p_t)$, and their returns should consider dividends, the price of the share next period, debt, and the interest on debt. Then, the equation giving the value of the firm changes to

$$V_t = B_t + n_t p_t = \frac{1}{1+\rho} [n_t d_{t+1} + n_t p_{t+1} + (1+r)B_t].$$

At the same time, the amount of capital raised externally $(m_t p_t + B_{t+1})$ is used to finance the investment and we must also consider the debt and the interest on debt:

$$m_{t+1} p_{t+1} + B_{t+1} = I_{t+1} - [X_{t+1} - D_{t+1}] + (1+r)B_t,$$

where r is the constant interest rate of debt. Then, by substitution of this second equation in the first one, also assuming that $n_{t+1} = n_t + m_{t+1}$, the value of the firm is given by

$$V_t = B_t + n_t p_t$$

$$= \frac{1}{1+\rho} \left[\begin{array}{l} D_{t+1} + n_{t+1} p_{t+1} + (1+r) B_t \\ + B_{t+1} - I_{t+1} + X_{t+1} - D_{t+1} - (1+r) B_t \end{array} \right]$$

$$= \frac{1}{1+\rho} [V_{t+1} - I_{t+1} + X_{t+1}].$$

This total return is, as before, independent of the current dividend. In an uncertain world, this completes the proof of the dividend's irrelevance proposition. (See page 29 of Miller and Modigliani, 1961.)

6. See page 169 of Litzenberger and Ramaswamy (1979).
7. In the presence of short-term traders, there might be some arbitrage profit around the ex-dividend day. Suppose the dividend per share is smaller than the expected price drop by more than transaction costs (C). Short-term traders could sell the stock short cum-dividend and buy it back ex-dividend, thereby gaining $(1-\tau)[P_b - P_a - D - C] > 0$ where τ is the marginal tax rate on ordinary income the short-term trader is subject to. On the other hand, if the dividend per share exceeded the ex-dividend expected price drop by more than the cost of buying and selling the stock, investors could buy the stock cum-dividend and sell it ex-dividend and gain $(1-\tau)[D - (P_b - P_a) - C] > 0$. The non-profit condition can be found by combining the preceding equations: $|D - (P_b - P_a)| \le C \Rightarrow$

$$1 - \frac{C}{D} \le \frac{P_b - P_a}{D} \le 1 + \frac{C}{D}.$$

From this nonprofit condition it can be seen that the tax rate cannot be inferred from the value of $(P_b - P_a)/D$. (See Kalay, 1982.)

C.4.2 Dividends and Information

1. The financing announcement effect is equal to the reversed dividend announcement effect, as negative values of the net dividend can be interpreted as a need for financing. The sign and size of the price change following an announcement of new financing will depend on the relation between I^* and the expected earnings.
2. See page 1042 of Miller and Rock (1985).

3. We will consider each parameter separately.

   (a) Start with γ. The first-order condition, denoted by $H(D, \gamma) = 0$, defines implicitly a relation between D and γ. By the implicit theorem function, $\frac{\partial D}{\partial \gamma} = -\frac{\partial H/\partial \gamma}{\partial H/\partial D}$, where $\partial H/\partial D < 0$ because it is the second-order condition of the problem. Then, as

$$\frac{\partial H}{\partial \gamma} = k\frac{1}{1+\rho}X' \geq 0,$$

   we have the result $\frac{\partial D}{\partial \gamma} > 0$. It means that, the higher the value of γ, other things equal, the higher the payout ratio and the lower the investment level in the signaling equilibrium. The reason for this relation is that a higher γ means that the gain in value for the fraction of shareholders planning to sell their shares is higher and they would be induced to pay more to the management to increase dividends and cut investment. In fact, the higher the value of γ, the stronger the persistence in earnings and the greater the predicted responsiveness of price to unexpected dividends, leading to a higher return for the sellers.

   (b) Using the same procedure as before,

$$\frac{\partial H}{\partial k} = \frac{1}{1+\rho}[F' + \gamma]X' \geq 0.$$

   It follows that $\frac{\partial D}{\partial K} > 0$. The effect of a change in k has the same sign as a change in γ. In this case, if k is the fraction of shareholders planning to sell, it can be seen as measuring the weight in the objective function of current price, as opposed to long-run return. Increasing dividends will benefit those planning to sell, reducing the long-run return since some projects with a positive value will be forgone.

4. The optimal level of investment is given by $1/I^* = 1+\rho \Leftrightarrow$

$$I^* = (1+\rho)^{-1}.$$

The maximizing problem of the management is $\max_D kV_1^2(D_1) + (1 - k)V_1^1(X_1, D_1)$. It follows that the first-order condition in equilibrium is

$$k\partial_x V_1^1(X(D), D)X'(D) + \partial_d V_1^1(X(D), D) = 0.$$

Since the value of the firm is given by

$$V_1 = D_1 + \frac{1}{1+\rho}F(X_1 - D_1) + \gamma[X_1 - F(I_o)],$$

we get

$$\partial_x V_1^1 = \frac{1}{1+\rho} F' + \gamma \frac{1}{1+\rho} = \frac{1}{1+\rho} (X-D)^{-1} + \gamma \frac{1}{1+\rho}$$

and

$$\partial_d V_1^1 = 1 - \frac{1}{1+\rho} F' = 1 - \frac{1}{1+\rho} (X-D)^{-1}.$$

Substituting in the first-order condition, and assuming $\gamma = 0$,

$$kX'(D) \frac{1}{1+\rho}(X-D)^{-1} + 1 - \frac{1}{1+\rho}(X-D)^{-1} = 0$$

$$\Leftrightarrow X'(D) = \frac{1}{k} - \frac{(1+\rho)}{k(X-D)^{-1}}$$

$$\Leftrightarrow X'(D) = \alpha - \beta(X-D),$$

where $\alpha = 1/k$ and $\beta = (1+\rho)k^{-1}$. The solution of this differential equation is

$$X(D) = \exp(-\beta D)\left(A + \int \alpha \exp(\beta D)dD + \int \beta D \exp(\beta D)dD\right)$$

$$\Leftrightarrow$$

$$X(D) = \exp(-\beta D)\left(A + \frac{1}{\beta}(\alpha - 1)\exp \beta D + D \exp(\beta D)\right),$$

where A is the integration constant. To compute the value of A we use the result that firms whose results are at the lower bound $\underline{X}$ choose I^*, so that $D^* = \underline{X} - I^*$ and $\underline{X}(D^*) = \underline{X}$ Then,

$$A = \beta^{-1} \exp(\beta D^*).$$

Finally,

$$X(D) = D + \beta^{-1} \exp(-\beta(D - D^*)) + \beta^{-1}(\alpha - 1). \qquad (C.5)$$

The optimal level of investment is then

$$X(D) - D = \beta^{-1} \exp(-\beta(D - D^*)) + \beta^{-1}(\alpha - 1)$$

$$\Leftrightarrow$$

$$X(D) - D = I^* - \frac{k}{1+\rho}[1 - \exp(-(1+\rho)k^{-1}(D - D^*))] \le I^*.$$

The last conclusion comes from the fact that $X'(D)$ from condition (C.5) is positive only if $D > D^*$.

C.5 Financial Contracting

C.5.1 Contracting and Allocation of Control

1. See footnote 8 of Aghion and Bolton (1992).
2. See page 482 of Aghion and Bolton (1992).
3. Without renegotiation the investor accepts only a contract $t_s = 0$, whatever signal is observed, and the entrepreneur will always choose a_g, independently of the state of nature. Denote the expected payoff to the entrepreneur without renegotiation by π_{wt}^E. Then $\pi_{wt}^E = q l_g^g + (1-q) l_g^b$. Because all the bargaining power is on the side of the entrepreneur in the negotiation, he/she will make the investor pay as much as he/she can, that is, $q y_g^g + (1-q) y_b^b - \pi_2 = (1-q)(y_b^b - y_g^b)$. So, the expected payoff to the entrepreneur with renegotiation π_w^E becomes

$$
\begin{aligned}
\pi_w^E &= q l_g^g + (1-q) l_b^b + (1-q)\left(y_b^b - y_g^b\right) \\
&= q l_g^g + (1-q)\left(y_b^b - l_b^b\right) + (1-q) y_g^b \\
&\geq q l_g^g + (1-q)\left(y_g^b - l_g^b\right) + (1-q) y_g^b \\
&= q l_g^g + (1-q) l_g^b = \pi_{wt}^E.
\end{aligned}
$$

4. In general, expected profit is defined by

$$
\begin{aligned}
\pi_i &= E[r] - E[g(r)] \\
&= E[r] - E[t_s r] \\
&= E[(1 - t_s) r]. \tag{C.6}
\end{aligned}
$$

As the incentive constraints are satisfied with $t_s = \hat{t}$, we obtain

$$
\pi_1 = q(1 - \hat{t}) y_g^g + (1-q)(1 - \hat{t}) y_b^b.
$$

If $t_s < \hat{t}$, the investor will only accept a contract with $t_s = 0$ whatever signal is observed. Therefore, the entrepreneur will always choose a_g independently of the state of nature. Equation (C.6) then reads

$$
\pi_2 = q y_g^g + (1-q) y_g^b.
$$

To obtain the expression for π_3, we rewrite equation (C.6) as

$$\pi_i = q \begin{bmatrix} \Pr(s=1|\theta=\theta_g)(1-t_s)y(s=1|\theta=\theta_g) \\ + \Pr(s=0|\theta=\theta_g)(1-t_s)y(s=0|\theta=\theta_g) \end{bmatrix}$$
$$+ (1-q) \begin{bmatrix} \Pr(s=1|\theta=\theta_b)(1-t_s)y(s=1|\theta=\theta_b) \\ + \Pr(s=0|\theta=\theta_b)(1-t_s)y(s=0|\theta=\theta_b) \end{bmatrix}$$

$$\Leftrightarrow$$

$$\pi_i = q\big[\beta_g(1-t_s)y(s=1|\theta=\theta_g) + (1-\beta_g)(1-t_s)y(s=0|\theta=\theta_g)\big]$$
$$+ (1-q)\big[\beta_g(1-t_s)y(s=1|\theta=\theta_b)$$
$$+ (1-\beta_g)(1-t_s)y(s=0|\theta=\theta_b)\big].$$

In this case $t_s = \hat{t}$ for $s=0$ and $t_s = 0$ for $s=1$. Thus, if $s=1$ and the state of nature is θ_b, the entrepreneur will be induced to choose the action a_g. For any other contingency he/she will choose the optimal one. Therefore,

$$\pi_3 = q\big[\beta_g y_g^g + (1-\beta_g)(1-\hat{t})y_g^g\big] + (1-q)\big[\beta_b y_g^b + (1-\beta_b)(1-\hat{t})y_b^b\big].$$

Now we find the expression for π_4. As we have $t_s = \hat{t}_s = 1 - (1-t_s)\frac{y_b^g}{y_g^g}$ in state θ_g (this will induce the investor to choose a_g in state θ_g) and $t_s = t$ in state θ_b, the expression is

$$\pi_4 = q(1-\hat{t}_s)y_g^g + (1-q)(1-t)y_b^b = q\left((1-t_s)\frac{y_b^g}{y_g^g}\right)y_g^g + (1-q)(1-t)y_b^b.$$

Knowing that $\hat{t}_s \geq 0$, we must have $(1-t_s) \leq \frac{y_b^g}{y_g^g}$. Substituting for $(1-t_s) = \frac{y_g^g}{y_b^g}$, we get

$$\pi_4 = \frac{y_g^g}{y_b^g}\big[q y_g^g + (1-q)y_b^b\big].$$

5. See page 483 of Aghion and Bolton (1992).
6. See page 484 of Aghion and Bolton (1992).

C.5.2 Debt Contract Design

1. Taking the derivative of β_0 with respect to q we obtain

$$\frac{\partial \beta_0}{\partial q} = \frac{-K\left(\frac{y}{2} - \frac{\alpha^2 y^2}{4\bar{c}}\right)}{\left[q\frac{y}{2} + (1-q)\frac{\alpha^2 y^2}{4\bar{c}}\right]^2} \leq 0.$$

As, by assumption, $\frac{\alpha y}{2} < \bar{c}$, then $\frac{\alpha^2 y}{2} < \bar{c}$ and the result is obtained.

2. See pages 10–13 of Bolton and Scharfstein (1996).
3. The expected value at $t = 0$ of the short-term debt is given by

$$P_u V_s^u + P_d V_s^d = f(1 - e)r_1 + [1 - f(1 - e)]V_s^d$$

where P_u (P_d) is the probability of the project to be upgraded (down-graded) for a borrower of unknown type. Then, if we equal this expected value to the expected return R required by one period lender, we obtain $f(1-e)r_1 + [1 - f(1-e)]V_s^d = R \Leftrightarrow r_1 = \frac{R - [1 - f(1-e)]V_s^d}{f(1-e)}$.

4. See the appendix (pages 732–733) of Diamond (1991).
5. See example 1 (pages 716–717) of Diamond (1991).
6. See examples 2 and 3 (pages 717–719) of Diamond (1991).

C.6 Going Public

C.6.1 The Going Public Decision

1. See Appendix A of Chemmanur and Fulghieri (1999).
2. See Appendix B of Chemmanur and Fulghieri (1999).

C.6.2 Underpricing and Information Asymmetries

1. Under a firm commitment underwriting agreement, the firm and the underwriter agree on a price and quantity for the firm's first issuance. Once the price is set, no further adjustments are allowed. If there is excess demand, the bank rations the shares among the interested; if there is excess supply, the offer concludes with unsold shares. The investment bank pays the shares to the firm, at the offering price, and disposes of them later at market prices.

    On the other hand, under a best-effort underwriting agreement, the investment bank acts only as a marketing agent for the firm. The underwriter does not agree to purchase the issue at a predetermined price, but he/she only sells the securities and takes a spread. All the residual shares are taken back by the firm.

    It is clear that the problem in an offering is the uncertainty about the market price. In the first case, the investment bank has an incentive to underprice to be sure that the all securities are sold and he/she doesn't lose with the operation. In the second case, if there is excess supply, it is the firm that gets the residual and may lose with the offering.

2. This private information ϕ may have the following interpretation: (i) It could have been obtained during his/her contacts with customers made to estimate the demand for the issue. (ii) It may represent the bank's superior knowledge of the covariance between the return on the securities to be issued and the return on the market portfolio.
3. See page 962 of Baron (1982).
4. See page 192 of Rock (1986).
5. In Rock's model, the incoming orders are assigned a lottery number upon arrival. These numbers are drawn at random and the corresponding orders are filled in their entirety. The drawings conclude when there are either no more orders or no more shares. Under this rationing scheme, the probability that an order is filled is independent of its size.

   Suppose that, instead of all orders being received on one day and filled by lot, the orders arrive over a period of many days and are filled in order of arrival, which is typical of a best-effort underwriting. If the issuer closes the offer as soon as the last share is subscribed, the rationing is invisible because the unfilled orders can't be seen. Nevertheless, they exist and this invisible rationing exerts the same downward pressure on the offering price. Uninformed investors who arrive in time suspect their success may be due to lack of interest on the part of informed investors. Conditional on getting some shares, the uninformed find the shares to be worth less than their unconditional value. Therefore the shares must be priced at a discount to attract uninformed buyers.
6. We want to show that $\frac{\partial \alpha}{\partial p_0} < 0$. In this model, the issuing firm maximizes the offer price subject to the constraint that the uninformed investors earn an expected return of zero:

$$\int_0^{p_0} n(p_0 - v) f(v) \, dv = (1 - \alpha) \int_{p_0}^{\infty} n(v - p_0) f(v) \, dv.$$

   The left (right) side of the equation represents the expected loss (profits) to uninformed investors from purchasing IPOs for more (less) than their secondary market equilibrium price. From this equation we know that as the proportion of informed investors rises, the offer price must fall to maintain equilibrium. When α increases, all else equal, less room is left for uninformed investors to get underpriced issues compensating for the overpriced issues they also buy. Then, this is not an equilibrium since they earn a negative expected return. Therefore, to get back to the equilibrium, there must be more underpriced issues— that is, the offer price (p_0) must fall.
7. See page 1050 of Carter and Manaster (1990).

8. Assuming that other investors also indicate their information truthfully, the expected profit of an investor with a piece of good information is the expected return between the premarket and the
aftermarket,

$$\sum_{h=0}^{H-1} \pi'_h(p_{h+1} - p_0(h+1))q_{g, h+1}.$$

On the other hand, the investor with a piece of good information who
falsely indicates bad information will only be allocated a b portion, and
the price will reflect one less piece of good information. Its expected
profit is

$$\sum_{h=0}^{H-1} \pi'_h(p_{h+1} - p_0(h))q_{b, h}.$$

To induce the investor to tell the truth, the first result must exceed
the second one, and, knowing that $p_0(h+1) = \alpha + p_0(h)$, we get

$$\sum_{h=0}^{H-1} \pi'_h(p_{h+1} - p_0(h+1))q_{g, h+1} \geq \sum_{h=0}^{H-1} \pi'_h(p_h - p_0(h) + \alpha)q_{b, h}.$$

9. On the premarket, the allocation to each g is $q_{g, h}$; and the allocation
to each b is $q_{b, h}$. Total shares presold are $hq_{g, h} + (H - h)q_{b, h}$. Then,
there are only $n - hq_{g, h} - (H - h)q_{b, h}$ left to be sold in the after
market sales. As for shares left to be sold in the aftermarket, sales
$= n - hq_{g, h} = (H - h)q_{b, h}$. Finally, the expected proceeds is $p_h n - [p_h - p_0(h)][hq_{g, h} + (H - h)q_{b, h}]$.

10. See page 354 of Benveniste and Spindt (1989).
11. See page 356 of Benveniste and Spindt (1989).

C.7 Going Private

C.7.1 Leveraged Buyouts

1. See page 357 of Elitzur et al. (1998).
2. Let $F(w_1, r) = 0$ denote the first-order condition with respect to w_1.
By the implicit function theorem,

$$\frac{\partial w_1}{\partial r} = -\frac{\partial F(w_1, r)/\partial r}{\partial F(w_1, r)/\partial w_1}$$

$$= -\frac{\sum_{t=1}^{\infty} \rho_t\{-(P_o + \phi)N(1 - \lambda)(1 + r)^{t-1}[1 + r(t - 1)(1 + r)^{-1}]\}}{\partial F(w_1, r)/\partial w_1}.$$

The denominator of this expression is simply the second-order condition, which must be negative if the problem has a maximum. It follows that $\frac{\partial w_1}{\partial r} < 0$. This result is intuitive. As the opportunity cost of funds left in the firm increases, the manager would prefer to decrease the investment in the firm and invest more in outside projects.

3. A number of explanations have been discussed. First are tax benefits since the high leverage provides the benefits of interest savings. Second are agency cost arguments. It is argued that under an LBO (or MBO) management's incentives are stronger for improved performance. Also, increasing debt commits free cash flows to debt payments rather than self-aggrandizing expenditures. Third, the payments of premiums may represent wealth transfers to shareholders from bondholders and preferred stockholders. Wealth may also be transferred from current employees since the number of employees grows more slowly or even decreases because of divestitures or more efficient use of labor. Fourth, large premiums are also consistent with the argument that managers have more information on the value of the firm than public shareholders. Finally, we have an efficiency argument. It is argued that the decision process is more efficient under private ownership; for instance, actions can be taken more speedily. Also, a public firm must publish information that may disclose important information to rival firms.

C.8 Mergers and Acquisitions

C.8.1 Tender Offers and the Free-Rider Problem

1. When the raider is not a shareholder before he/she makes the raid, and $p \geq v$, the raider makes no profit since he/she pays at least as much for the firm's shares as they are worth to him/her. In fact, if we also consider the cost of the raid, the raider will make a loss.

   Suppose now that the raider has a fraction x of the shares of the firm. He/she will have profits if what he/she gets after the bid $(v + px)$ is higher than its costs $(p + c)$. That is, if its profit is positive, $\pi = v - p[1 - x] - c > 0 \Leftrightarrow x > 1 + \frac{c-v}{p}$.

2. See footnote 8 of Grossman and Hart (1980).
3. See page 50 of Grossman and Hart (1980).
4. See page 51 of Grossman and Hart (1980).
5. The model analyzed is the one by Shleifer and Vishny.

   (a) See pages 468 and 483 of Shleifer and Vishny (1986).
   (b) See pages 469 and 483 of Shleifer and Vishny (1986).
   (c) See pages 469 and 483 of Shleifer and Vishny (1986).

In this model, $\pi^*(\alpha)$ is the smallest π satisfying the condition

$$\pi - E[Z|Z - (1 - 2\alpha) - 2c \geq 0] \geq 0, \tag{C.7}$$

which is the condition to be satisfied if small shareholders tender their shares; and $Z^c(\alpha)$ is the smallest Z satisfying the condition

$$0.5Z(\alpha) - (0.5 - \alpha)\pi(\alpha) - c \geq 0, \tag{C.8}$$

which is the condition for large shareholders to bid. When $F(Z)$ follows a uniform distribution, we can solve directly for $Z^c(\alpha)$. Following C.7,

$$\pi^*(\alpha) = E[Z|Z \geq Z^c(\alpha)] = \frac{1 + Z^c(\alpha)}{Z}.$$

Then, since $Z^c(\alpha)$ is the smallest Z that will allow a bid, it will be such that (C.8) equals zero, given this $\pi^*(\alpha)$,

$$0.5Z^c(\alpha) - (0.5 - \alpha)\pi^*(\alpha) = 0$$

$$\Leftrightarrow$$

$$Z^c(\alpha) = \frac{0.5 - \alpha}{0.5 + \alpha}$$

and

$$\pi^*(\alpha) = \frac{1}{1 + 2\alpha}.$$

Then

$$\frac{\partial \pi^*(\alpha)}{\partial \alpha} = -\frac{2}{(1 + 2\alpha)^2} < 0$$

and

$$\frac{\partial Z^c(\alpha)}{\partial \alpha} = -\frac{1}{(0.5 + \alpha)^2} < 0,$$

as stated in the beginning of the exercise.

6. A dilution by $a + bZ$ means that, after obtaining control, the bidder reduces the value of the shares to $Z(1-b)-a$. Since target shareholders do not know Z, this implies that they do not know the value of their shares after the raid. In equilibrium, shareholders will be indifferent about whether to tender if they receive a bid they believe to be equal to the posttakeover price

$$\pi = Z(1 - b) - a. \tag{C.9}$$

The bidder's objective function is now

$$\max_{\pi}[\alpha Z + \omega(Z - \pi) + 0.5(a + bZ)]P(\pi, a, b)$$

and the first-order condition is

$$\frac{\partial G}{\partial \pi} = P'[\alpha Z + \omega(Z - \pi) + 0.5(a + bZ] - \omega P = 0. \qquad (C.10)$$

If we substitute the value of Z given in C.9 in C.10, we obtain a differential equation for $P(\pi)$:

$$\frac{P'}{P} = \frac{\omega(1 - b)}{a + \pi[\alpha + b(1 - \alpha)]}.$$

We use the condition $P(Z_{max}) = 1$ and solve the differential equation to get

$$P(\pi) = \left(\frac{\delta_0 \delta_1 + \pi}{\delta_0 \delta_1 + Z_{max}}\right)^{\delta_1}$$

where $\delta_0 = \frac{a}{\omega(1-b)}$ and

$$\delta_1 = \frac{\omega(1 - b)}{w + b(1 - \alpha)}.$$

The probability of success is uniformly higher than it is in the basic model and increases with the dilution. Profits increase with dilution both directly in the profit function and as an indirect result of the increased probability of success. As a result, Z^c decreases.

For the solution of the differential equation,

$$\int \frac{P'}{P} = \int \frac{\omega(1 - b)}{a + \pi[\alpha + \beta(1 - \alpha)]}$$

$$\Leftrightarrow$$

$$\ln P + C = \frac{\omega(1 - b)}{[\alpha + \beta(1 - \alpha)]} \ln\left(\frac{\pi[\alpha + \beta(1 - \alpha)]}{\omega(1 - b)} + \frac{a}{\omega(1 - b)}\right) + D,$$

where C and D are constants. This simplifies to

$$Pe^C = \left(\frac{a}{\omega(1 - b)} + \frac{\pi[\alpha + \beta(1 - \alpha)]}{\omega(1 - b)}\right)^{\frac{\omega(1-b)}{[\alpha+\beta(1-\alpha)]}} e^D$$

$$\Leftrightarrow$$

$$P = \left(\delta_0 + \frac{\pi}{\delta_1}\right)^{\delta_1} \frac{e^D}{e^C}.$$

Then, if $\frac{e^D}{e^C} = F$, and knowing that $P(Z_{max}) = 1$,

$$F = \left(\delta_0 + \frac{Z_{max}}{\delta_1}\right)^{-\delta_1}$$

and we get to the final solution:

$$P(\pi) = \left(\frac{\delta_0 \delta_1 + \pi}{\delta_0 \delta_1 + Z_{\max}} \right)^{\delta_1}.$$

7. Result 1 says that the value of bidding high is increasing in the bidder's type Z:

$$\frac{\partial}{\partial Z}[G(\pi', \alpha; Z) - G(\pi, \alpha; Z)] > 0, \quad \forall \pi < \pi'.$$

Substituting the value of

$$G(.) = P(\pi)[0.5Z - (0.5 - \alpha)\pi],$$

we get

$$\frac{\partial}{\partial Z}[G(\pi', \alpha; Z) - G(\pi, \alpha; Z)] = 0.5[P(\pi') - P(\pi)] > 0.$$

Result 2 says that the cost of choosing any level of initial α is identical for the bidder regardless of his/her value of Z; that is,

$$\frac{\partial}{\partial \alpha}[G(\pi, \alpha; Z)]$$

is independent of Z. In fact, given

$$G(.) = P(\pi)[0.5Z - (0.5 - \alpha)\pi],$$

we take the partial derivative and arrive at

$$\frac{\partial}{\partial \alpha}[G(\pi, \alpha; Z)] = \pi P(\pi).$$

8. To show that there is no pooling equilibrium, we must show that α has no signaling value. Suppose $\alpha_{pool} = \alpha_m = 0.3$. Then,

$$\pi = E(Z_{pool} \mid \pi_{pool}, \alpha_{pool}) = Z_M = 0.4 \times 40 + 0.6 \times 80 = 64.$$

The value of each type is

$$G(\pi, \alpha; Z) = [0.5Z - (0.5 - \alpha)\pi]P(\pi).$$

The value of the high-Z type is

$$G(64, 0.3; 80) = [0.5 \times 80 - (0.5 - 0.3)64]\ln 64 = 113.1216.$$

The value of the low-Z type is

$$G(64, 0.3; 40) = [0.5 \times 40 - (0.5 - 0.3)64]\ln 64 = 29.944.$$

The high-value type is better off, but the low-value type could improve his/her value by bidding less. The optimal α for the low-value type (α') is the one that makes the high-value type indifferent between bidding 64 and 40, which the low-value bidder prefers—that is, α' solves the equation

$$G(40, \alpha'; Z_H) = G(64, 0.3; Z_H)$$

$$\Leftrightarrow$$

$$\alpha' = 0.2667.$$

By bidding 40 and acquiring $\alpha' = 0.2667$, the low-value bidder is strictly better off since

$$G(40, 0.2667; 40) = \ln 40[0.5 \times 40 - (0.5 - 0.2667)40]39.337 > 29.944.$$

Therefore signaling through α does have an effect, and the pooling equilibrium fails to exist.

9. Both models try to solve the problem of free riding that occurs when bids are made to atomistic shareholders. Jegadeesh and Chowdhry (JC) and Shleifer and Vishny (SV) try to solve this problem assuming the existence of a large shareholder prior to the offer. However, since they deal with the question assuming different hypotheses, they will arrive at different conclusions: JC predict a negative relationship between the initial shareholding and the bid premium, while SV predict a positive relationship.

The main difference between these two works is that SV assume an exogenously fixed share ownership by the bidder (a large shareholder) and JC relax this assumption and consider the initial shareholding to be determined endogenously.

SV assume that the firm is owned by one large shareholder and a fringe of small ones. They do not consider strategic interactions between large shareholders. The bid premium decreases with α since the more shares L owns, the easier is to convince small shareholders that a low bid indicates a small rise in price after the takeover, rather than an attempt to profit at their expenses. On the other hand, if $\alpha = 0$, the bid premium is higher as no one will tender unless the large shareholder offers a price greater or equal to the value of the firm after the takeover.

JC assume strategic interaction between bidders. They assume that there are large shareholders with different valuations of the target. Then, bidders will choose different values of initial shares to keep on hand before the takeover since α is used as a signal to the market for the different valuations of the target. The low bidder does not buy so many shares before the takeover in order to credibly signal its type and bid a lower amount in the tender offer. Therefore, when α is high, it is because this shareholder has a high valuation of the target and will pay a large bid premium.

C.8.2 Merger Bids

1. The signaling equilibrium is not fully revealing since bidder 2 only learns whether $v \leq \tilde{v}_1 < r$ or $\tilde{v}_1 \geq r$, not the precise value of v_1. If $\tilde{v}_1$ were directly observable, bidder 1 would make an initial offer of v (if $\tilde{v}_1 \geq v$). Bidder 2 would then compete if $v \leq \tilde{v}_1 < w$ where $E\pi_2(w, \tilde{v}_2, v, 1) = 0$. By the definition of r, we have $r < w$. Therefore, for realizations of $\tilde{v}_1$ such that $r \leq \tilde{v}_1 < w$, bidder 2 is deterred in the signaling equilibrium, but he/she would not be if $\tilde{v}_1$ could be observed directly.

2. See page 96 of Fishman (1988).

3. If an amount of C is offered, the acquirer expects to receive assets worth only $0.75C$. To see this, notice that the target accepts the offer if and only if $v \leq C$. Then the expected value of the target's assets to the acquirer conditional on the offer being accepted is $0.75C$. Consider now a stock deal in which the acquirer offers an ownership of β of the combined firm. For this case, we can find a stock trade that is mutually beneficial for all v. To be beneficial to the target, the condition

$$\beta(x + 1.5v) \geq v$$

should be satisfied for all v. This is satisfied for all v when it is satisfied for $v = 100$ (because p is increasing in v). Thus, we must have

$$\beta(x + 150) \geq 100.$$

The trade should also be beneficial to the acquirer, conditional on the target always accepting the offer. This occurs when the expected wealth of the acquirer is no smaller than x. Since the expected value of the target's assets to the acquirer conditional on the offer always being accepted is 75, the condition to the acquirer should be

$$(1 - \beta)(x + 75) \geq x$$

or

$$p \leq \frac{75}{x + 75}.$$

Then, the two conditions are mutually consistent when $x \leq 150$. This example shows that stock can effect trade even when cash cannot.

4. See page 80 of Hansen (1987).
5. See the proof on page 81 of Hansen (1987). The explanation is the following: If the acquirer's firm is too large relative to the target, the acquirer misses a larger fraction of the value of his/her own firm compared to a situation where the offer is made in cash. At the same time, as the acquirer gets bigger, the target's assets become a less significant addition to the acquirer.
6. Hansen studies the process of a merger to formulate a model for the choice of the exchange medium (either cash or stock). Throughout the analysis, the target firm has private information on its value. He/she first considers the case where the acquirer's premerger value is publicly known. In this case it is shown that a stock offer can affect trade even when a cash offer cannot.

   Later he considers that the acquiring firm has private information on its own value. Then, the acquirer will not offer stock when the target underestimates the value of its offer. This implies that stock will not necessarily dominate cash. Hansen argues that there generally exists a critical value of x below which the "overvalued" stock is offered and above which cash is offered.

   If the target price decreases (increases) if an offer is accepted (rejected), it may be because the market does not agree with the valuation made about the acquirer's value. That is, Hansen's model predicts that if x is large, it is difficult to convince the target that the acquirer is overvalued, so it is better to offer cash instead of undervalued shares. However, the market may think that, in fact, the acquirer is overvalued and receiving cash is worse, to the target, than receiving shares.

   On the other hand, Hansen's model predicts that if x is small, the acquirer prefers to pay with shares of its overvalued firm. If the target price decreases after the offer is accepted, it may be because the market views the acquirer as undervalued and it would have been better to the target to receive cash instead of shares of an undervalued firm.
7. See page 45 of Fishman (1989).
8. We need to show that
$$p_c(v_1) < p_d(v_1).$$

Notice that this is equivalent of proving

$$\gamma E \min\left[\max\left(v, v_2^+\right), v_1^+\right] + (1 - \gamma)v_1^- < E \min\left[\max\left(v, v_2^+\right), v_1^+\right].$$

This expression simplifies to

$$(\gamma - 1)\left[E \min\left[\max\left(v, v_2^+\right), v_1^+\right] - v_1^-\right] < 0,$$

which is true since $\gamma < 1$ and $E \min[\max(v, v_2^+), v_1^+] > v_1^-$. In fact, if $\gamma = 1$, the target effectively possesses no private information.

In this case, $p_c(v_1) = p_d(v_1)$ since then cash is equivalent to debt. If $\gamma < 1$, the target possesses private information and $p_c(v_1) < p_d(v_1)$.

9. An increase in the cost of bidder 2 has the same effect as in Fishman's previous work. Consider a decrease in bidder 2's cost. Since its cost of competing is lower, its expected payoff is higher. Bidder 1's expected payoff is lower since a higher valuation must be signaled to deter bidder 2, and this is more costly. Bidder 2 is preempted less often, and when it is preempted, the bid is higher. Both effects benefit the target, and its expected payoff is higher.

10. Harris and Raviv make the following assumption:

$$E_2(D) + K_2(D) \geq E_1(D);$$

that is, there is an incentive to control the firm, even if the management has lower ability. I and R want to vote for themselves, in each case, regardless of their private signals and the debt level. The worst payoff either I or R can receive if in control of the firm is $\alpha_i E_2(D) + K_2(D)$, $i = I, R$; the best payoff either I or R can receive if not in control of the firm is $\alpha_i E_1(D)$, $i = I, R$. If they always vote for themselves, it is because $\alpha_i E_2(D) + K_2(D) > \alpha_i E_1(D)$, which is true by the assumption that $E_2(D) + K_2(D) \geq E_1(D)$.

Notes

Chapter One

1. See Duffie (1988), page 71.
2. See the excellent textbook of Trigeorgis (1996) and references therein for more details.

Chapter Two

1. See Bradley, Jarrell, and Kim (1984), Titman and Wessels (1988), and Barclay, Smith, and Watts (1995).
2. See Miller and Scholes (1978) among others.

Chapter Three

1. The seminal papers in this area were written by Ross (1973,1977) and Jensen and Meckling (1976). Since then an extensive literature in the same vein has been produced. An exhaustive list of references of the subsequent works can be found in the survey by Harris and Raviv (1991).
2. This solution was presented in an earlier paper by Ross (1973).
3. See Ross (1977).
4. This assumption, known as the free cash flow hypothesis, was first presented by Jensen (1986).
5. This type of conflict was introduced by Jensen and Meckling (1976).
6. This argument was pointed out by Myers (1977).
7. To see how that happens, it suffices to notice that the marginal utilities should be equal at the optimal value of the firm. Therefore, a decrease in utility at that point by reducing the fraction of ownership should be compensated by an increase of the fringe benefits.
8. The schedule f could also be considered as a function of the state of the world, for instance. For simplicity, this factor is avoided here. See Ross (1973) for a discussion of this point.
9. See equation 9 of Ross (1973).
10. See Cox and Rubinstein (1985), Chapter 7, especially Section 7.3.
11. Basically, there will be fewer states of the world compatible with the payment of K. As $K \to \infty$, the set of states of the world at which the debtholders will be conveniently paid has measure zero and, hence, the present value of that debt is also zero.

12. Otherwise, bankruptcy is certain.

13. This is true as far as it is an internal optimum—that is, as far as the optimal level of B satisfies $0 < B < t$.

14. What leads to the uniqueness of this relation is the Spence-Mirrlees condition (see Appendix B for a discussion), burried in equations (3.10) and (3.11). That is why one obtains perfect separation of types (i.e., a unique debt level for each type): The management changes perceived value because managers of better firms are relatively more immune to taking on debt, and this happens in a monotonic way.

15. The demand for an asset is said to be *normal* if, in a portfolio choice situation without signaling, the demand is a decreasing function of price.

16. Saying that Jensen (1986) and Myers and Majluf (1984) are direct competitors is correct, as far as predictions are concerned. It should be stressed, however, that these two papers refer to different problems. Jensen refers to a moral hazard story, in the sense that managers pursue their own objectives unless cash is removed from their hands. The conflict is between managers and inside shareholders. In the case of Myers and Majluf, there is a cost of issuing securities, caused by the asymmetry of information between management and (outside) investors. In the former case, one must prevent management from taking on negative-NPV projects; in the latter, positive projects are passed by because of the adverse selection cost—no matter how well intentioned management is. In a sense, these are complementary aspects of the same debate.

17. $E(x|\Omega)$ denotes the expected value of the random variable x with respect to the joint probability of $(\widetilde{A}, \widetilde{B})$ conditioned to a set $\Omega \subset M \cup M'$.

18. If debt is default–risk-free, for instance, it follows that $\Delta B = 0$. The fact that in such a case the management is sure of no capital loss implies that it will invest in any project with positive net present value. That is why the ability to raise funds in this way is included in the definition of slack.

19. Not discussed here is the role of beliefs of outside investors and the possibility of multiple equilibria depending on these beliefs. One can have equilibria where equity is preferred to debt, or in which different types issue different securities in a nonmonotonic fashion (see, for example, Noe, 1988), independently of the risk of the securities.

20. See Chapter 7, page 63, and footnote 10 of Masulis (1988).

21. The assumption that the derivative of W is positive is natural. The higher the value of information perceived by the market, the larger is the benefit of signaling to the management.

22. See Viswanath (1993) for a discussion of this point.

23. See Barclay and Smith (1999) for further discussion on the interpretation of these results.

Chapter Four

1. See Campbell, Lo, and MacKinlay (1997) for a discussion of these empirical problems in some detail.

2. See, among others, Asquith and Mullins (1983), Brickley (1983), Healey and Palepu (1988), and Michaely, Thaler, and Womack (1995).
3. This assumption is shown to hold true in Miller and Rock (1985) if the $X(D)$ schedule is Pareto dominating.
4. Actually, it implies that D is an increasing function of X and therefore that the same holds for the inverse function $X(D)$. Notice that at a certain point, $X(D)$ was assumed to be single-valued.
5. Actually, an average of the daily returns over the five consecutive trading days after t is used.
6. Here again, an average of the daily returns of the S&P index over the five consecutive trading days after t is used.

Chapter Five

1. Take γ and δ as the expected values conditioned on θ and a of two random variables. If $\gamma_g^g > \gamma_b^g$ and $\gamma_b^b > \gamma_g^b$, then δ is said to be comonotonic with γ if $\delta_g^g > \delta_b^g$ and $\delta_b^b > \delta_g^b$.
2. The results generated are without loss of generality. See Aghion and Bolton (1992).
3. This is left as an exercise.

Chapter Six

1. The model here presented has been developed by Chemmanur and Fulghieri (1999).
2. See Ibbotson, Sindelar, and Ritter (1988) for an extensive survey of the empirical literature.
3. See, for example, Ibbotson (1975), who was nevertheless unable to provide a convincing explanation for the fact.
4. See the works by Baron (1982), Beatty and Ritter (1986), Rock (1986), Tiniç (1988), Allen and Faulhaber (1989), Welch (1989), and Carter and Manaster (1990) among others.
5. See Ritter (1984).
6. Note this distinction from the assumptions made in the model developed by Chemmanur and Fulghieri (1999).

Chapter Seven

1. See Section 3.2.4.
2. Note that the existence of correlation between two variables does not define any causal relationship among them. The same data could be used to argue, for example, that the increase of stock repurchases for whatever other reason independent of takeovers would induce potential bidders to anticipate

their takeover actions. If that were the case, the causal relationship would be reversed.

3. Vermaelen (1981) computes returns around the announcement of the repurchases both in the case of a tender offer and in the case of an open market purchase. The positive numbers reported here refer to the tender offer case.

4. The *true market price* refers to the value at which the managers have access by their privileged information, and which they should try to pass to the market through the signaling mechanism. Such mechanism, however, works under the assumption of market efficiency. Therefore, the hypothesis that the transfer of information is compatible with the expropriation of the outsiders implies market inefficiencies.

5. See page 472 of Lakonishok and Vermaelen (1990), in particular Table IX.

6. See Bennett Stewart (1990), for example.

Chapter Eight

1. See Jensen and Ruback (1983), for example.

2. See Jensen and Warner (1988), for example.

3. Examples are by paying a high salary to the future management after the acquisition, and by making special commercial agreements with other firms of the bidder.

4. See Jensen and Warner (1988).

5. It is asked that this fact be shown in an exercise.

6. Note that the objective function that follows is identical to the function G defined before equation (8.4). The only difference is that it will be maximized in two variables, since the optimal α is to be determined endogenously through this process.

7. This last inequality is easily verified, as we notice that by construction of α',

$$G(Z_L, \alpha'; Z_H) = G(Z_M, \alpha_m; Z_H) > G(Z_M, \alpha_m; Z_L)$$

where use was made of the fact that $G(\pi, \alpha; Z)$ is strictly decreasing on Z.

8. See also the arguments used by Myers and Majluf (1984) discussed at the end of Chapter 3.

Appendix B

1. Suitable regularity conditions must be imposed on $U(\cdot)$ and $V(\cdot)$. In particular, $U(\cdot)$ is strictly increasing in P, while $V(\cdot)$ is strictly increasing in θ and increasing in y.

2. To see why is easy: The equilibrium signaling function is determined from the seller's first-order conditions, which usually include $\theta'(y)$, and by the requirement that the signal is truthful—that is, $\theta(y) = \theta$.

3. There is more than a slight abuse of language here, since we have not formally defined what strategy is in this context. (Some of the more attentive readers might even wonder whether we actually have defined a game.) We ignore this and other (legitimate) considerations for the purpose of brevity and easiness of exposition. For a rigorous textbook treatment of the revelation principle, see Fudenberg and Tirole (1991).

Bibliography

Aghion, P., and P. Bolton, 1989, "The Financial Structure of the Firm and the Problem of Control," *European Economic Review* 33, 286–93.

———, 1992, "An 'Incomplete Contracts' Approach to Financial Contracting," *Review of Economic Studies* 59, 473–94.

Aharony, J., and I. Swary, 1980, "Quarterly Dividends and Earnings Announcements and Stockholders' Returns: An Empirical Analysis," *Journal of Finance* 35, 1–12.

Akerlof, G., 1970, "The Market for Lemons: Qualitative Uncertainty and the Market Mechanism," *Quarterly Journal of Economics* 84, 488–500.

Allen, F., and G. Faulhaber, 1989, "Signalling by Underpricing in the IPO Market," *Journal of Financial Economics* 23, 303–23.

Allen, F., and R. Michaely, 1995, "Dividend Policy," in R. A. Jarrow, V. Maksimovic, and W. T. Ziemba (eds.), *Handbooks in Operations Research and Management Science 9*, Amsterdam: North-Holland,

Allen, F., and S. Morris, 2001, "Finance Applications of Game Theory," in Kalyan Chatterjee and William F. Samuelson, (eds.), *Game Theory and Business Applications*, Boston: Kluwer Academic Publishers.

Allen, J., 1996, "LBOs—The Evolution of Financial Structures and Strategies," *Journal of Applied Corporate Finance* 8, 18–29.

Altman, E., 1989, "Measuring Corporate Bond Mortality and Performance," *Journal of Finance* 44, 909–22.

Arrow, K., 1964, "Le Rôle des Valeurs Boursières pour la Repartition la Meilleure des Risques," translated as "The Role of Securities in the Optimal Allocation of Risk-Bearing," *Review of Economic Studies* 31, 91–96.

Asquith, P., and D. Mullins, Jr, 1983, "The Impact of Initiating Dividend Payments on Shareholders' Wealth," *Journal of Business* 56, 77–96.

Asquith, P., and T. Wizman, 1990, "Event Risk, Covenants and Bondholder Returns in Leveraged Buyouts," *Journal of Financial Economics* 27, 195–214.

Bagwell, L., 1991, "Share Repurchase and Takeover Deterrence," *Rand Journal of Economics* 22, 72–88.

———, 1992, Dutch Auction Repurchases: An Analysis of Shareholder Heterogeneity," *Journal of Finance* 47, 71–105.

Bagwell, L., and J. Shoven, 1989, "Cash Distributions to Shareholders," *Journal of Economic Perspectives* 3, 129–40.

Baker, G., M. Jensen, and K. Murphy, 1988, "Compensation and Incentives: Practice vs. Theory," *Journal of Finance* 43, 593–616.

Barclay, J., and C. Smith, 1999, "The Capital Structure Puzzle: Another Look at the Evidence," *Journal of Applied Corporate Finance* 12, 8–20.

Barclay, J., C. Smith, and R. Watts, 1995, "The Determinants of Corporate Leverage and Dividend Policies," *Journal of Applied Corporate Finance* 7, 4–19.

Baron, D. P., 1982, "A Model of the Demand for Investment Banking Advising and Distribution Services for New Issues," *Journal of Finance* 37, 955–76.

Beatty, R. P., and J. R. Ritter, 1986, "Investment Banking, Reputation, and Underpricing of Initial Public Offerings," *Journal of Financial Economics* 15, 213–32.

Bennett Stewart, G, 1990, "Remaking the Public Corporation from Within," *Harvard Business Review* 68, 126–37.

Benveniste, L. M., and P. A. Spindt, 1989, "How Investment Bankers Determine the Offer Price and Allocation of New Issues," *Journal of Financial Economics* 24, 343–61.

Berglöf, E., and E. von Thadden, 1994, "Short-Term versus Long-Term Interests: Capital Structure with Multiple Investors," *The Quarterly Journal of Economics* 109, 1055–84.

Bhattacharya, S., 1979, "Imperfect Information, Dividend Policy, and 'The Bird in the Hand Fallacy'," *Bell Journal of Economics* 10, 259–70.

Bhattacharya, S., and G. M. Constantinides (eds.), 1989a, *Theory of Valuation. Frontiers of Modern Financial Theory, Vol. 1.* Savage, MD: Rowman and Littlefield.

———— (eds.), 1989b, *Financial Markets and Incomplete Information. Frontiers of Modern Financial Theory, Vol. 2.* Savage, MD: Rowman and Littlefield.

Black, F., and M. Scholes, 1973, "The Pricing of Options and Corporate Liabilities," *Journal of Political Economy* 81, 637–54.

Bolton, P., and D. Scharfstein, 1990, "A Theory of Predation Based on Agency Problems in Financial Contracting," *American Economic Review* 80, 94–106.

Bolton, P., and D. Scharfstein, 1996, "Optimal Debt Structure and the Number of Creditors," *Journal of Political Economy* 104, 1–25.

Bradley, M., G. Jarrell, and E. Kim, 1984, "On the Existence of an Optimal Capital Structure: Theory and Evidence," *Journal of Finance* 39, 857–78.

Bradley, M., and E. Kim, 1985, "The Tender Offer as a Takeover Device: Its Evolution, the Free Rider Problem and the Prisoner's Dilemma." Unpublished manuscript.

Bradley, M., and L. Wakeman, 1983, "The Wealth Effects of Targeted Share Repurchases," *Journal of Financial Economics* 11, 301–28.

Brennan, M., 1973, "Taxes, Market Valuation and Corporate Financial Policy," *National Tax Journal* 23, 417–27.

Brennan, M. (ed.), 1996, *The Theory of Corporate Finance. International Library of Critical Writings in Financial Economics*, Vols. I and II. Edward Elgar.

Brickley, J., 1983, "Shareholder Wealth, Information Signaling, and the Specially Designated Dividend: An Empirical Study," *Journal of Financial Economics* 12, 187–210.

Buser, S., and P. Hess, 1986, "Empirical Determinants on the Relative Yields on Taxable and Tax-Exempt Securities," *Journal of Financial Economics* 17, 335–56.

Campbell, J., A. Lo, and A. C. MacKinlay, 1997, "The Econometrics of Financial Markets." Princeton, NJ: Princeton University Press.

Carter, R., and S. Manaster, 1990, "Initial Public Offerings and Underwriter Reputation," *Journal of Finance* 45, 1045–67.

Castanias, R., 1983, "Bankruptcy Risk and Optimal Capital Structure," *Journal of Finance* 38, 1617–36.

Chang, C., 1992, "Capital Structure as an Optimal Contract between Employees and Investors," *Journal of Finance* 47, 1141–58.

Charest, G., 1978, "Dividend Information, Stock Returns and Market Efficiency," *Journal of Financial Economics* 6, 297–330.

Chemmanur, T., and P. Fulghieri, 1999, "A Theory of Going Public Decision," *Review of Financial Studies* 12, 249–79.

Chowdhry, B., and A. Sherman, 1996, "The Winner's Curse and International Methods of Allocating Initial Public Offerings," *Pacific-Basin Finance Journal* 4, 15–30.

Comment, R., and G. Jarrell, 1987, "Two Tier Tender Offers: The Imprisonment of the Free Riding Shareholder," *Journal of Financial Economics* 19, 283–310.

———, 1991, "The Relative Signaling Power of Dutch-Auction and Fixed-Price Self-Tender Offers and Open-Market Share Repurchases," *Journal of Finance* 46, 1243–71.

Cox, J., and M. Rubinstein, 1985, *Options Markets.* Englewood Cliffs, NJ: Prentice-Hall.

Dann, L., 1981, "Common Stock Repurchases: An Analysis of Returns to Bondholders and Stockholders," *Journal of Financial Economics* 9, 113–28.

Dann, L., and H. DeAngelo, 1983, "Standstill Agreements, Privately Negotiated Stock Repurchases, and the Market for Corporate Control," *Journal of Financial Economics* 11, 275–300.

Dann, L., R. Masulis, and D. Mayers, 1991, "Repurchase Tender Offers and Earnings Information," *Journal of Accounting and Economics* 14, 217–51.

DeAngelo, H., L. DeAngelo, and E. Rice, 1984, "Going Private: Minority Freezouts and Stockholder Wealth," *Journal of Law and Economics* 27, 367–401.

DeAngelo, H., and R. Masulis, 1980, "Optimal Capital Structure under Corporate and Personal Taxation," *Journal of Financial Economics* 8, 3–29.

Degeorge, F., and R. Zeckhauser, 1993, "The Reverse LBO Decision and Firm Performance: Theory and Evidence," *Journal of Finance* 48, 1323–48.

Dewatripont, M., and J. Tirole, 1994, "A Theory of Debt and Equity: Diversity of Securities and Manager–Shareholder Congruence," *Quarterly Journal of Economics* 109, 1027–54.

Diamond, D., 1991, "Debt Maturity Structure and Liquidity Risk," *Quarterly Journal of Economics*, 709–37.

Diamond, D., 1993, "Seniority and Maturity of Debt Contracts," *Journal of Financial Economics* 33, 341–68.

Dixit, A., and R. Pindyck, 1994, *Investment under Uncertainty.* Princeton, NJ: Princeton University Press.

Dothan, M., 1990, *Prices in Financial Markets.* Oxford, England: Oxford University Press.

Duffie, D., 1988, *Security Markets—Stochastic Models.* Boston, MA: Academic Press.

———, 1996, *Dynamic Asset Pricing Theory.* Princeton, NJ: Princeton University Press.

Dunn, K., and C. Spatt, 1984, "A Strategic Analysis of Sinking Fund Bonds," *Journal of Financial Economics* 13, 399–423.

Eckbo, B., 1986, "Information Asymmetries and Valuation Effects of Corporate Debt Offerings," *Journal of Financial Economics* 15, 119–51.

Elitzur, R., P. Halpern, R. Kieschnick, and W. Rotenberg, 1998, "Managerial Incentives and the Structure of Management Buyouts," *Journal of Economic Behavior and Organization* 36, 347–67.

Elton, E., and M. Gruber, 1970, "Marginal Stockholders' Tax Rates and the Clientele Effect," *Review of Economics and Statistics* (February), 68–74.

Fama, E., and H. Babiak, 1968, "Dividend Policy: An Empirical Analysis," *American Statistical Association Journal* (December), 1132–61.

Field, L. C., 1997, "Is Institutional Investment in Initial Public Offerings Related to the Long-Run Performances of These Firms?" Working paper, Penn State University.

Fishman, M., 1988, "A Theory of Preemptive Takeover Bidding," *Rand Journal of Economics* 19, 88–101.

———, 1989, "Preemptive Bidding and the Role of the medium of Exchange in Acquisitions," *Journal of Finance* 44, 41–57.

Franks, J., R. S. Harris, and C. Mayer, 1988, "Means of Payment in Takeovers: Results for the United Kingdom and the United States," in *Corporate Takeovers: Causes and Consequences*, A. J. Auerbach, (ed.), Chicago: The University of Chicago Press.

Fudenberg, D., and J. Tirole, 1991, *Game Theory.* Cambridge, MA: The MIT Press.

Galai, D., and R. Masulis, 1976, "The Option Pricing Model and the Risk Factor of Stock," *Journal of Financial Economics* 3, 53–81.

Gibbons, R., 1992, *Game Theory for Applied Economists*. Princeton, NJ: Princeton University Press.

Graham, J., 1996, "Debt and Marginal Tax Rate," *Journal of Financial Economics* 41, 41–73.

Grossman, S., and O. Hart, 1980, "Takeover Bids, the Free Rider Problem, and the Theory of the Corporation," *Bell Journal of Economics* (Spring), 42–64.

———, 1986, "The Costs and Benefits of Ownership: A Theory of Vertical and Lateral Integration," *Journal of Political Economics* 20, 175–202.

———, 1990, "Takeover Bids, the Free Rider Problem and the Theory of the Corporation," *Bell Journal of Economics*, 42–64.

Grullon, G., and R. Michaely, 2000, "Dividends, Share Repurchases, and the Substitution Hypothesis," Working paper, Cornell University.

Guedes, J., and T. Opler, 1996, "The Determinants of the Maturity of Corporate Debt Issues," *Journal of Finance* 51, 1809–33.

Hamada, R., and M. Scholes, 1985, "Taxes and Corporate Financial Management," in E. I. Altman and M. G. Subrahmanyan, (eds.), *Recent Advances in Corporate Finance*, Homewood, IL, Irwin Press.

Hanley, K. W., and W. J. Wilhelm, 1995, "Evidence on the Strategic Allocation of Initial Public Offerings," *Journal of Financial Economics* 37, 239–57.

Hansen, R., 1987, "A Theory for the Choice of Exchange Medium in Mergers and Acquisitions," *Journal of Business* 60, 75–95.

Harris, R., and A. Raviv, 1988, "Corporate Control Contests and Capital Structure," *Journal of Financial Economics* 20, 55–86.

———, 1991, "The Theory of Capital Structure," *Journal of Finance* 46, 297–355.

Hart, O., 1995, *Firms, Contracts and Financial Structure*. New York: Oxford University Press.

Hart, O., and J. Moore, 1989, "Default and Renegotiation: A Dynamic Model of Debt," MIT working paper 520.

———, 1990, "Property Rights and the Nature of the Firm," *Journal of Political Economy* 98, 1119–58.

———, 1995, "Debt and Seniority: An Analysis of the Role of Hard Claims in Constraining Management," *American Economic Review* 85(3), 567–85.

Hausch, D., and J. Seward, 1993, "Signaling with Dividends and Share Repurchases: A Choice between Deterministic and Stochastic Cash Disbursements," *Review of Financial Studies* 6, 121–54.

Hayn, C., 1989, "Tax Attributes as Determinants of Shareholder Gains in Corporate Acquisitions," *Journal of Financial Economics* 23, 121–53.

Healey, P., and K. Palepu, 1989, "Earnings Information Conveyed by Dividend Initiation and Omissions," *Journal of Financial Economics* 21, 149–76.

Hertzel, M., and P. Jain, 1991, "Earnings and Risk Changes around Stock Repurchase Tender Offers," *Journal of Accounting and Economics* 14, 253–74.

Hertzel, M., and R. Smith, 1993, "Market Discounts and Shareholder Gains for Placing Equity Privately," *Journal of Finance*, 459–85.

Hirshleifer, J., 1958, "On the Theory of Optimal Investment Decisions," *Journal of Political Economy*, 239–352.

———, 1970, *Investment, Interest, and Capital.* Englewood Cliffs, NJ: Prentice-Hall.

Hirshleifer, D., and S. Titman, 1990, "Share Tendering Strategies and the Success of Hostile Takeover Bids," *Journal of Political Economy* 98, 295–324.

Holthausen, R. W., and D. F. Larcker, 1996, "The Financial Performance of Reverse Leveraged Buyouts," *Journal of Financial Economics* 42, 293–332.

Huang, C. F., and R. Litzenberger, 1988, *Foundations for Financial Economics*. New York: North-Holland.

Huang, Y.-S., and R. Walking, 1987, "Target Abnormal Returns Associated with Acquisition Announcements: Payment, Acquisition Form and Managerial Resistance," *Journal of Financial Economics* 19, 329–50.

Ibbotson, R., 1975, "Price Performance of Common Stock New Issues," *Journal of Financial Economics* 2, 235–72.

Ibbotson, R., J. Sindelar, and J. Ritter, 1988, "Initial Public Offerings," *Journal of Applied Corporate Finance* 1, 37–45.

Israel, R., 1991, "Capital Structure and the Market for Corporate Control: The Defensive Role of Debt Financing," *Journal of Finance* 46, 1391–1410.

Jegadeesh, N., and B. Chowdhry, 1994, "Pre-Tender Offer Share Acquisition Strategy in Takeovers," *Journal of Financial and Quantitative Analysis* 29, 117–29.

Jensen, M., 1986, "Agency Costs of Free Cash Flow, Corporate Finance and Takeovers," *American Economic Review* 76, 323–29.

———, 1989, "The Eclipse of the Public Corporation," *Harvard Business Review* 67, 61–74.

Jensen, M., and W. Meckling, 1976, "Theory of the Firm: Managerial Behaviour, Agency Costs and Ownership Structure," *Journal of Financial Economics* 3, 305–60.

Jensen, M., and R. Ruback, 1983, "The Market for Corporate Control: The Scientific Evidence," *Journal of Financial Economics* 11, 5–50.

Jensen, M., and J. Warner, 1988, "The Distribution of Power among Corporate Managers, Shareholders and Directors," *Journal of Financial Economics* 20, 3–24.

John, K., and J. Williams, 1985, "Dividends, Dilution and Taxes: A Signaling Equilibrium," *Journal of Finance* 40, 1053–70.

Kalay, A., 1982, "The Ex-Dividend Day Behavior of Stock Prices: A Reexamination of the Clientele Effect," *Journal of Finance* 37, 1059–70.

Kaplan, S., 1989a, "The Effects of Management Buyouts on Operating Performance and Value," *Journal of Financial Economics* 24, 217–54.

———, 1989b, "Management Buyouts: Evidence on Taxes as a Source of Value," *Journal of Finance* 44, 611–32.

———, 1991, "The Staying Power of Leveraged Buyouts," *Journal of Financial Economics* 29, 287–313.

Kaplan S., and J. C. Stein, 1993, "The Evolution of Buyout Pricing and Financial Structure," *Quarterly Journal of Economics* 108, 313–57.

Kato, K., and J. Schallheim, 1993, "Private Equity Financing in Japan and Corporate Grouping (Keiretsu)," *Pacific-Basin Finance Journal*, 287–307.

Keloharju, M., 1997, "The Distribution of Information among Institutional and Retail Investors and the Impact of Past Investment Performance on the Demand for IPOs." Working paper 175, Helsinki School of Economics and Business Administration, Helsinki, Finland.

Kester, C., 1986, "Capital and Ownership Structure: A Comparison of United States and Japanese Manufacturing Corporations," *Financial Management* 15, 5–16.

Kieschnick, R. L., 1998, "Free Cash Flow and Stockholder Gains in Going Private Transactions Revisited," *Journal of Business Finance and Accounting* 25, 187–202.

Kim, E., 1989, "Optimal Capital Structure," in *Financial Markets and Incomplete Information*, Vol. 2, S. Bhattacharya and G. Constantinides, (eds.), Savage, MD: Rowman & Littlefield.

Krigman, L., W. H. Shaw, and K. L. Womack, 1999, "The Persistence of IPO Mispricing, and the Predictive Power of Flipping," *Journal of Finance* 54, 1015–44.

Lakonishok, J., and T. Vermaelen, 1986, "Tax-Induced Trading around Ex-Dividend Days," *Journal of Financial Economics* 16, 287–319.

Lakonishok, J., and T. Vermaelen, 1990, "Anomalous Price Behavior around Repurchase Tender Offers," *Journal of Finance* 45, 455–77.

Lambert, R., 1986, "Executive Effort and Selection of Risky Projects," *Rand Journal of Economics* 17, 77–88.

Lease, R., K. John, A. Kalay, U. Loewenstein, and O. Sarig, 2000, *Dividend Policy*. Boston: Harvard Business School Press.

Lee, P. J., S. L. Taylor, and T. S. Walter, 1996, "Expected and Realized Returns for Singaporean IPOs: Initial and Long-Run Analysis," *Pacific-Basin Finance Journal* 4, 153–80.

———, 1999, "IPO Underpricing Explanations: Implications from Investor Application and Allocation Schedules," *Journal of Financial and Quantitative Analysis* 34, 425–44.

Lehn, K., and A. Poulsen, 1989, "Free Cash-Flow and Stockholder Gains in Going Private Transactions," *Journal of Finance* 44, 771–88.

Leland, H., and D. Pyle, 1977, "Information Asymmetry, Financial Structure and Financial Intermediation," *Journal of Finance* 32, 371–87.

Lerner, J., 1994, "Venture Capitalists and the Decision to Go Public," *Journal of Financial Economics* 35, 293–316.

Lintner, J., 1956, "Distribution of Incomes of Corporations among Dividends, Retained Earnings and Taxes," *American Economic Review* 46, 97–113.

Litzenberger, R., and K. Ramaswamy, 1979, "The Effects of Personal Taxes and Dividends on Capital Asset Prices: Theory and Empirical Tests," *Journal of Financial Economics* 7, 163–95.

Long, M., and I. Malitz, 1985, "The Investment-Financing Nexus: Some Empirical Evidence," *Midland Corporate Finance Journal* 3, 53–59.

Loughran, T., and J. R. Ritter, (1997), "The Operating Performance of Firms Conducting Seasoned Equity Offerings," *Journal of Finance*, 52, 1823–50.

Lowenstein, L., 1985, "Management Buyouts," *Columbia Law Review* 85, 730–84.

Mackie-Mason, J., 1990, "Do Taxes Affect Corporate Financing Decisions?" *Journal of Finance* 45, 1471–94.

Masulis, R., 1988, *The Debt/Equity Choice.* Cambridge, MA: Ballinger.

Michaely, R., R. Thaler, and K. Womack, 1995, "Price Reactions to Dividend Initiations and Omissions: Overreaction or Drift?" *Journal of Finance* 50, 573–608.

Mikkelson, W., and M. M. Partch, 1986, "Valuation Effects of Security Offerings and the Issuance Process," *Journal of Financial Economics* 15, 31–60.

Mikkelson, W., and R. Ruback, 1991, "Targeted Repurchases and Common Stock Returns," *Rand Journal of Economics* 22, 544–61.

Miller, M., 1977, "Debt and Taxes," *Journal of Finance* 32, 261–75.

Miller, M., and F. Modigliani, 1961, "Dividend Policy, Growth, and the Valuation of Shares," *Journal of Business* 34, 411–33.

Miller, M., and K. Rock, 1985, "Dividend Policy under Asymmetric Information," *Journal of Finance* 40, 1031–51.

Miller, M., and M. Scholes, 1978, "Dividends and Taxes," *Journal of Financial Economics* 6, 333–64.

———, 1982, "Dividends and Taxes: Some Empirical Evidence," *Journal of Political Economy* 90, 1118–41.

Modigliani, F., and M. Miller, 1958, "The Cost of Capital, Corporation Finance and the Theory of Investment," *American Economic Review* 48, 261–97.

———, 1963, "Corporate Income Taxes and the Cost of Capital: A Correction," *American Economic Review*, 433–43.

Muscarella, C., and M. Vetsuypens, 1989, "A Simple Test of Baron's Model of IPO Underpricing," *Journal of Financial Economics* 24, 125–36.

———, 1990, "Efficiency and Organizational Structure: A Study of Reverse LBOs," *Journal of Finance* 45, 1389–413.

Myers, S., 1977, "Determinants of Corporate Borrowing," *Journal of Financial Economics* 5, 147–75.

Myers, S., and N. Majluf, 1984, "Corporate Financing and Investment Decisions when Firms Have Information That Investors Do Not Have," *Journal of Financial Economics* 13, 187–221.

Myerson, R., 1979, "Incentive Compatibility and the Bargaining Problem," *Econometrica* 47, 61–73.

———, 1986, "Multistage Games with Communication," *Econometrica* 54, 323–58.

Noe, T., 1988, "Capital Structure and Signaling Equilibria," *Review of Financial Studies* 1, 331–56.

Ofer, A., and A. Thakor, 1987, "A Theory of Stock Price Responses to Alternative Corporate Cash Disbursements Methods: Stock Repurchases and Dividends," *Journal of Finance* 42, 365–94.

Osborne, M., and A. Rubinstein, 1994, "A Course in Game Theory," Cambridge, MA: The MIT Press.

Pagano, M., F. Panetta, and L. Zingales, 1988, "Why Do Companies Go Public? An Empirical Analysis," *Journal of Finance* 53, 27–64.

Pagano, M., and A. Röell, (eds.), 1996, "The decision to go public and the stock market as a source of capital," *Quaderni di Ricerche*, numero 19, Rome: Bancaria Editrice.

———, 1998, "The Choice of Stock Ownership Structure: Agency Costs, Monitoring and the Decision to Go Public," *Quarterly Journal of Economics* 113, 187–226.

Parrino, R., and M. Weisbach, 1999, "Measuring Investments Distortions Arising from Stockholders–Bondholders Conflicts," *Journal of Financial Economics* 53, 3–42.

Pettit, R., 1972, "Dividends Announcements, Security Performance, and Capital Market Efficiency," *Journal of Finance* 27, 993–1007.

———, 1976, "The Impact of Dividends and Earnings Announcements: A Reconciliation," *Journal of Business* 49, 86–96.

———, 1977, "Taxes, Transaction Costs and the Clientele Effect of Dividends," *Journal of Financial Economics* 5, 419–36.

Pliska, S., 1997, *Introduction to Mathematical Finance.* Oxford, England: Blackwell Publishers.

Rajan, R., and L. Zingales, 1995, "What Do We Know about Capital Structure? Some Evidence from International Data," *Journal of Finance* 50, 1421–60.

Rappaport, A., 1990, "The Staying Power of the Public Corporation," *Harvard Business Review* 68, 96–104.

Rasmusen, E., 1994, *Games and Information: An Introduction to Game Theory,* 2nd ed., Cambridge, MA: Basil Blackwell.

Riley, J., 1979, "Informational Equilibrium," *Econometrica* 47(2), 331–59.

Ritter, J., 1984, "The 'Hot Issue' Market of 1980," *Journal of Business* 57, 215–40.

———, 1994, "The Long-Run Performance of Initial Public Offerings," *Journal of Finance* 46, 3–27.

Rock, K., 1986, "Why New Issues Are Underpriced?" *Journal of Financial Economics* 15, 187–212.

Roden, D., and W. Lewellen, 1995, "Corporate Capital Structure Decisions: Evidence from Leveraged Buyouts," *Financial Management* 24, 76–87.

Ross, S., 1973, "The Economic Theory of Agency: The Principal's Problem," *American Economic Review* 63, 134–39.

———, 1977, "The Determination of Financial Structure: The Incentive Signaling Approach," *Bell Journal of Economics*, 23–40.

Rydqvist, K., and K. Hogholm, 1994, "Going Public in the 1980s: Evidence from Sweden," *European Financial Management* 1, 287–316.

Schartwz, E., and R. Aronson, 1967, "Some Surrogate Evidence in Support of a Concept of Optimal Financial Structure," *Journal of Finance* 22, 10–18.

Shavell, S., 1979, "Risk Sharing and Incentives in the Principal and Agent Relationship," *Bell Journal of Economics* 10, 55–73.

Shleifer, A., and R. Vishny, 1986, "Large Shareholders and Corporate Control," *Journal of Political Economy* 94, 461–88.

Shyam-Sunder, L., and S. C. Myers, 1999, "Testing Static Trade-off Against Pecking Order Models of Capital Structure," *Journal of Financial Economics* 51, 219–44.

Smith, A., 1990, "Corporate Ownership Structure and Performance: The Case of Management Buyouts," *Journal of Financial Economics* 27, 143–64.

Smith, C., 1986, "Investment Banking and the Capital Acquisition Process," *Journal of Financial Economics* 15, 3–29.

Smith C., and J. Warner, 1979, "On Financial Contracting: An Analysis of Bond Covenants," *Journal of Financial Economics* 7, 117–61.

Spence, M., 1974, *Market Signaling*, Cambridge, MA: Harvard University Press.

Stultz, R., R. Walking, and M. Song, 1990, "The distribution of Target Ownership and the Division of Gains in Successful Takeovers," *Journal of Finance*, 817–34.

Thakor, A., 1991, "Game Theory in Finance," *Financial Management* (Spring), 71–94.

———, 1993, "Information, Investment Horizons and Price Reactions," *Journal of Financial and Quantitative Analysis*, 28.

Thatcher, J. S., 1985, "The Choice of Call Provision Terms: Evidence of the Existence of Agency Costs of Debt," *Journal of Finance* 40, 549–61.

Tiniç, S., 1988, "Anatomy of Initial Public Offerings of Common Stock," *Journal of Finance* 43, 789–822.

Tirole, J., 1999, "Incomplete Contracts: Where Do We Stand," *Econometrica* 67, 741–81.

Titman S., and R. Wessels, 1988, "The Determinants of Capital Structure Choice," *Journal of Finance* 43, 1–19.

Travlos, N., and M. Cornett, 1993, "Going Private Buyouts and Determinants of Shareholders' Returns," *Journal of Accounting, Auditing and Finance* 8, 1–25.

Trigeorgis, L., 1996, *Real Options.* Cambridge, MA: The MIT Press.

Vermaelen, T., 1984, "Common Stock Repurchases and Market Signaling: An Empirical Study," *Journal of Financial Economics* 9, 139–83.

————, 1981, "Repurchase Tender Offers, Signaling, and Managerial Incentives," *Journal of Financial and Quantitative Analysis* 19, 163–81.

————, 1992, "Corporate Restructuring: Evidence from the Stock Market," in *European Industrial Restructuring in the 1990s,* Karel Cool, Damien Neven, and Ingo Walter, (eds.), London: Macmillan.

Viswanath, P., 1993, "Strategic Considerations, the Pecking Order Hypothesis, and Market Reactions to Equity Financing," *Journal of Financial and Quantitative Analysis* 28, 213–34.

von Neumann, J., and O. Morgenstern, 1947, *The Theory of Games and Economic Behavior,* 2nd ed. Princeton, NJ: Princeton University Press.

Warner, J., 1977, "Bankruptcy Costs: Some Evidence," *Journal of Finance* 32, 337–47.

Watts, R., 1973, "The Information Content of Dividends," *Journal of Business* 46, 191–211.

————, 1976, "Comments on The Impact of Dividends and Earnings Announcements: A Reconciliation," *Journal of Business* 49, 97–106.

Welch, I., 1989, "Seasoned Offerings, Imitation Costs, and the Underpricing of Initial Public Offerings," *Journal of Finance* 44, 421–49.

Weston, J. F., J. A. Siu, and B. A. Johnson, 2001, *Takeovers, Restructuring, and Corporate Governance,* 3rd ed. Englewood Cliffs, NJ: Prentice Hall.

Williams, J., 1988, "Efficient Signaling with Dividends, Investment, and Stock Repurchases," *Journal of Finance* 43, 737–47.

Williamson, O., 1988, "Corporate Finance and Corporate Governance," *Journal of Finance* 43, 567–91.

Wruck, K., 1989, "Equity Ownership Concentration and Firm Value: Evidence from Private Equity Financings," *Journal of Financial Economics* 23, 3–28.

Zender, J., 1991, "Optimal Financial Instruments," *Journal of Finance* 26, 1645–65.

Index

absence of arbitrage opportunities, 4
accessible consumption paths, 3
acquisitions and mergers, 191–223,
   271–278
after-tax equilibrium, 52–53
agency costs, 61–77
  in choice of payment for mergers,
   220
  of debt, 71–75
  outside equity, 64–66
  role in capital structure, 255–260
aggregate debt, 49
allocation of control, contracting
  and, 126–134, 266–268
alternative valuations, 100–101
antitakeover devices, 192
arbitrage opportunities, 22–23
  investment and, 23–24
arcs, 30
average cost of capital, 43

bankruptcy, 41
before-tax equilibrium debt, 53–54
before-tax rates of return, 52
beta-evaluation, 4
beta values, 26–28
bidder, suits against, 222
bidder competition
  cash as a preemptive instrument,
   212–214
  in merger bids, 206–207
binomial tree, multiperiod setting,
  30–32
bondholders, 40

bonding, costs of, 74
bonds
  demand for, 49–50
  supply of, 50
boundary condition, 81
budget constraint, 83
buybacks
  as an antitakeover device, 177
  regulations for, 178–179

callability provision, 75
call option, 34
capitalizing dividends, dividend
  policy and, 101
capital markets
  consumption and investment with,
   11–13
  multiperiod economy with, 15–17
  role of, 9–11
capital structure, 39–58
  implications, 61–91, 255–261
  informational asymmetries, 78–91
  optimal, 251–255
cash, as a preemptive instrument in
  merger bids, 212–214
cash effect, 220
certain consumption plan, 19
certainty, valuation under, 5–17
certainty equivalent, 19
competitive-rationality condition, 240
constrained optimization, 228–232
consumption, time preferences, 7
consumption paths, 3–4
consumption plan, 18
contingent control, 133–134

contracting, allocation of control
  and, 126–134
contracts
  debt (*see* debt contracts)
  efficient, 129
  feasible, 129
  financing (*see* financing contracts)
  incomplete (*see* incomplete
    contracts)
control
  allocation of, 126–134
  contingent, 133–134
  entrepreneur, 129–131
  investor, 131–133
convertible debt, 75
corporate governance, 126–134
costless separation, 236
costly separation, 236
cost of capital, 12, 42–43
  after taxation, 45–46
cost of debt, 42–43
cost of equity, 43
cost of opportunity of capital (*see*
  cost of capital)
creditors, 40
  number, nature, and type, 137–139
current wealth, 10

debt contracts
  design, 134–148, 267–268
  duration of, 139–145
debtholders, 40
debt tax shield, 46–47
default premium, 57
demand rate of return, bonds, 50
direct mechanism, 238
disclosure regulations, 207
discounted cash flow, dividend policy
  and, 101
divestitures, 192
dividend policy (*see* Payout policy)
dividends
  information and, 110–119, 263–265
  taxes and, 104–105
  trade around ex-dividend dates
    and, 108–109

dual class recapitalizations, 222
duration, in debt contracts, 139–145

effective personal tax rate, 52
efficient contract, 129
endowments, current and future, 9
entrepreneur, 127–128
  control, 129–131
equilibrium
  alternative, 54–57
  bonds, 51–53
  pooling, 79
  rate of return on bonds, 53
  separating, 79
equity carve-out, 192
equityholders, 41
equivalence, 4
executive stock options, 70–71
exercise price, 34
expected utility function, 19

fair price amendments, 222
feasible contract, 129
fee schedules, 62
  managers' signaling because of,
    79–82
  optimal, determination of, 66–70
financial contracting, 125–148
  allocation of control and, 266–268
financial markets, 11
financing
  announcement effect, 112
  choice between public and private,
    154–160
financing contracts, 133–134
Fisher separation principle, 12–13, 16
flipping, 174–175
free-rider problem, tender offers
  and, 192–205, 271–276
fund raising, financing for LBO,
  179–180
future uncertainty in a one-period
  economy, 18
future value of X, 9
future wealth, 10

games of incomplete information, 233
game theory, 233–240
GHM approach, 125
going private, 177–189, 270–271
going public, 151–175, 268–270
    decision, 152–160
    equilibrium, 154–160
governance structure, 127
Greenmail, 192, 223
growth rates, dividend policies and, 102–103

hostile takeover, 192

incentive compatible direct mechanisms, 238
incomplete contracts, 126
    allocation of control in a firm and, 127–131
indirect game, equilibrium strategies of, 239
inference function, 234
information
    differences between investors, 173–175
    disclosure as unexpected value, 112
    dividends and, 110–119
informational asymmetries
    in capital structure, 78–91
    economic agents, 233
    between investors, 163–164
    between issuers and underwriters, 162–163
    perceived value of firm and, 82
    role in capital structure, 260–261
    underpricing, 160–175, 268–270
informational equilibrium, 233–237
informed party, 233
initial endowment, investment of, 3
initial public offering (IPO), 151–175
    investment bank, 151
    investors, 151
    issuing firm, 151
    underwriters, 151
interest rate, 9

intertemporal consumption path, 13
inverse function, 51
investment, arbitrage opportunities and, 23–24
investment banker, uncertainty and, 165–167
investment opportunities
    dividend policy and, 101
    signals conditioned by, 85–89
investment policy, 3–38
investment project, value of, 14–15
investment schedule, 4, 8, 11–15
investors, 127–128
    in an IPO, 151
    asymmetry between, 163–164
    control, 131–133
    informational differences between, 173–175
    managers as, 82–85
irrelevancy statement, MM propositions, 40–43, 98–100
issuing firm
    asymmetry between underwriters, 162–163
    IPOs, 151

jawboning, 199

Lagrangian function, 13, 230
largely diffused ownership, 193–196
legal liabilities, in underpricing, 171–172
leveraged buyouts (LBOs), 177, 179–189, 270–271
    mechanisms of, 179–181
    reverting of, 180
levered, 40
limited liability, 41
liquidity default, 137
long-term debt, 139–145

management buyout (MBO), 177
management changes, in LBOs, 180
manager and shareholder conflict, 62–63

managers
  as investors, 82–85
  signaling from, 79–82
marginal rate of substitution, 7
market completeness, 23
market incompleteness, 23
market line, 11
Martingale measure, value and, 24–25
maturity, 34
mechanism design, game theory, 233,
  238
merger, definition, 191
merger bids, 205–223, 276–278
  bidder competition, 206–207
  cash as a preemptive instrument,
    212–214
  choosing means of payment,
    207–212
  takeover methods, 214–218
mergers and acquisitions, 191–223,
  271–278
MM propositions, 39–48
  comparison, 53–54
  dividend policy, 98–109
  irrelevancy statement, 40–43,
    98–100
  optimal capital structure, 251–255
  with taxes, 44–46
mode, 30
Modigliani and Miller (*see* MM
  propositions)
monitoring, costs of, 74
multiperiod economy, capital markets
  with, 15–17
multiperiods, 4
  flexibility under uncertainty and,
    29–38
  real options, 33–34
multiplicity of equilibria, 237

net present value (NPV), 15
nonmimicry constraints, 239

observable action, 67
one-period economy, 3, 16
one-period model, 18–21

optimization principles, 227–232
  equality constraints, 228–231
  inequality constraints, 231–232
option premium, 33
options, 33–34
  general properties of, 34–38
outside equity, agency costs of, 64–66
overinvestment, 147
  cost of, 73
overinvestment problem, 63
ownership, largely diffused, 193–196

Pareto dominating price function,
  237
payment, choice of means in merger
  bids, 207–212
payout policy, 97–124
  dividend policy, 261–265
  dividends and information,
    263–265
  recent trends, 120
poison pills, 222–223
pooling equilibrium, 79
present value of Y, 9
pricing function, 234
  informationally consistent, 235
principal-agent problems, 66–71
private benefits, 128
private financing, 154–156
production opportunities, 8
proxy fight, 198
public equity market, 151
public equity offering, reverting the
  LBO, 180
public financing, 156–160
put-call parity relation, 35
put option, 34

recombining, 30
region of admissible consumptions, 5
  with investment schedule, 8
  with investment schedule and
    capital markets, 14
  presence of capital markets, 9
regressing the returns, dividend
  policy, 106–107

relaxing certainty, dividend policies and, 103–104
revelation principle
  incomplete information, 238–240
  Myerson, 233
Riley outcome, 237
risk-averse, 19
risk-seeking, 19
risk shifting, 63
Robinson Crusoe economy, 5–7

separating equilibrium, 79
shareholder and debtholder conflict, 62–63
shareholders, 41
  dilution of rights, 194
  large, role of, 196–199
shares, 41
short-term debt, 139–145
signal function, 234
signaling
  in choice of payment for mergers, 220
  conditioned by investment opportunities, 85–89
  credible, 236
  false type, 81
  managers', 79–82
  stock repurchase in, 89–93
signaling model
  consistent, 114–116
  dividends and information, 111–114
signal space, 237
similarity condition, 68
Spence-Mirrlees condition, 235
Spence/Riley methodology, 233
spinoff, 192
split-off, 192
state-price deflator, 25
stock buyout, in LBOs, 179–180
stock repurchase, 177–179
  in payout policy, 119–124
    reasons, 121–122
  as a signal, 89–93
strategic default, 137
suits against the bidder, 222

supermajority provisions, 222
supplied rate of return, bonds, 50
systematic risk, 54

takeover
  choice of methods, 214–218
  hostile, 192
  optimal size before, 201–205
  uncertain outcome of, 199–201
targeted repurchases (greenmail), 223
taxation
  changes in, 54–57
  personal and corporate, 48–58, 255
taxes
  in choice of payment for mergers, 220
  dividends and, 104–105
  MM propositions with, 44–46
tax-exempt investors, 49
tender offer, 191
  effect, 220
  free-rider problem and, 192–205, 271–276
  successful, 216
  unsuccessful, 216
time preferences
  current and future consumption, 7
  trading, 9
trade around ex-dividend dates, dividends and, 108–109
truth telling constraints, 238–239
two-period economy, 15
two-tier offer, 195

uncertain stream of cash flows, 4
uncertainty
  flexibility under, 29–38
  reputation of bankers and, 165–167
  valuation under, 18–29
unconstrained optimization, 227–228
underinvestment, 147
  cost of, 73
underinvestment problem, 63
underpriced shares, 89

underpricing
  informational asymmetries and, 268–270
  legal liabilities in, 171–172
underwriters, 151
  asymmetry with issuers, 162–163
  how they become informed, 167–171
uninformed party, 233
unlevered, 40
unobservable action, 66
utility function, 5–6

valuation, 3–38
  under certainty, 5–17, 241–244
  under uncertainty, 18–29, 244–250
variability of returns, investment decision effects, 73
venture capitalist, 151
von Neumann-Morgenstern utility function, 19

welfare of limiting types, 236
white knight, 192